TENJHO TENGE

Maya Natsume

Aya Natsume

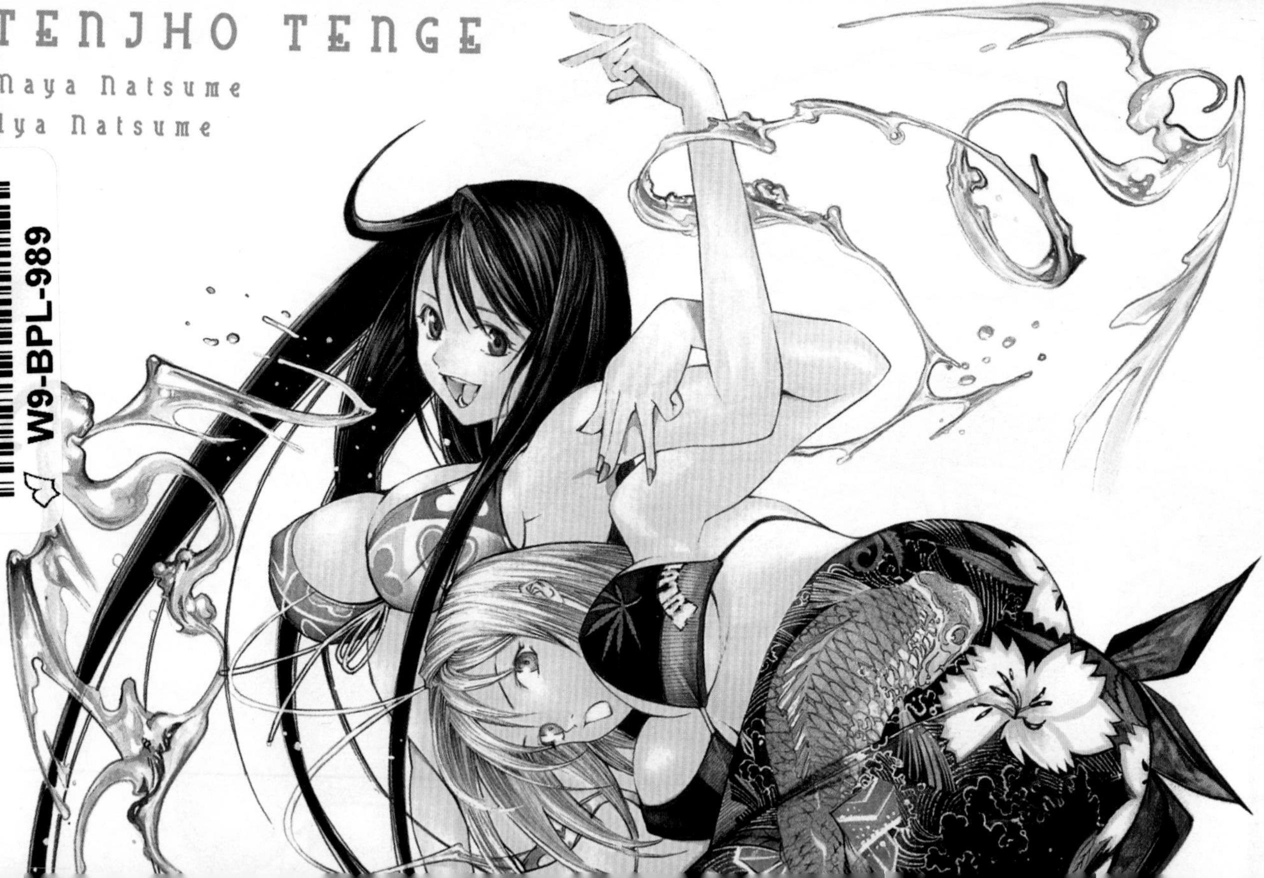

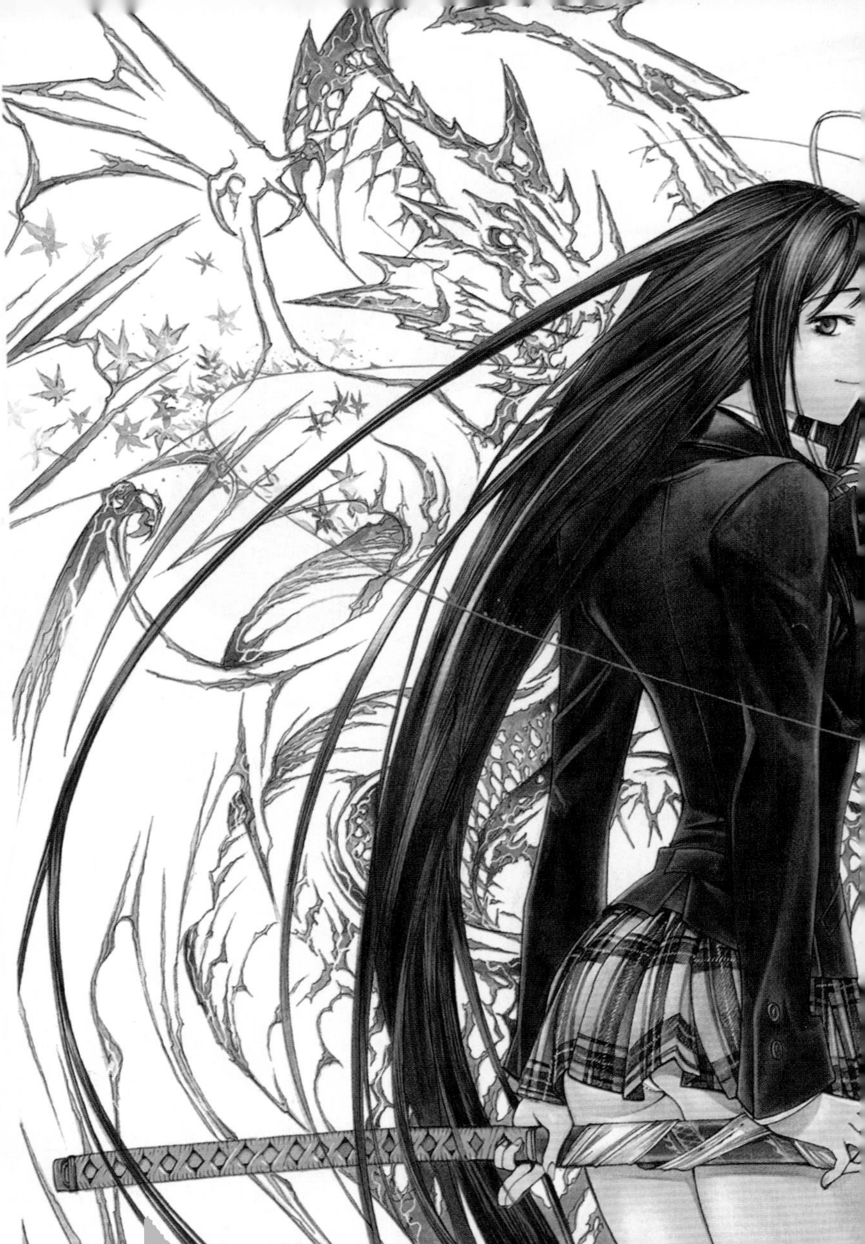

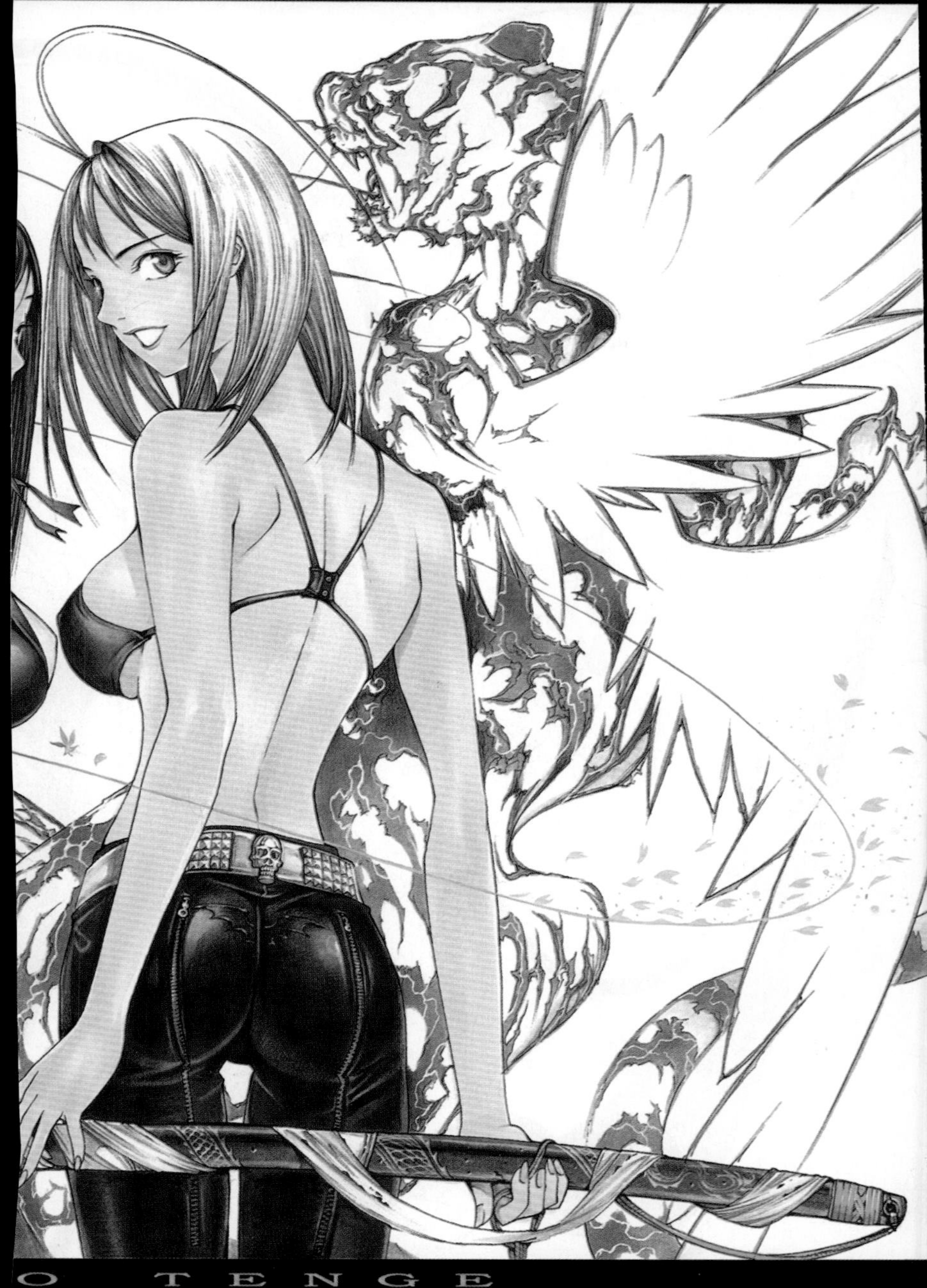
O TENGE

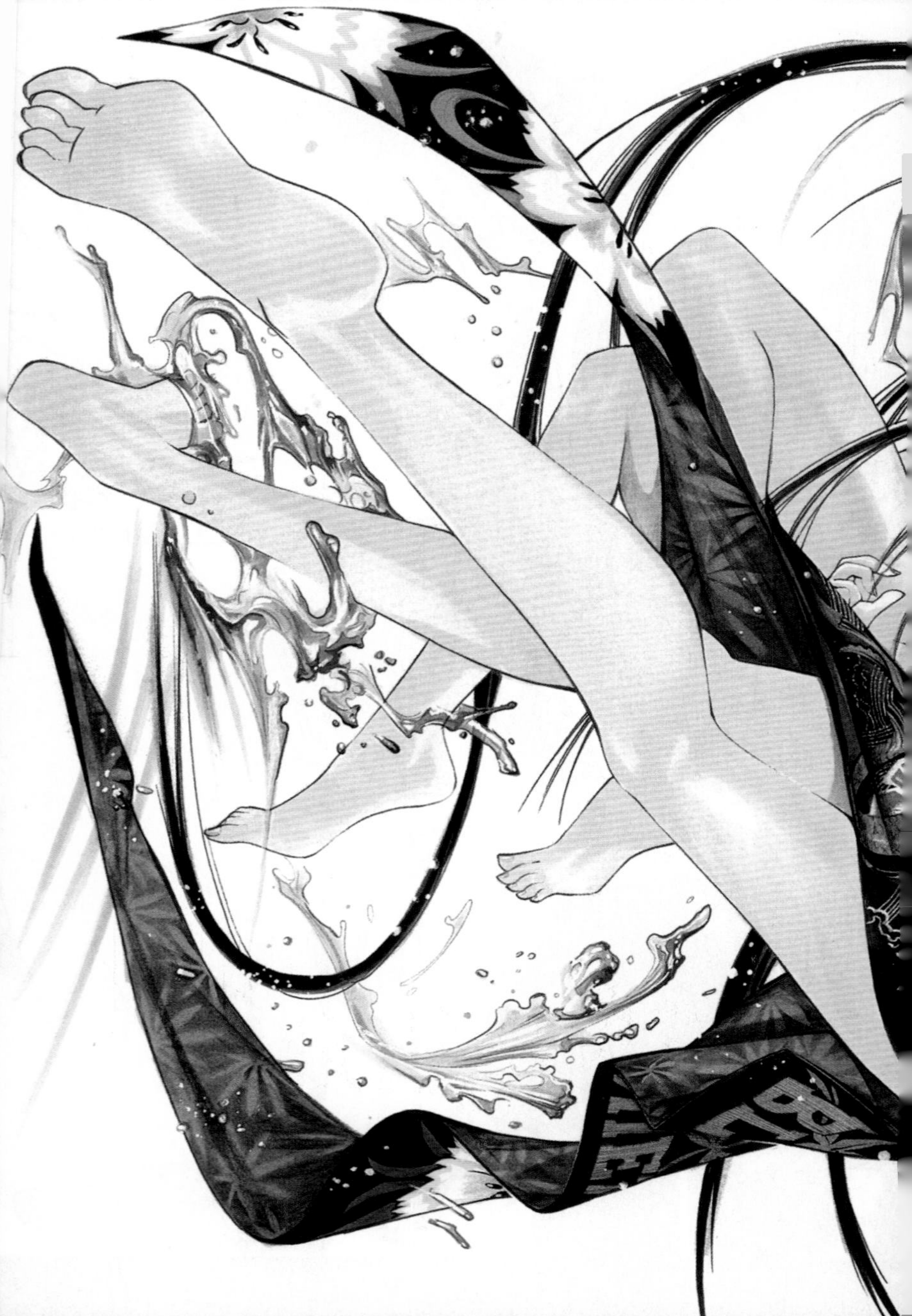

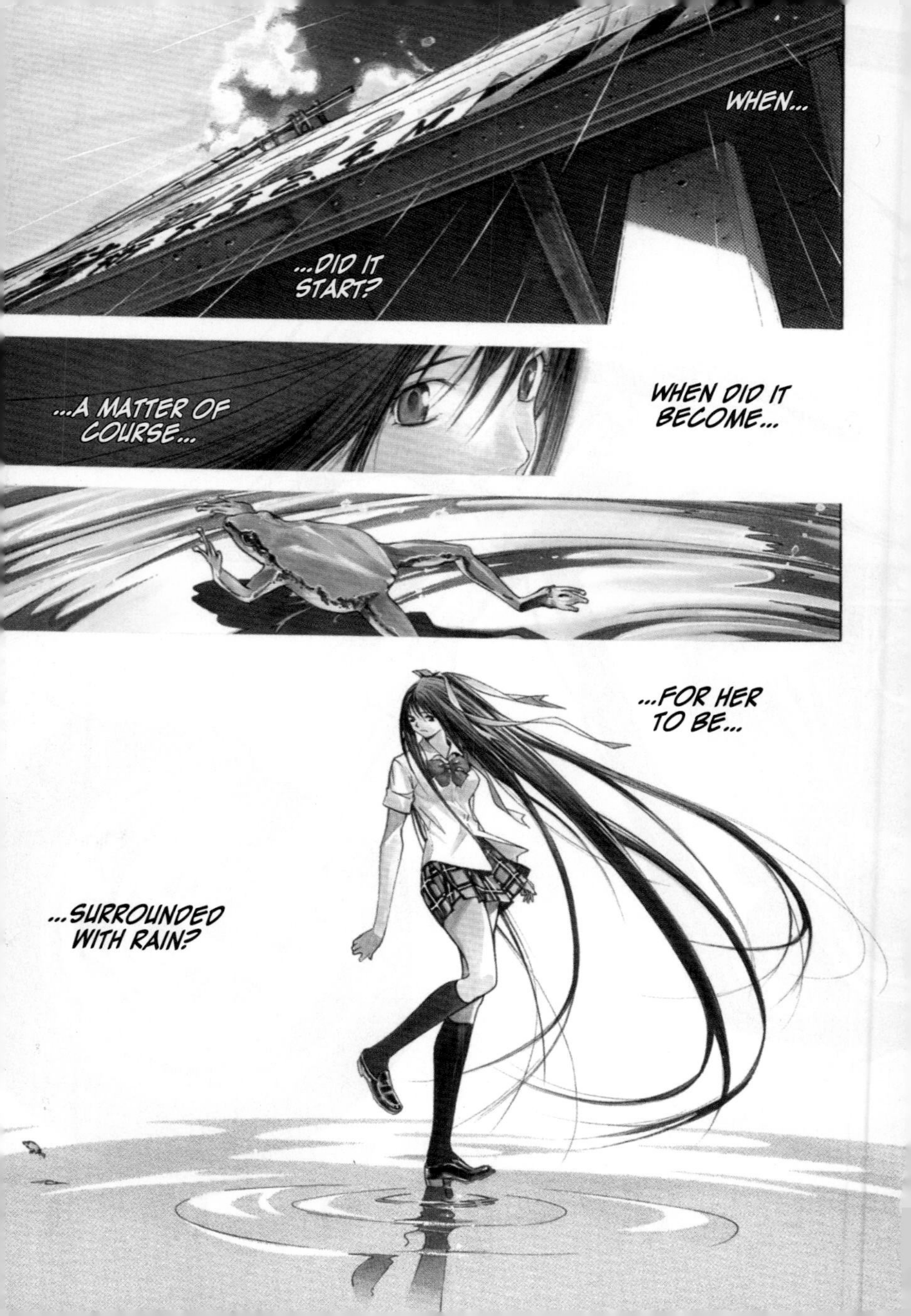
WHEN...
...DID IT START?
WHEN DID IT BECOME...
...A MATTER OF COURSE...
...FOR HER TO BE...
...SURROUNDED WITH RAIN?

FIGHT:76

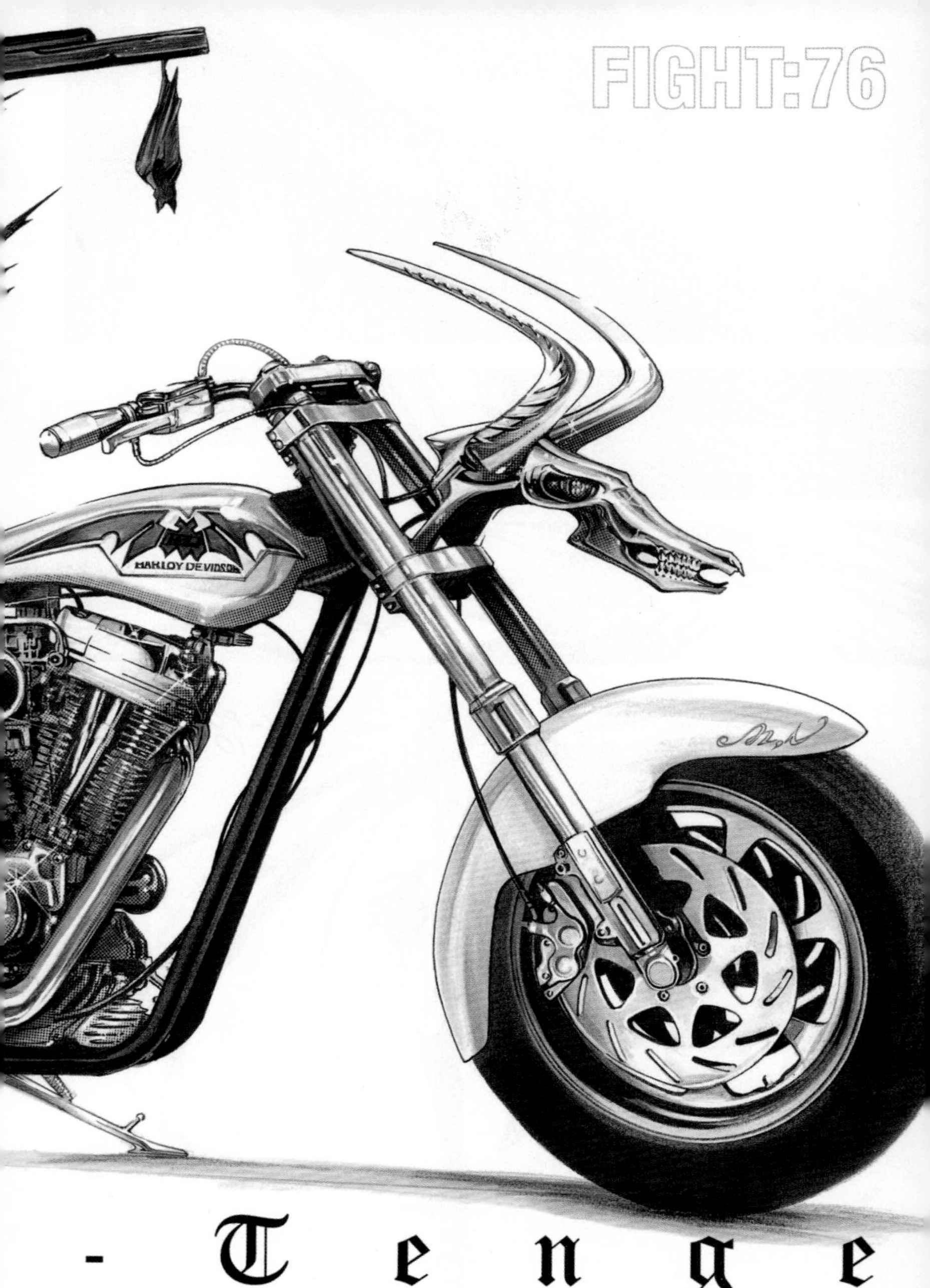
HARLOY DEVIDSON

- Tenge

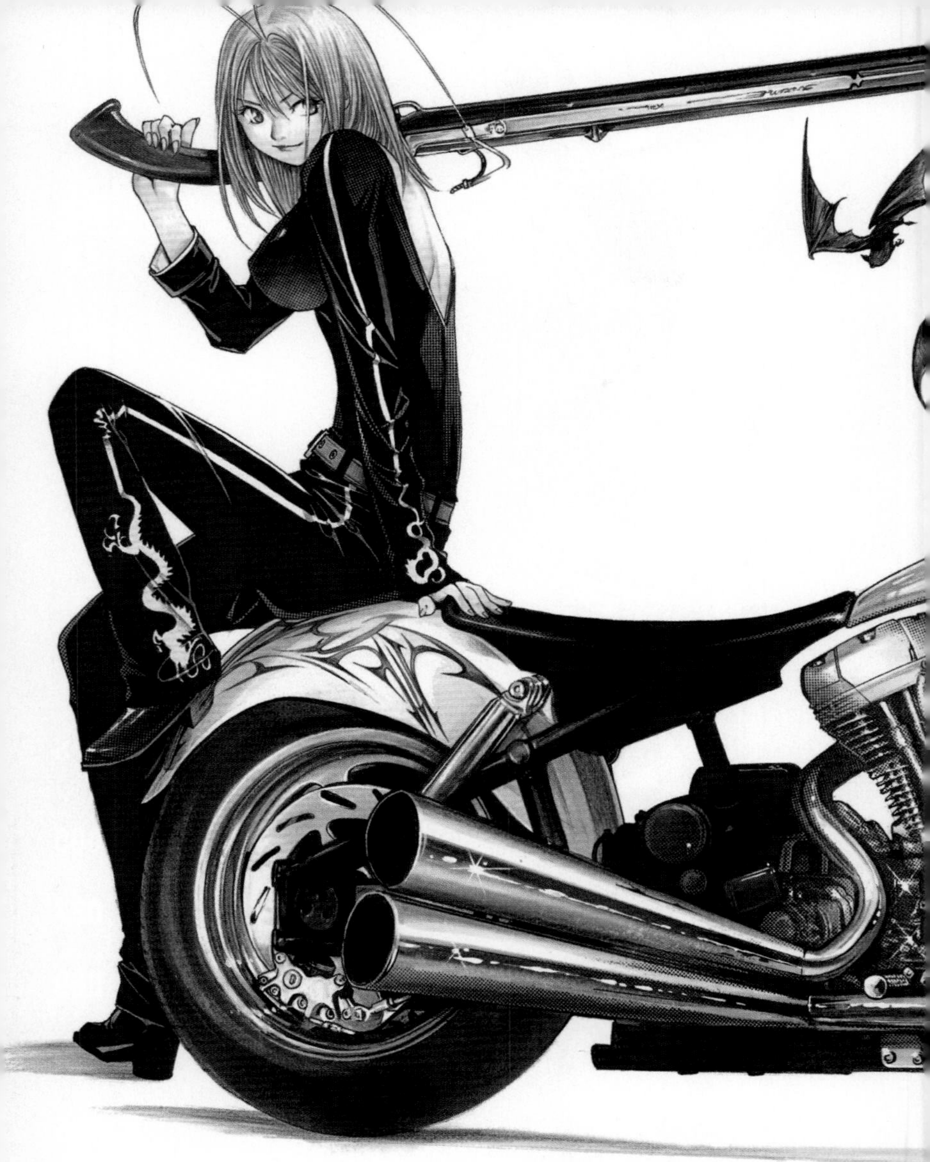

Tenjho

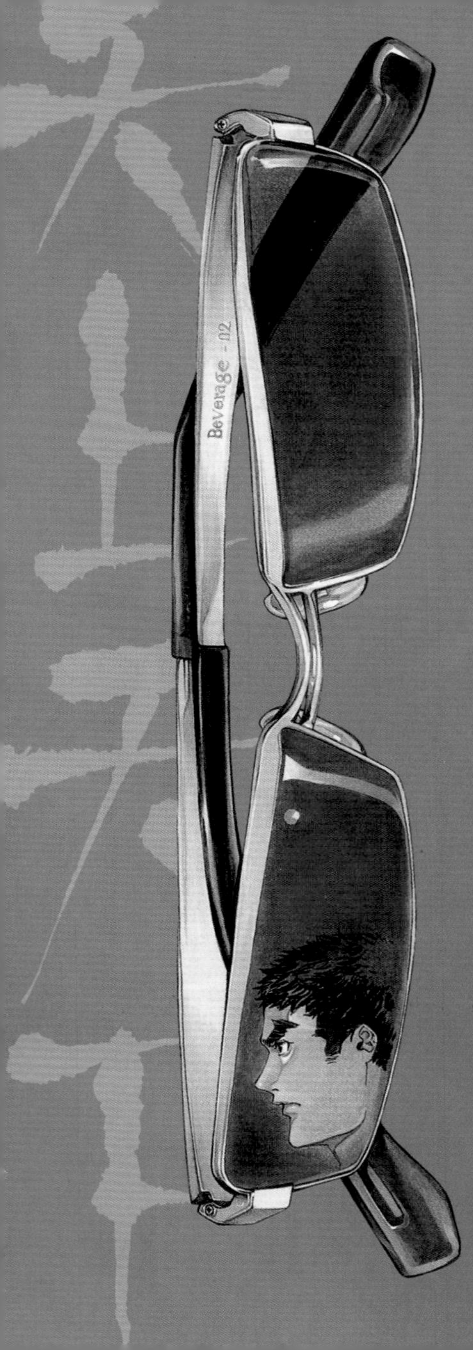
Beverage -02

13 CONTENTS

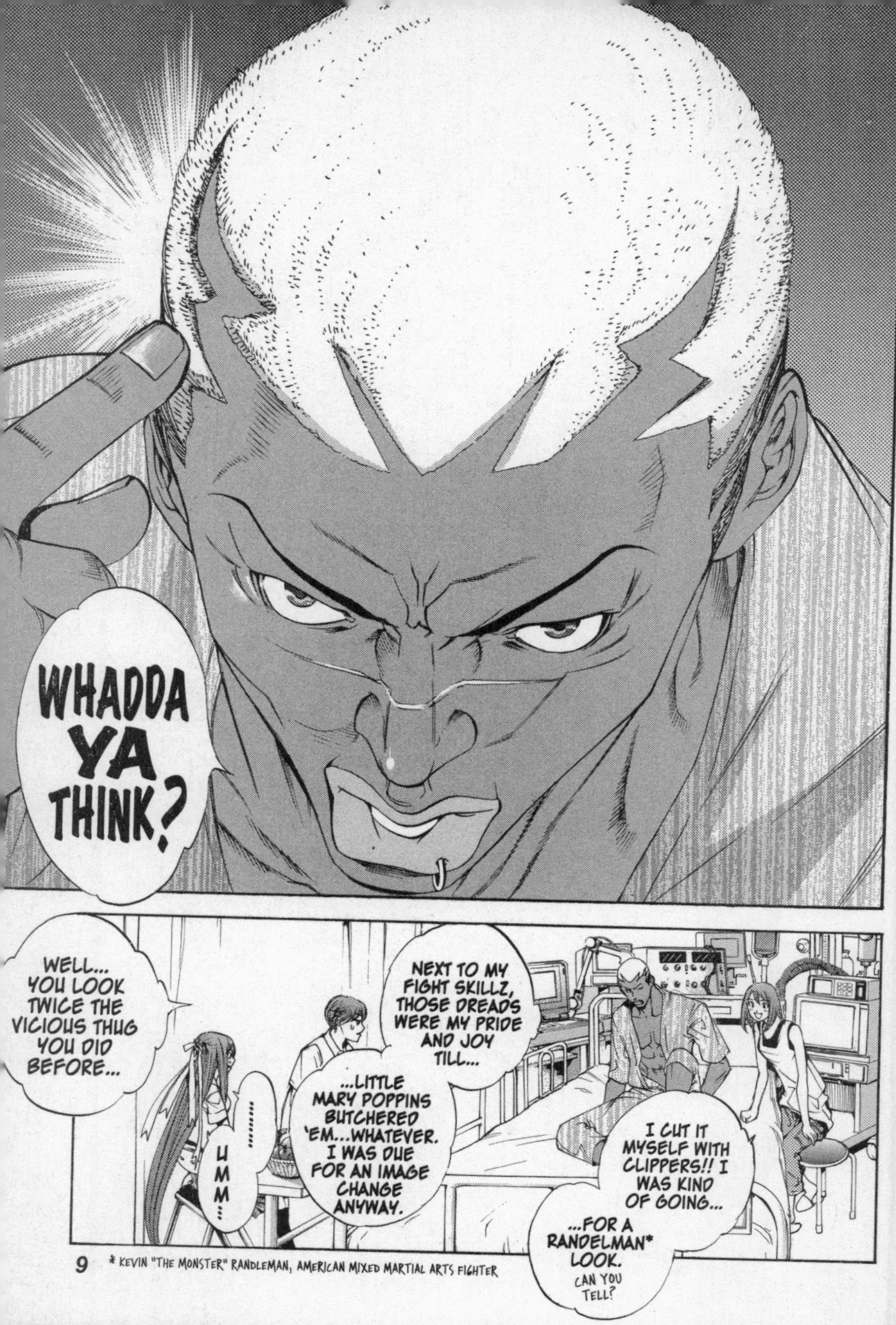
WHADDA YA THINK?
NEXT TO MY FIGHT SKILLZ, THOSE DREADS WERE MY PRIDE AND JOY TILL...
...LITTLE MARY POPPINS BUTCHERED 'EM...WHATEVER. I WAS DUE FOR AN IMAGE CHANGE ANYWAY.
I CUT IT MYSELF WITH CLIPPERS!! I WAS KIND OF GOING...
...FOR A RANDELMAN* LOOK.
CAN YOU TELL?
UMM...
....
WELL... YOU LOOK TWICE THE VICIOUS THUG YOU DID BEFORE...

* KEVIN "THE MONSTER" RANDLEMAN, AMERICAN MIXED MARTIAL ARTS FIGHTER

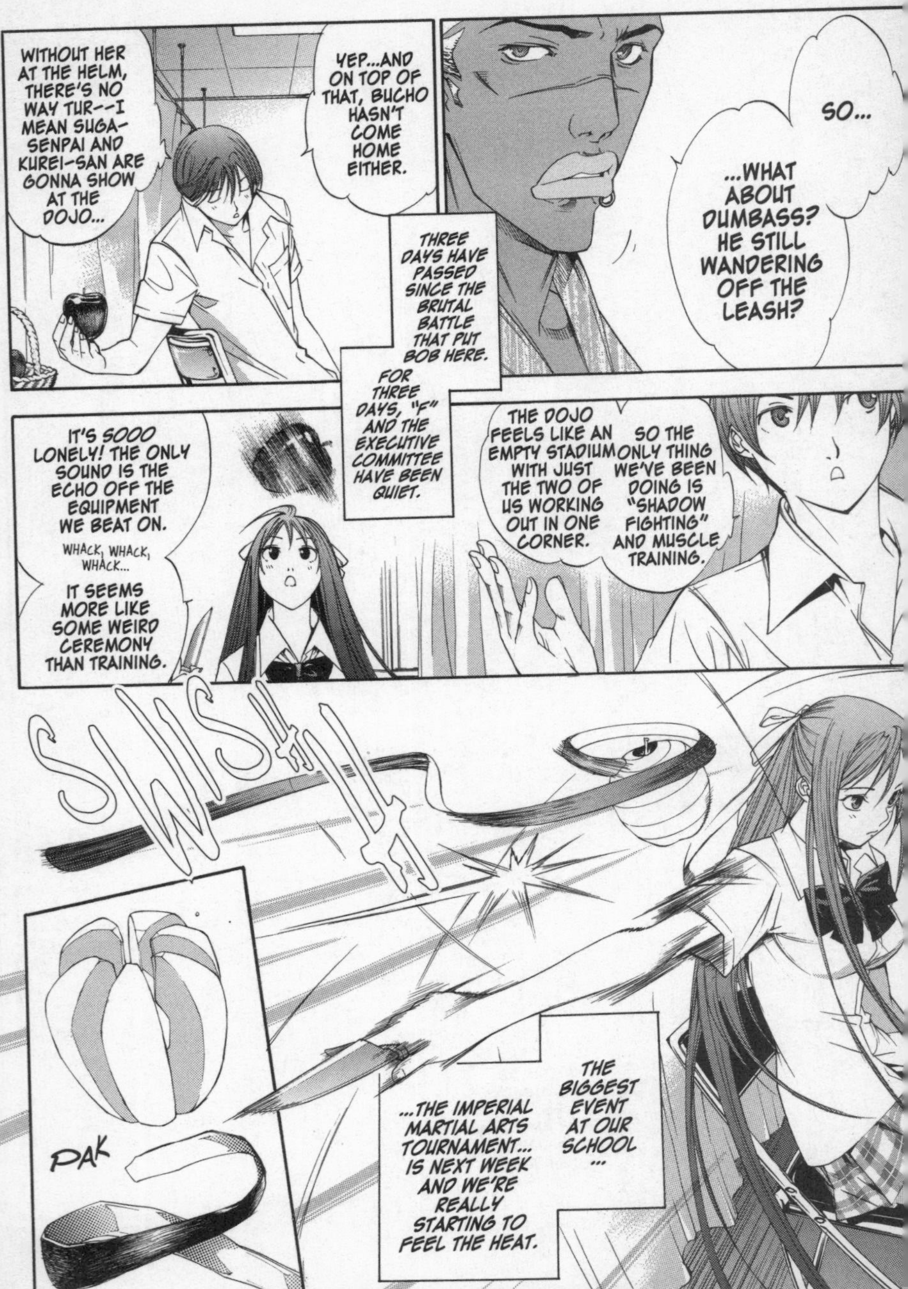
SO...
...WHAT ABOUT DUMBASS? HE STILL WANDERING OFF THE LEASH?
YEP...AND ON TOP OF THAT, BUCHO HASN'T COME HOME EITHER.
WITHOUT HER AT THE HELM, THERE'S NO WAY TUR--I MEAN SUGA-SENPAI AND KUREI-SAN ARE GONNA SHOW AT THE DOJO...
THREE DAYS HAVE PASSED SINCE THE BRUTAL BATTLE THAT PUT BOB HERE.
FOR THREE DAYS, "F" AND THE EXECUTIVE COMMITTEE HAVE BEEN QUIET.
THE DOJO FEELS LIKE AN EMPTY STADIUM WITH JUST THE TWO OF US WORKING OUT IN ONE CORNER.
SO THE ONLY THING WE'VE BEEN DOING IS "SHADOW FIGHTING" AND MUSCLE TRAINING.
IT'S SOOO LONELY! THE ONLY SOUND IS THE ECHO OFF THE EQUIPMENT WE BEAT ON.
WHACK, WHACK, WHACK...
IT SEEMS MORE LIKE SOME WEIRD CEREMONY THAN TRAINING.
SWISH
THE BIGGEST EVENT AT OUR SCHOOL...
...THE IMPERIAL MARTIAL ARTS TOURNAMENT... IS NEXT WEEK AND WE'RE REALLY STARTING TO FEEL THE HEAT.
PAK

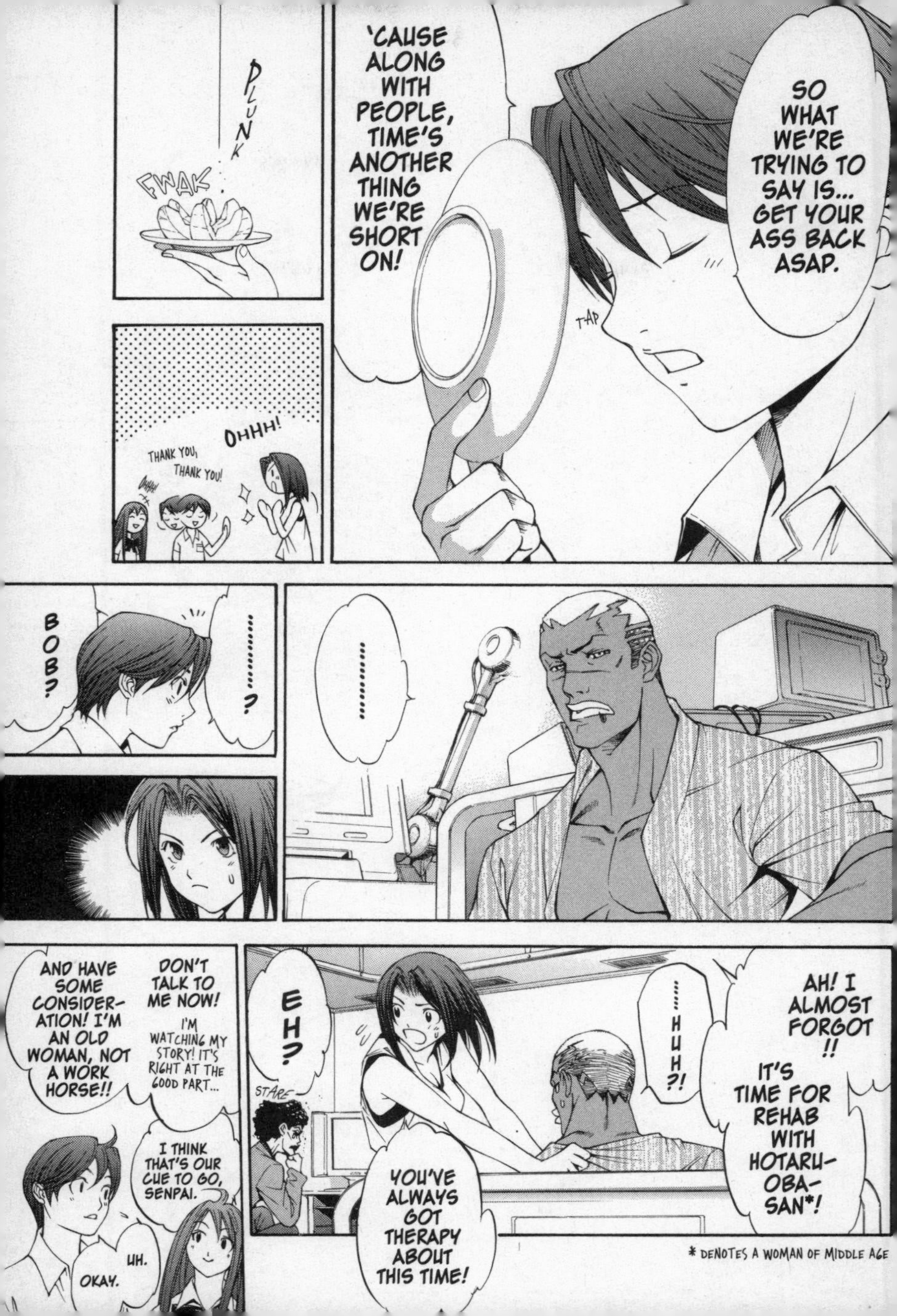
SO WHAT WE'RE TRYING TO SAY IS... GET YOUR ASS BACK ASAP.
TAP
'CAUSE ALONG WITH PEOPLE, TIME'S ANOTHER THING WE'RE SHORT ON!
PLUNK
FWAK
OHHH!
THANK YOU, THANK YOU!
OHHH!
....
BOB?
........?
AH! I ALMOST FORGOT!! IT'S TIME FOR REHAB WITH HOTARU-OBA-SAN*!
....HUH?!
EH?
STARE
YOU'VE ALWAYS GOT THERAPY ABOUT THIS TIME!
DON'T TALK TO ME NOW! I'M WATCHING MY STORY! IT'S RIGHT AT THE GOOD PART...
AND HAVE SOME CONSIDERATION! I'M AN OLD WOMAN, NOT A WORK HORSE!!
I THINK THAT'S OUR CUE TO GO, SENPAI.
UH. OKAY.

* DENOTES A WOMAN OF MIDDLE AGE

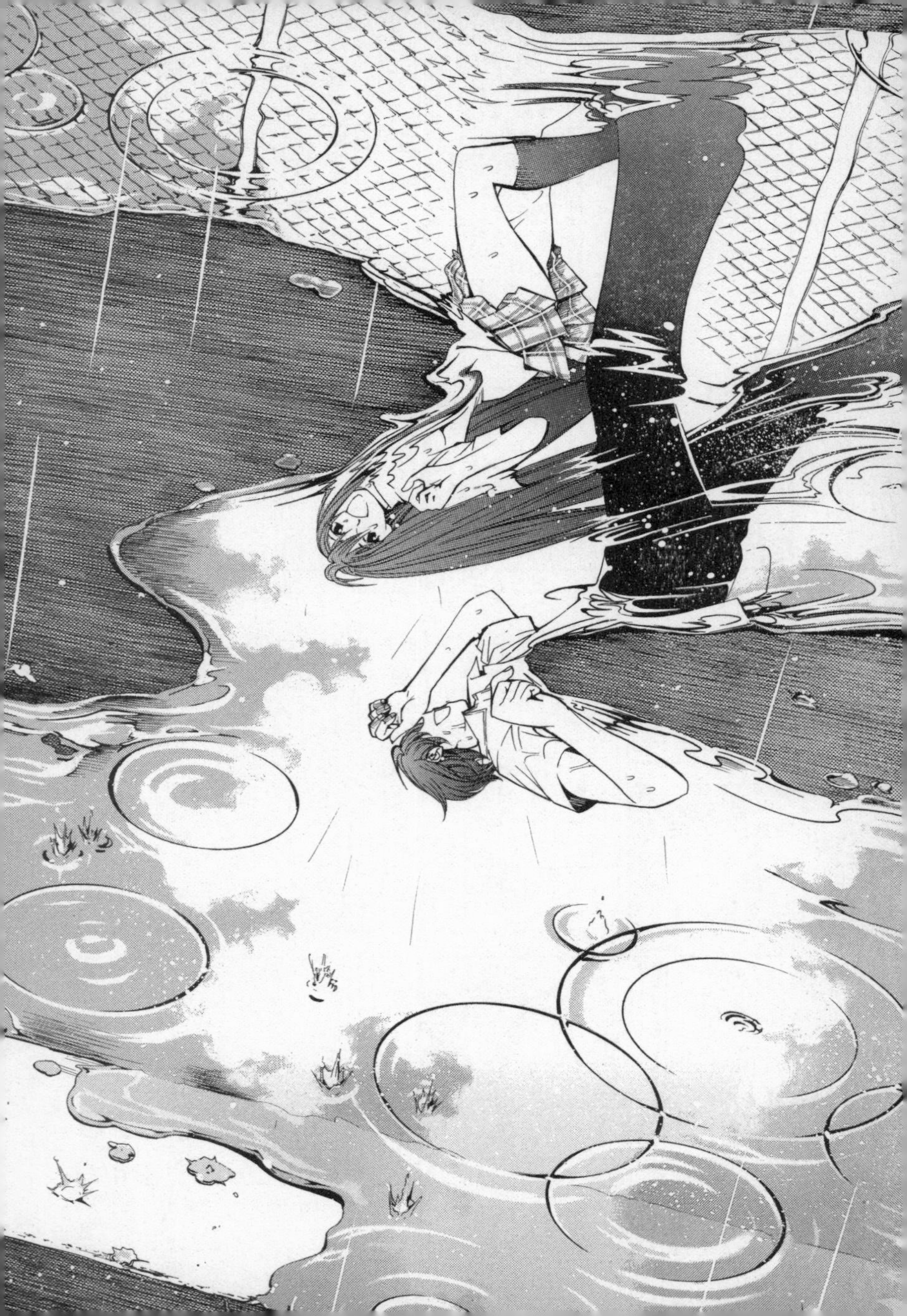

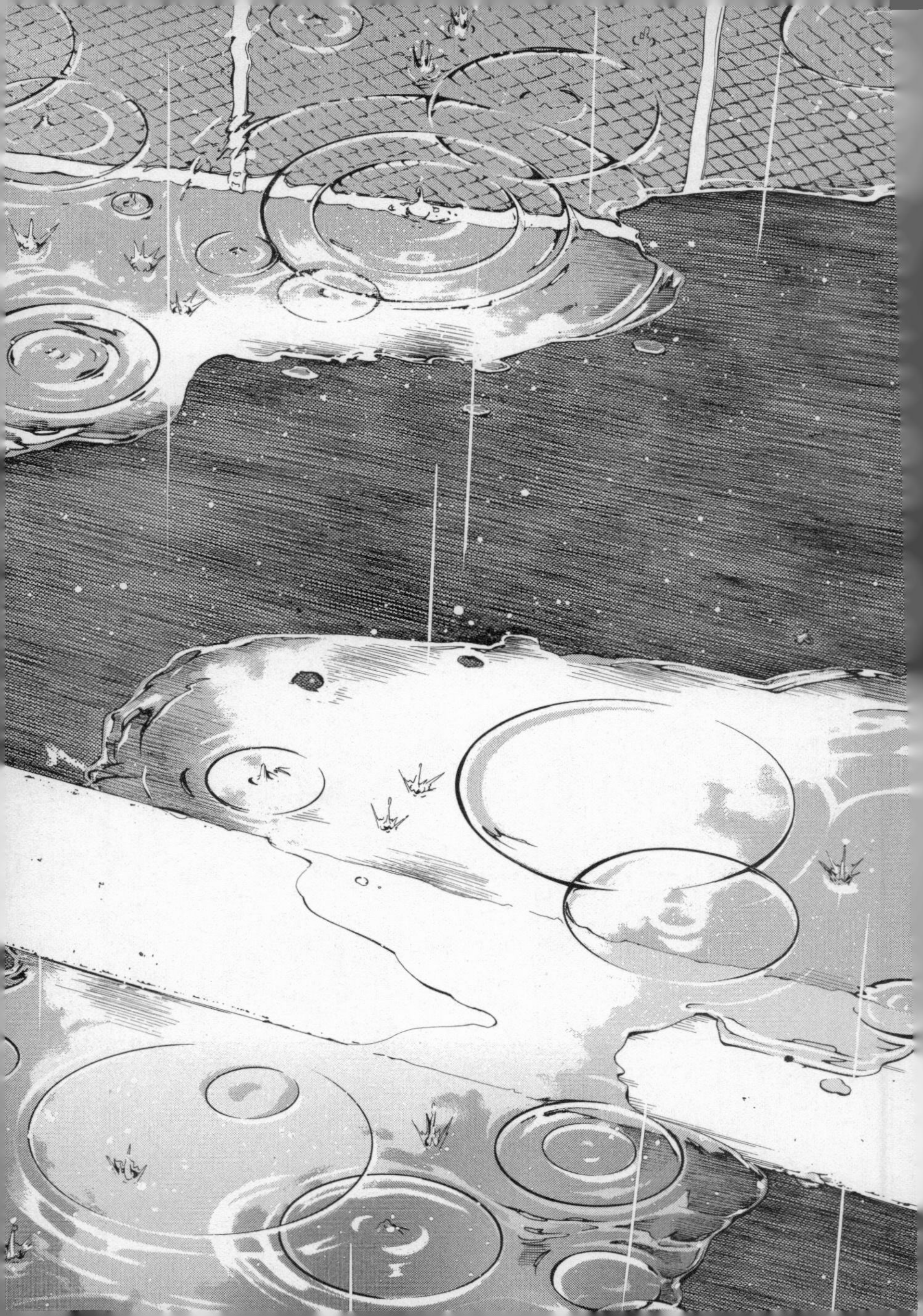

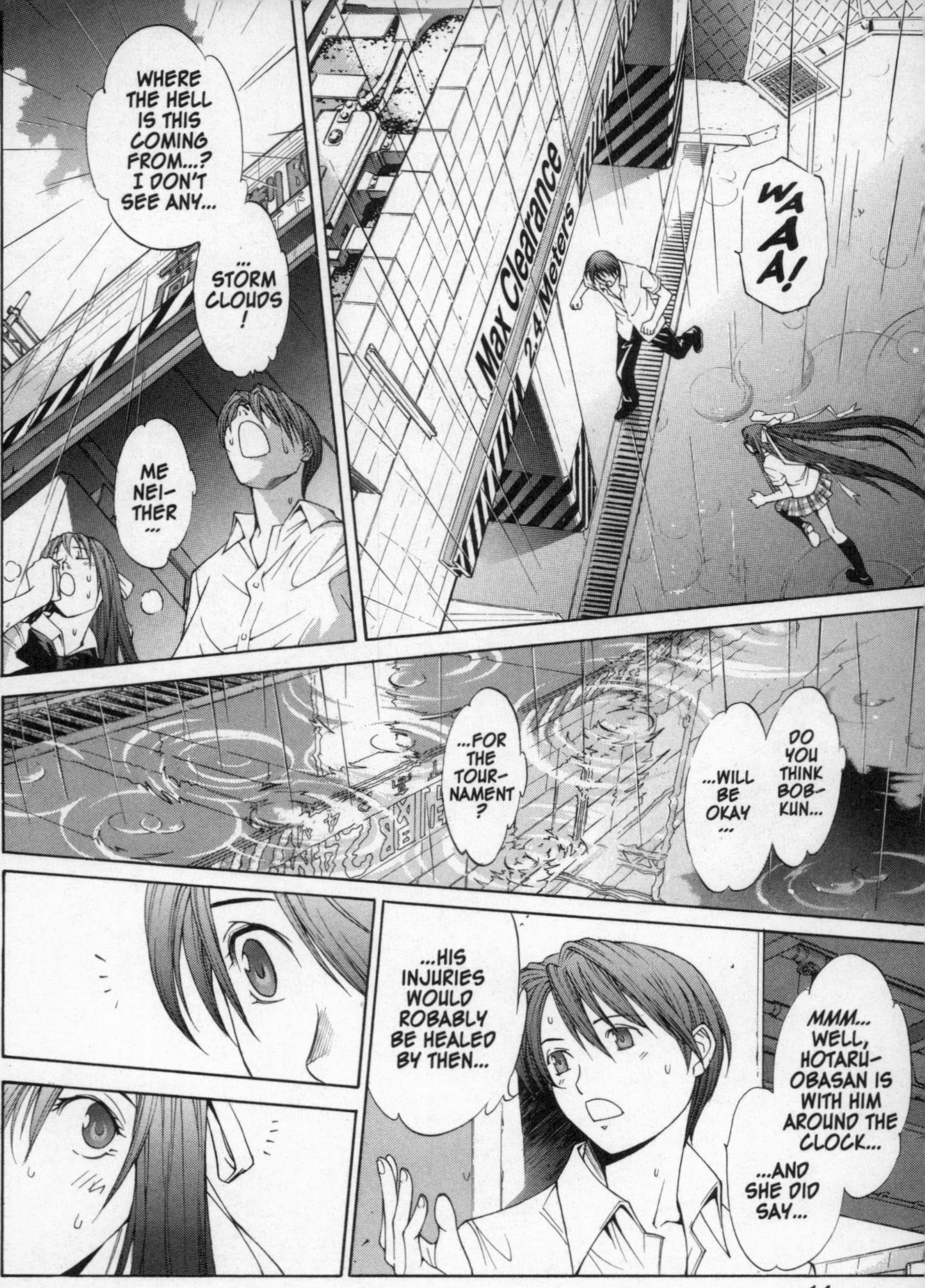
WAAA!
Max Clearance
2.4 Meters
WHERE THE HELL IS THIS COMING FROM...? I DON'T SEE ANY...
...STORM CLOUDS!
ME NEI-THER...
DO YOU THINK BOB-KUN...
...WILL BE OKAY...
...FOR THE TOUR-NAMENT?
MMM... WELL, HOTARU-OBASAN IS WITH HIM AROUND THE CLOCK...
...AND SHE DID SAY...
...HIS INJURIES WOULD ROBABLY BE HEALED BY THEN...

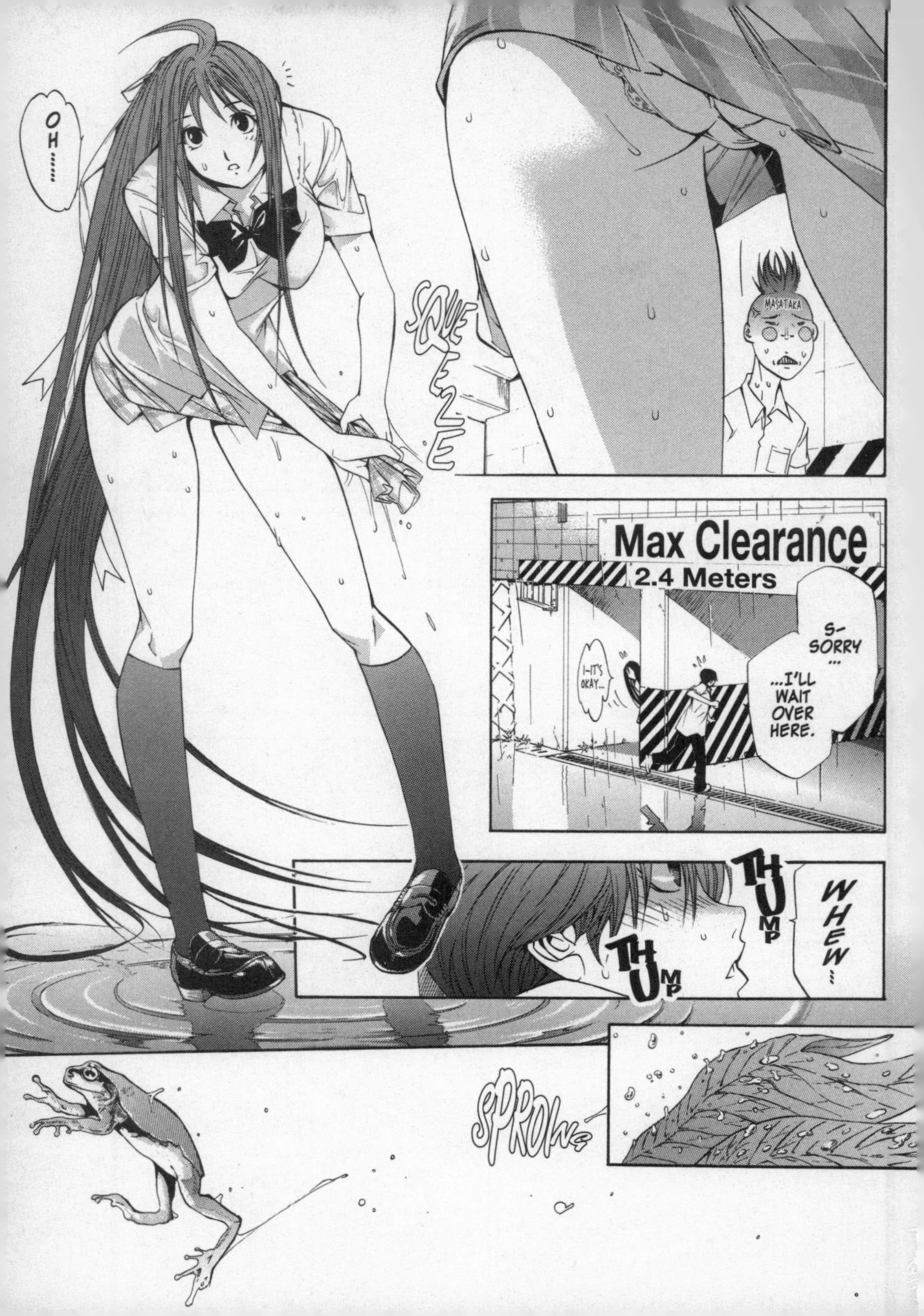
MASATAKA
Max Clearance
2.4 Meters
S-SORRY... ...I'LL WAIT OVER HERE.
I-IT'S OKAY...
THUMP
WHEW...
THUMP
OH......
SQUEEZE
SPROING

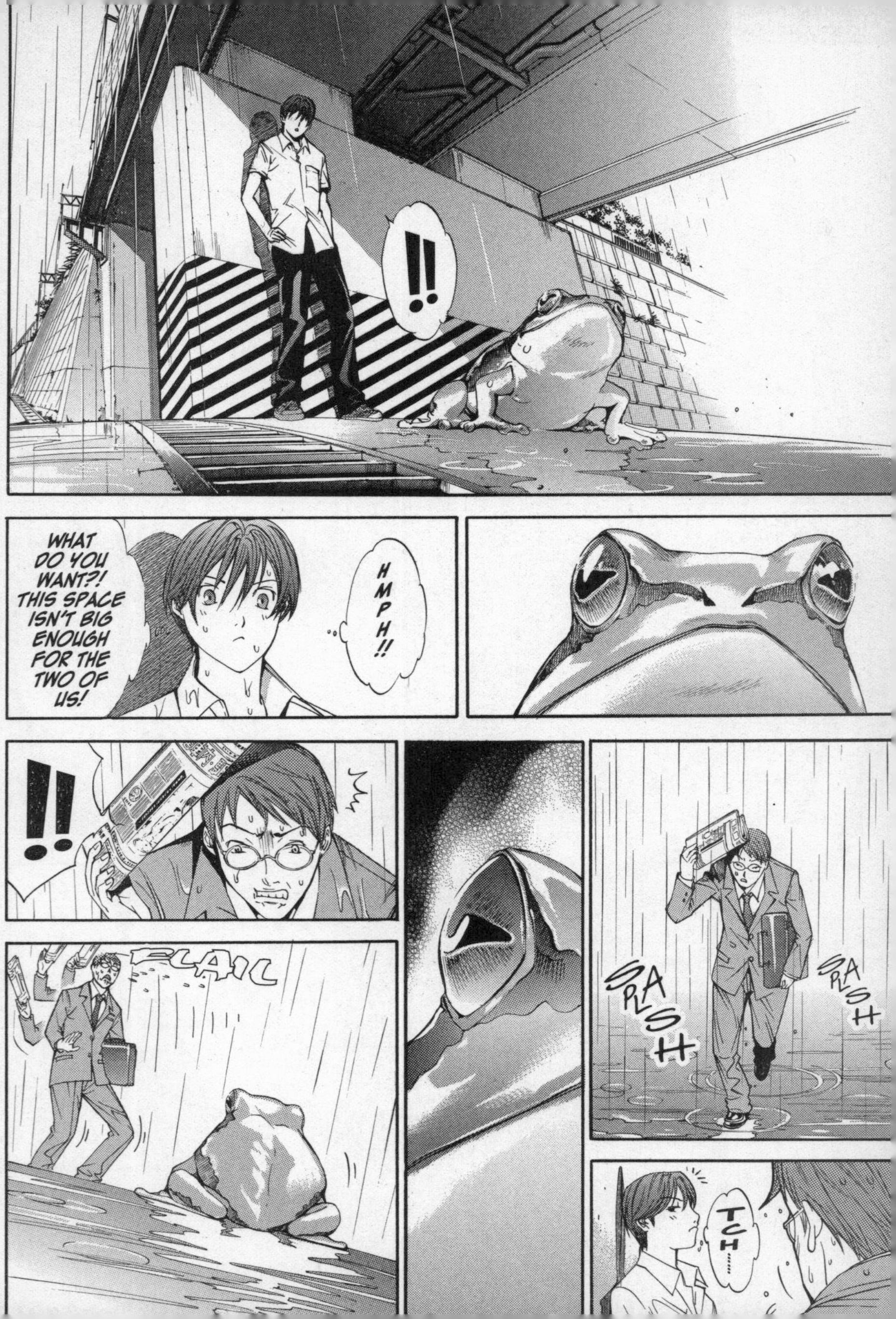
!!
HMPH!!
WHAT DO YOU WANT?! THIS SPACE ISN'T BIG ENOUGH FOR THE TWO OF US!
SPLASH
SPLASH
TCH......
!!
FLAIL

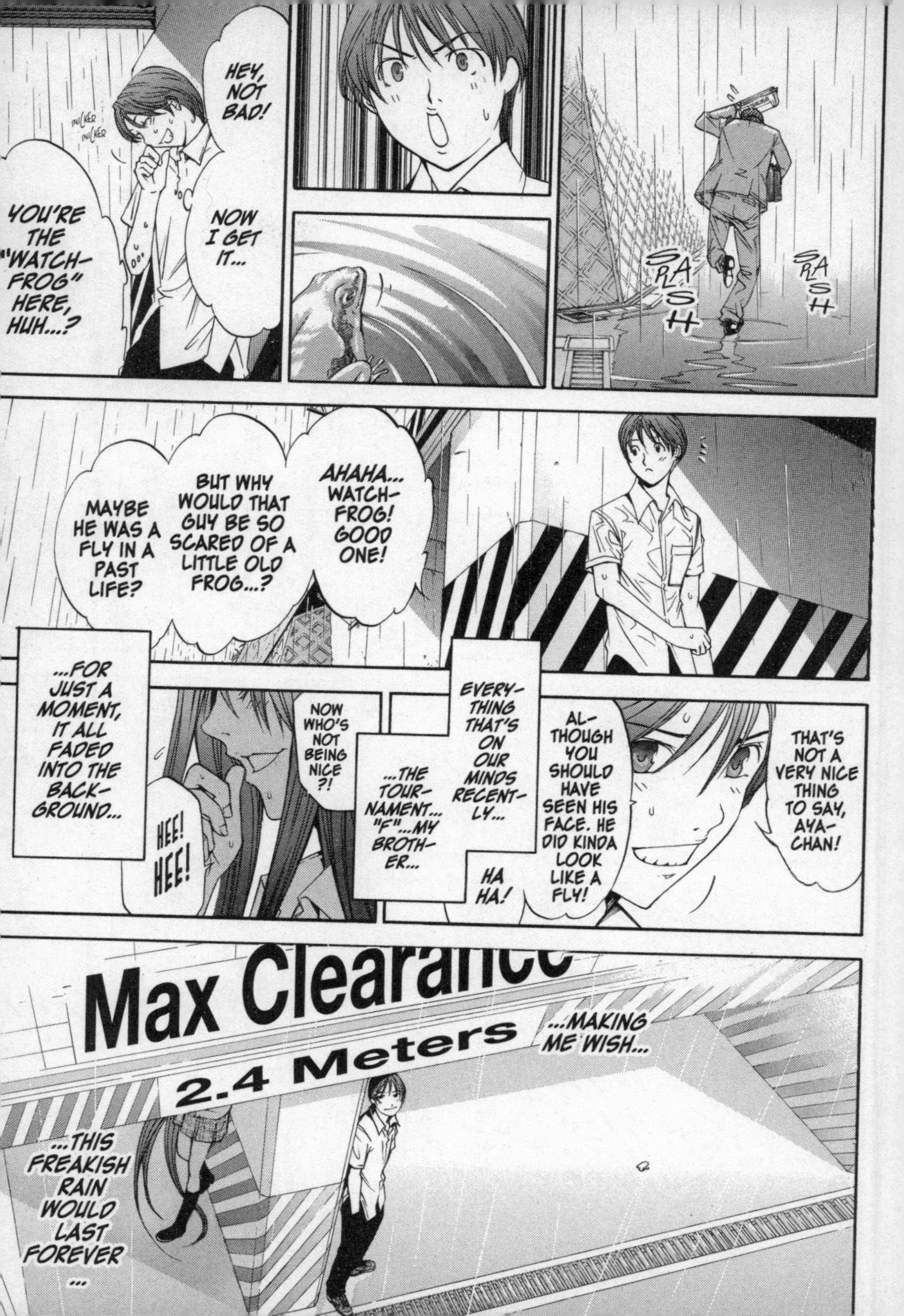
SPLASH
SPLASH
HEY, NOT BAD!
NOW I GET IT...
SNICKER SNICKER
YOU'RE THE "WATCH-FROG" HERE, HUH...?
AHAHA... WATCH-FROG! GOOD ONE!
BUT WHY WOULD THAT GUY BE SO SCARED OF A LITTLE OLD FROG...?
MAYBE HE WAS A FLY IN A PAST LIFE?
THAT'S NOT A VERY NICE THING TO SAY, AYA-CHAN!
ALTHOUGH YOU SHOULD HAVE SEEN HIS FACE. HE DID KINDA LOOK LIKE A FLY!
HA HA!
EVERYTHING THAT'S ON OUR MINDS RECENTLY...
...THE TOURNAMENT... "F"...MY BROTHER...
NOW WHO'S NOT BEING NICE?!
HEE! HEE!
...FOR JUST A MOMENT, IT ALL FADED INTO THE BACKGROUND...
Max Clearance
2.4 Meters
...MAKING ME WISH...
...THIS FREAKISH RAIN WOULD LAST FOREVER...

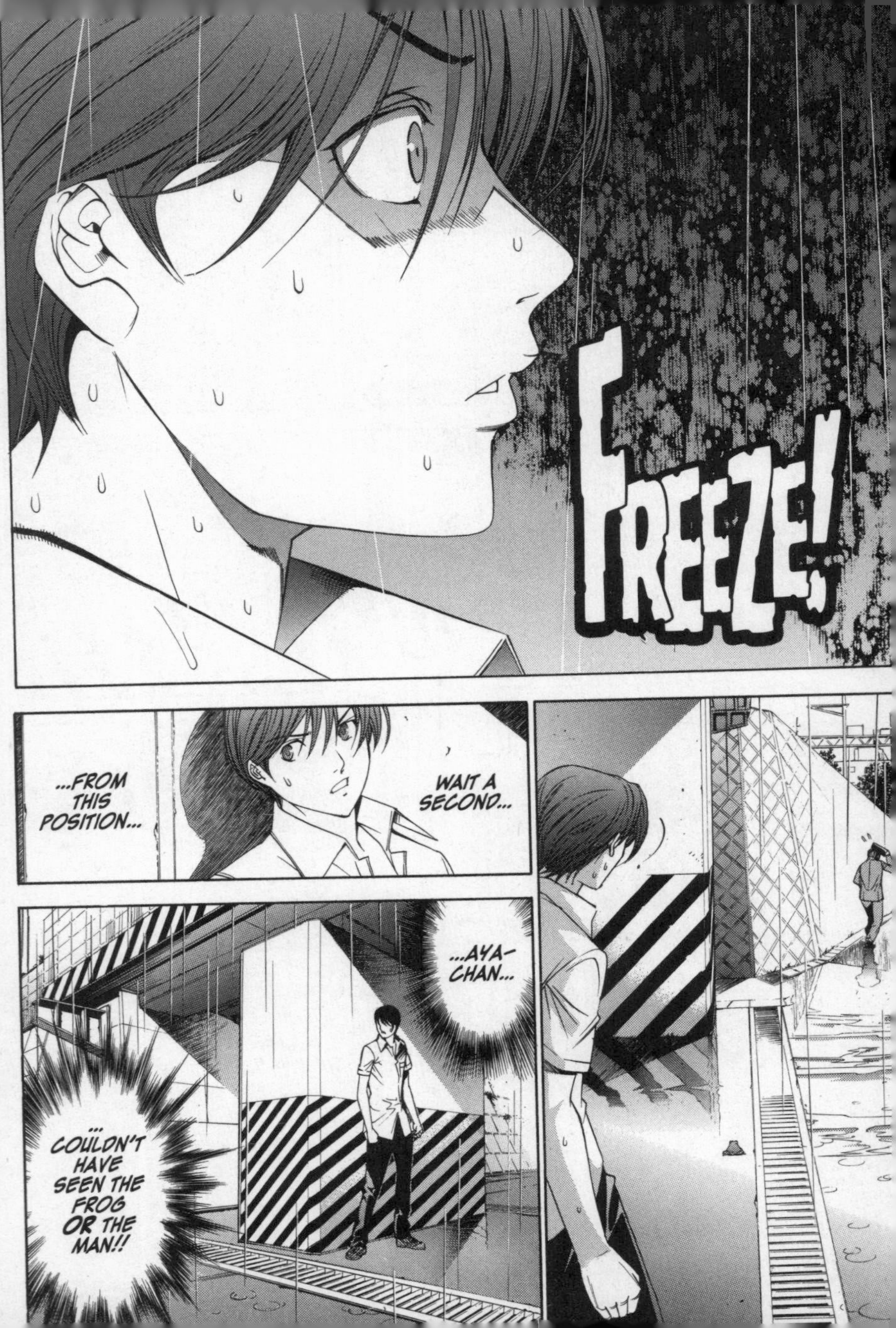
FREEZE!
WAIT A SECOND...
...FROM THIS POSITION...
...AYA-CHAN...
...COULDN'T HAVE SEEN THE FROG OR THE MAN!!

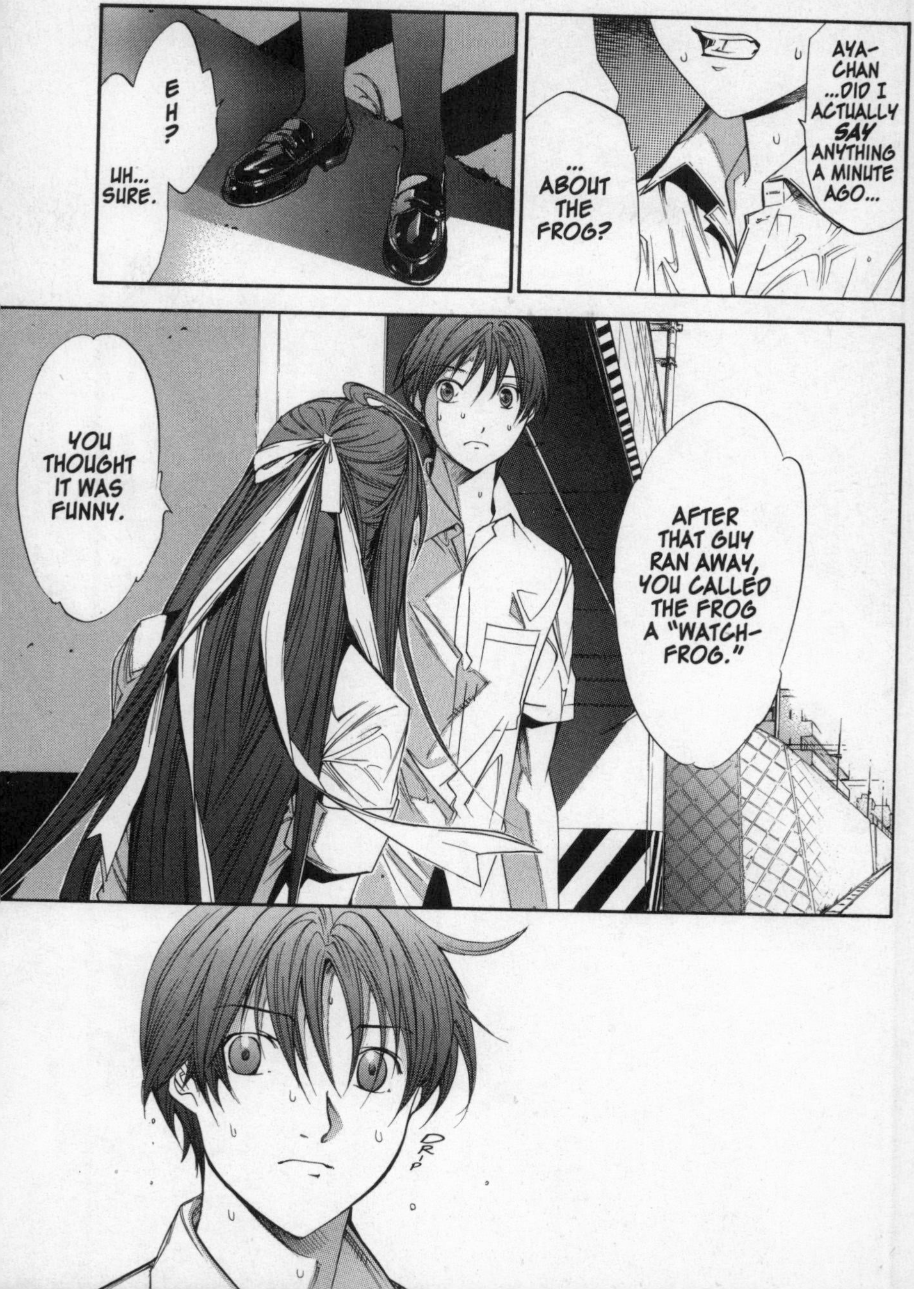
AYA-CHAN ...DID I ACTUALLY SAY ANYTHING A MINUTE AGO...
...ABOUT THE FROG?
EH?
UH... SURE.
AFTER THAT GUY RAN AWAY, YOU CALLED THE FROG A "WATCH-FROG."
YOU THOUGHT IT WAS FUNNY.
DRIP

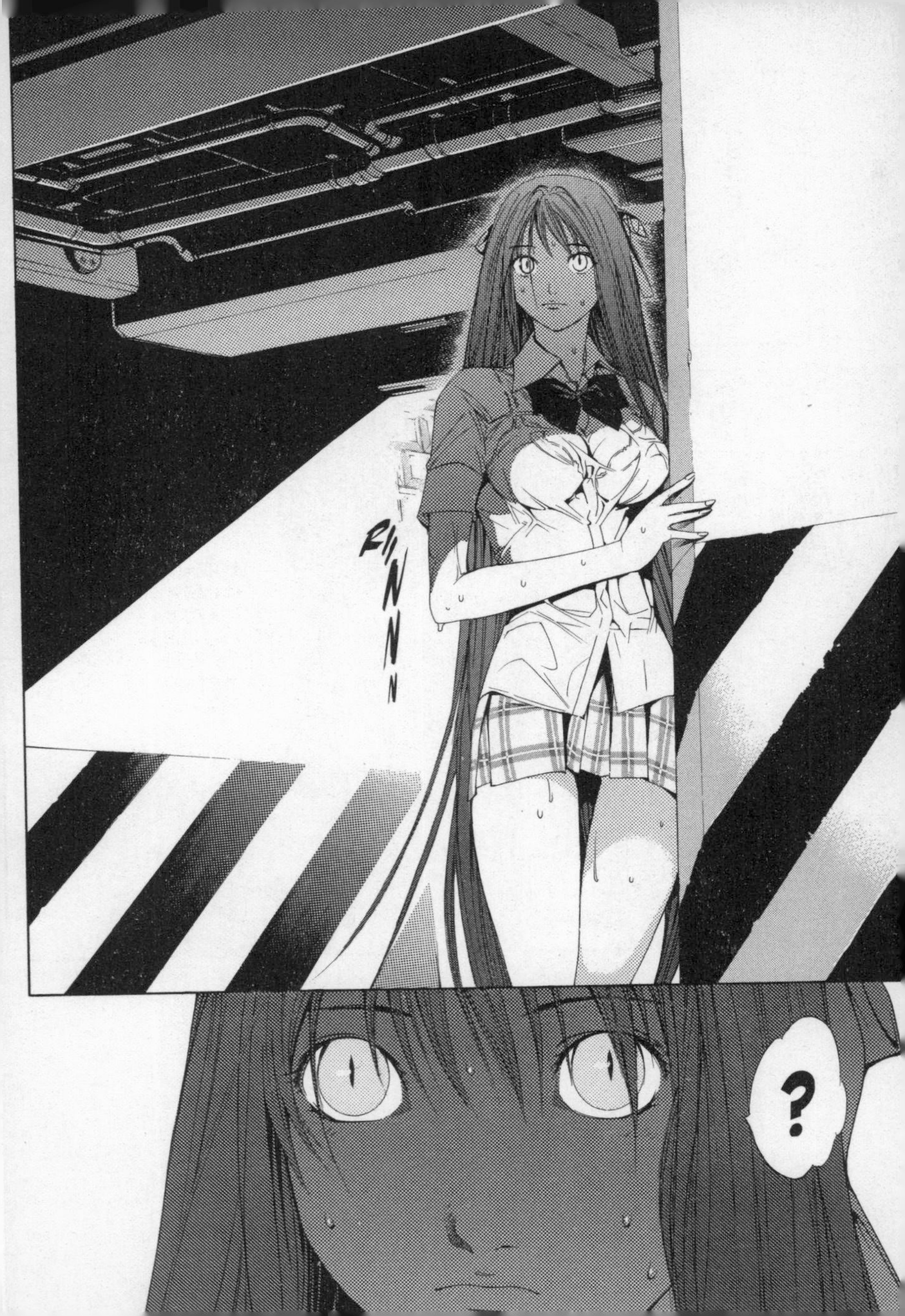
RIIINNNN
?

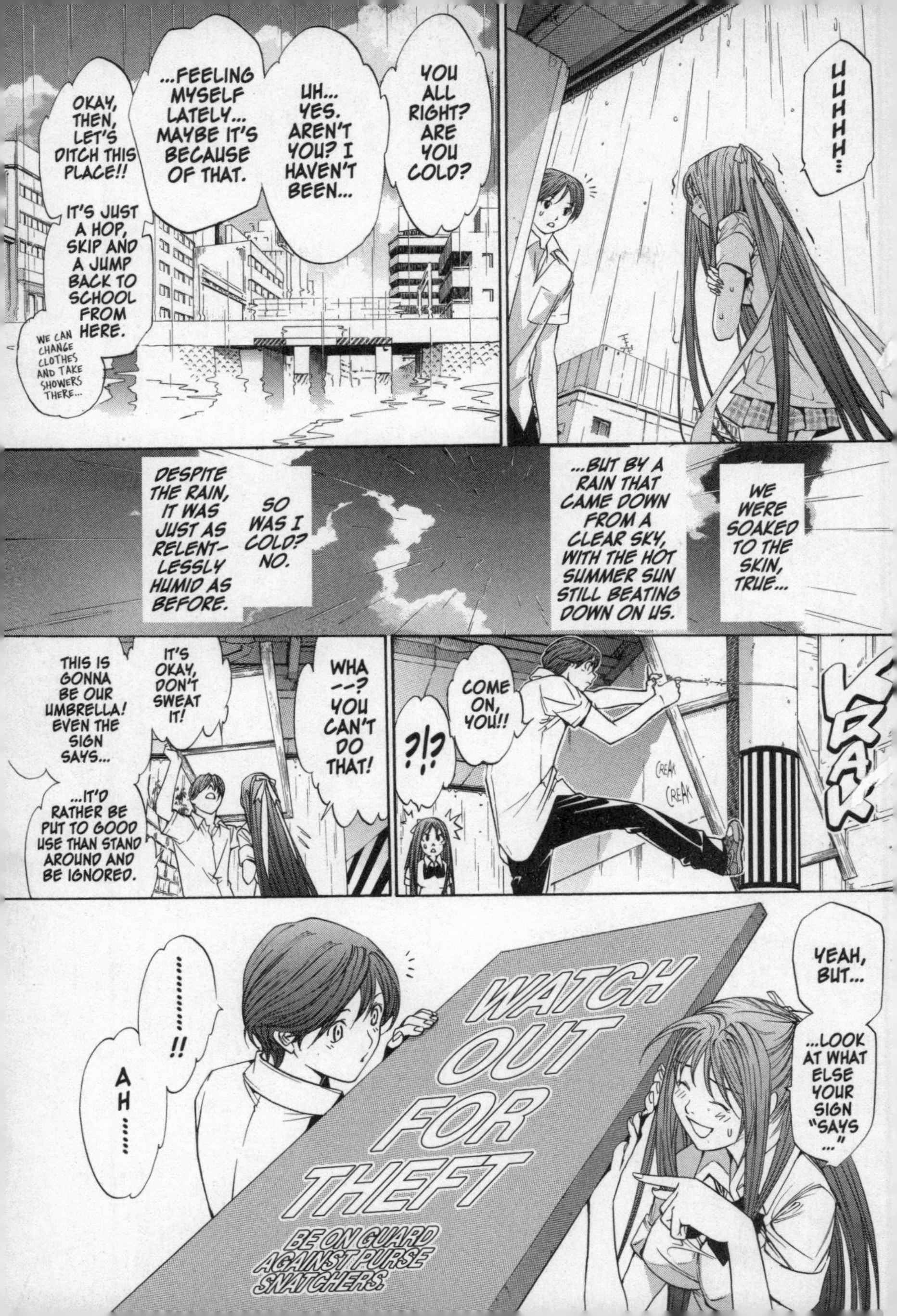
UUHHH...
YOU ALL RIGHT? ARE YOU COLD?
UH... YES. AREN'T YOU? I HAVEN'T BEEN...
...FEELING MYSELF LATELY... MAYBE IT'S BECAUSE OF THAT.
OKAY, THEN, LET'S DITCH THIS PLACE!!
IT'S JUST A HOP, SKIP AND A JUMP BACK TO SCHOOL FROM HERE.
WE CAN CHANGE CLOTHES AND TAKE SHOWERS THERE...
WE WERE SOAKED TO THE SKIN, TRUE...
...BUT BY A RAIN THAT CAME DOWN FROM A CLEAR SKY, WITH THE HOT SUMMER SUN STILL BEATING DOWN ON US.
SO WAS I COLD? NO.
DESPITE THE RAIN, IT WAS JUST AS RELENTLESSLY HUMID AS BEFORE.
KRAK
CREAK CREAK
COME ON, YOU!!
?!?
WHA--? YOU CAN'T DO THAT!
IT'S OKAY, DON'T SWEAT IT!
THIS IS GONNA BE OUR UMBRELLA! EVEN THE SIGN SAYS...
...IT'D RATHER BE PUT TO GOOD USE THAN STAND AROUND AND BE IGNORED.
YEAH, BUT...
...LOOK AT WHAT ELSE YOUR SIGN "SAYS"...
WATCH OUT FOR THEFT
BE ON GUARD AGAINST PURSE SNATCHERS.
..........!!
AH ......

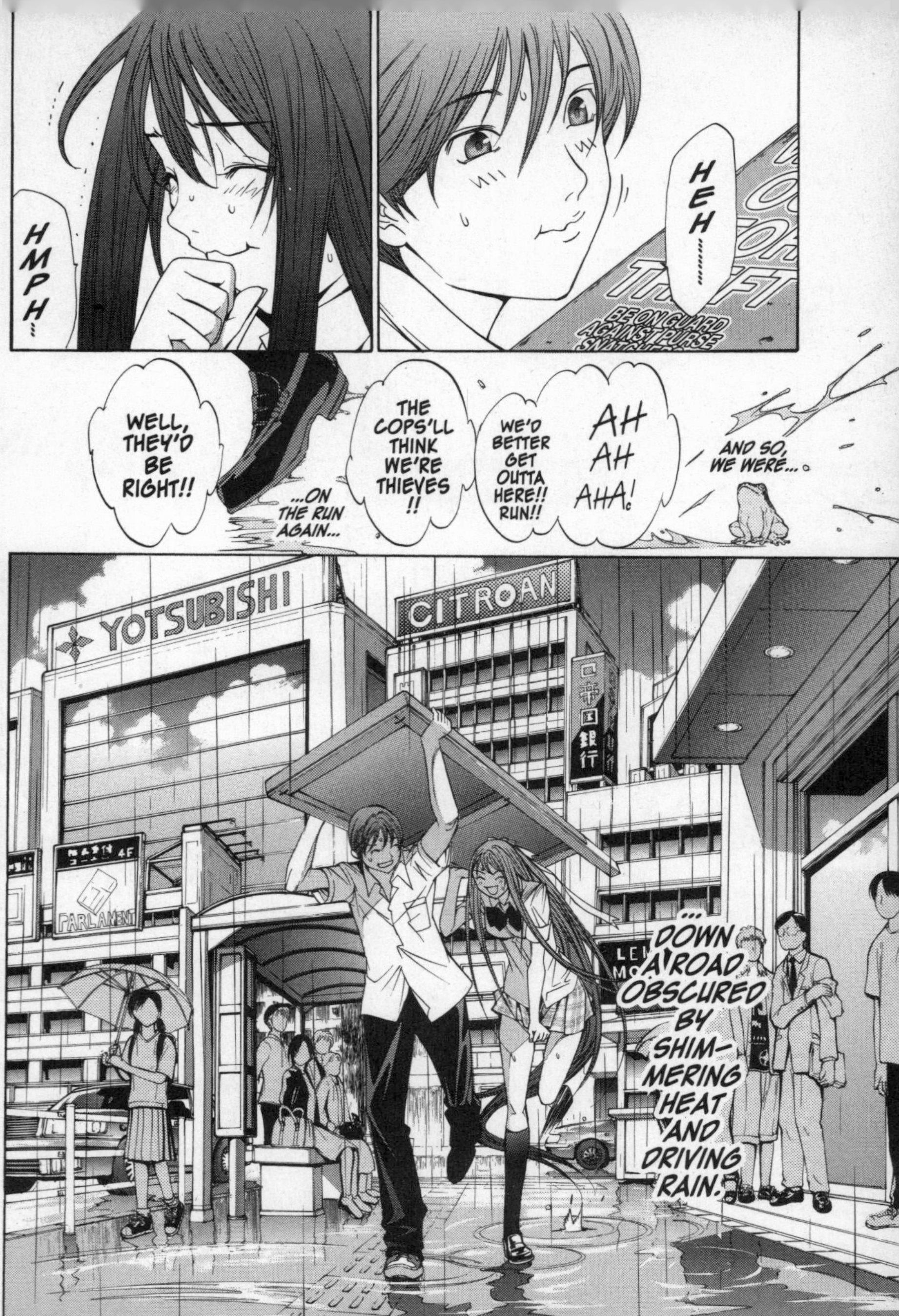
HEH......
THEFT
BE ON GUARD AGAINST PURSE
HMPH..
AND SO, WE WERE...
AH AH AHA!
WE'D BETTER GET OUTTA HERE!! RUN!!
THE COPS'LL THINK WE'RE THIEVES!!
...ON THE RUN AGAIN...
WELL, THEY'D BE RIGHT!!
CITROAN
YOTSUBISHI
4F
PARLAMENT
...DOWN A ROAD OBSCURED BY SHIMMERING HEAT AND DRIVING RAIN.

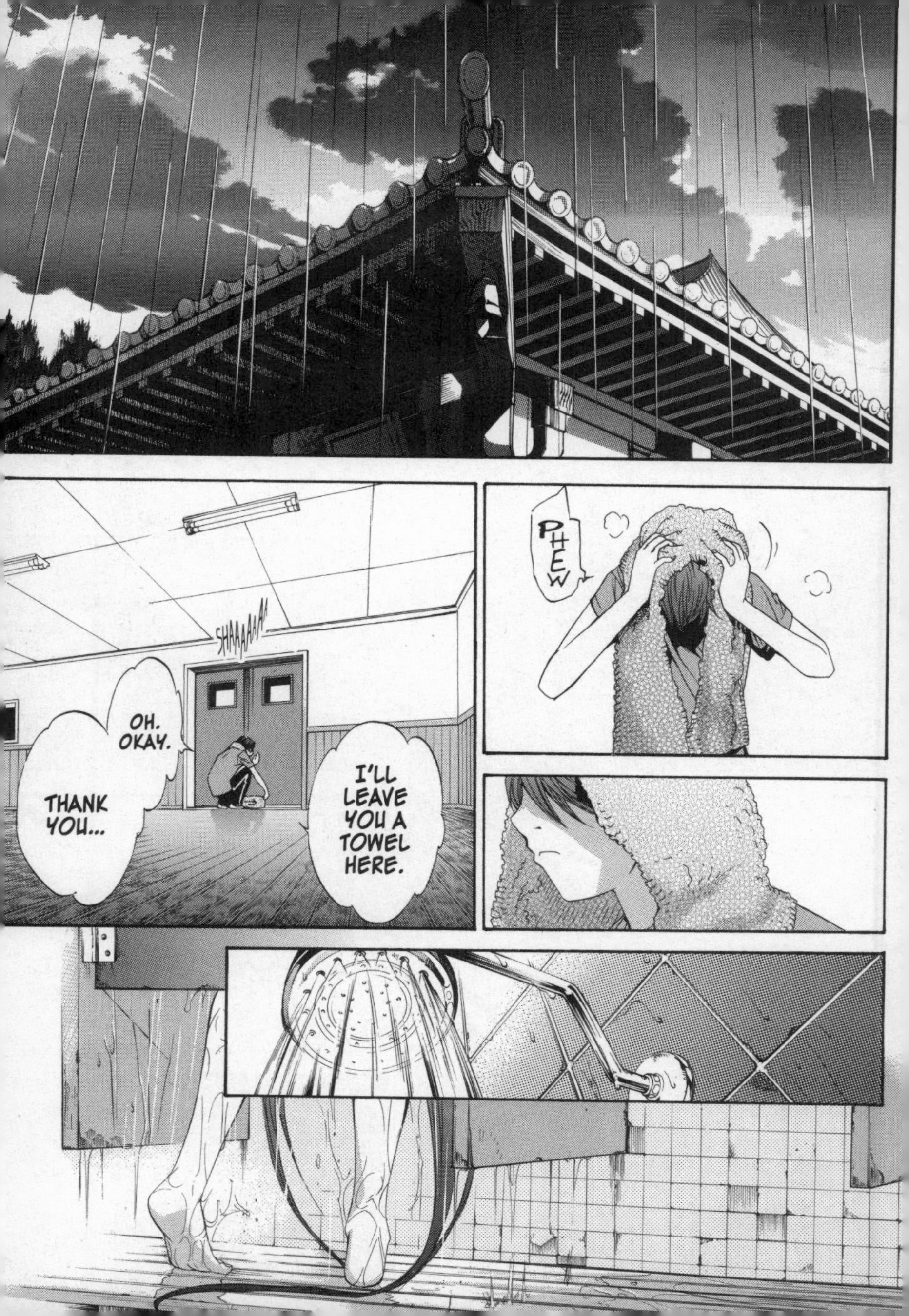
PHEW
SHAAAAAA
I'LL LEAVE YOU A TOWEL HERE.
OH. OKAY.
THANK YOU...

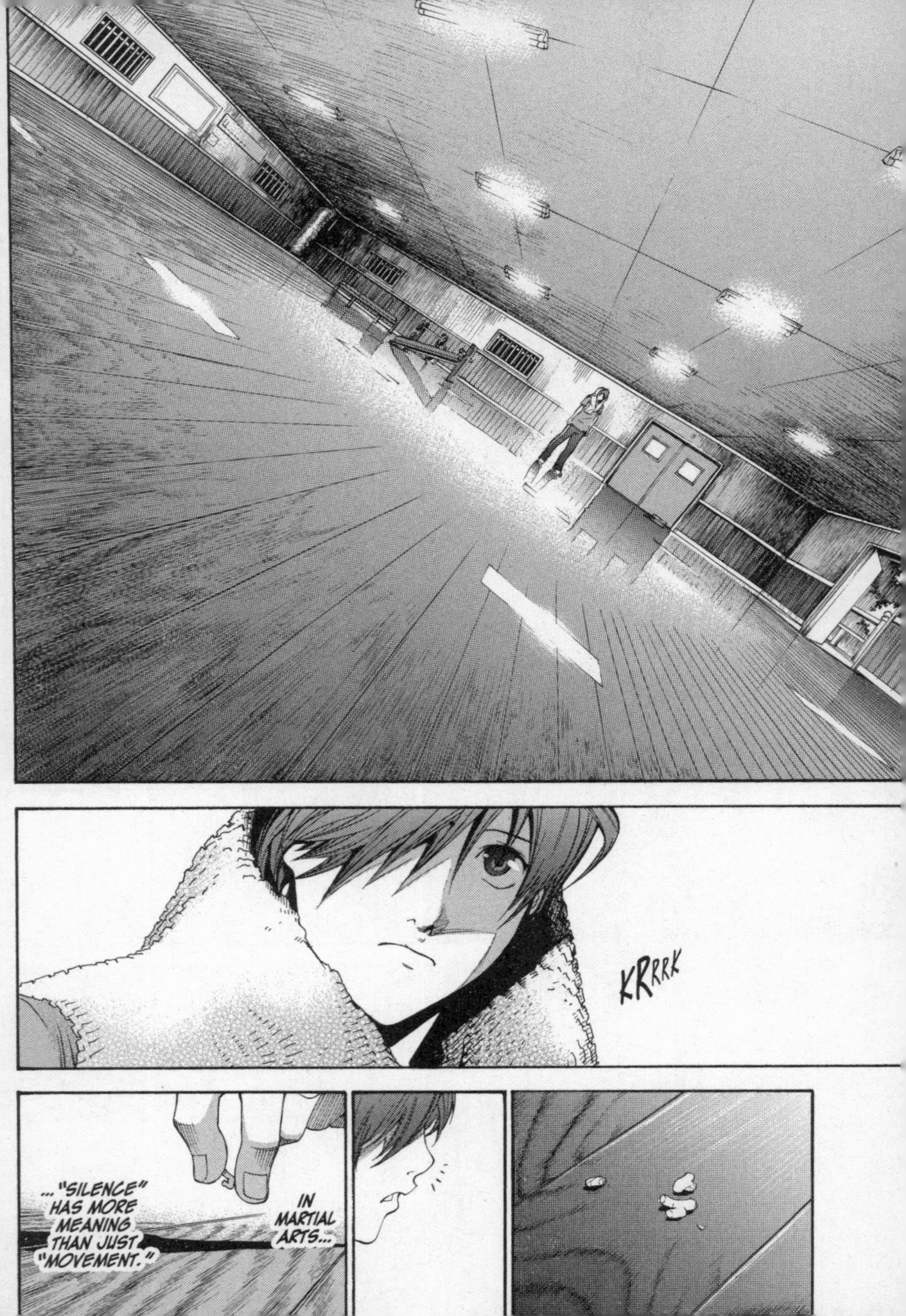
KRRRK
IN MARTIAL ARTS...
..."SILENCE" HAS MORE MEANING THAN JUST "MOVEMENT."

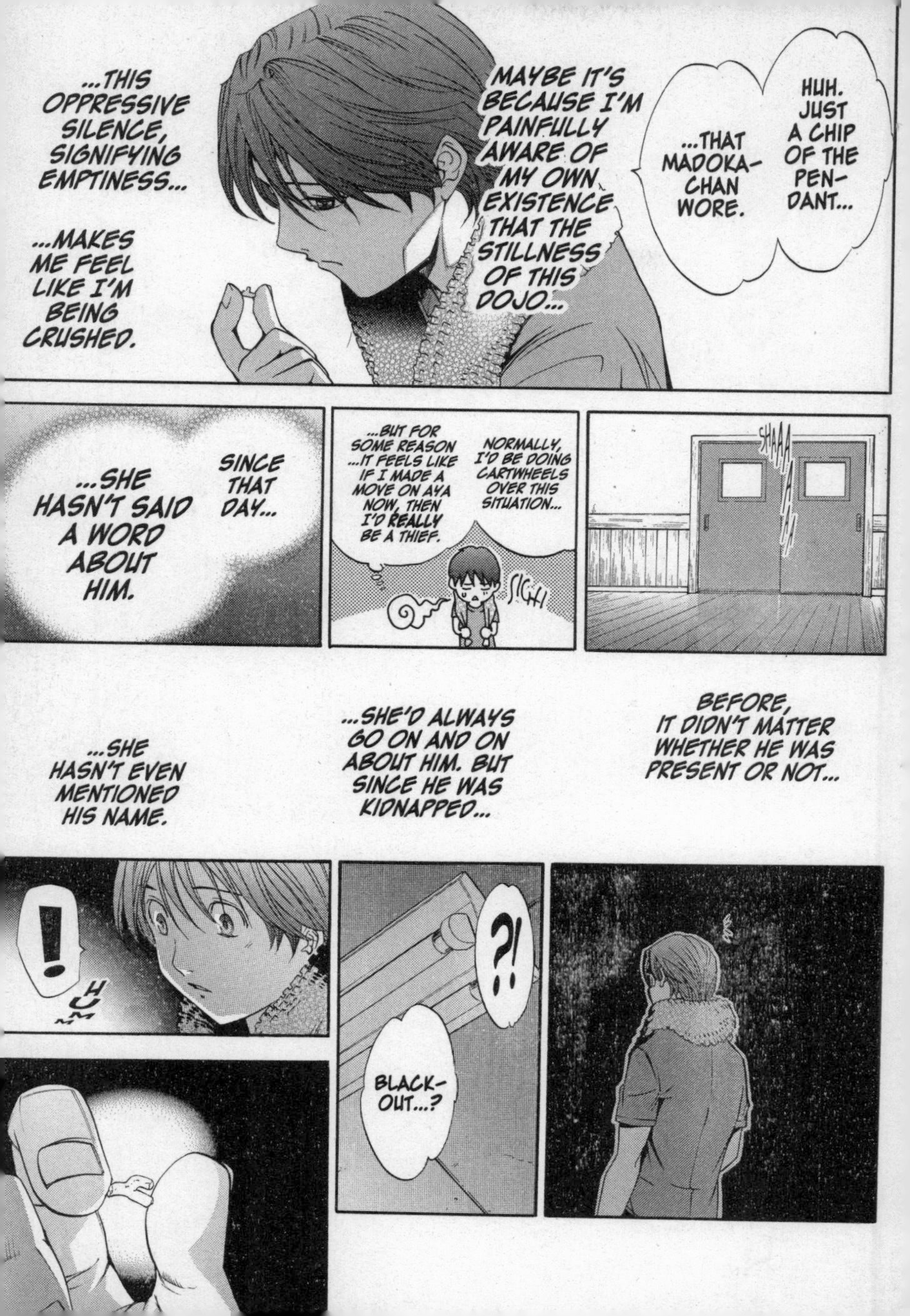
HUH. JUST A CHIP OF THE PEN-DANT...
...THAT MADOKA-CHAN WORE.
MAYBE IT'S BECAUSE I'M PAINFULLY AWARE OF MY OWN EXISTENCE THAT THE STILLNESS OF THIS DOJO...
...THIS OPPRESSIVE SILENCE, SIGNIFYING EMPTINESS...
...MAKES ME FEEL LIKE I'M BEING CRUSHED.
NORMALLY, I'D BE DOING CARTWHEELS OVER THIS SITUATION...
...BUT FOR SOME REASON ...IT FEELS LIKE IF I MADE A MOVE ON AYA NOW, THEN I'D REALLY BE A THIEF.
SIGH
SINCE THAT DAY...
...SHE HASN'T SAID A WORD ABOUT HIM.
BEFORE, IT DIDN'T MATTER WHETHER HE WAS PRESENT OR NOT...
...SHE'D ALWAYS GO ON AND ON ABOUT HIM. BUT SINCE HE WAS KIDNAPPED...
...SHE HASN'T EVEN MENTIONED HIS NAME.
?!
BLACK-OUT...?
!
HUM

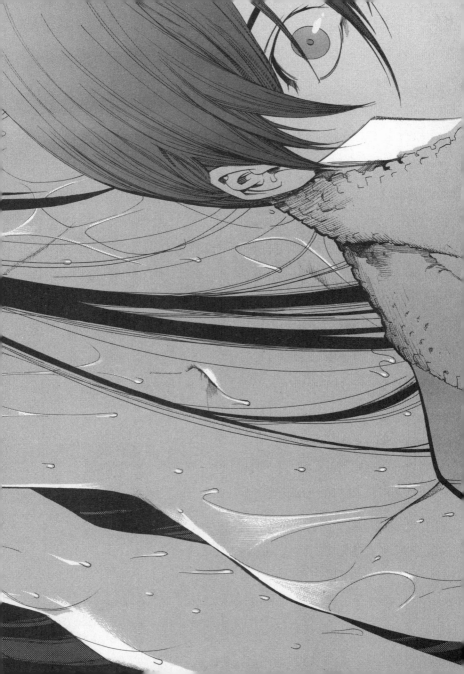

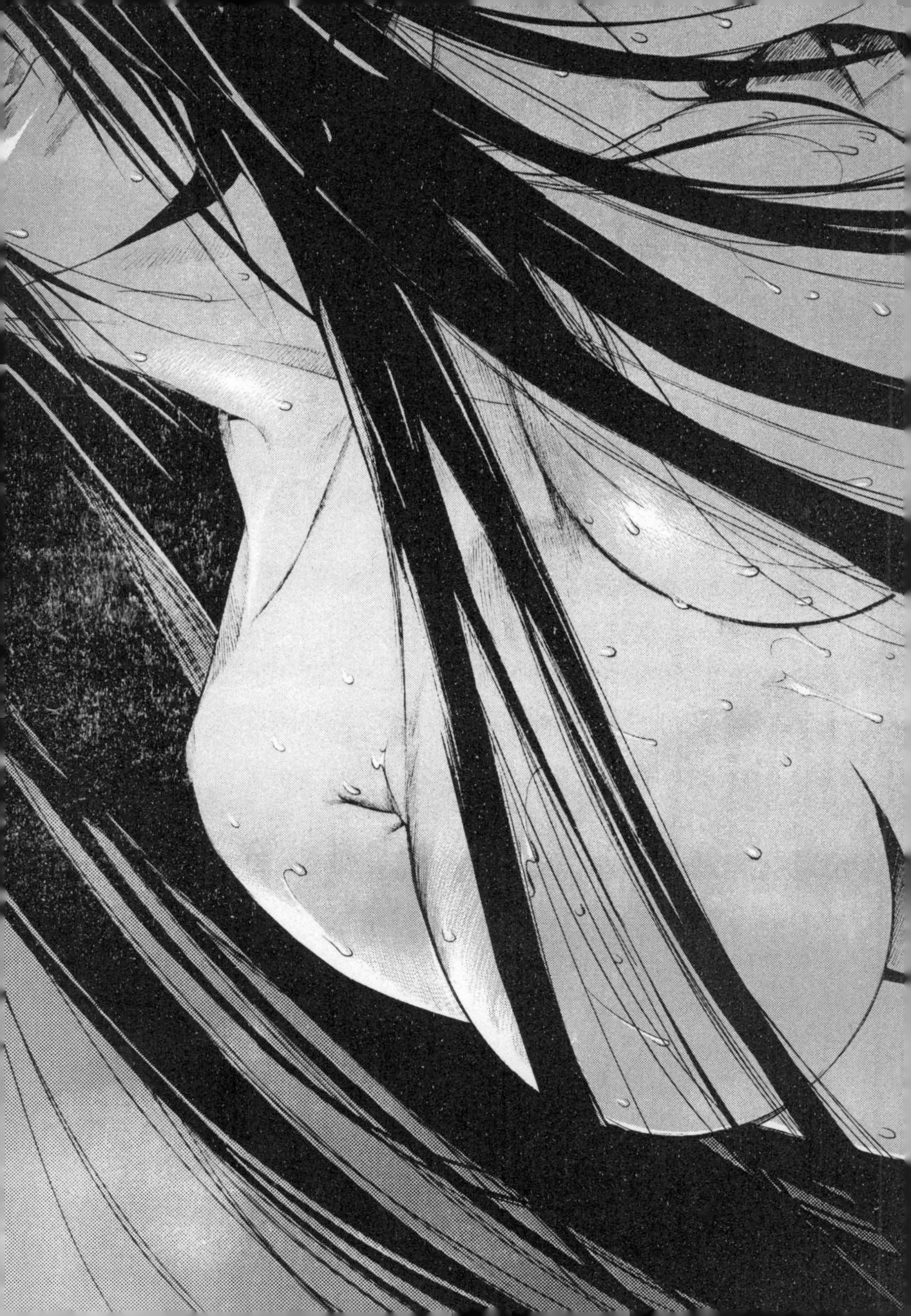

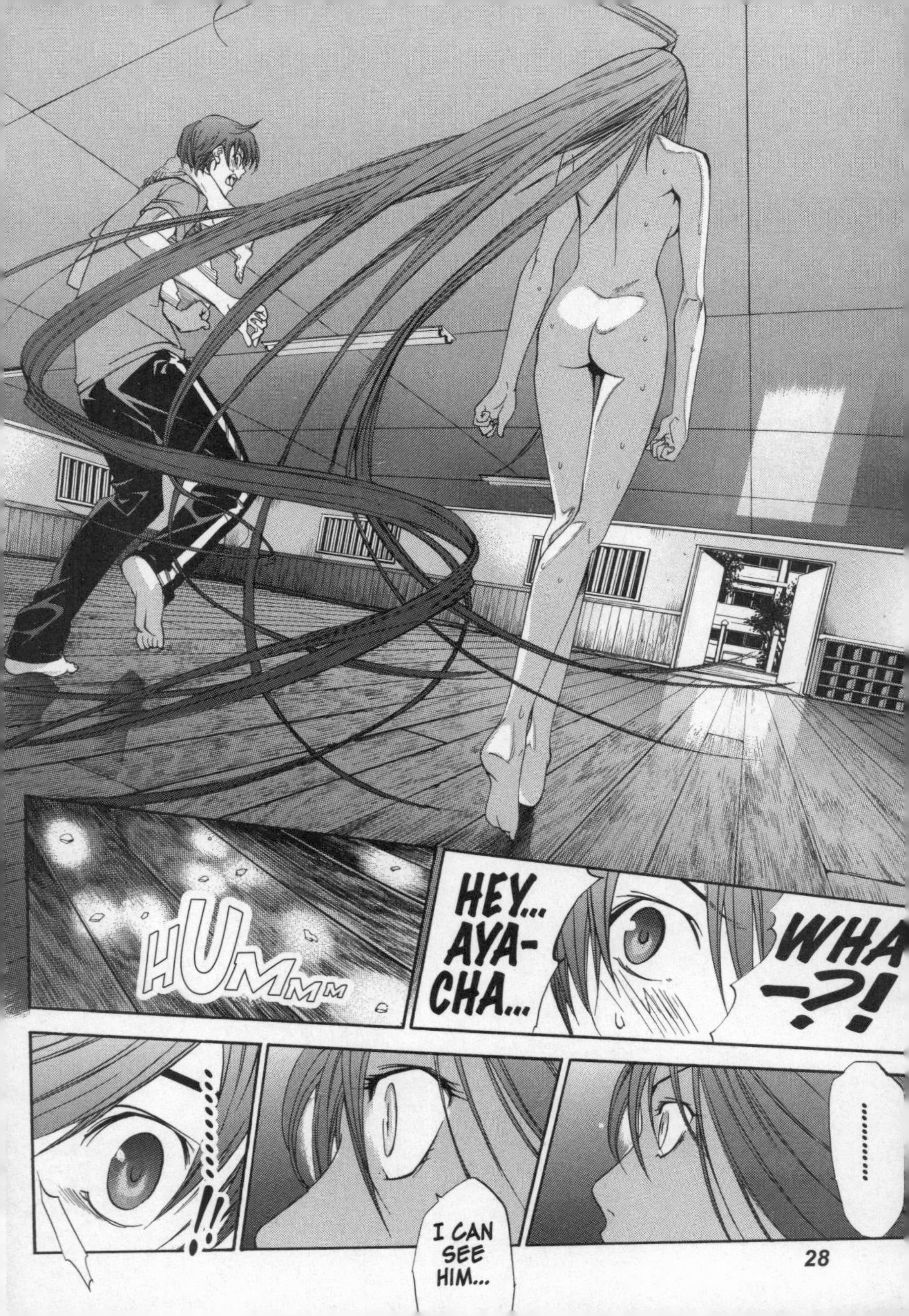
WHA--?!
HEY... AYA-CHA...
HUMMM
......
I CAN SEE HIM...
..........!!

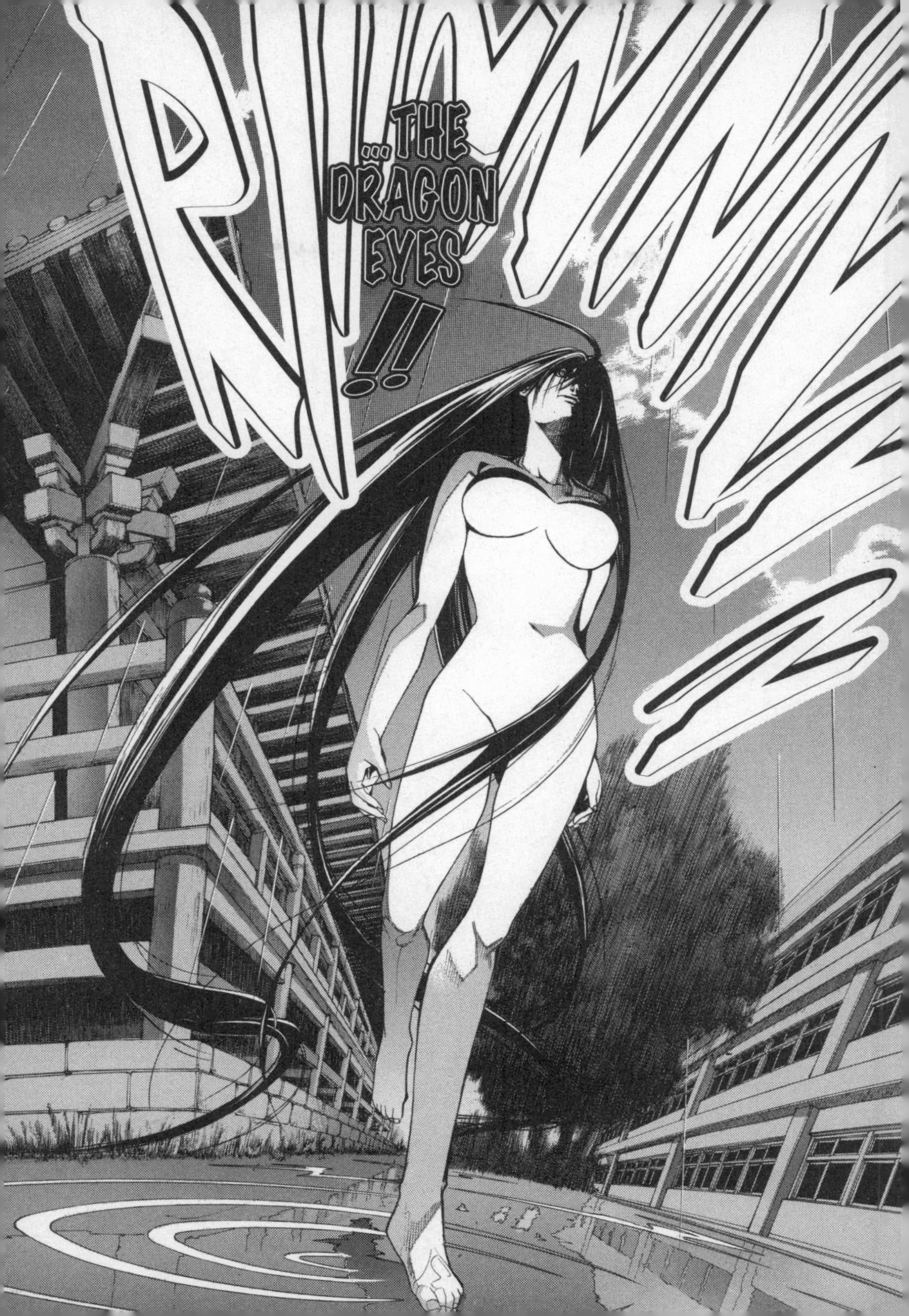
...THE DRAGON EYES!!

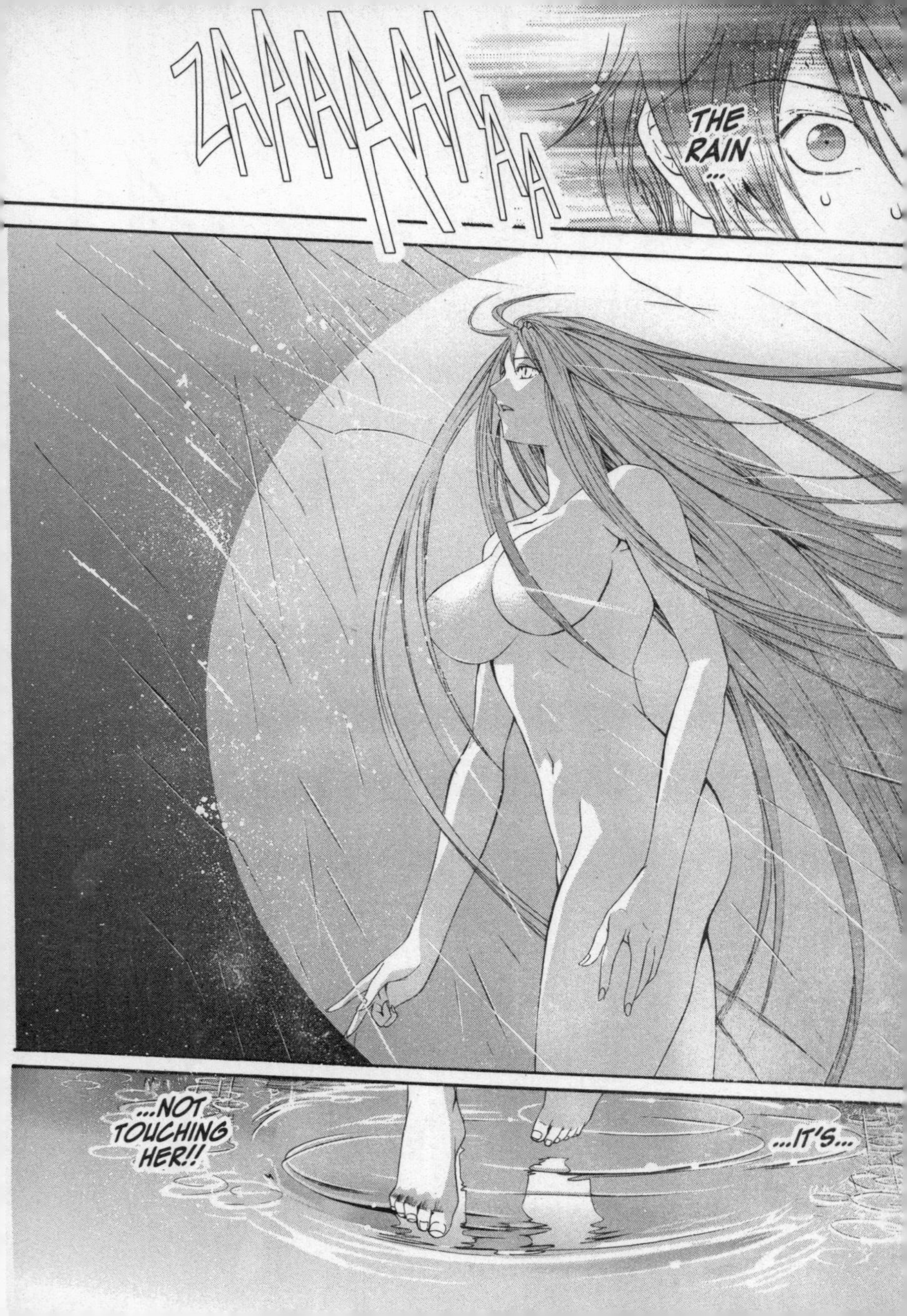
THE RAIN ...
ZAAAAAAAAA
...IT'S...
...NOT TOUCHING HER!!

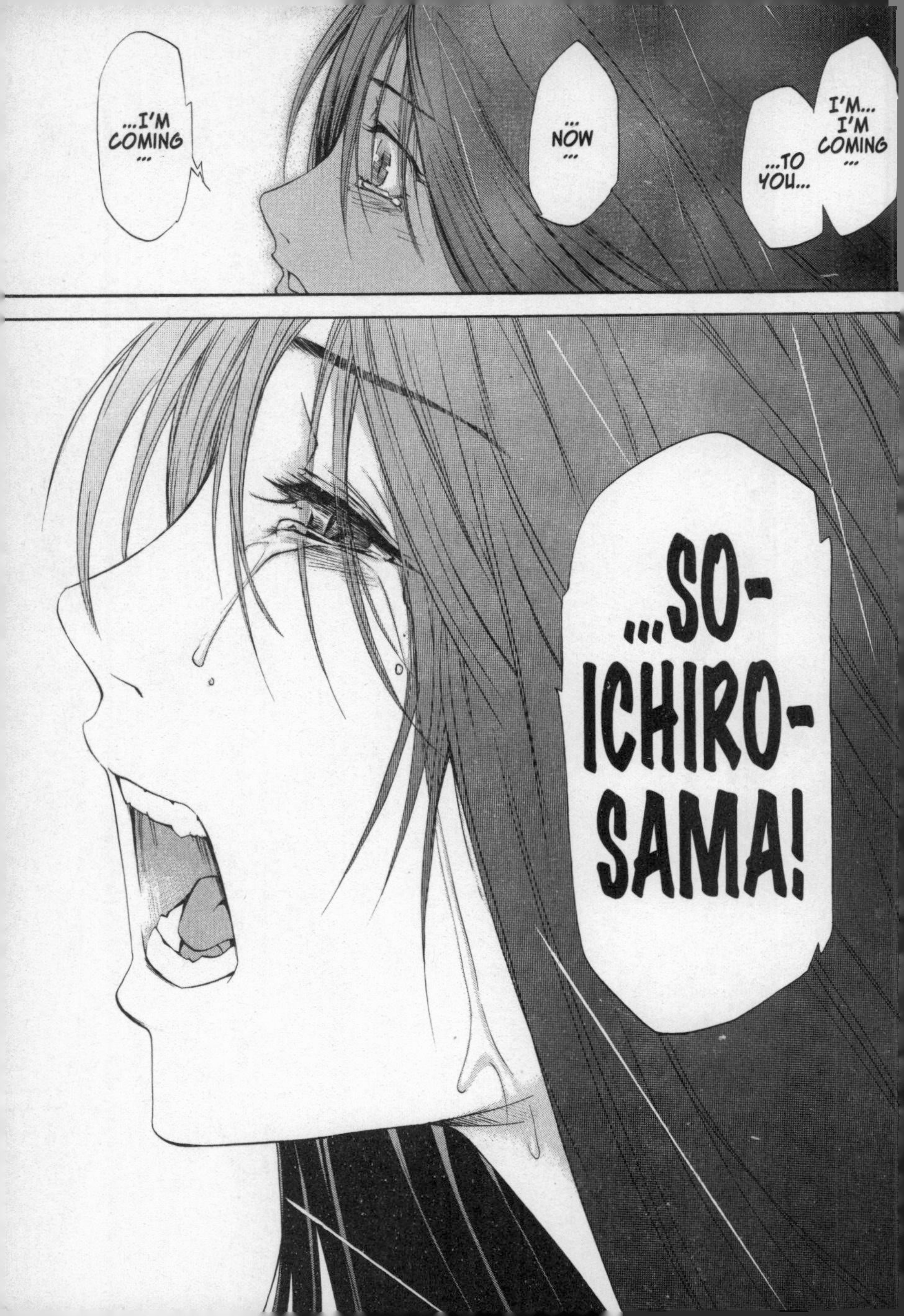
I'M... I'M COMING...
...TO YOU...
...NOW...
...I'M COMING...
...SO-ICHIRO-SAMA!

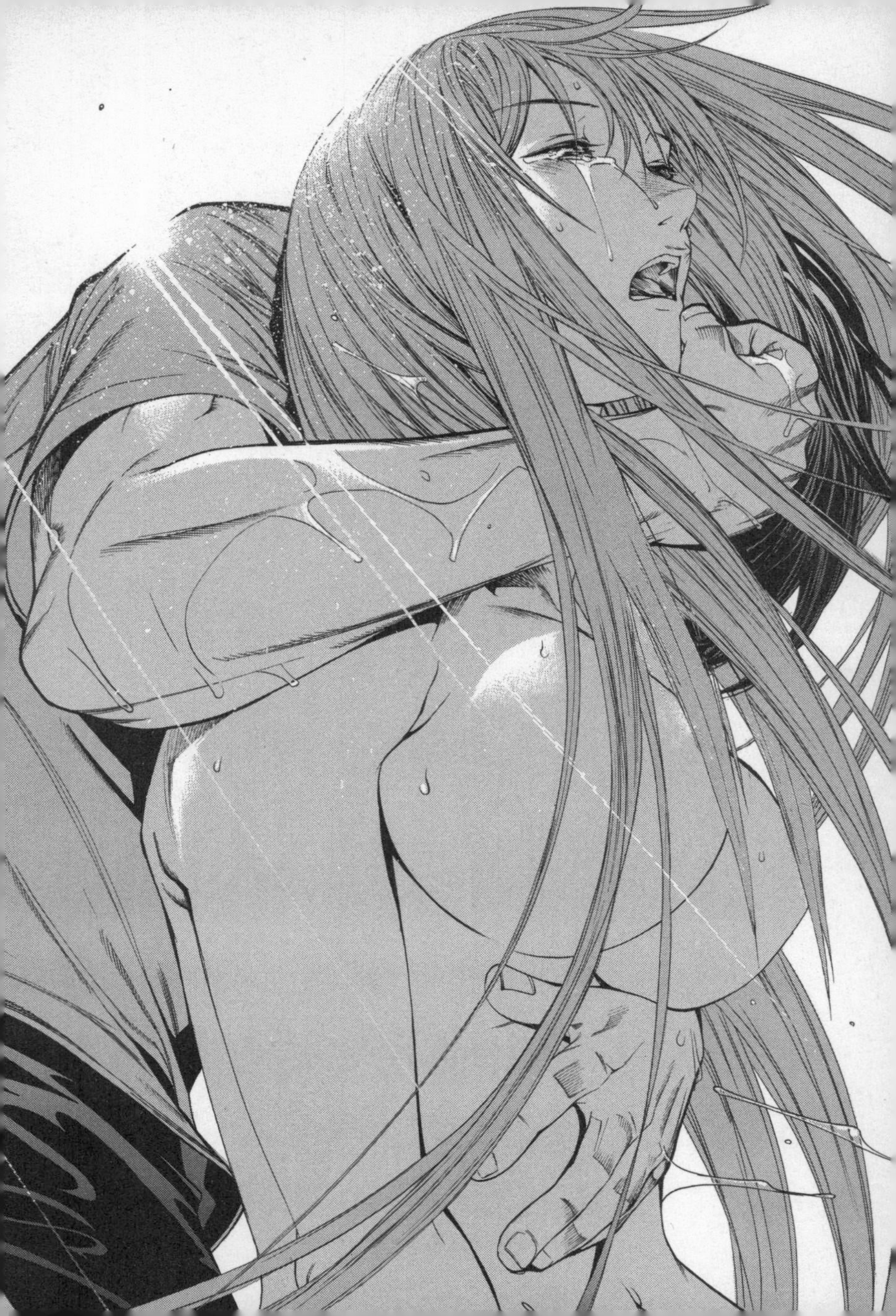

....
HE'S NOT HERE...

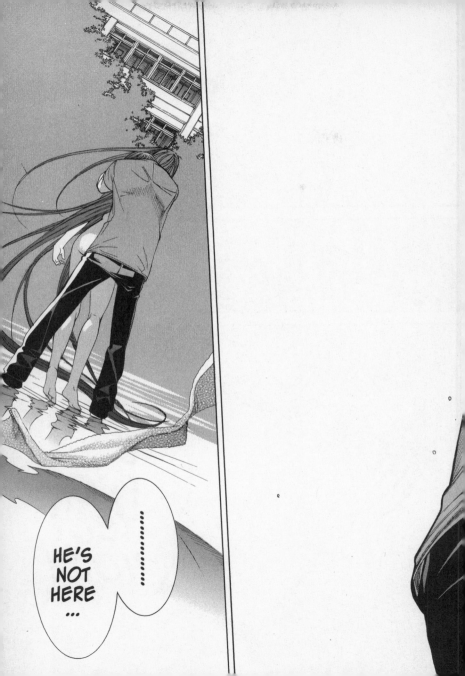

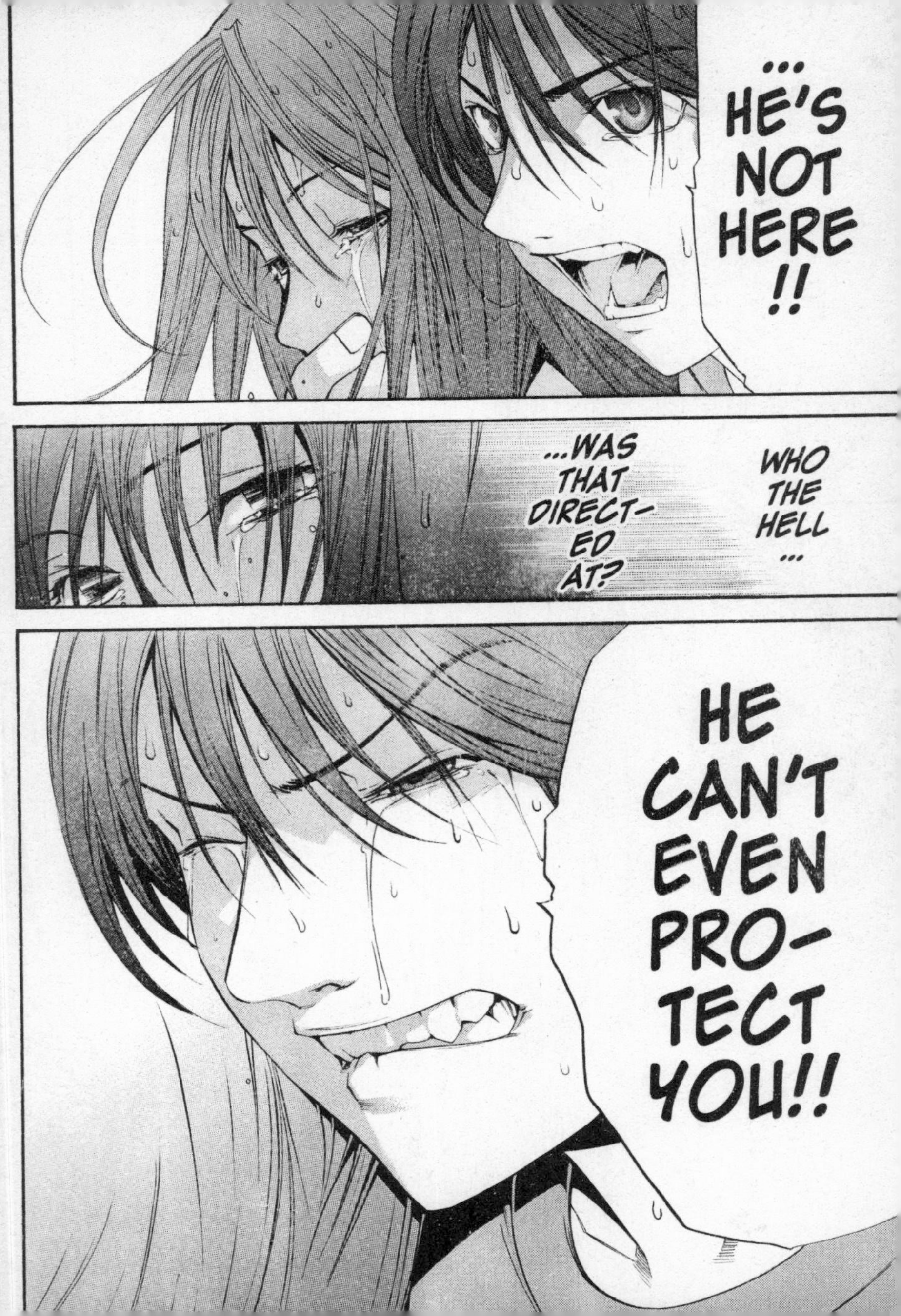
...HE'S NOT HERE!!
WHO THE HELL...
...WAS THAT DIRECT-ED AT?
HE CAN'T EVEN PRO-TECT YOU!!

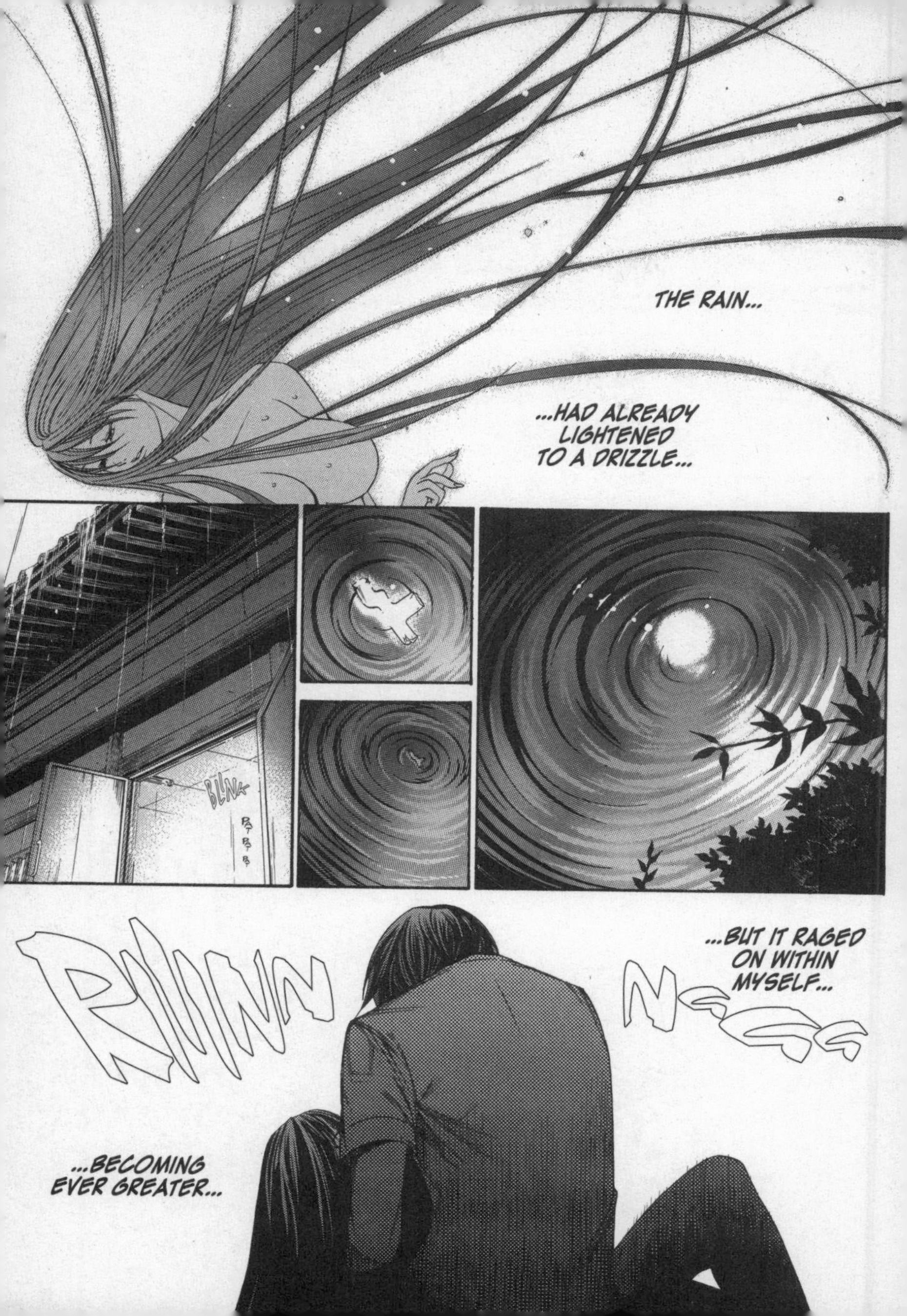
THE RAIN...
...HAD ALREADY LIGHTENED TO A DRIZZLE...
BLINK
PAT PAT PAT
...BUT IT RAGED ON WITHIN MYSELF...
...BECOMING EVER GREATER...

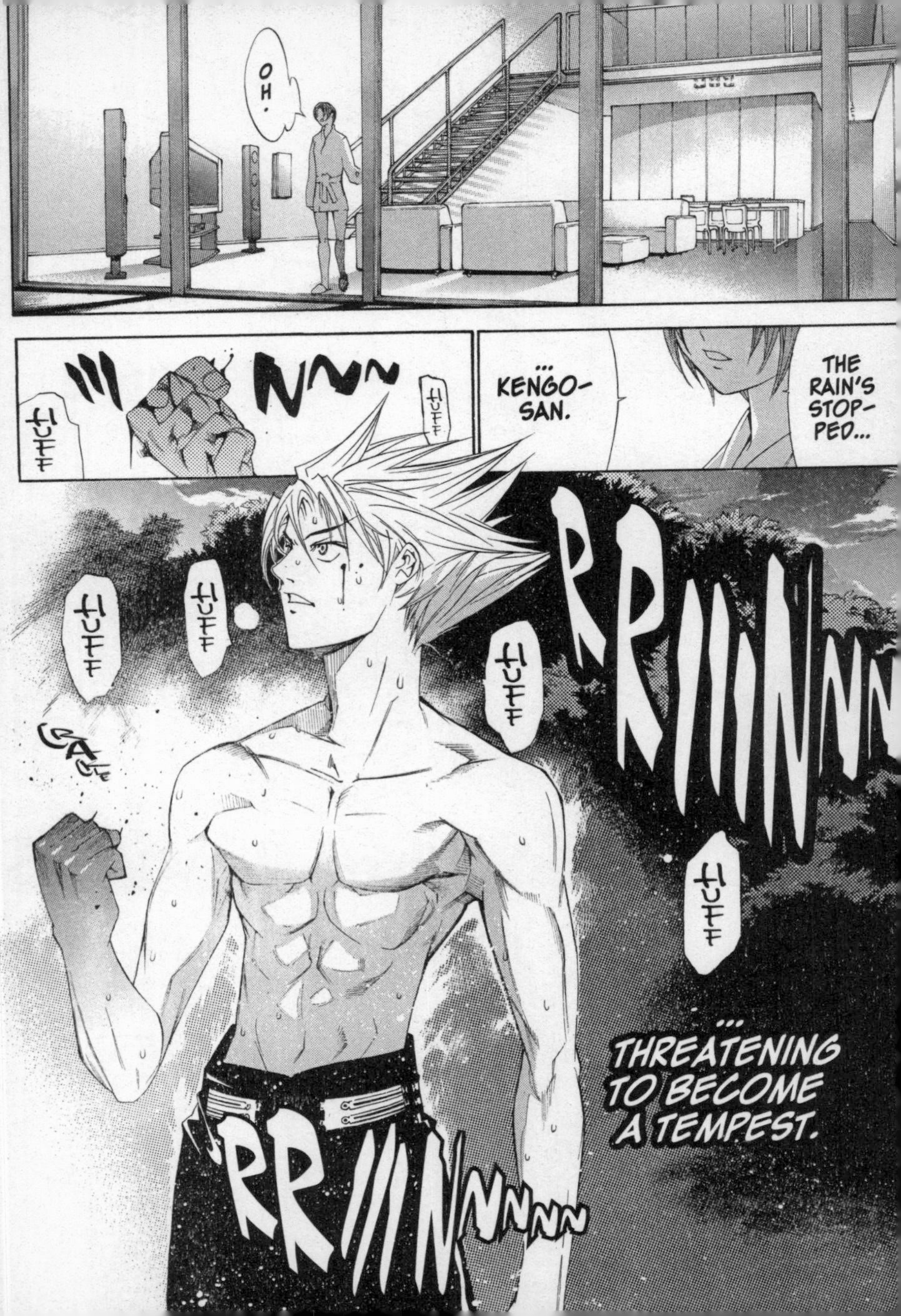
OH.
THE RAIN'S STOP-PED...
...KENGO-SAN.
HUFF
NNN
HUFF
RRIIIINNNN
HUFF
HUFF
HUFF
HUFF
...THREATENING TO BECOME A TEMPEST.
RRIINNNNN

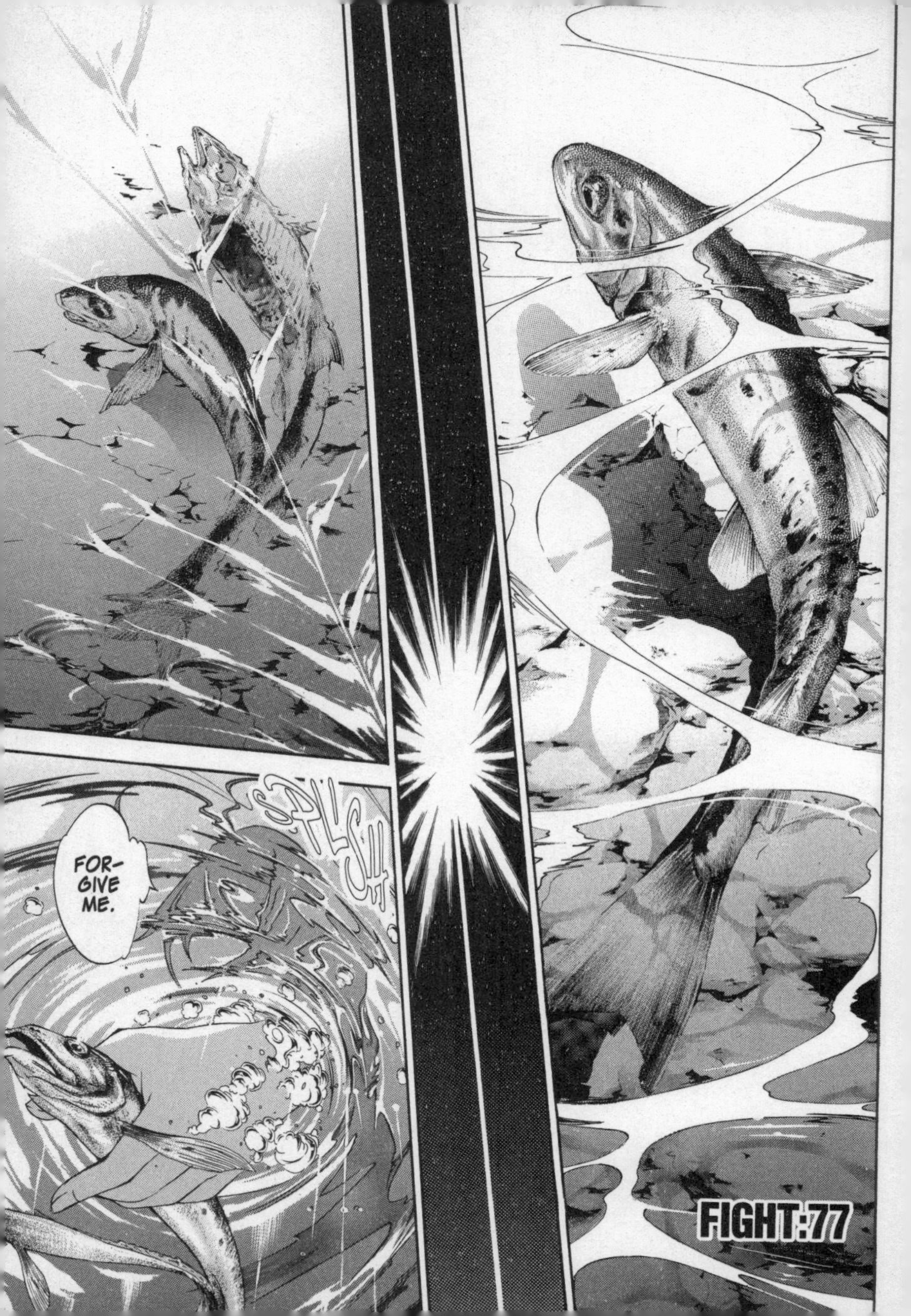
FIGHT:77
SPLSH
FOR-GIVE ME.

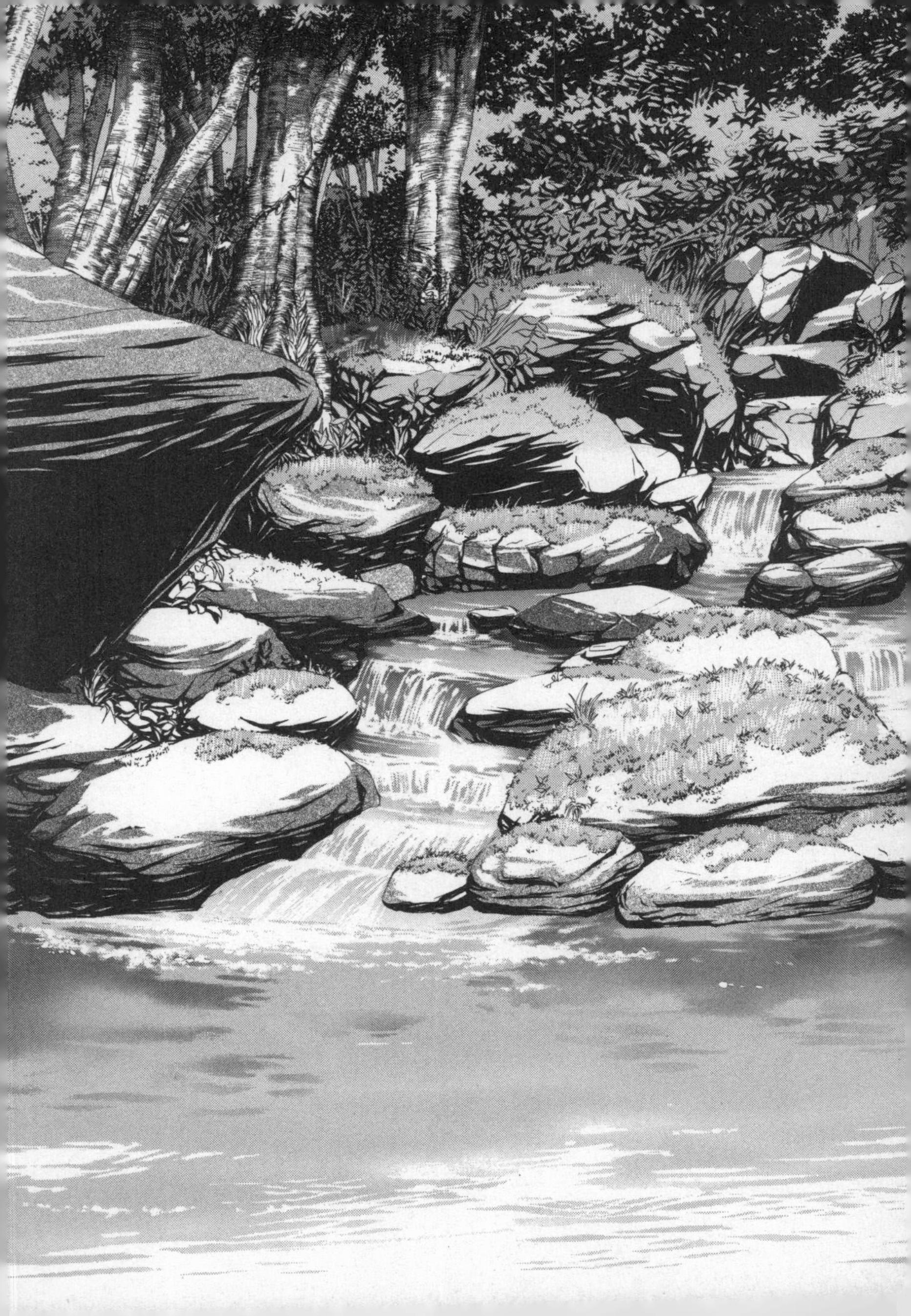

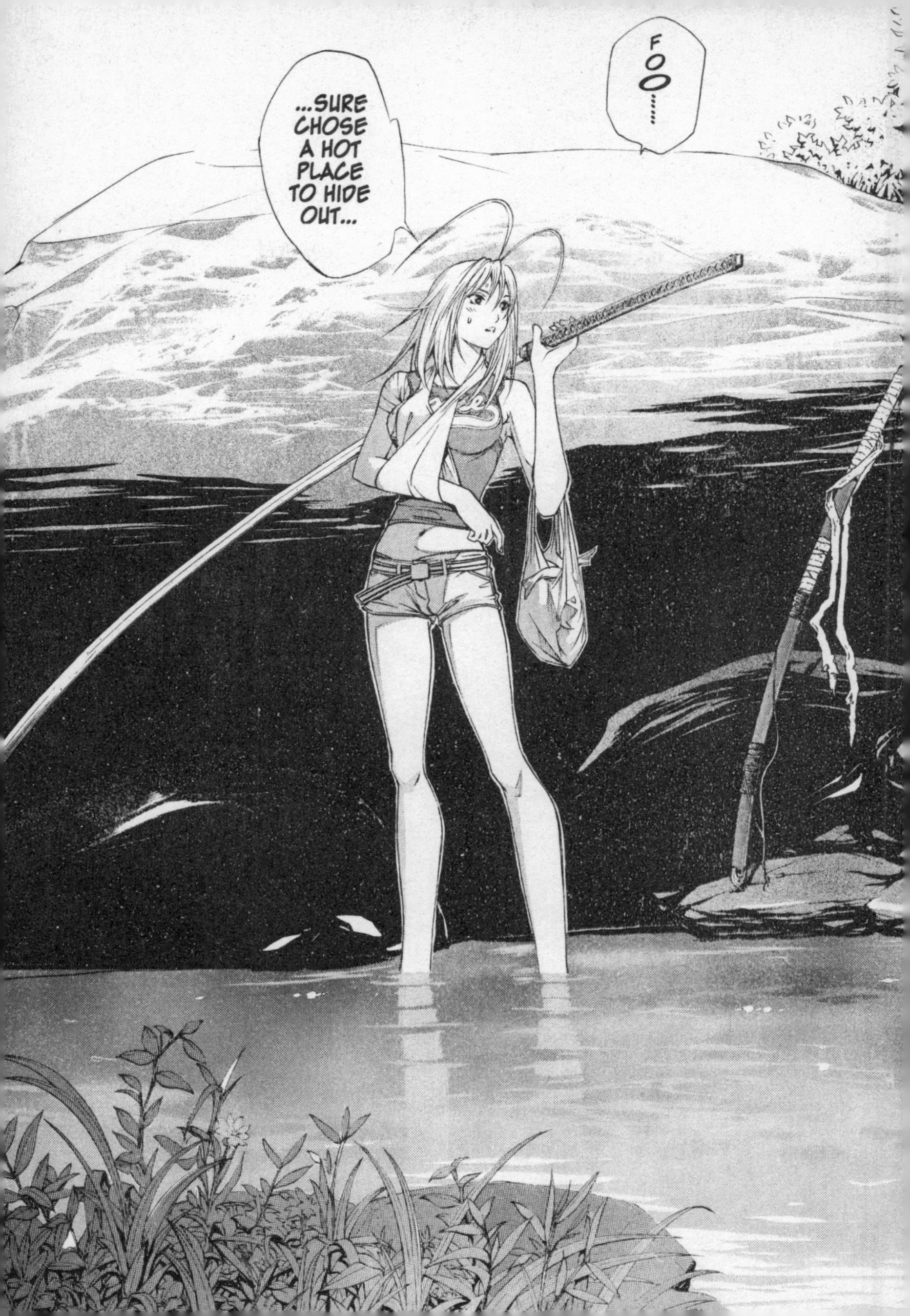
FOO......
...SURE CHOSE A HOT PLACE TO HIDE OUT...

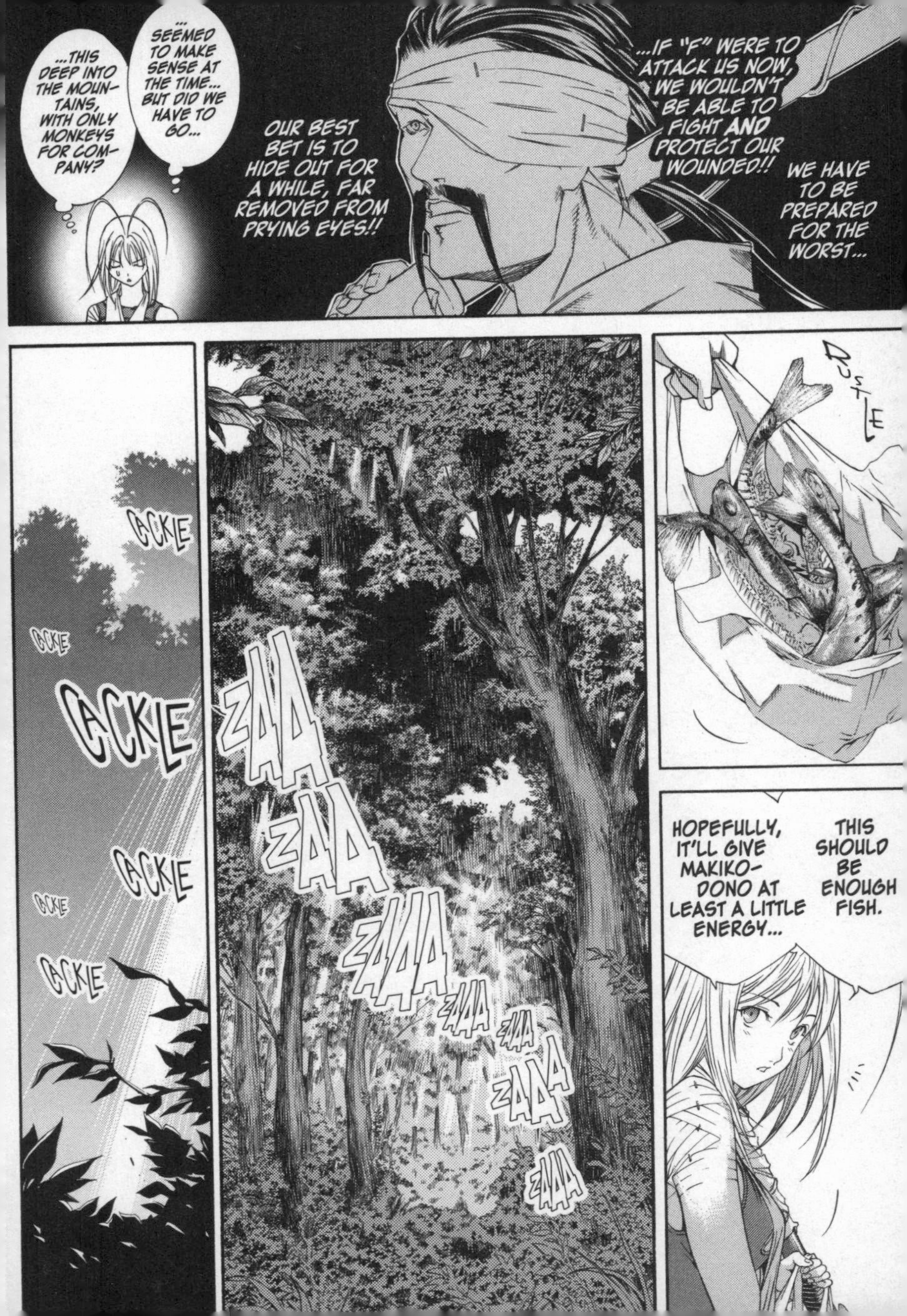
...IF "F" WERE TO ATTACK US NOW, WE WOULDN'T BE ABLE TO FIGHT AND PROTECT OUR WOUNDED!!
WE HAVE TO BE PREPARED FOR THE WORST...
OUR BEST BET IS TO HIDE OUT FOR A WHILE, FAR REMOVED FROM PRYING EYES!!
...SEEMED TO MAKE SENSE AT THE TIME... BUT DID WE HAVE TO GO...
...THIS DEEP INTO THE MOUN-TAINS, WITH ONLY MONKEYS FOR COM-PANY?
RUSTLE
THIS SHOULD BE ENOUGH FISH.
HOPEFULLY, IT'LL GIVE MAKIKO-DONO AT LEAST A LITTLE ENERGY...
ZAAA ZAAA ZAAA ZAAA ZAAA ZAAA ZAAA
CACKLE CACKLE CACKLE CACKLE CACKLE CACKLE

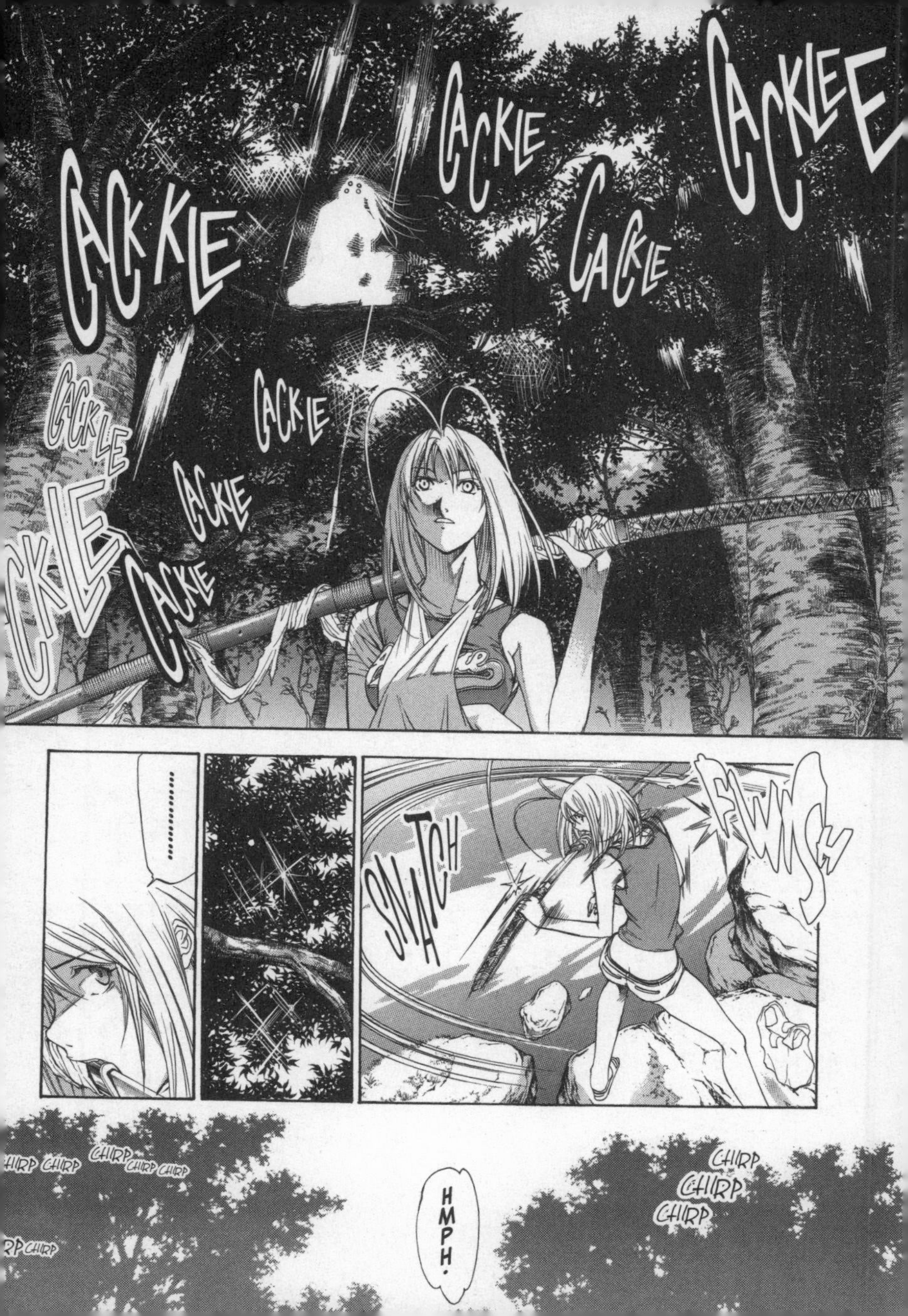
CACKLEE
CACKLE
CACKLE
CACKLE
CACKLE
CACKLE
CACKLE
CACKLE
FWUNCH
SNATCH
......
CHIRP
CHIRP
CHIRP
HMPH.
CHIRP CHIRP
CHIRP CHIRP CHIRP

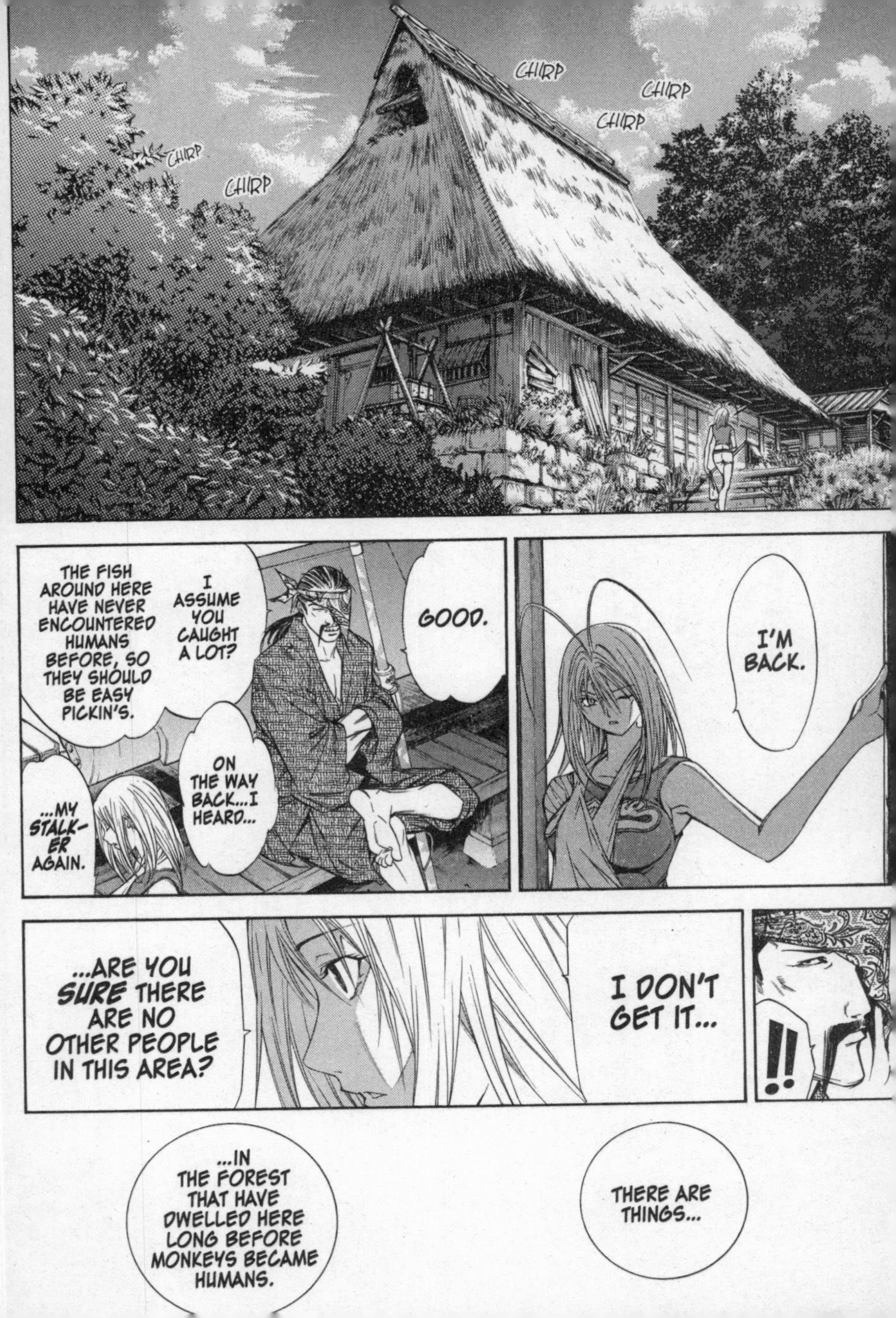
CHIRP
CHIRP
CHIRP
CHIRP
CHIRP
I'M BACK.
GOOD.
I ASSUME YOU CAUGHT A LOT?
THE FISH AROUND HERE HAVE NEVER ENCOUNTERED HUMANS BEFORE, SO THEY SHOULD BE EASY PICKIN'S.
ON THE WAY BACK...I HEARD...
...MY STALKER AGAIN.
!!
I DON'T GET IT...
...ARE YOU SURE THERE ARE NO OTHER PEOPLE IN THIS AREA?
THERE ARE THINGS...
...IN THE FOREST THAT HAVE DWELLED HERE LONG BEFORE MONKEYS BECAME HUMANS.

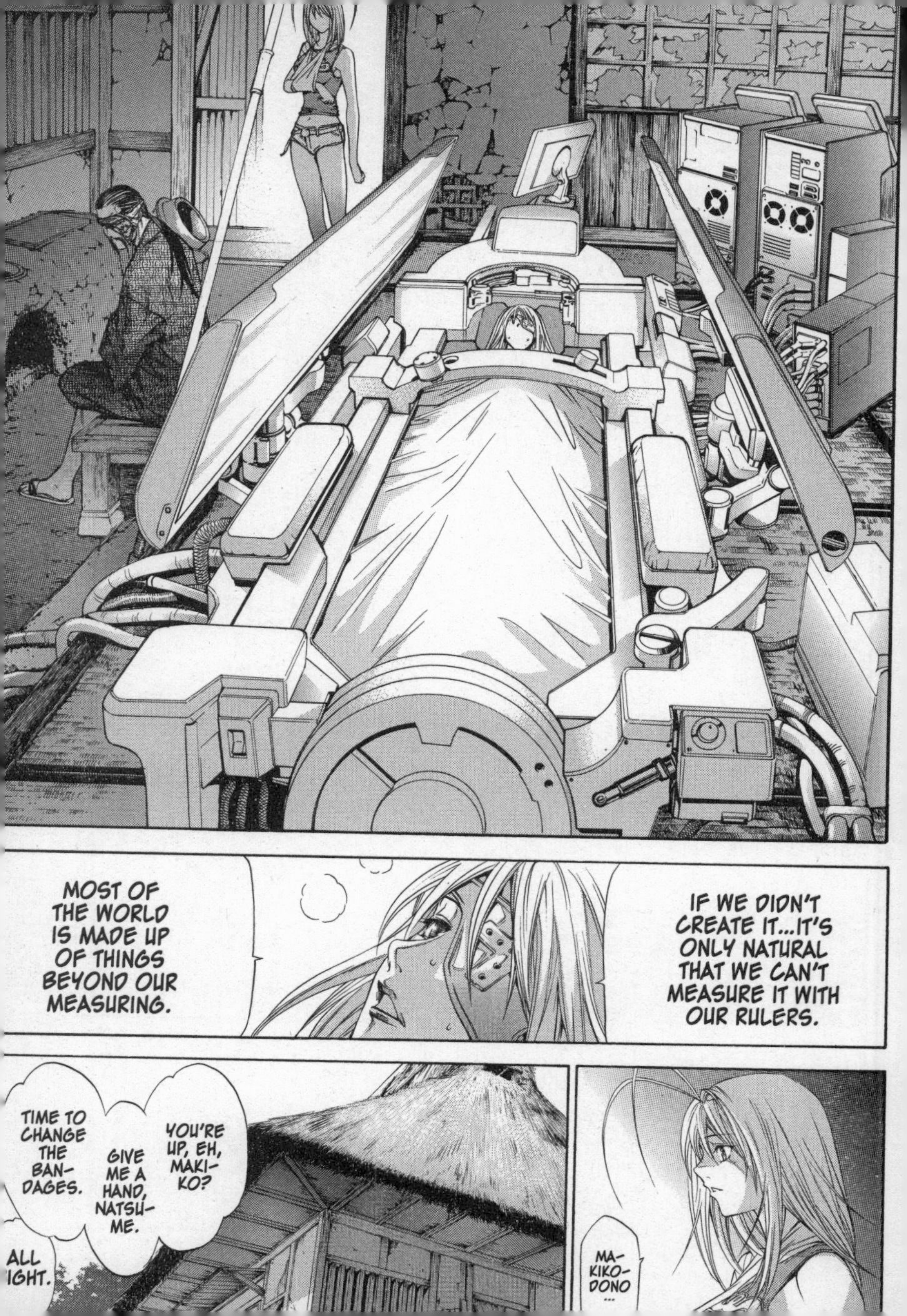
IF WE DIDN'T CREATE IT...IT'S ONLY NATURAL THAT WE CAN'T MEASURE IT WITH OUR RULERS.
MOST OF THE WORLD IS MADE UP OF THINGS BEYOND OUR MEASURING.
MA-KIKO-DONO ...
YOU'RE UP, EH, MAKI-KO?
GIVE ME A HAND, NATSU-ME.
TIME TO CHANGE THE BAN-DAGES.
ALL IGHT.

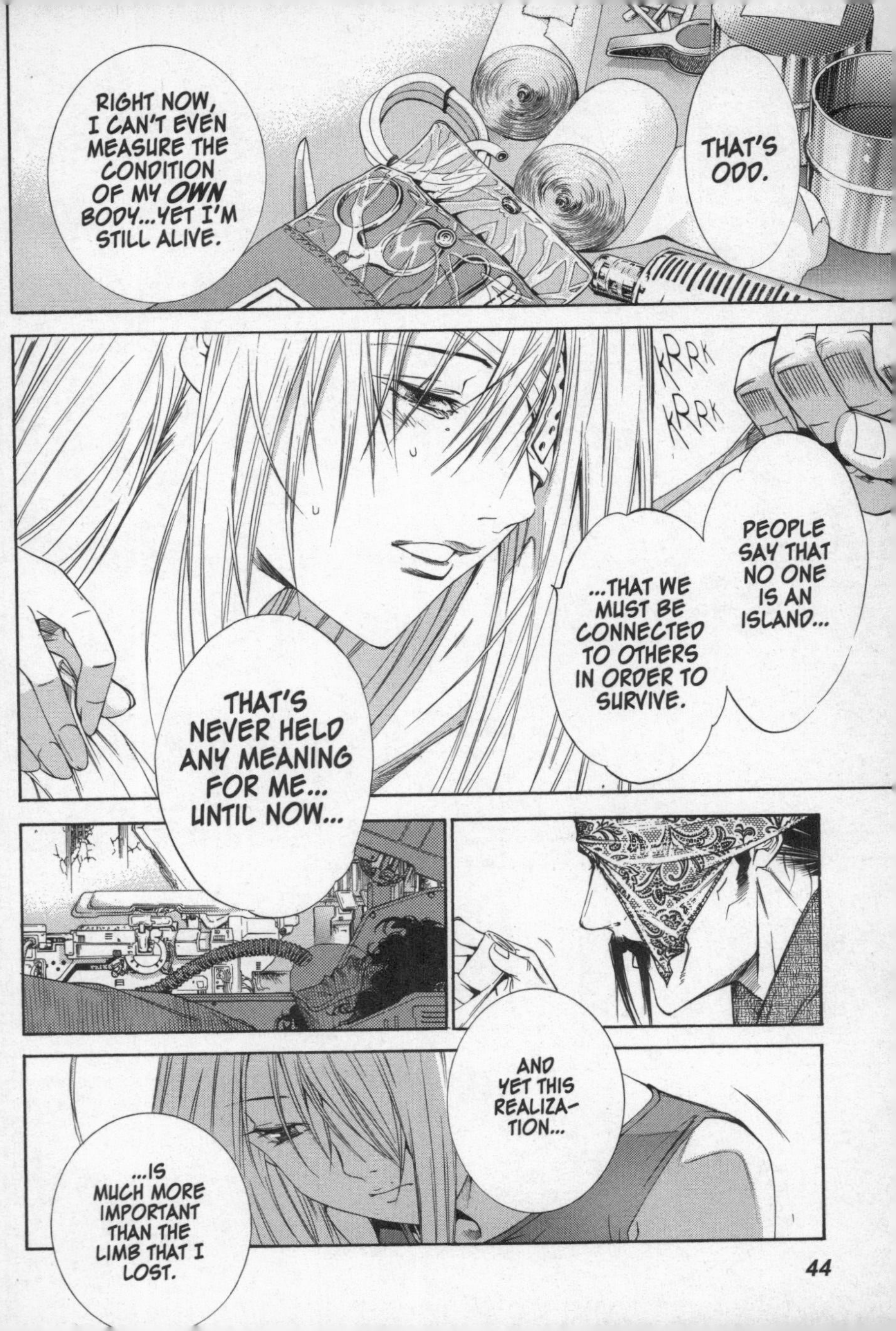

THAT'S ODD.
RIGHT NOW, I CAN'T EVEN MEASURE THE CONDITION OF MY OWN BODY...YET I'M STILL ALIVE.
KRRK KRRK
PEOPLE SAY THAT NO ONE IS AN ISLAND...
...THAT WE MUST BE CONNECTED TO OTHERS IN ORDER TO SURVIVE.
THAT'S NEVER HELD ANY MEANING FOR ME... UNTIL NOW...
AND YET THIS REALIZATION...
...IS MUCH MORE IMPORTANT THAN THE LIMB THAT I LOST.

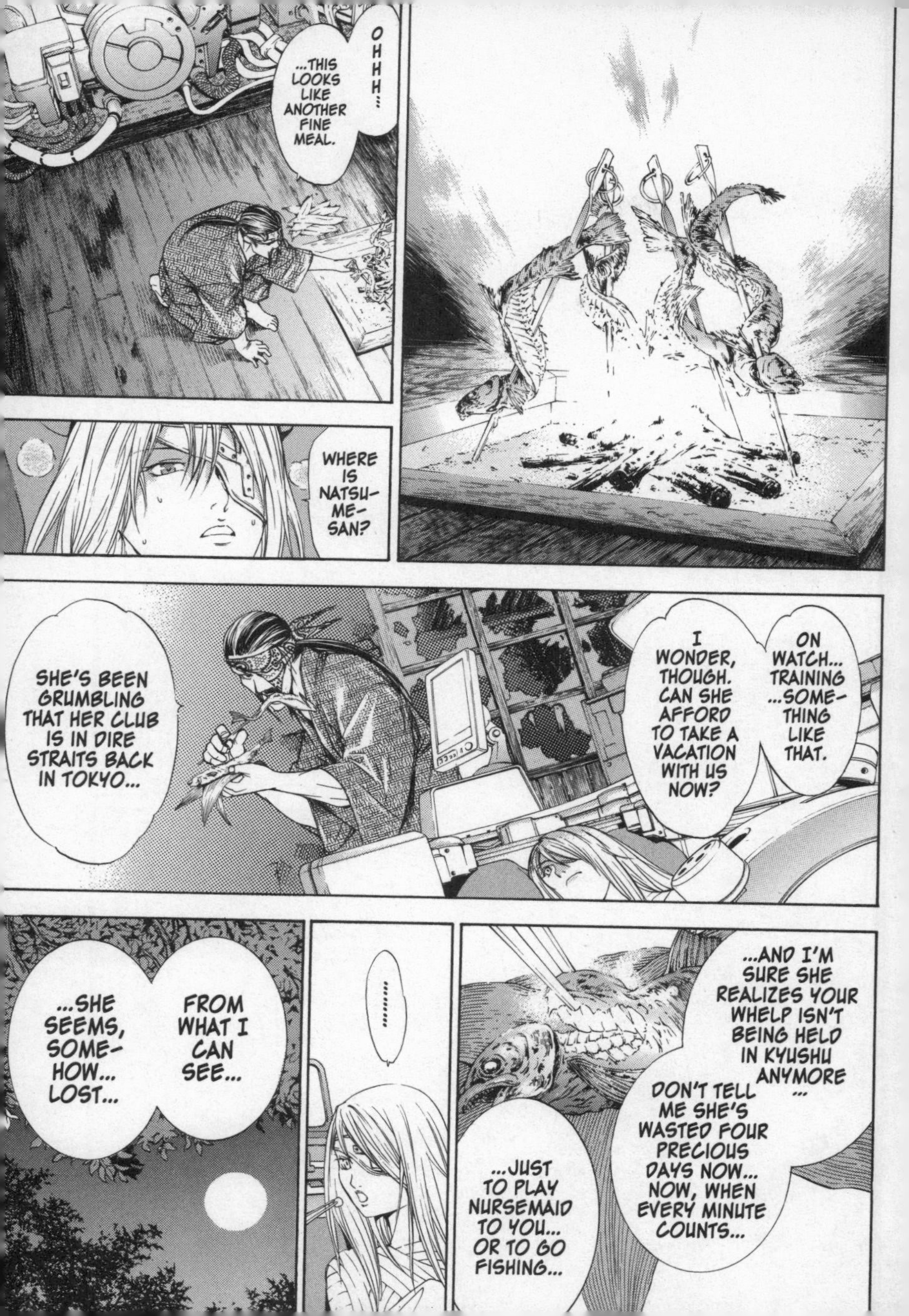
OHHH...
...THIS LOOKS LIKE ANOTHER FINE MEAL.
WHERE IS NATSUME-SAN?
ON WATCH... TRAINING ...SOMETHING LIKE THAT.
I WONDER, THOUGH. CAN SHE AFFORD TO TAKE A VACATION WITH US NOW?
SHE'S BEEN GRUMBLING THAT HER CLUB IS IN DIRE STRAITS BACK IN TOKYO...
...AND I'M SURE SHE REALIZES YOUR WHELP ISN'T BEING HELD IN KYUSHU ANYMORE...
DON'T TELL ME SHE'S WASTED FOUR PRECIOUS DAYS NOW... NOW, WHEN EVERY MINUTE COUNTS...
...JUST TO PLAY NURSEMAID TO YOU... OR TO GO FISHING...
....
FROM WHAT I CAN SEE...
...SHE SEEMS, SOMEHOW... LOST...

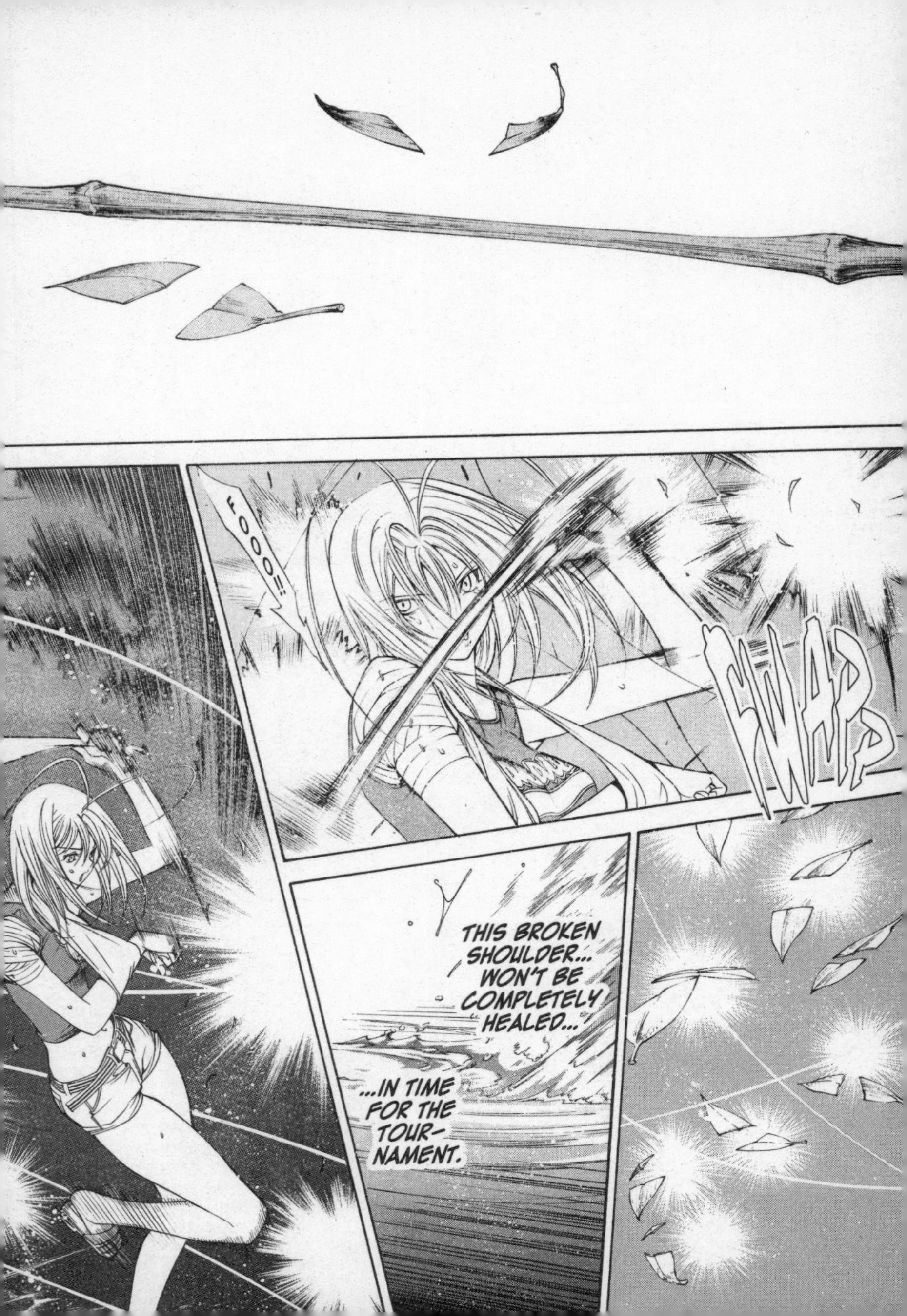
FOOOO!!
SWAP
THIS BROKEN SHOULDER... WON'T BE COMPLETELY HEALED...
...IN TIME FOR THE TOUR-NAMENT.

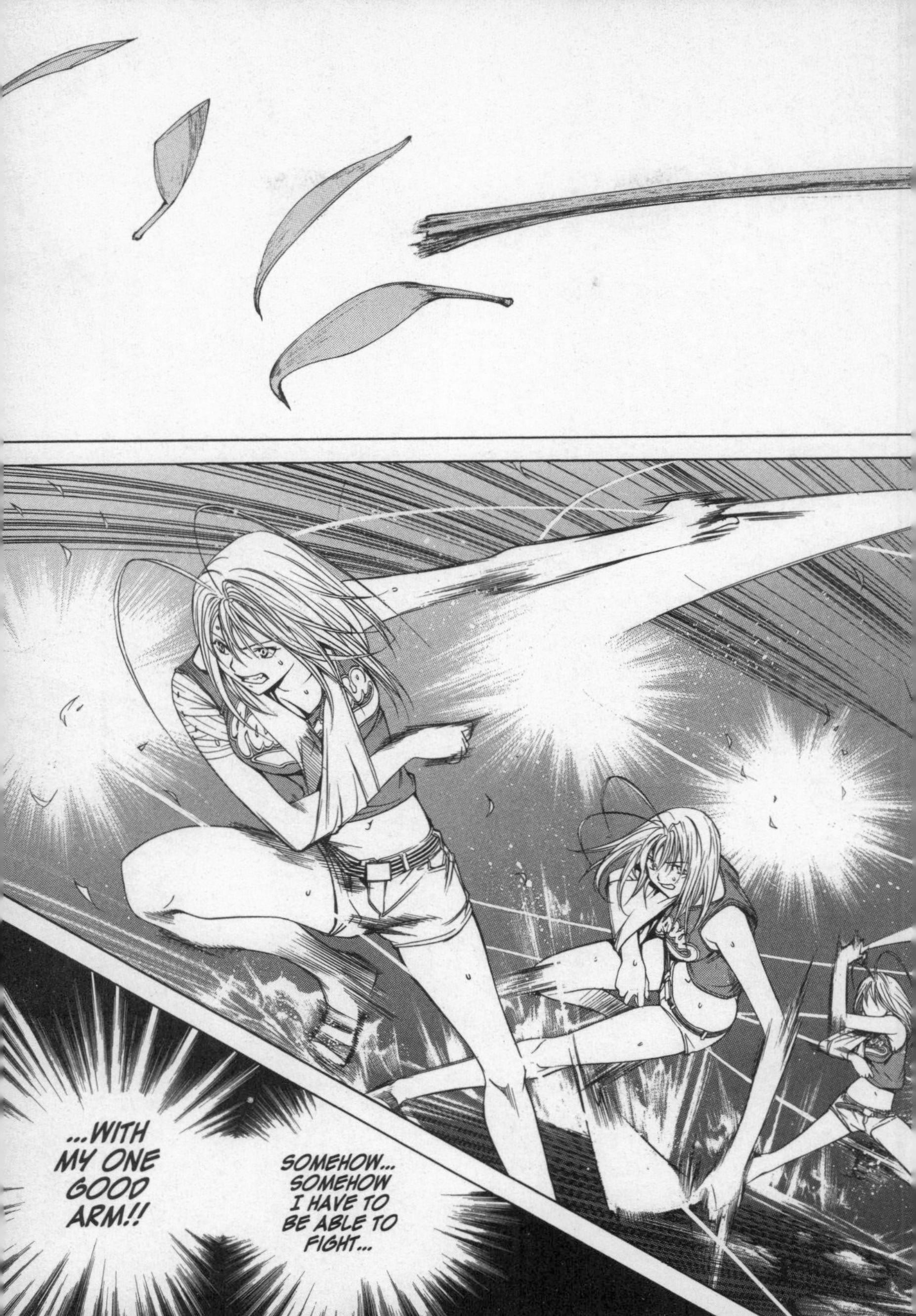
SOMEHOW... SOMEHOW I HAVE TO BE ABLE TO FIGHT...
...WITH MY ONE GOOD ARM!!

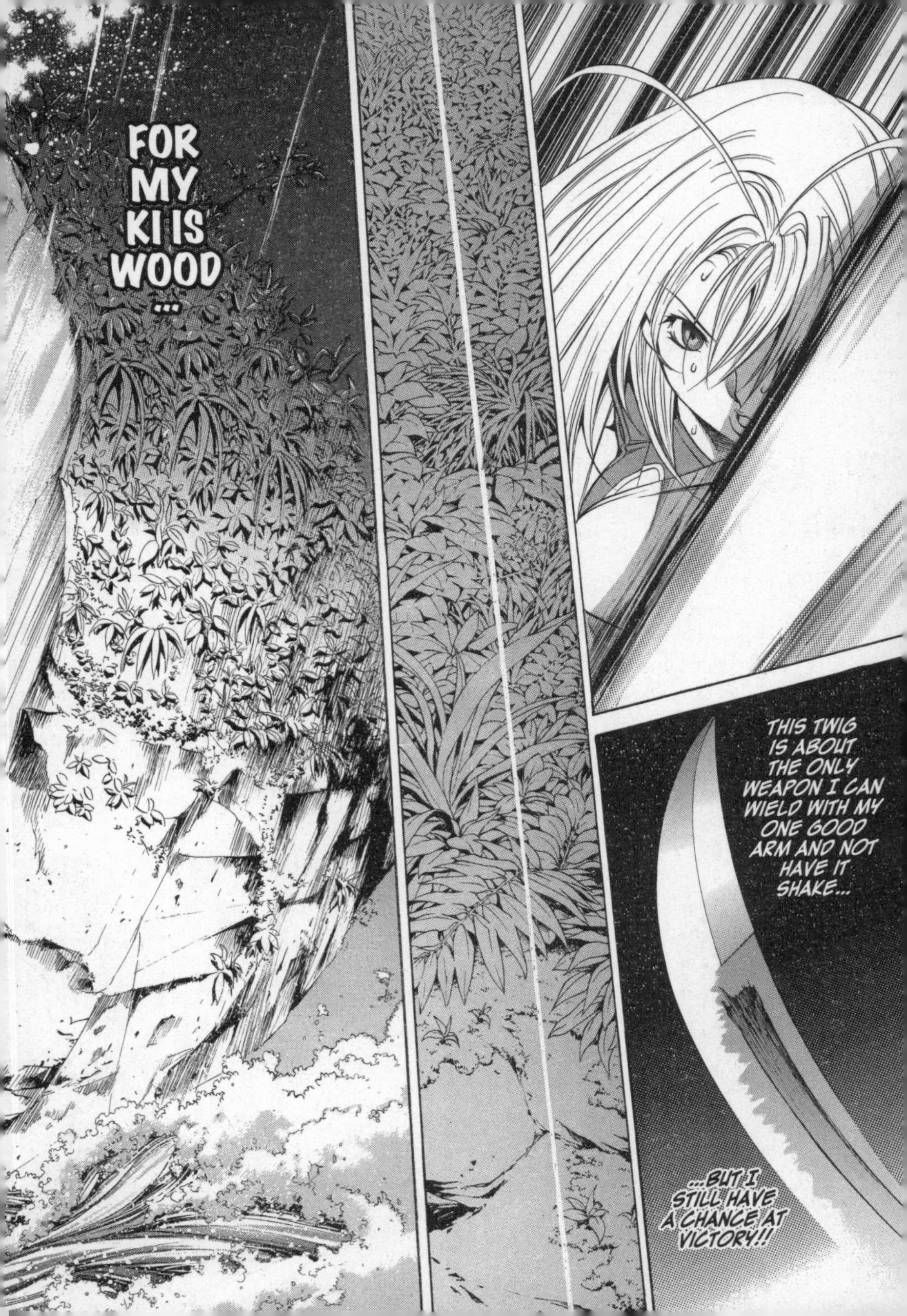
THIS TWIG IS ABOUT THE ONLY WEAPON I CAN WIELD WITH MY ONE GOOD ARM AND NOT HAVE IT SHAKE...
...BUT I STILL HAVE A CHANCE AT VICTORY!!
FOR MY KI IS WOOD...

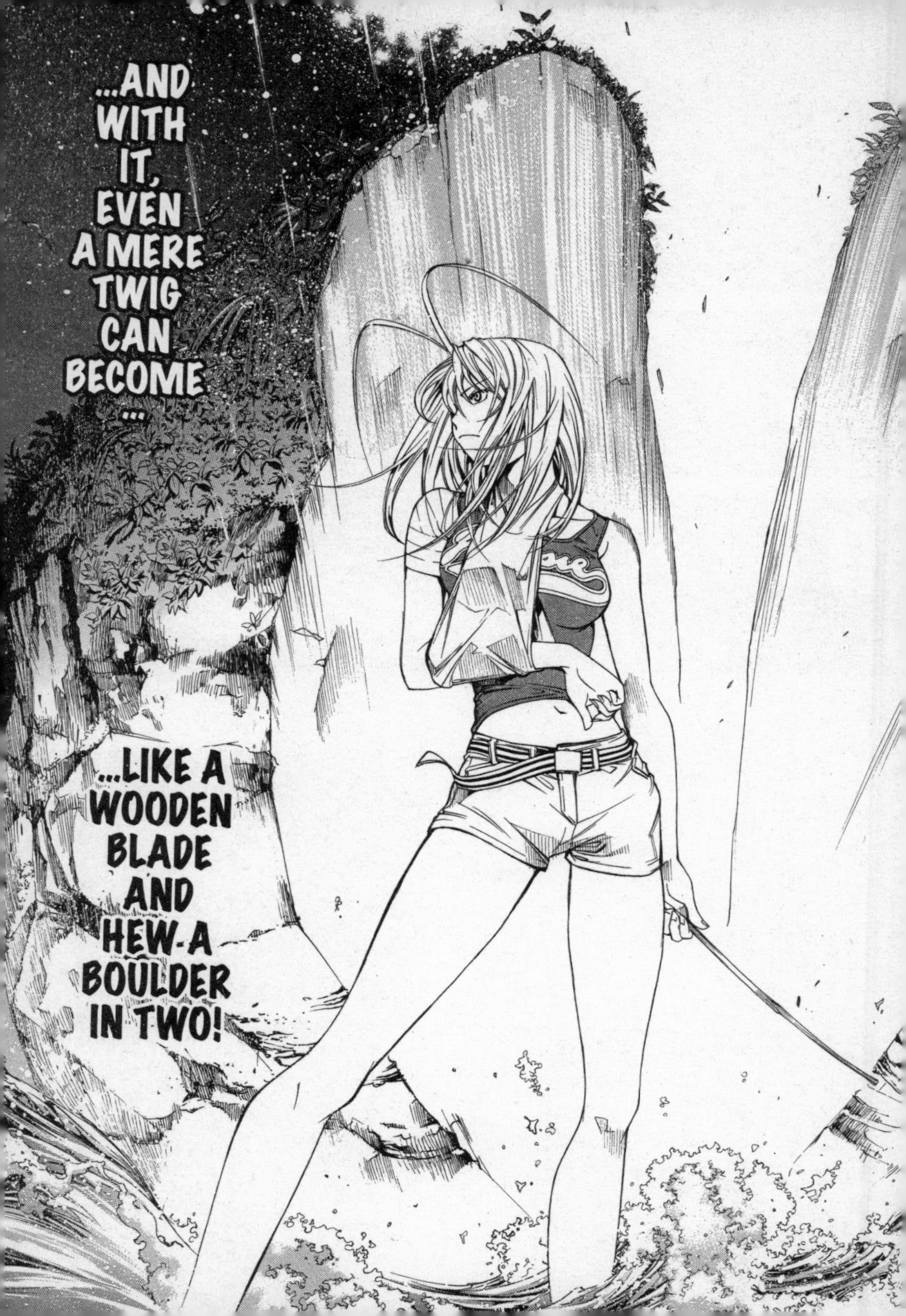
...AND WITH IT, EVEN A MERE TWIG CAN BECOME ...
...LIKE A WOODEN BLADE AND HEW-A BOULDER IN TWO!

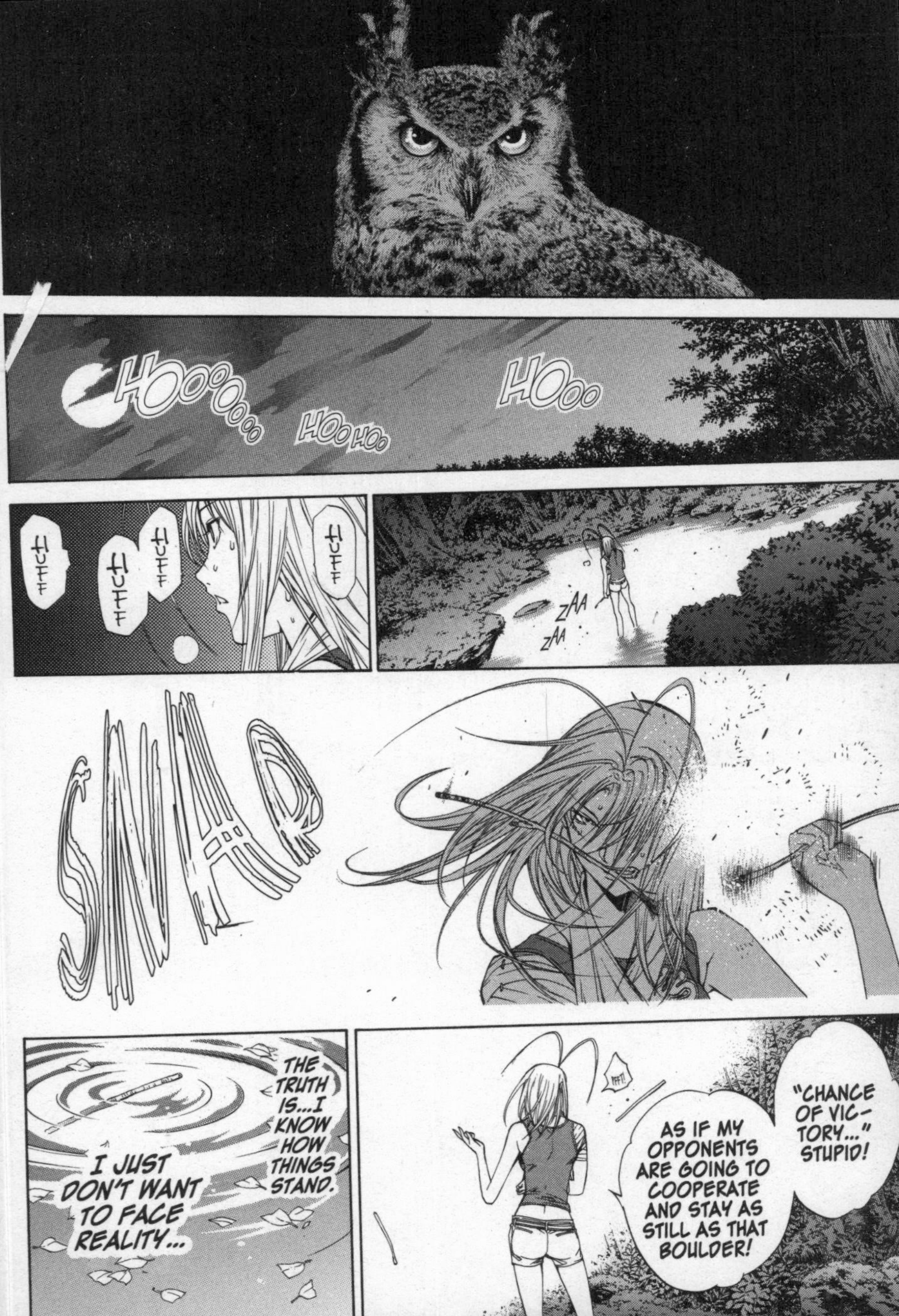
HOOoo
HOOoooooo
HOO HOO
HUFF
HUFF
HUFF
HUFF
ZAA
ZAA
SNAP
"CHANCE OF VICTORY..." STUPID!
AS IF MY OPPONENTS ARE GOING TO COOPERATE AND STAY AS STILL AS THAT BOULDER!
THE TRUTH IS...I KNOW HOW THINGS STAND.
I JUST DON'T WANT TO FACE REALITY...

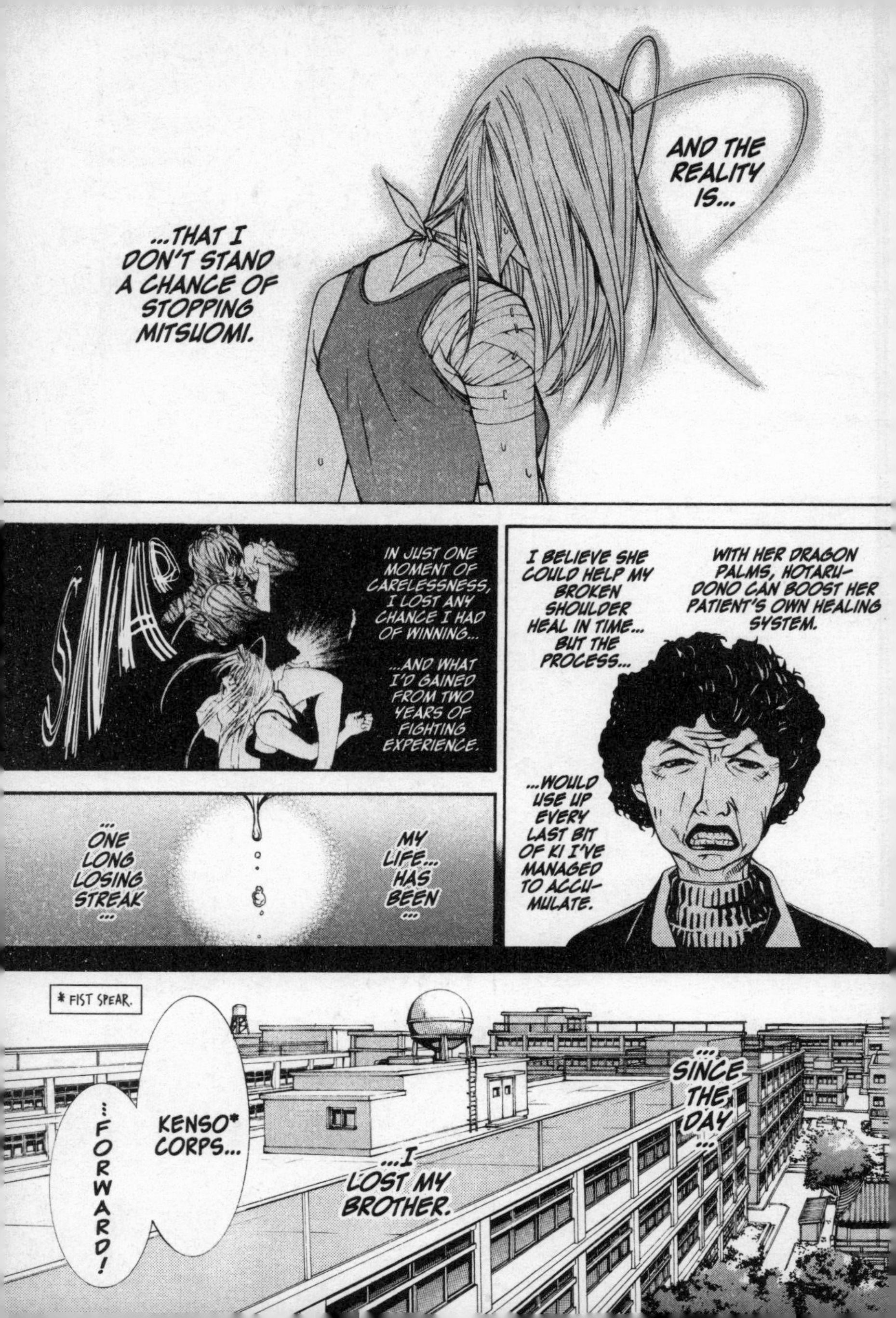
AND THE REALITY IS...
...THAT I DON'T STAND A CHANCE OF STOPPING MITSUOMI.
WITH HER DRAGON PALMS, HOTARU-DONO CAN BOOST HER PATIENT'S OWN HEALING SYSTEM.
I BELIEVE SHE COULD HELP MY BROKEN SHOULDER HEAL IN TIME... BUT THE PROCESS...
...WOULD USE UP EVERY LAST BIT OF KI I'VE MANAGED TO ACCUMULATE.
SNAP
IN JUST ONE MOMENT OF CARELESSNESS, I LOST ANY CHANCE I HAD OF WINNING...
...AND WHAT I'D GAINED FROM TWO YEARS OF FIGHTING EXPERIENCE.
MY LIFE... HAS BEEN...
...ONE LONG LOSING STREAK...
...SINCE THE DAY...
...I LOST MY BROTHER.
KENSO* CORPS...
...FORWARD!
* FIST SPEAR.

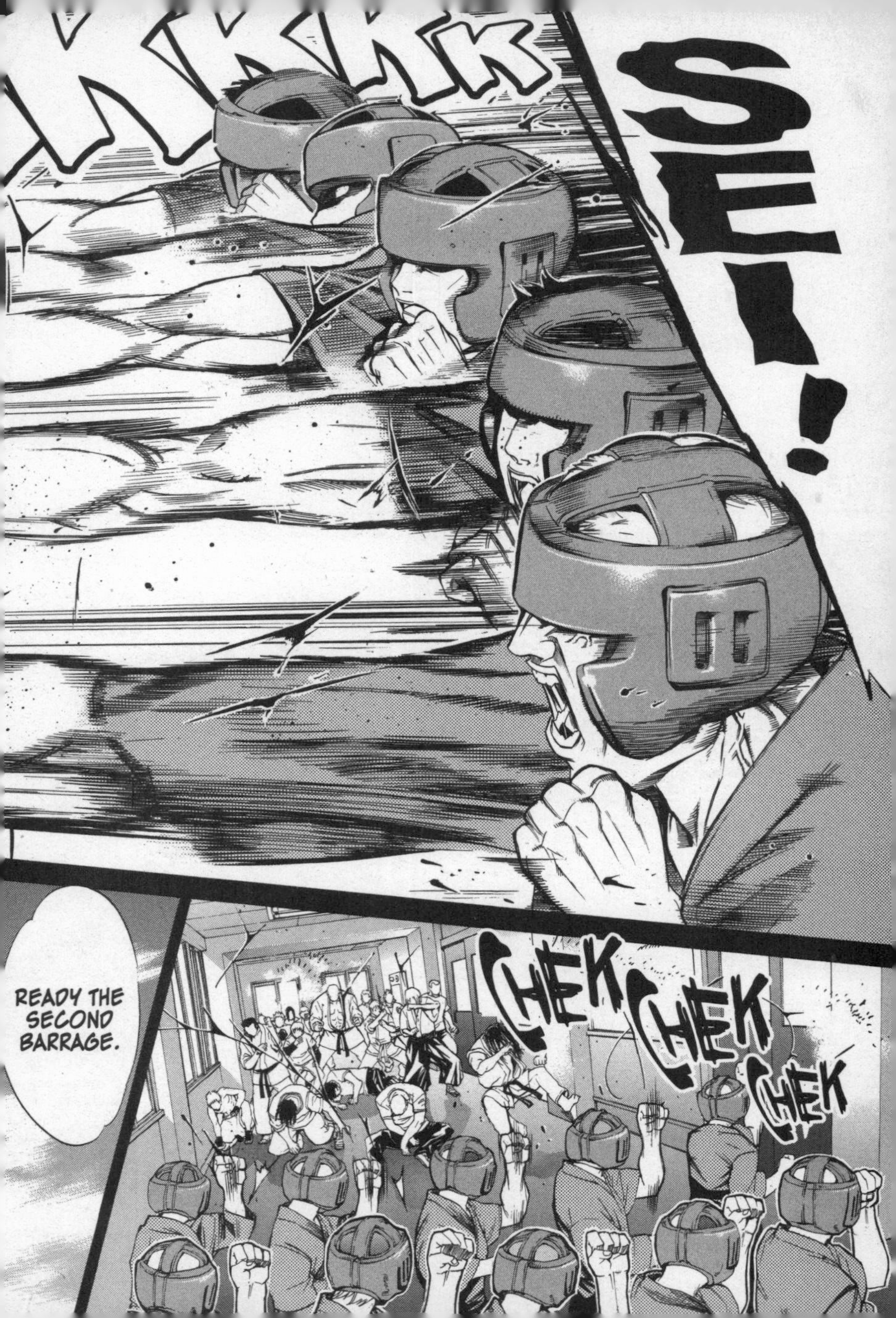
SEI!
CHEK CHEK CHEK
READY THE SECOND BARRAGE.

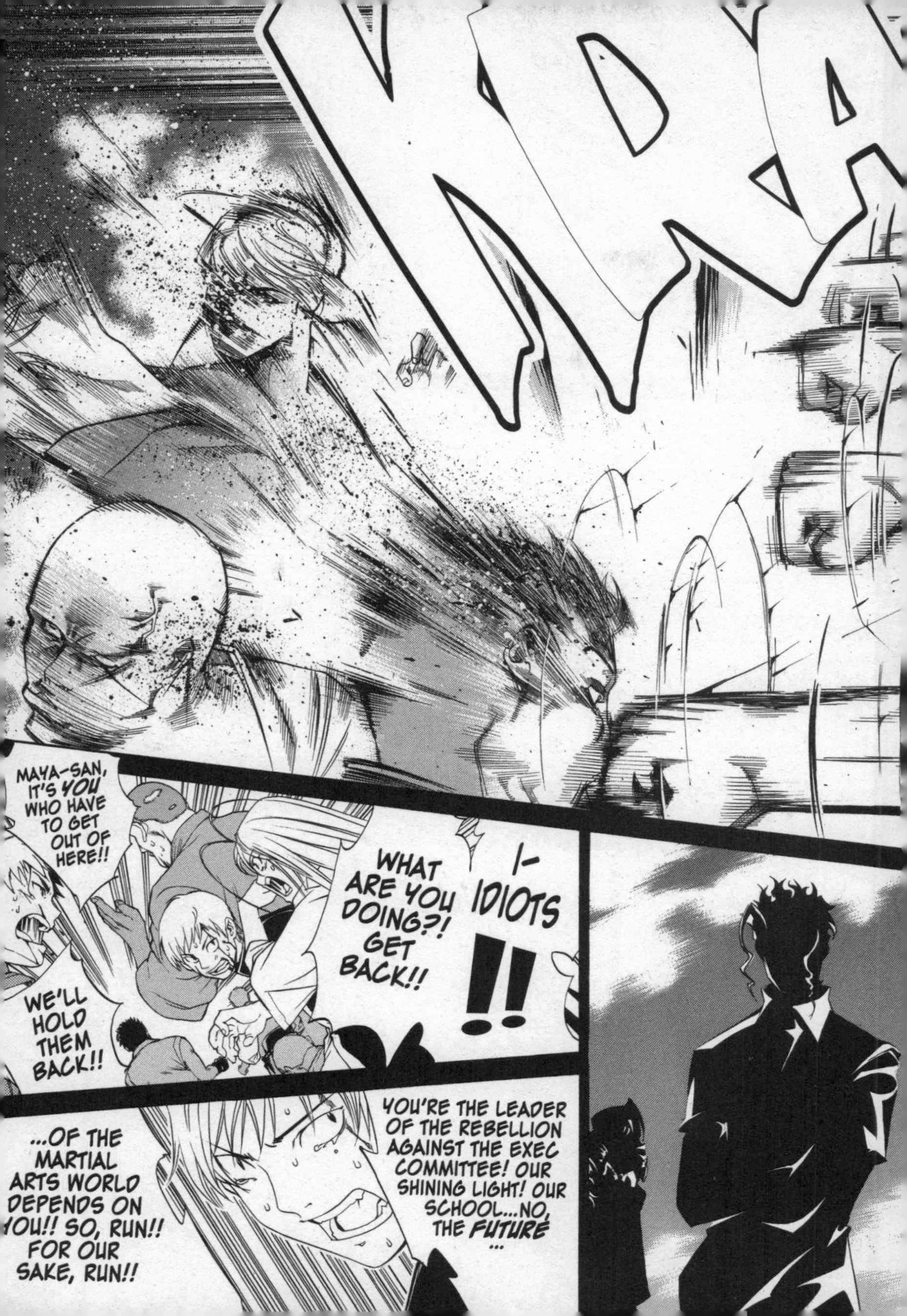
I- IDIOTS!!
WHAT ARE YOU DOING?! GET BACK!!
MAYA-SAN, IT'S YOU WHO HAVE TO GET OUT OF HERE!!
WE'LL HOLD THEM BACK!!
YOU'RE THE LEADER OF THE REBELLION AGAINST THE EXEC COMMITTEE! OUR SHINING LIGHT! OUR SCHOOL...NO, THE FUTURE ...
...OF THE MARTIAL ARTS WORLD DEPENDS ON YOU!! SO, RUN!! FOR OUR SAKE, RUN!!

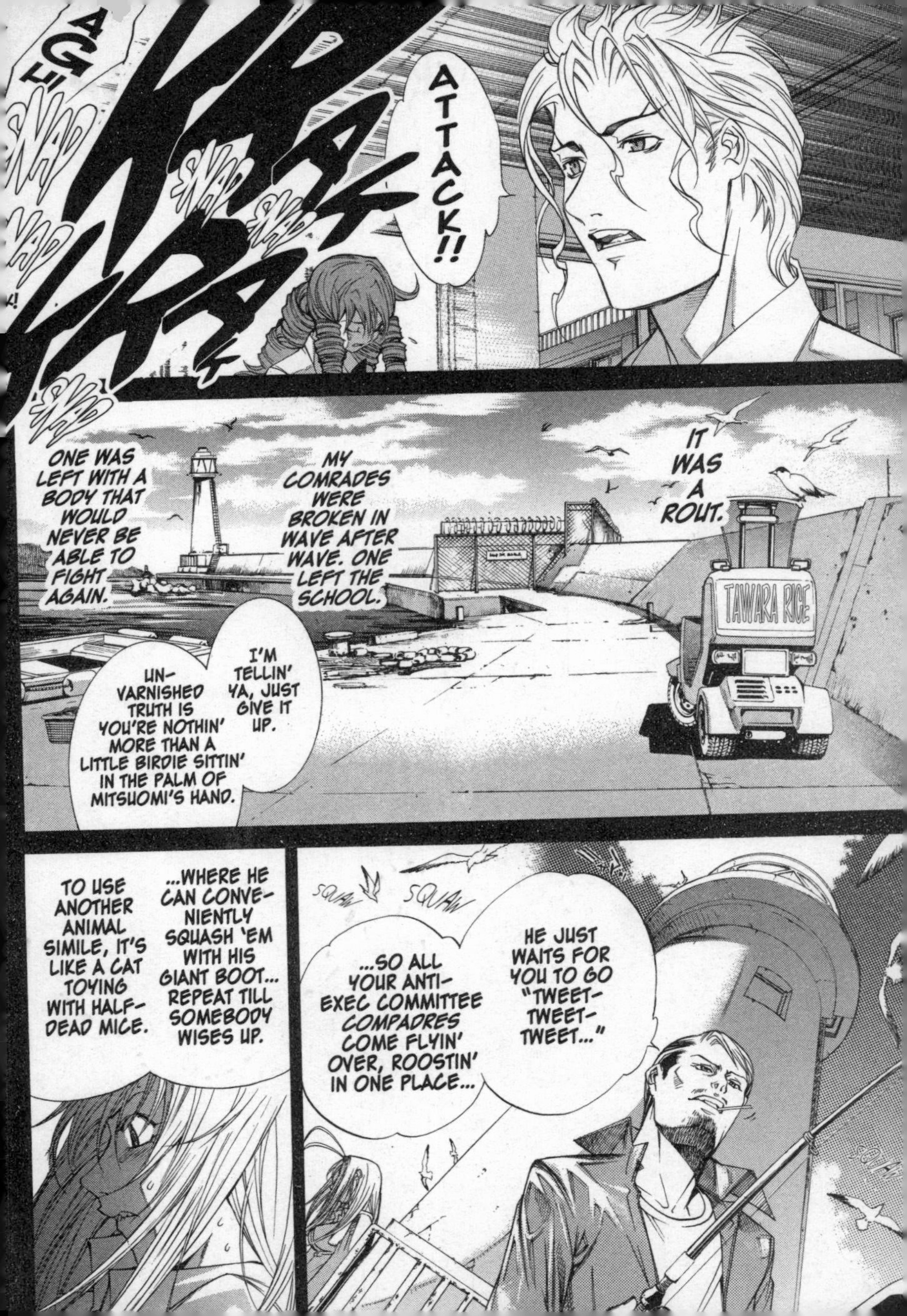
ATTACK!!
AGH
IT WAS A ROUT.
MY COMRADES WERE BROKEN IN WAVE AFTER WAVE. ONE LEFT THE SCHOOL.
ONE WAS LEFT WITH A BODY THAT WOULD NEVER BE ABLE TO FIGHT AGAIN.
TAWARA RICE
I'M TELLIN' YA, JUST GIVE IT UP.
UN-VARNISHED TRUTH IS YOU'RE NOTHIN' MORE THAN A LITTLE BIRDIE SITTIN' IN THE PALM OF MITSUOMI'S HAND.
HE JUST WAITS FOR YOU TO GO "TWEET-TWEET-TWEET..."
...SO ALL YOUR ANTI-EXEC COMMITTEE COMPADRES COME FLYIN' OVER, ROOSTIN' IN ONE PLACE...
SQUAWK
SQUAWK
...WHERE HE CAN CONVE-NIENTLY SQUASH 'EM WITH HIS GIANT BOOT... REPEAT TILL SOMEBODY WISES UP.
TO USE ANOTHER ANIMAL SIMILE, IT'S LIKE A CAT TOYING WITH HALF-DEAD MICE.

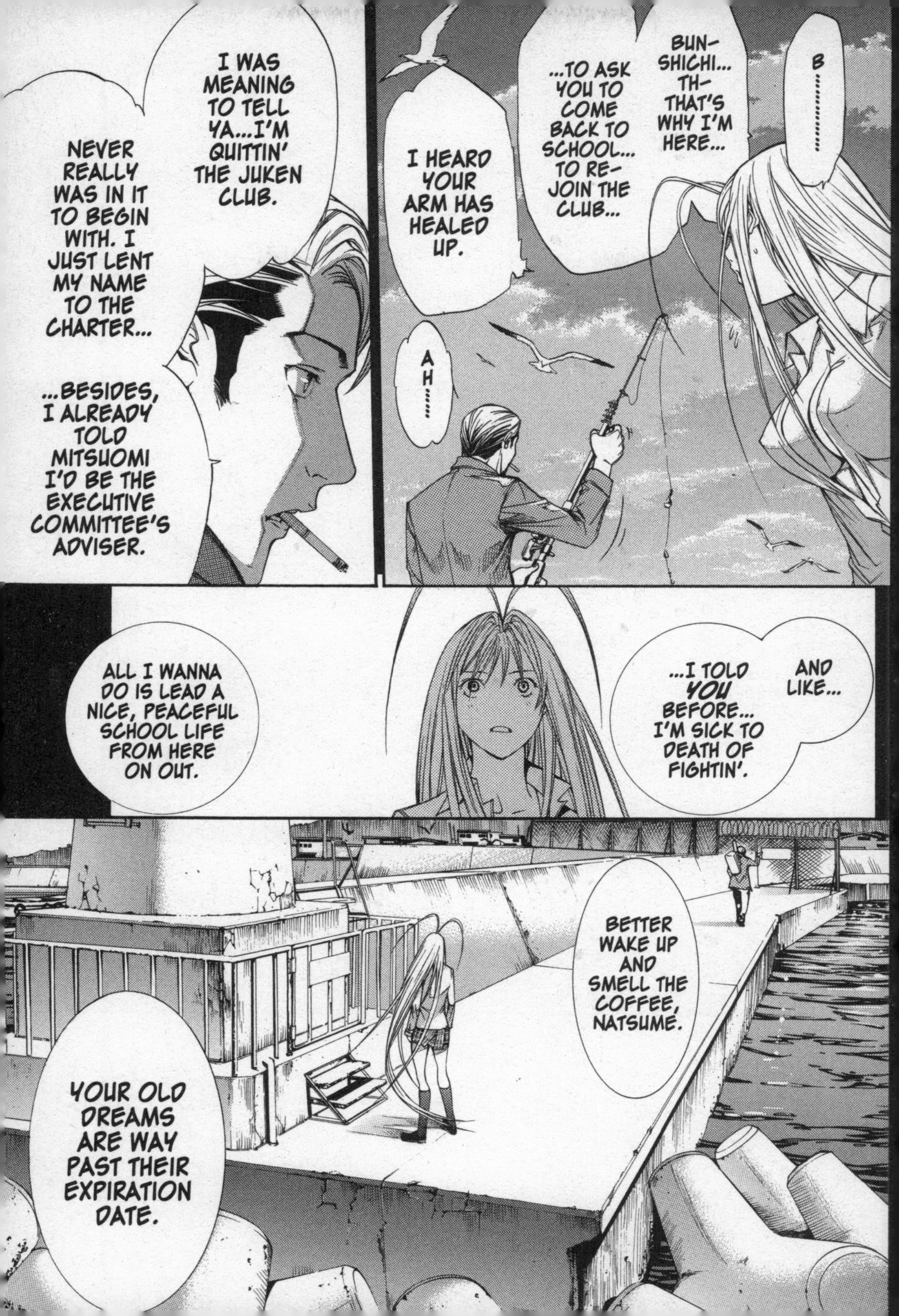
B........
BUN-SHICHI... TH-THAT'S WHY I'M HERE...
...TO ASK YOU TO COME BACK TO SCHOOL... TO RE-JOIN THE CLUB...
I HEARD YOUR ARM HAS HEALED UP.
AH......
I WAS MEANING TO TELL YA...I'M QUITTIN' THE JUKEN CLUB.
NEVER REALLY WAS IN IT TO BEGIN WITH. I JUST LENT MY NAME TO THE CHARTER...
...BESIDES, I ALREADY TOLD MITSUOMI I'D BE THE EXECUTIVE COMMITTEE'S ADVISER.
AND LIKE...
...I TOLD *YOU* BEFORE... I'M SICK TO DEATH OF FIGHTIN'.
ALL I WANNA DO IS LEAD A NICE, PEACEFUL SCHOOL LIFE FROM HERE ON OUT.
BETTER WAKE UP AND SMELL THE COFFEE, NATSUME.
YOUR OLD DREAMS ARE WAY PAST THEIR EXPIRATION DATE.

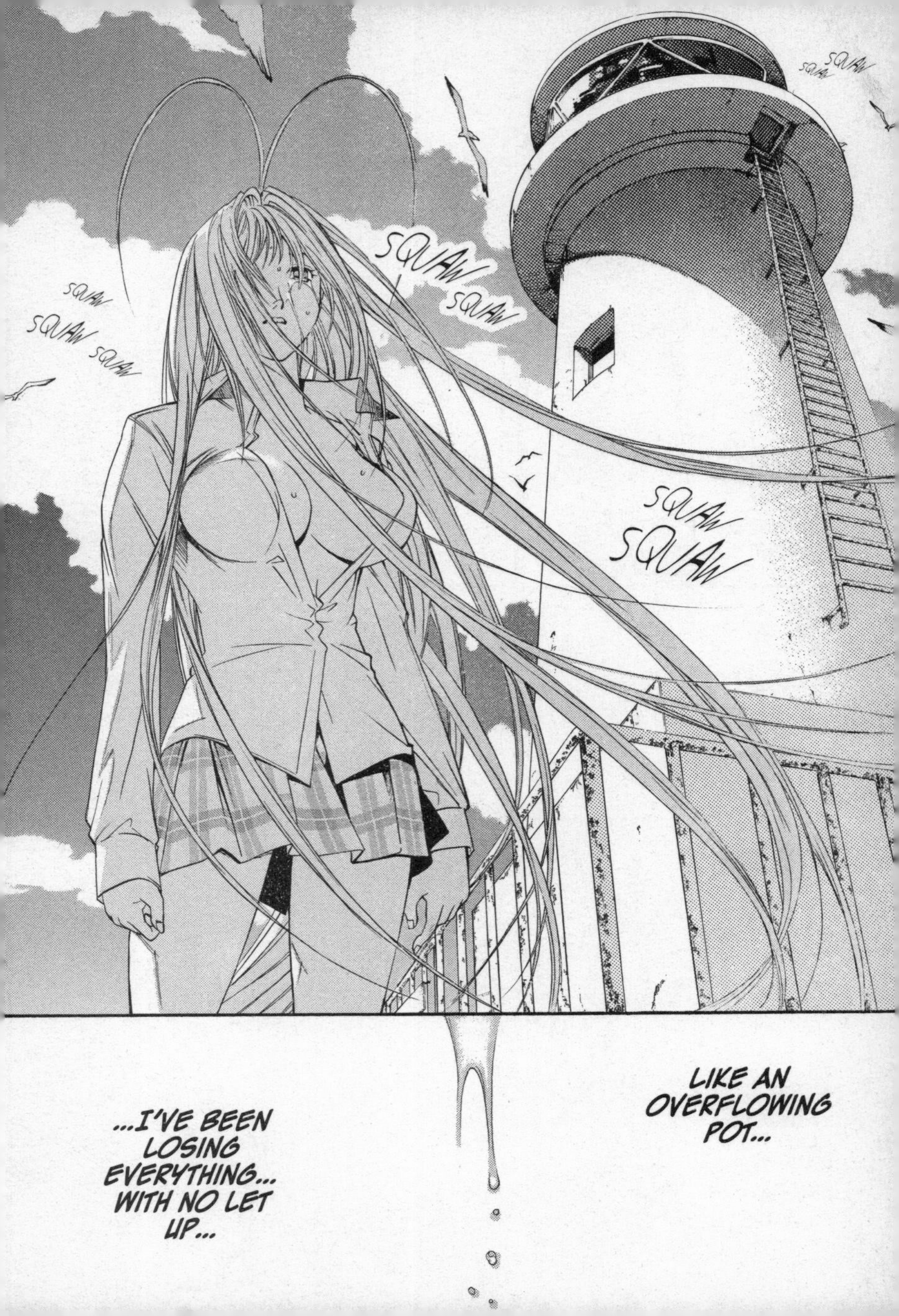
SQUAW SQUAW
SQUAW SQUAW
SQUAW SQUAW
SQUAW SQUAW SQUAW
LIKE AN OVERFLOWING POT...
...I'VE BEEN LOSING EVERYTHING... WITH NO LET UP...

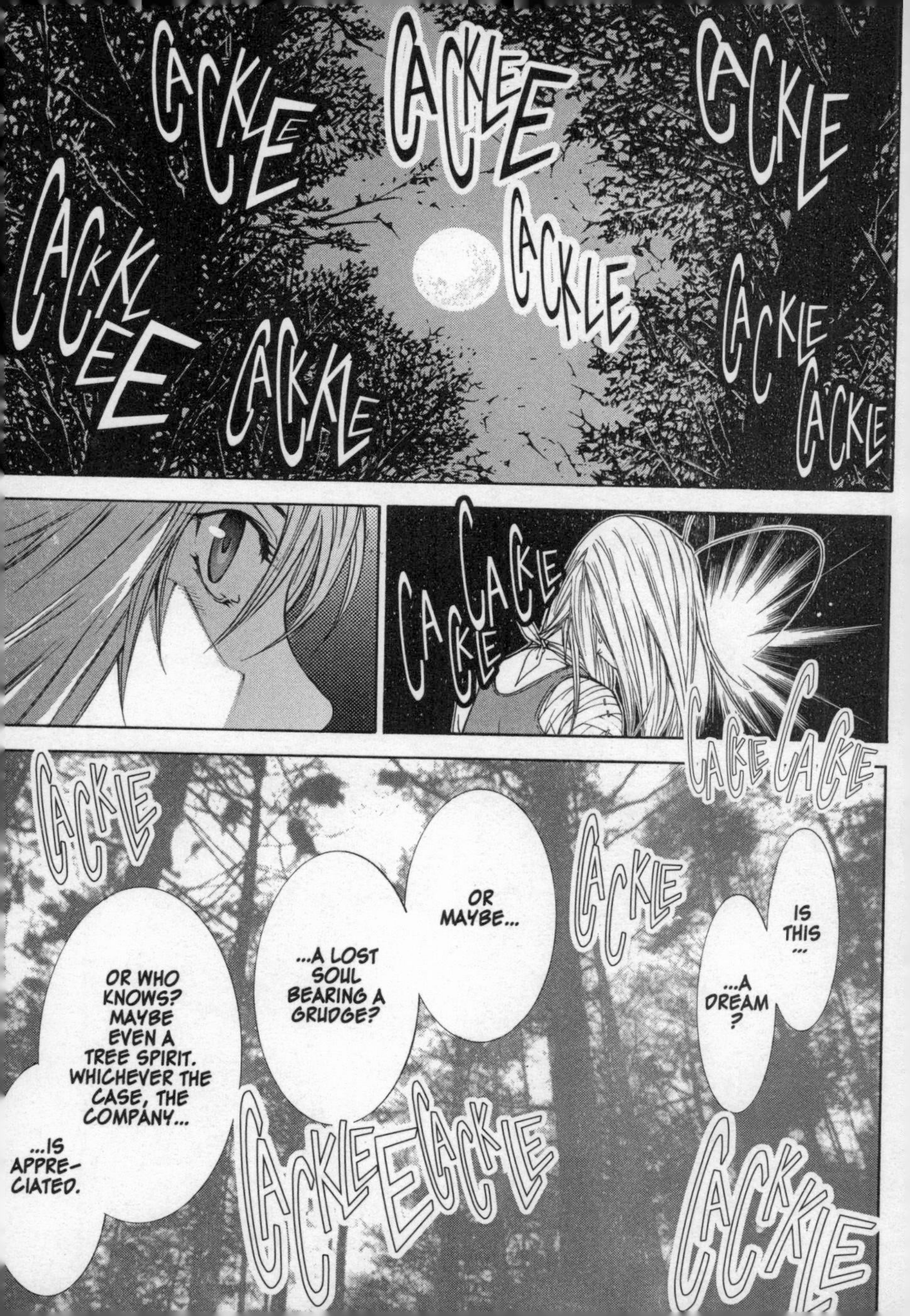
CACKLE
CACKLE
CACKLE
CACKLE
CACKLE
CACKLE
CACKLE
CACKLE
CACKLE
CACKLE
CACKLE CACKLE
CACKLE CACKLE
CACKLE
IS THIS...
...A DREAM?
CACKLE
OR MAYBE...
...A LOST SOUL BEARING A GRUDGE?
OR WHO KNOWS? MAYBE EVEN A TREE SPIRIT. WHICHEVER THE CASE, THE COMPANY...
...IS APPRE-CIATED.
CACKLE
CACKLE CACKLE
CACKLE

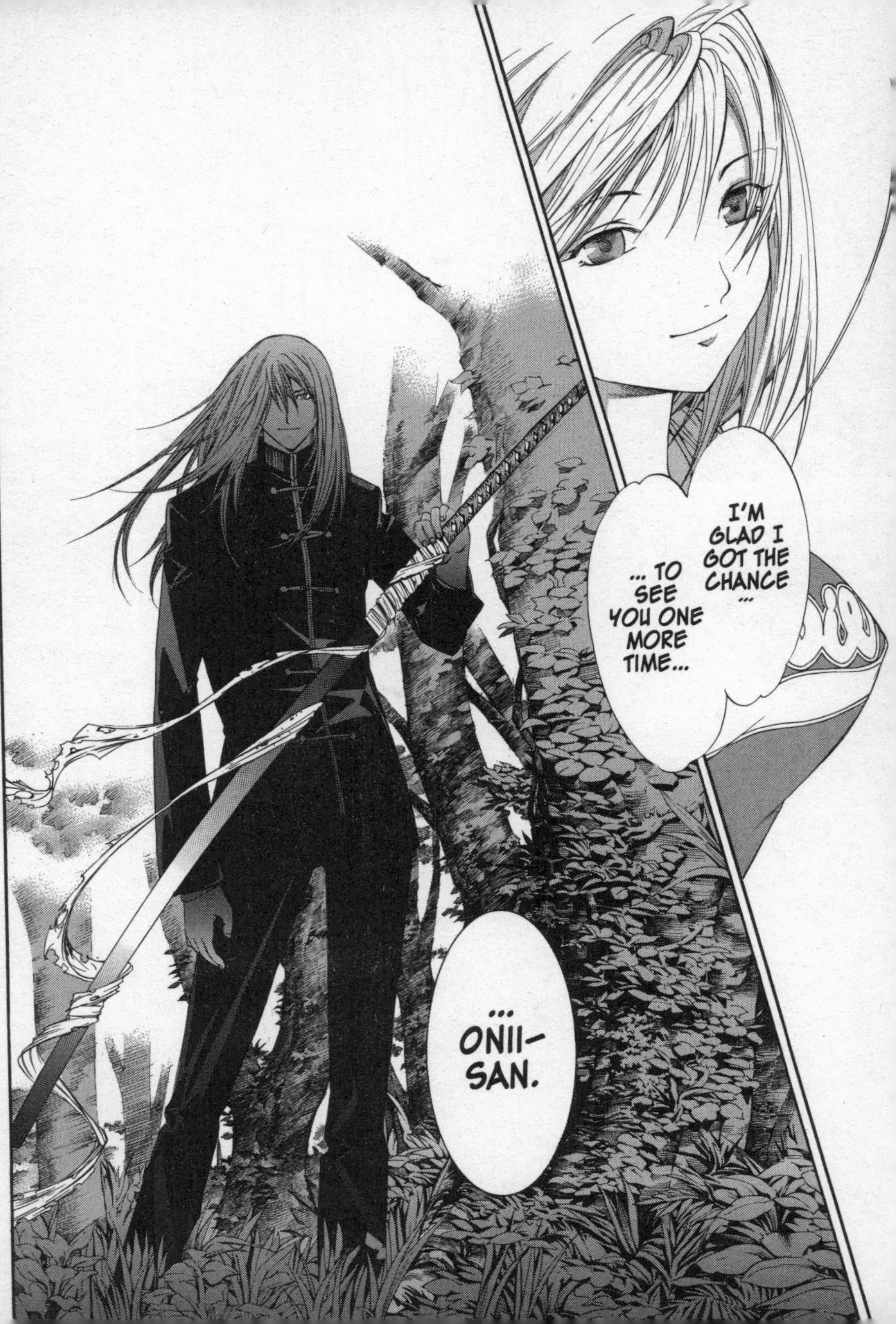
I'M GLAD I GOT THE CHANCE ...
... TO SEE YOU ONE MORE TIME...
... ONII-SAN.

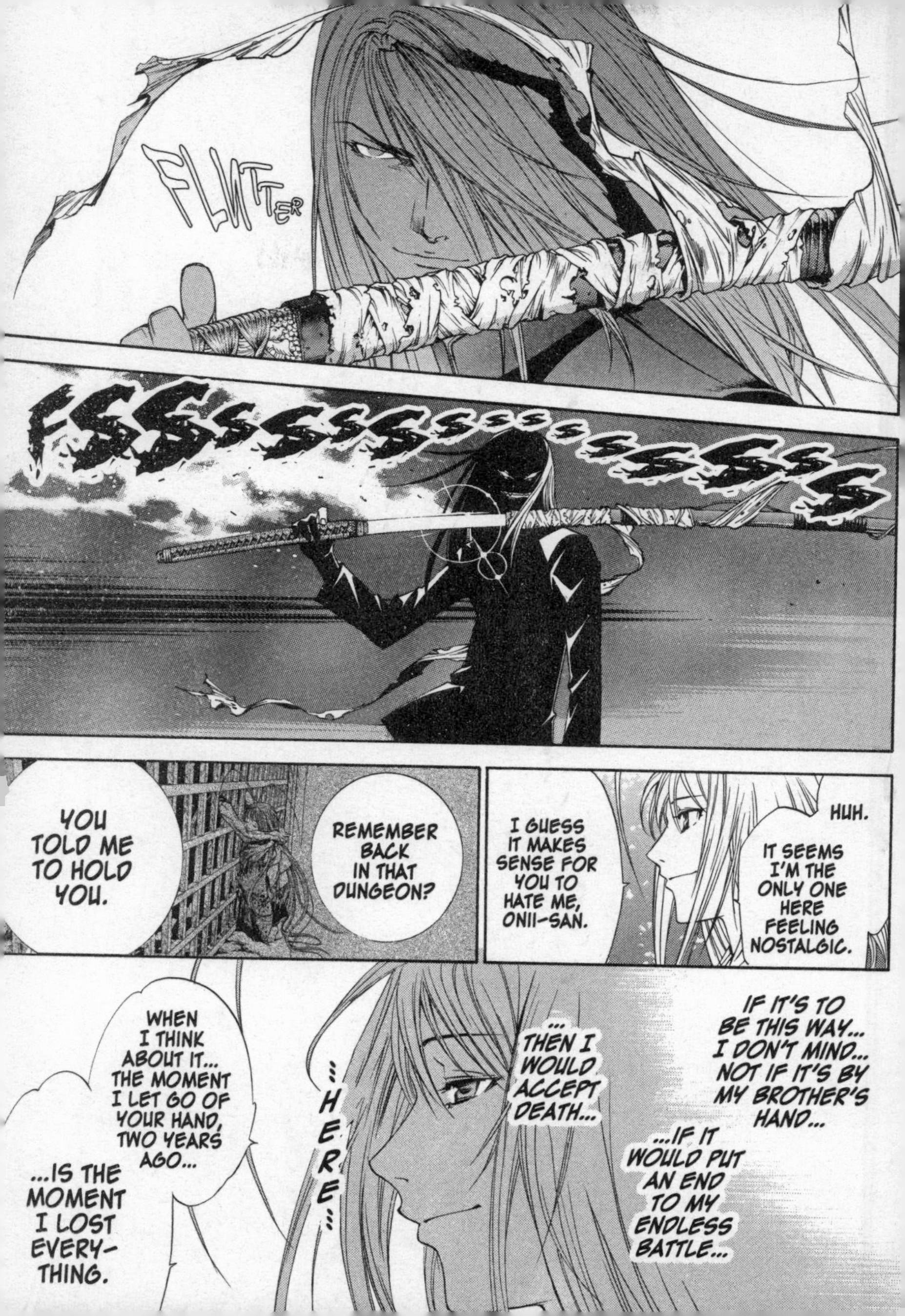
FLUTTER
FSSSSSSSSSSSSSSSS
HUH.
IT SEEMS I'M THE ONLY ONE HERE FEELING NOSTALGIC.
I GUESS IT MAKES SENSE FOR YOU TO HATE ME, ONII-SAN.
REMEMBER BACK IN THAT DUNGEON?
YOU TOLD ME TO HOLD YOU.
IF IT'S TO BE THIS WAY... I DON'T MIND... NOT IF IT'S BY MY BROTHER'S HAND...
...IF IT WOULD PUT AN END TO MY ENDLESS BATTLE...
...THEN I WOULD ACCEPT DEATH...
...HERE...
WHEN I THINK ABOUT IT... THE MOMENT I LET GO OF YOUR HAND, TWO YEARS AGO...
...IS THE MOMENT I LOST EVERY-THING.

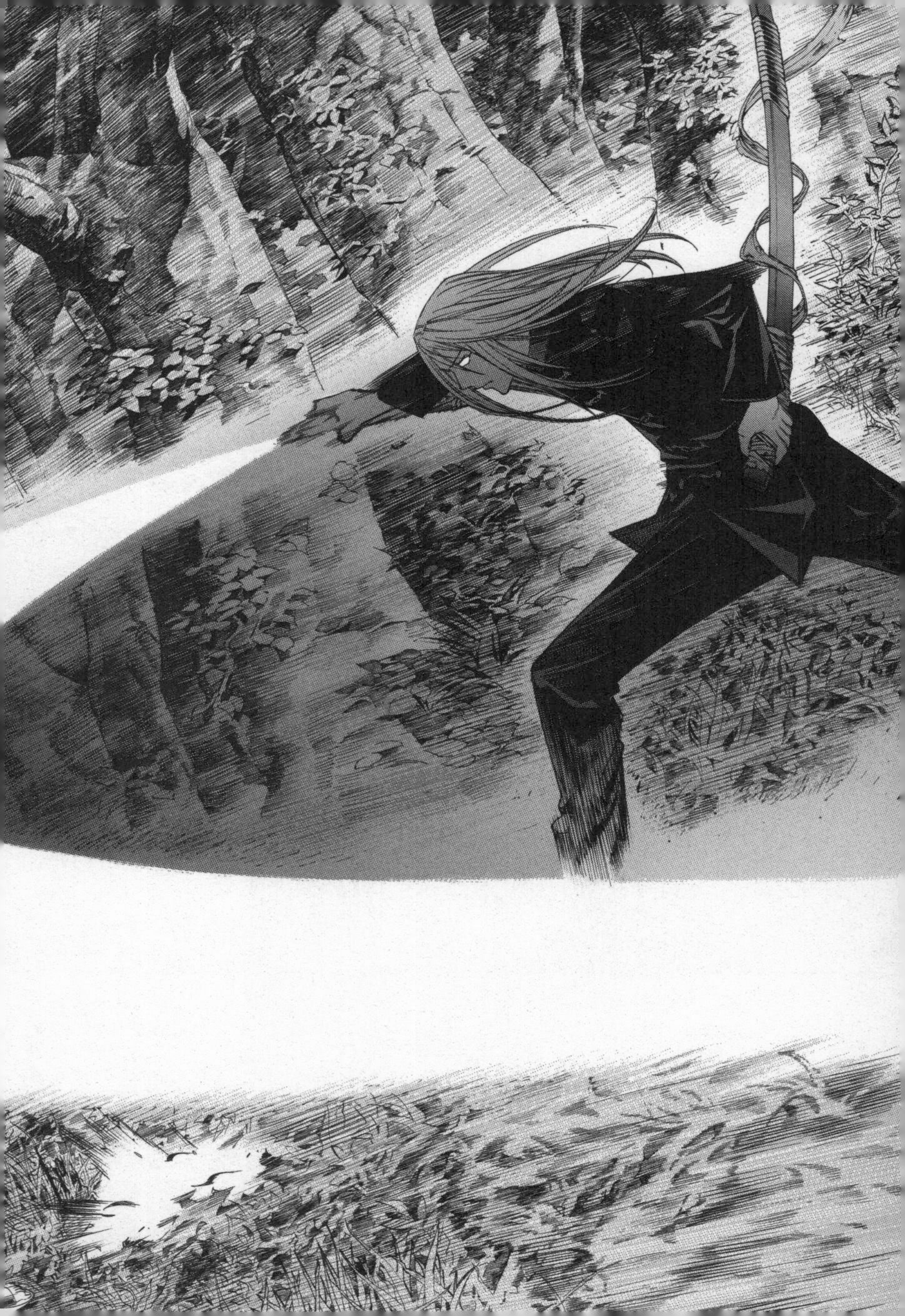

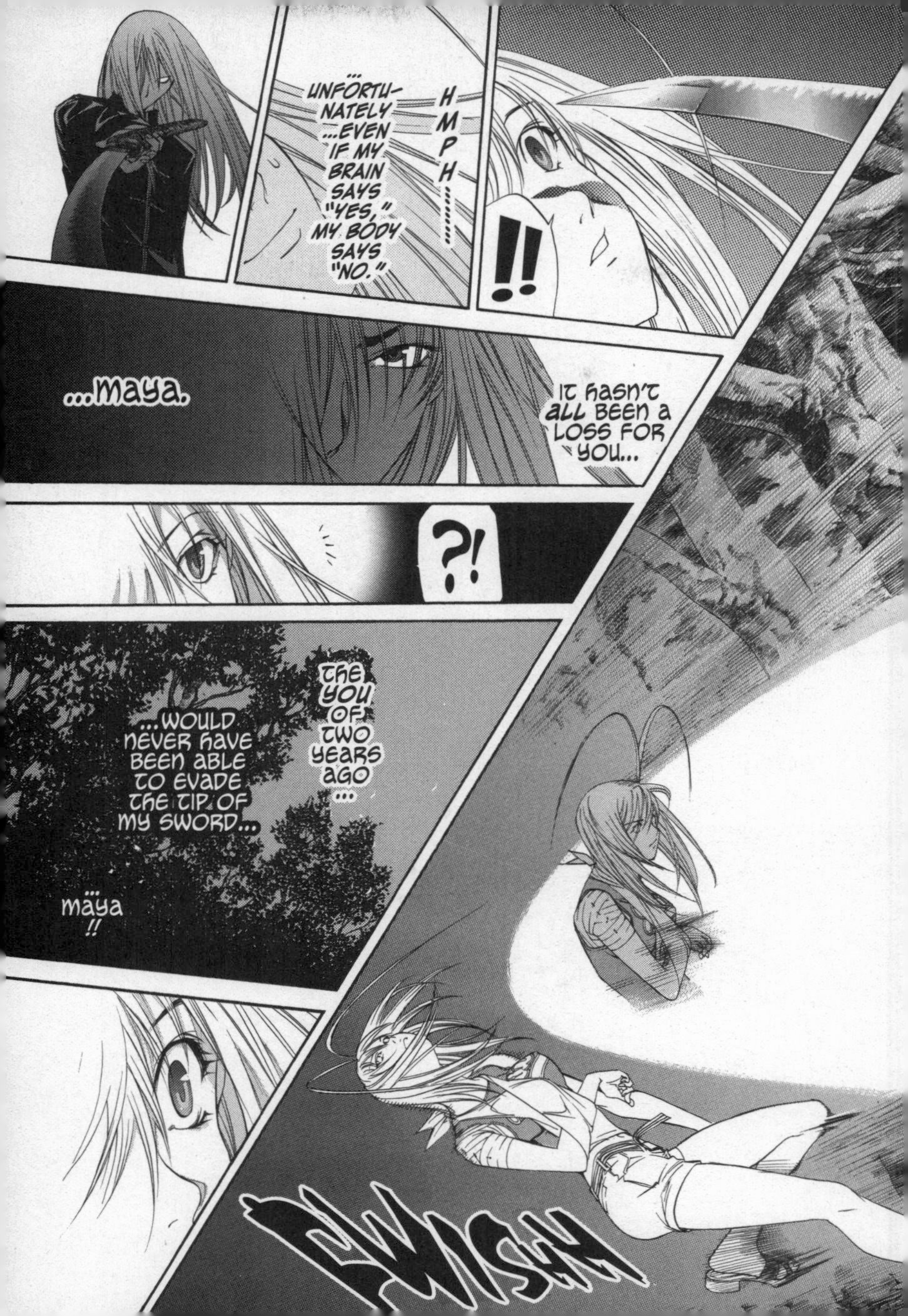
!!
HMPH......
...UNFORTUNATELY ...EVEN IF MY BRAIN SAYS "YES," MY BODY SAYS "NO."
IT HASN'T ALL BEEN A LOSS FOR YOU...
...MAYA.
?!
THE YOU OF TWO YEARS AGO...
...WOULD NEVER HAVE BEEN ABLE TO EVADE THE TIP OF MY SWORD...
...MAYA !!
SWISH

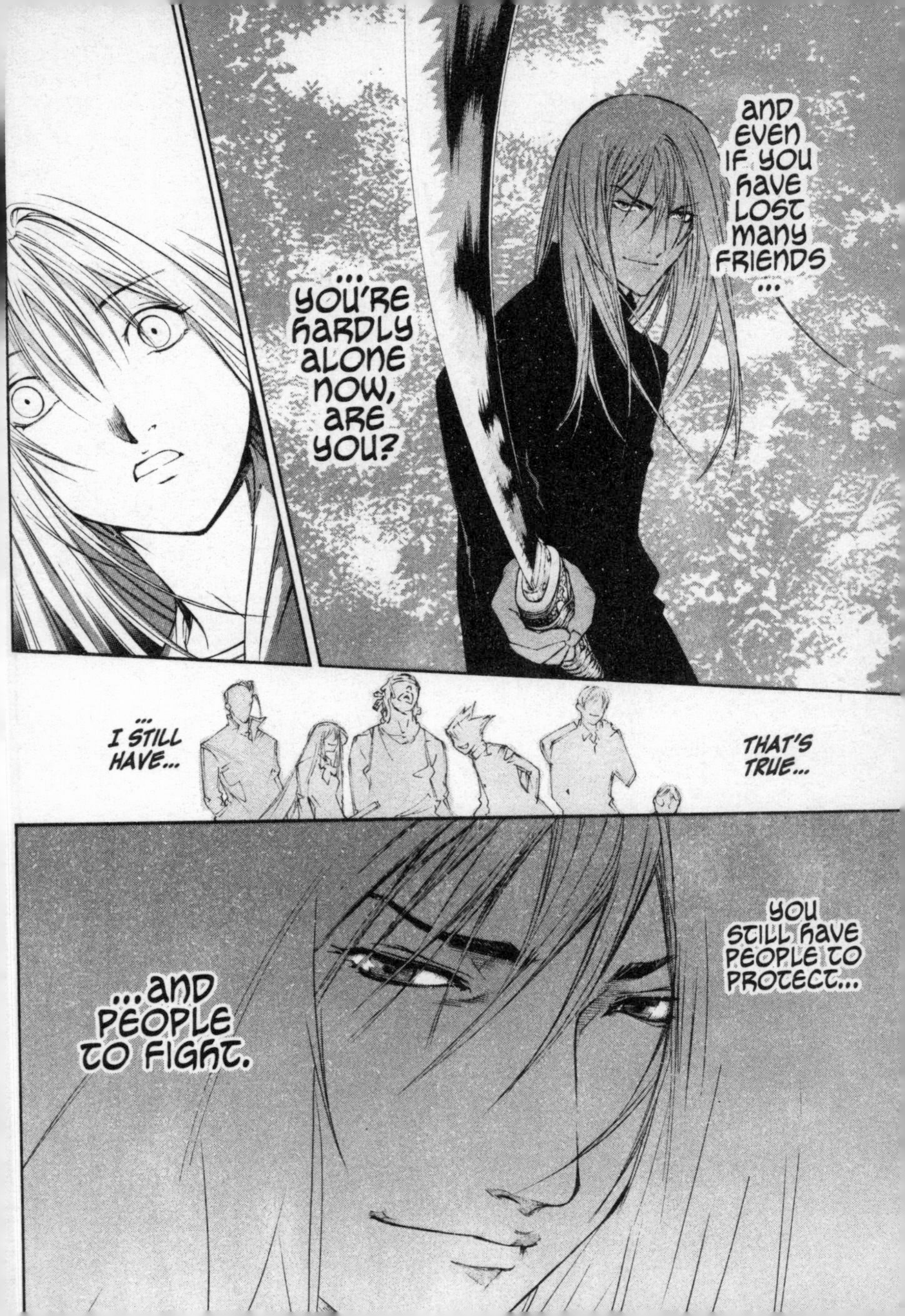
AND EVEN IF YOU HAVE LOST MANY FRIENDS...
...YOU'RE HARDLY ALONE NOW, ARE YOU?
THAT'S TRUE...
...I STILL HAVE...
YOU STILL HAVE PEOPLE TO PROTECT...
...AND PEOPLE TO FIGHT.

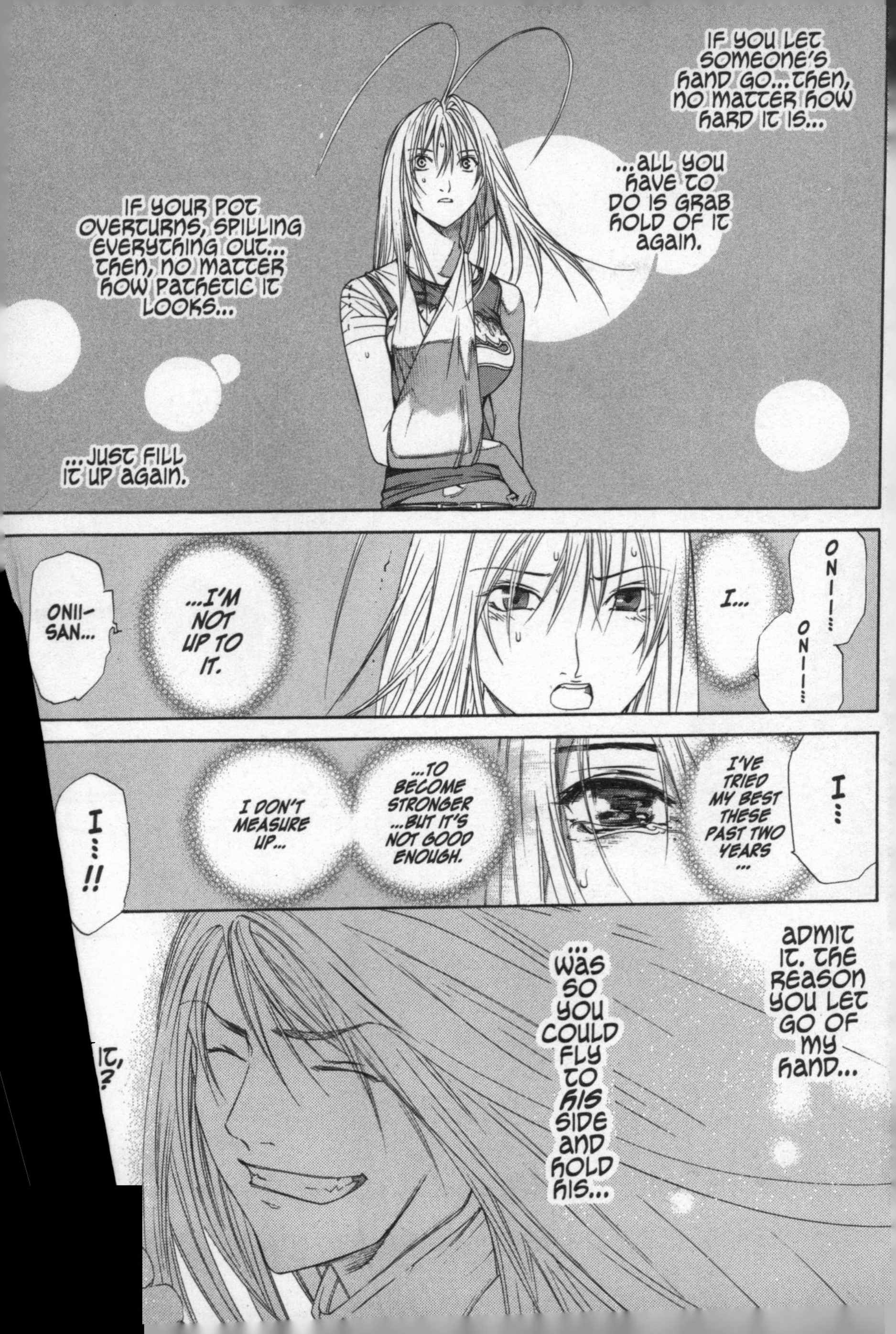
IF YOU LET SOMEONE'S HAND GO...THEN, NO MATTER HOW HARD IT IS...
...ALL YOU HAVE TO DO IS GRAB HOLD OF IT AGAIN.
IF YOUR POT OVERTURNS, SPILLING EVERYTHING OUT... THEN, NO MATTER HOW PATHETIC IT LOOKS...
...JUST FILL IT UP AGAIN.
ONII!... ONII!...
I...
...I'M NOT UP TO IT.
ONII-SAN...
I...
I'VE TRIED MY BEST THESE PAST TWO YEARS...
...TO BECOME STRONGER ...BUT IT'S NOT GOOD ENOUGH.
I DON'T MEASURE UP...
I...!!
ADMIT IT. THE REASON YOU LET GO OF MY HAND...
...WAS SO YOU COULD FLY TO HIS SIDE AND HOLD HIS...

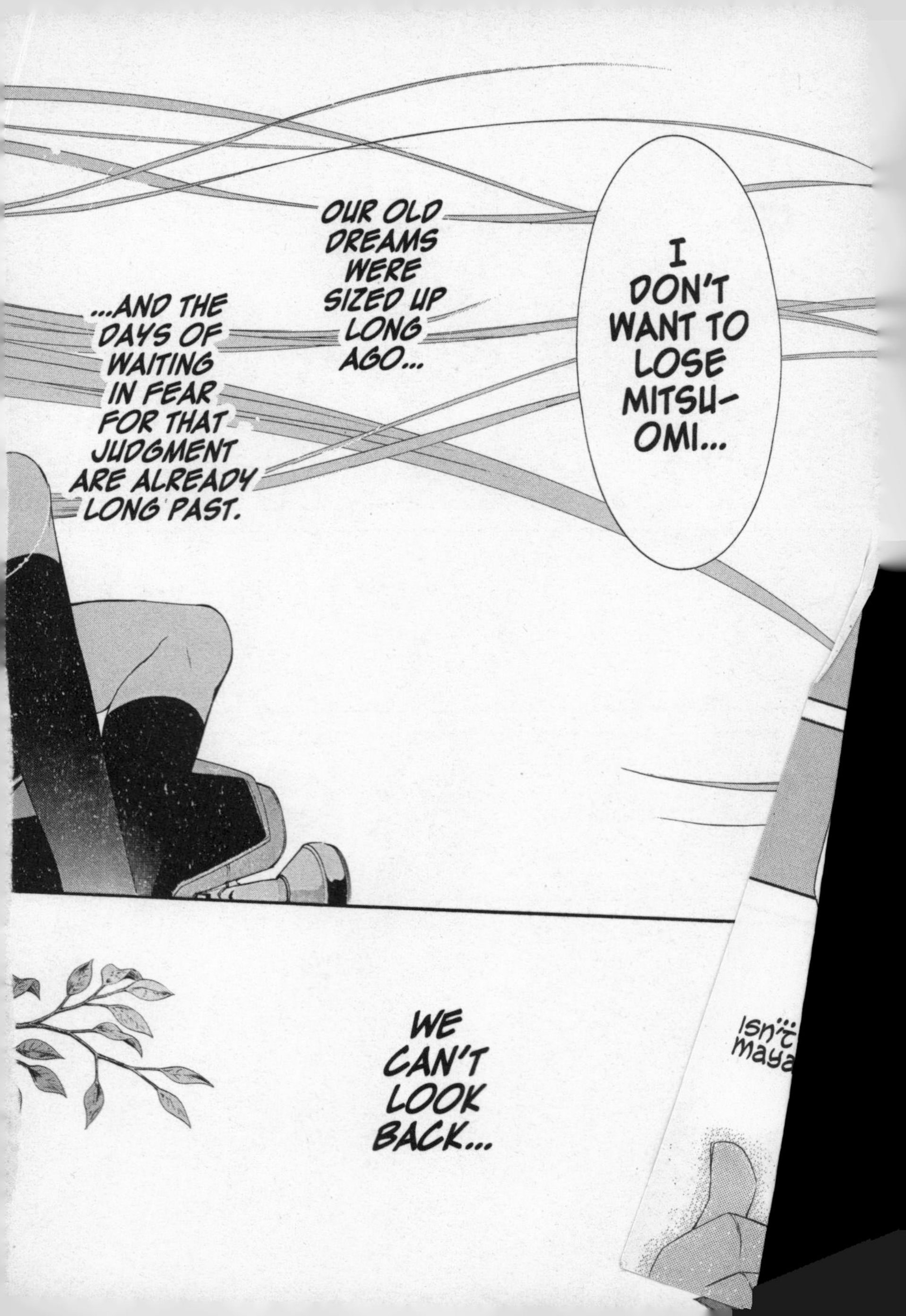
I DON'T WANT TO LOSE MITSUOMI...
OUR OLD DREAMS WERE SIZED UP LONG AGO...
...AND THE DAYS OF WAITING IN FEAR FOR THAT JUDGMENT ARE ALREADY LONG PAST.
WE CAN'T LOOK BACK...

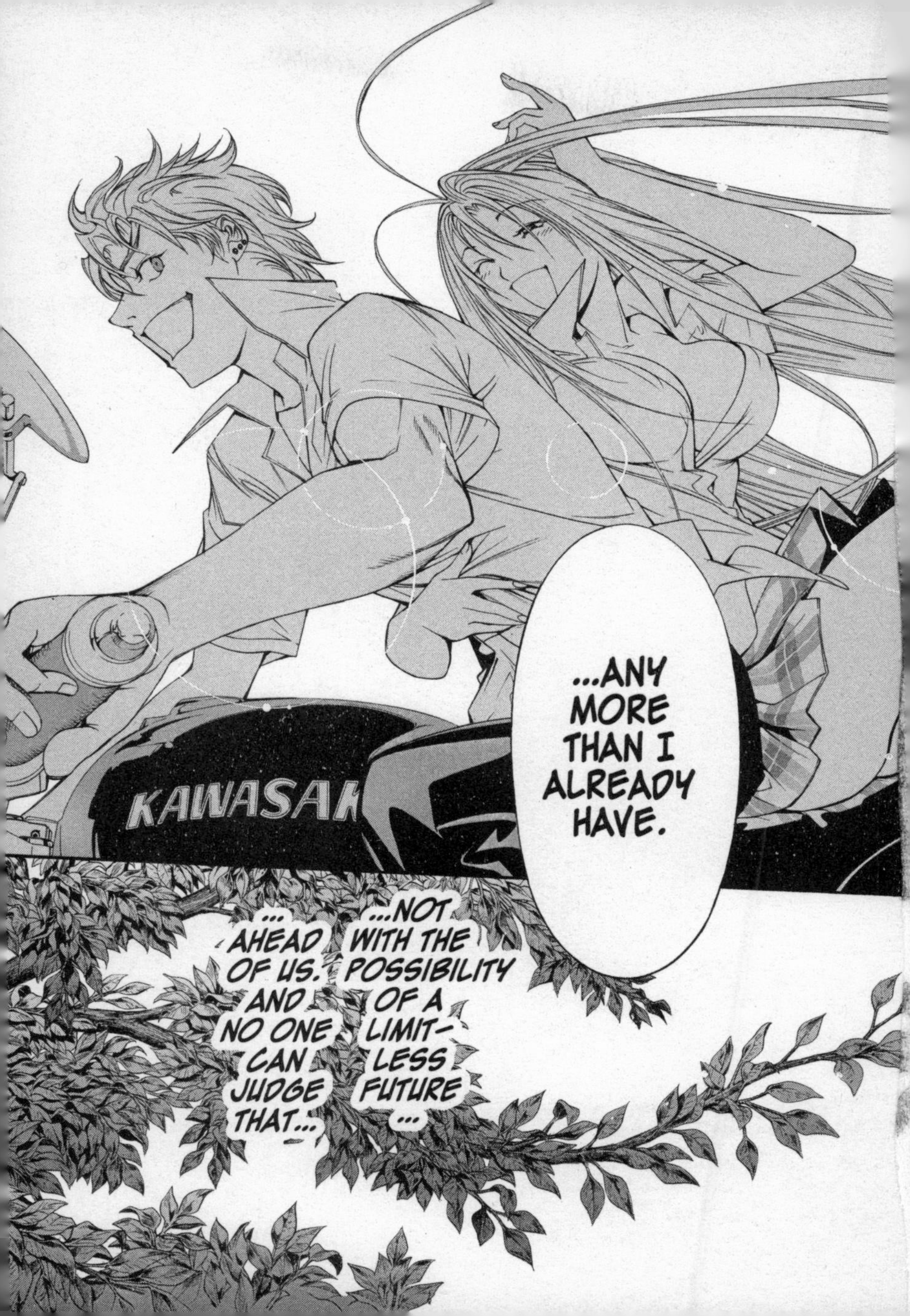
...ANY MORE THAN I ALREADY HAVE.
KAWASAK
...NOT WITH THE POSSIBILITY OF A LIMIT-LESS FUTURE ...
... AHEAD OF US. AND NO ONE CAN JUDGE THAT...

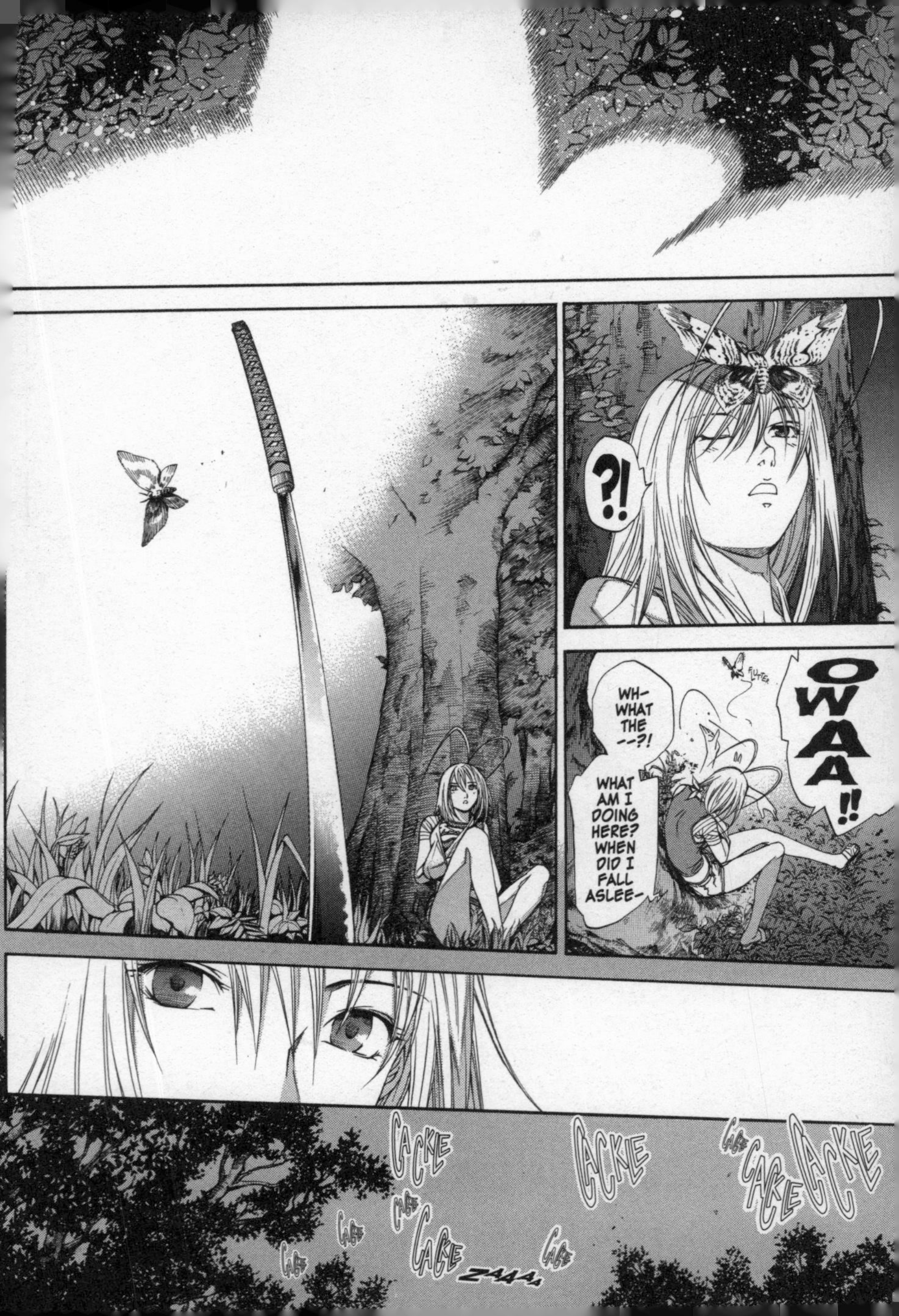
?!
OWAA!!
FLUTTER
WH- WHAT THE --?!
WHAT AM I DOING HERE? WHEN DID I FALL ASLEE-
CACKLE
CACKLE
CACKLE CACKLE CACKLE
CACKLE
ZAAAA

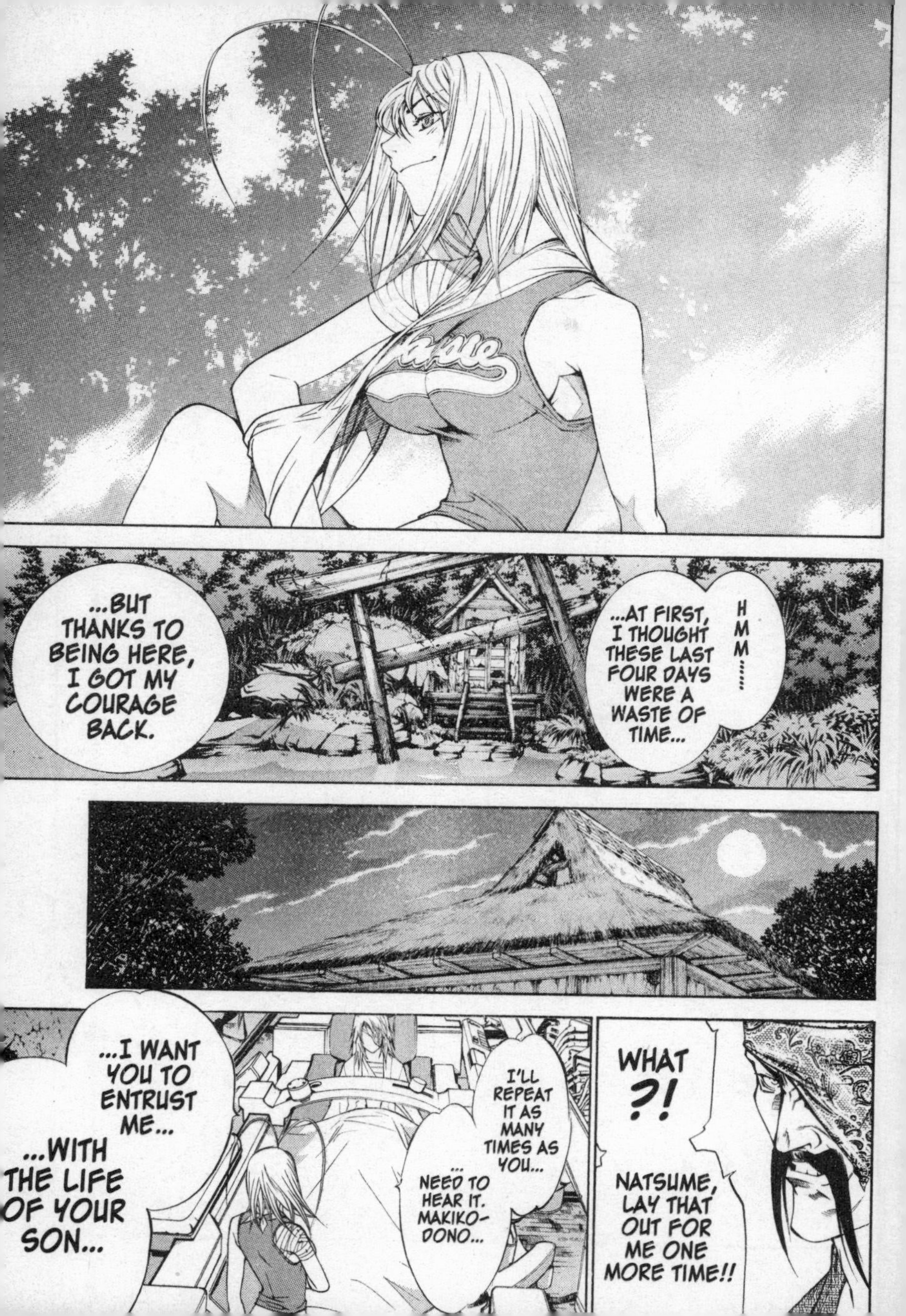
H M M ......
...AT FIRST, I THOUGHT THESE LAST FOUR DAYS WERE A WASTE OF TIME...
...BUT THANKS TO BEING HERE, I GOT MY COURAGE BACK.
WHAT ?!
NATSUME, LAY THAT OUT FOR ME ONE MORE TIME!!
I'LL REPEAT IT AS MANY TIMES AS YOU...
... NEED TO HEAR IT. MAKIKO-DONO...
...I WANT YOU TO ENTRUST ME...
...WITH THE LIFE OF YOUR SON...

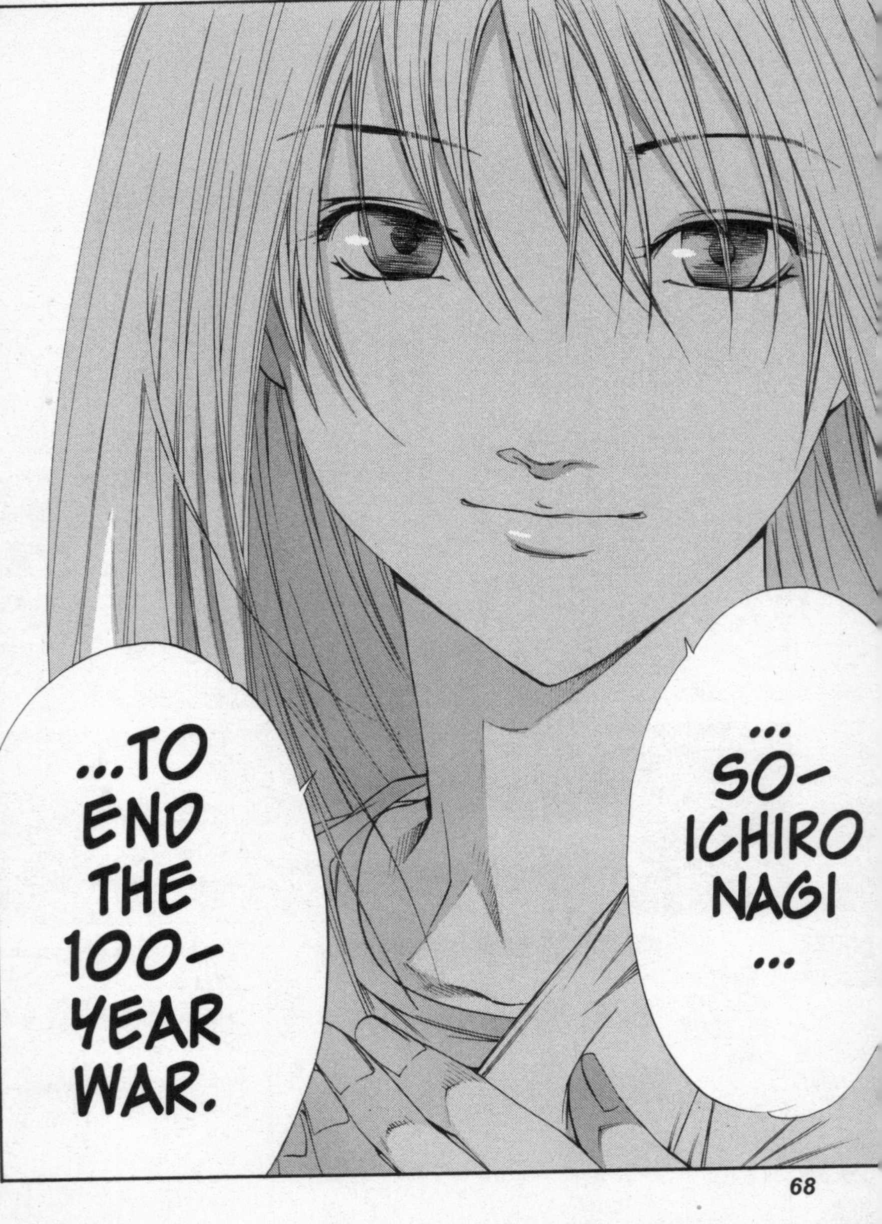
...SÕ-ICHIRO NAGI...
...TO END THE 100-YEAR WAR.

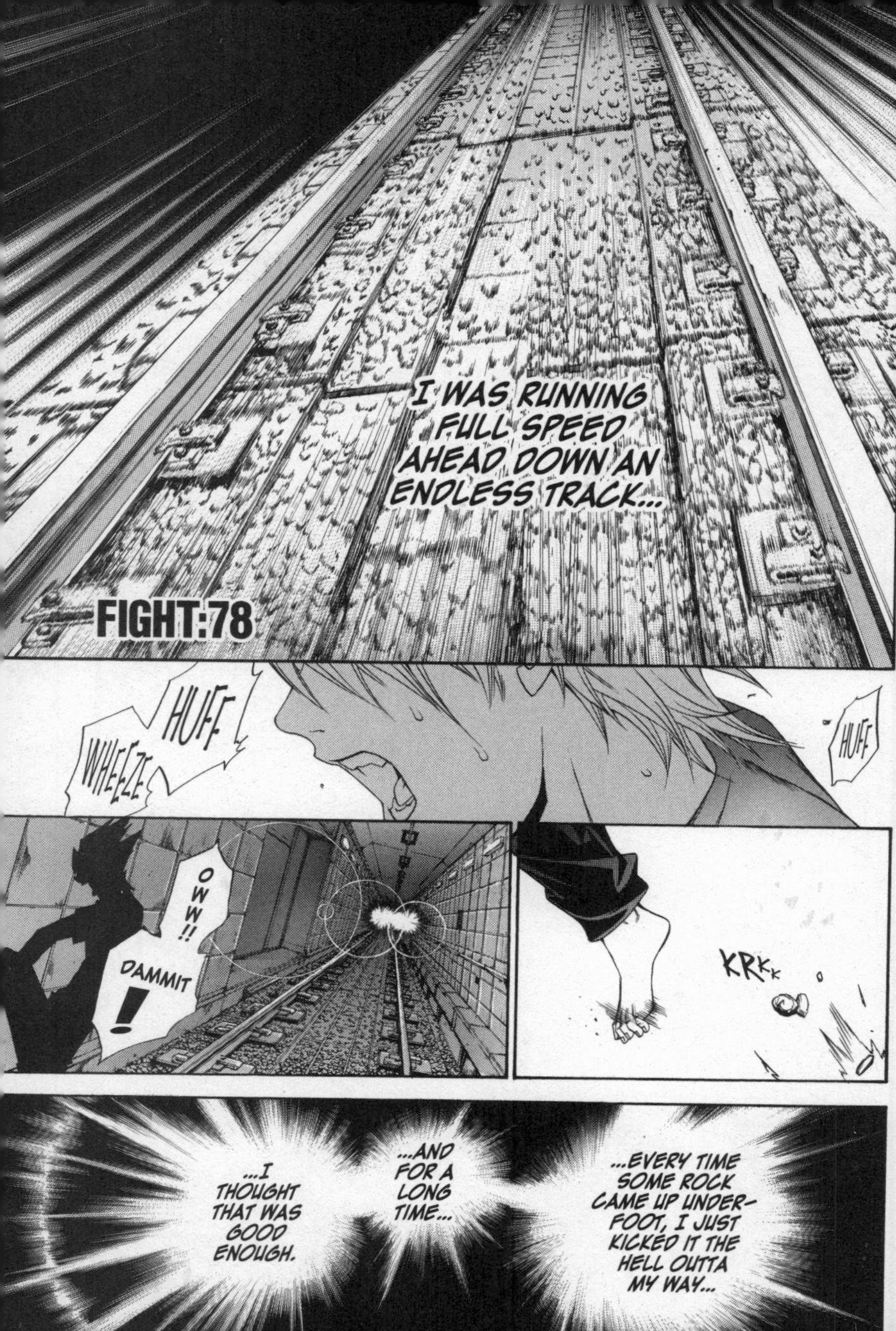
FIGHT:78
I WAS RUNNING FULL SPEED AHEAD DOWN AN ENDLESS TRACK...
HUFF
HUFF
WHEEZE
KRKK
OWW!!
DAMMIT!
...EVERY TIME SOME ROCK CAME UP UNDER-FOOT, I JUST KICKED IT THE HELL OUTTA MY WAY...
...AND FOR A LONG TIME...
...I THOUGHT THAT WAS GOOD ENOUGH.

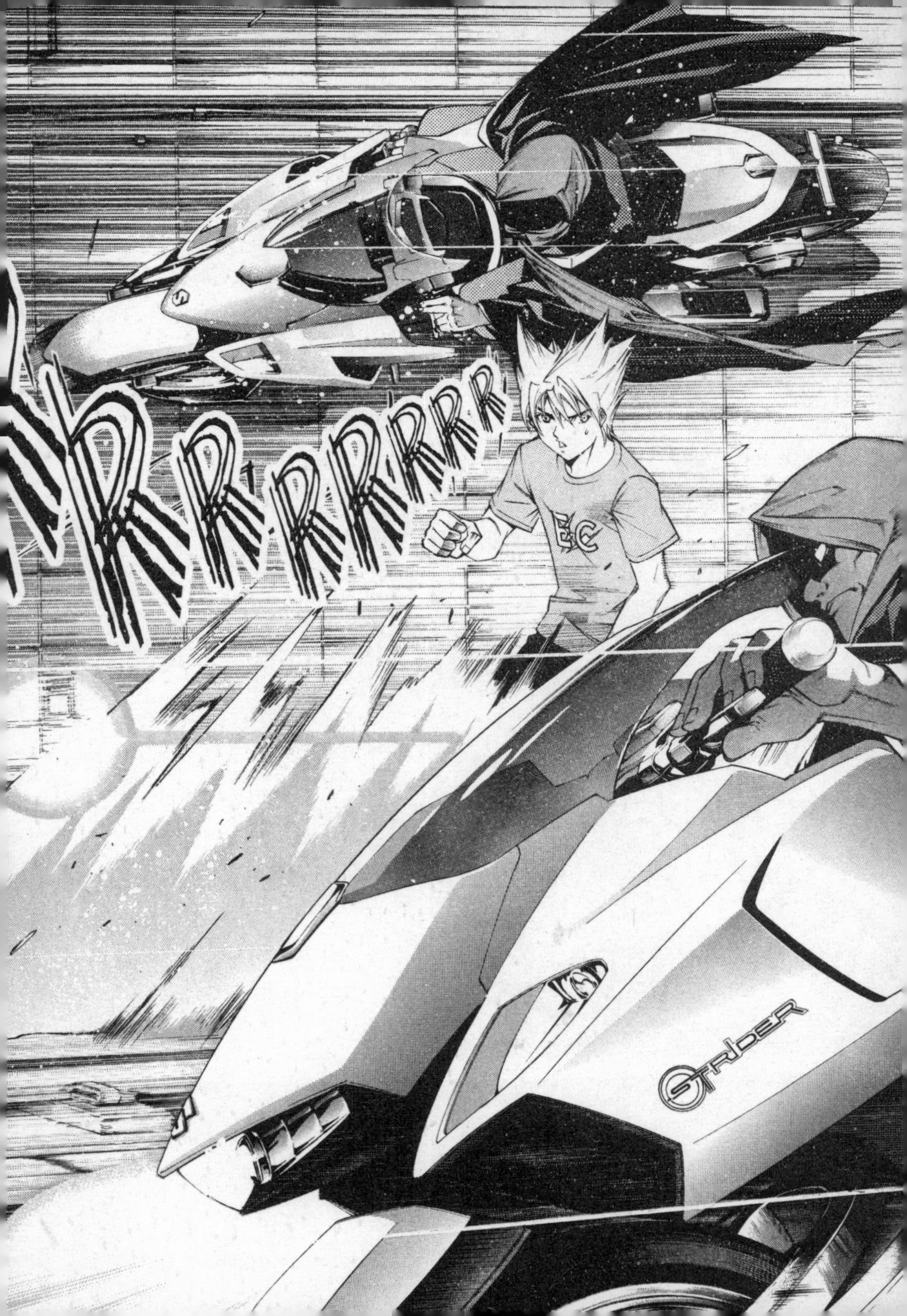
RRRRRRRR
EC
STRIDER

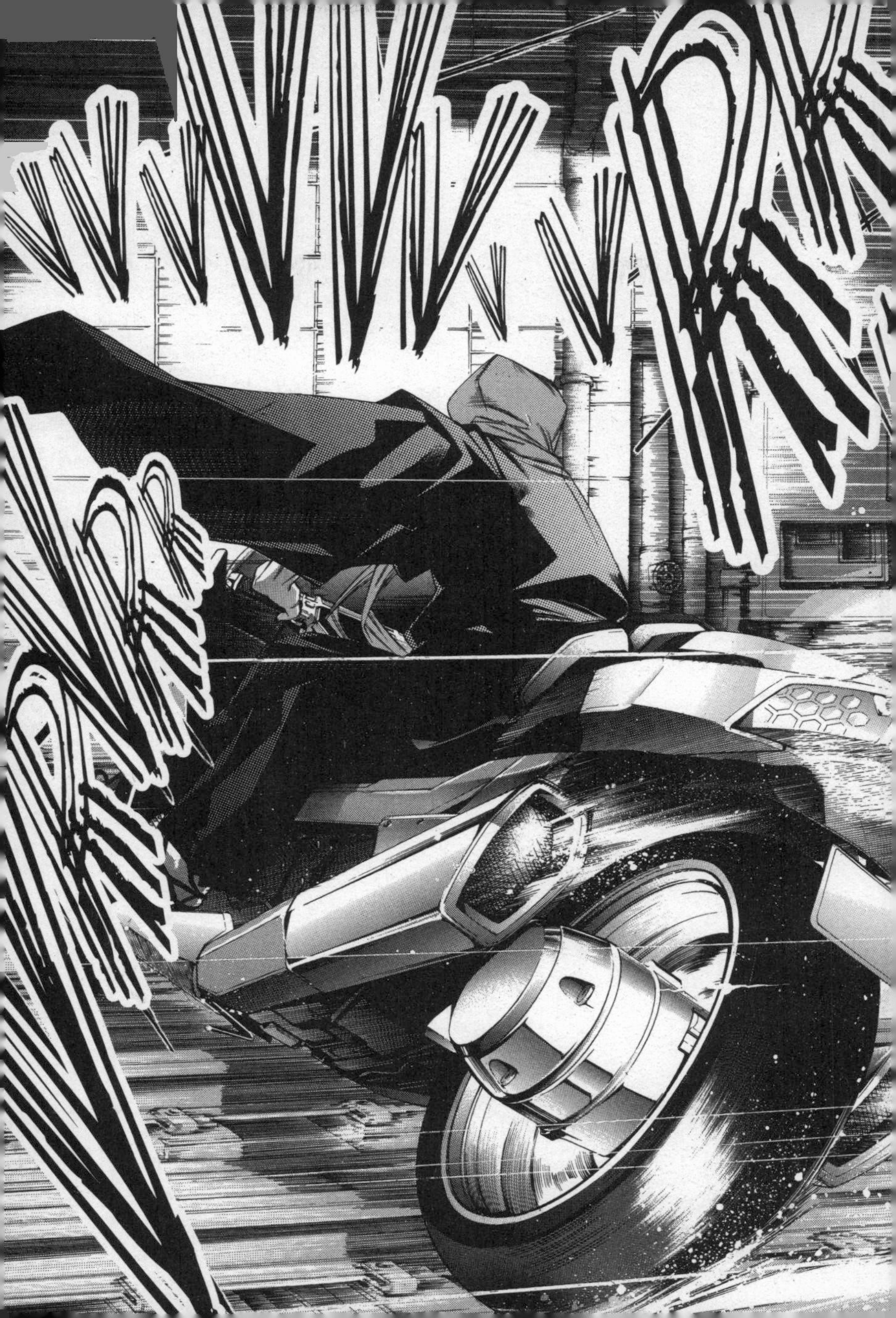

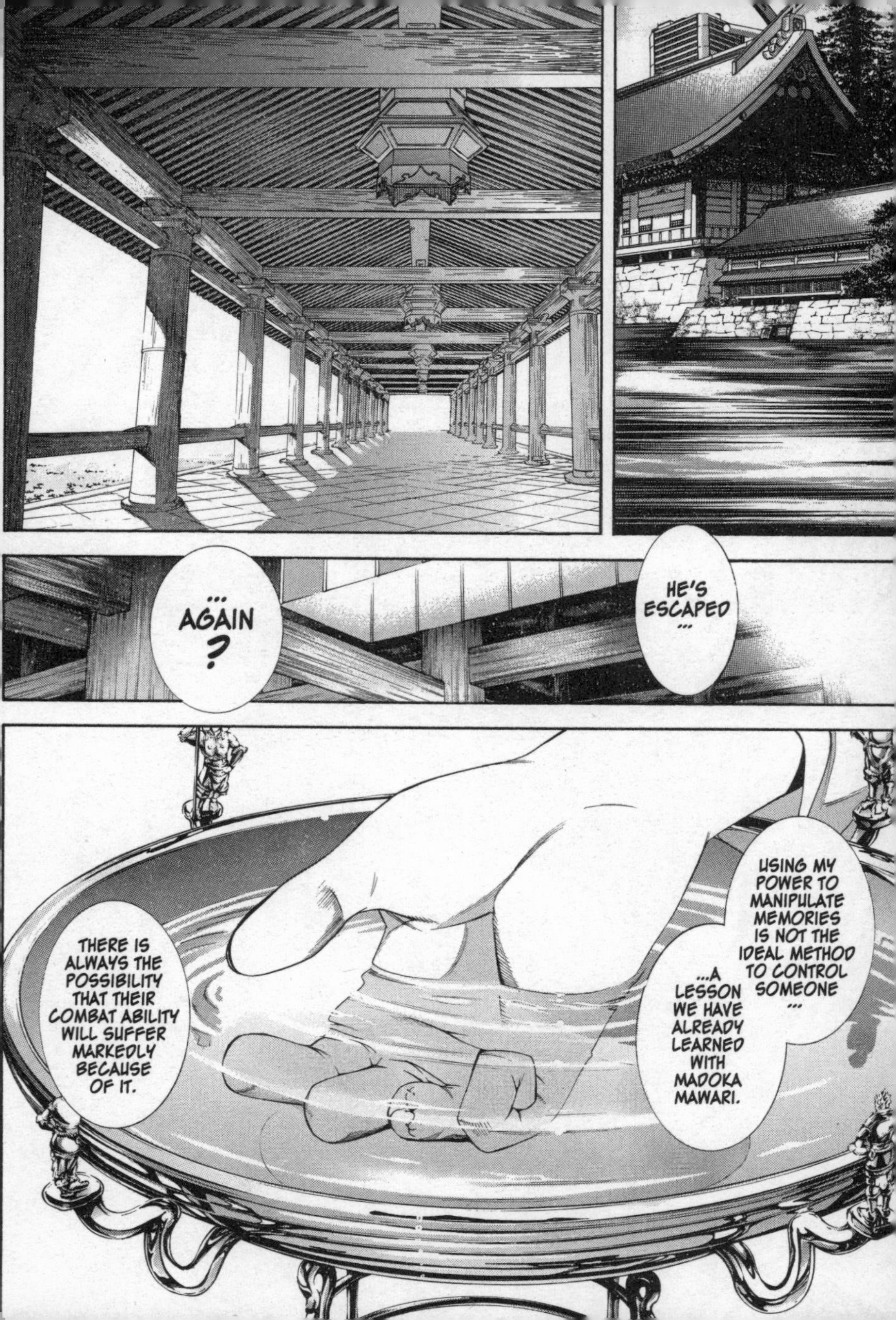
HE'S ESCAPED...
...AGAIN?
USING MY POWER TO MANIPULATE MEMORIES IS NOT THE IDEAL METHOD TO CONTROL SOMEONE...
...A LESSON WE HAVE ALREADY LEARNED WITH MADOKA MAWARI.
THERE IS ALWAYS THE POSSIBILITY THAT THEIR COMBAT ABILITY WILL SUFFER MARKEDLY BECAUSE OF IT.

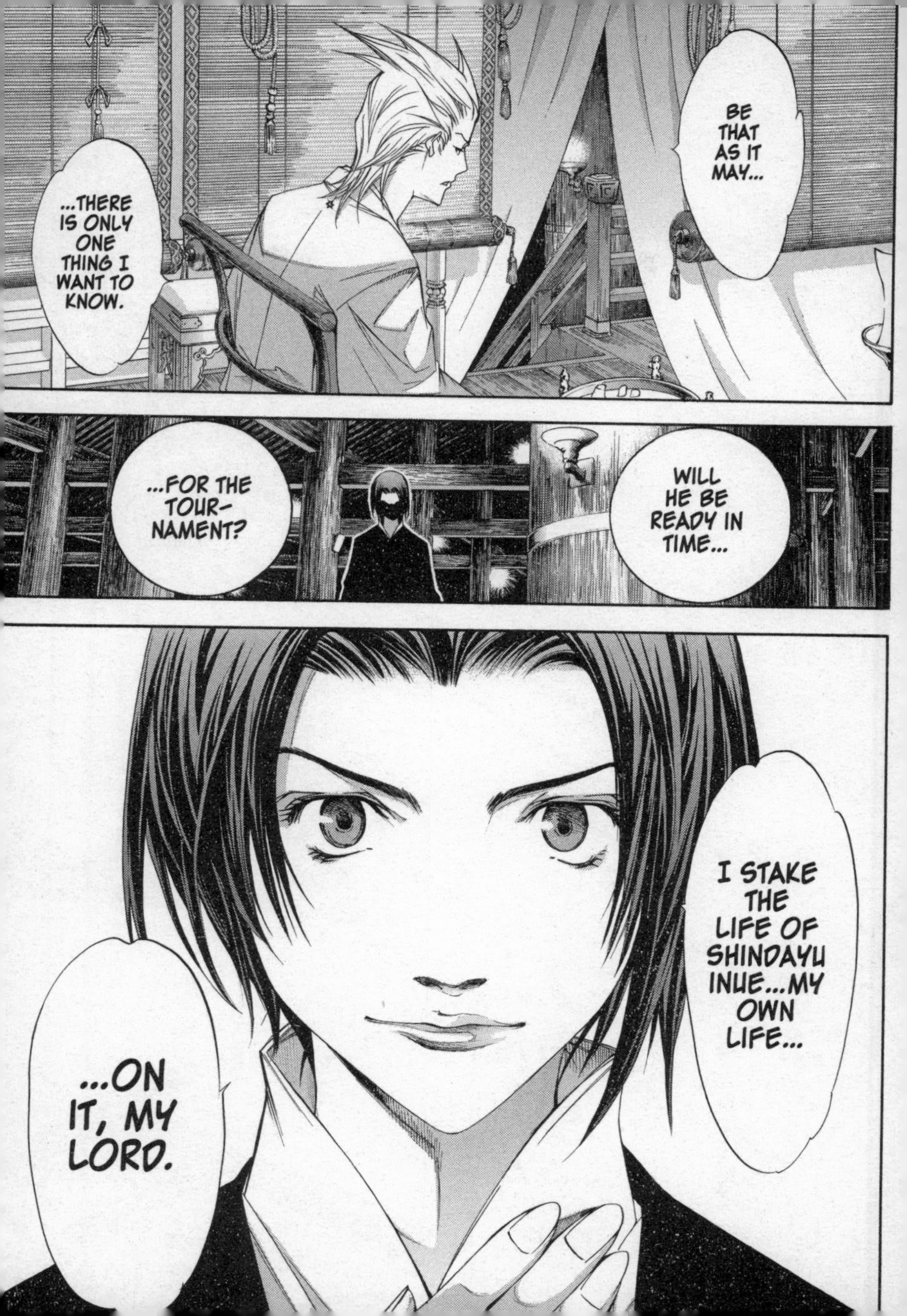
BE THAT AS IT MAY...
...THERE IS ONLY ONE THING I WANT TO KNOW.
WILL HE BE READY IN TIME...
...FOR THE TOURNAMENT?
I STAKE THE LIFE OF SHINDAYU INUE...MY OWN LIFE...
...ON IT, MY LORD.

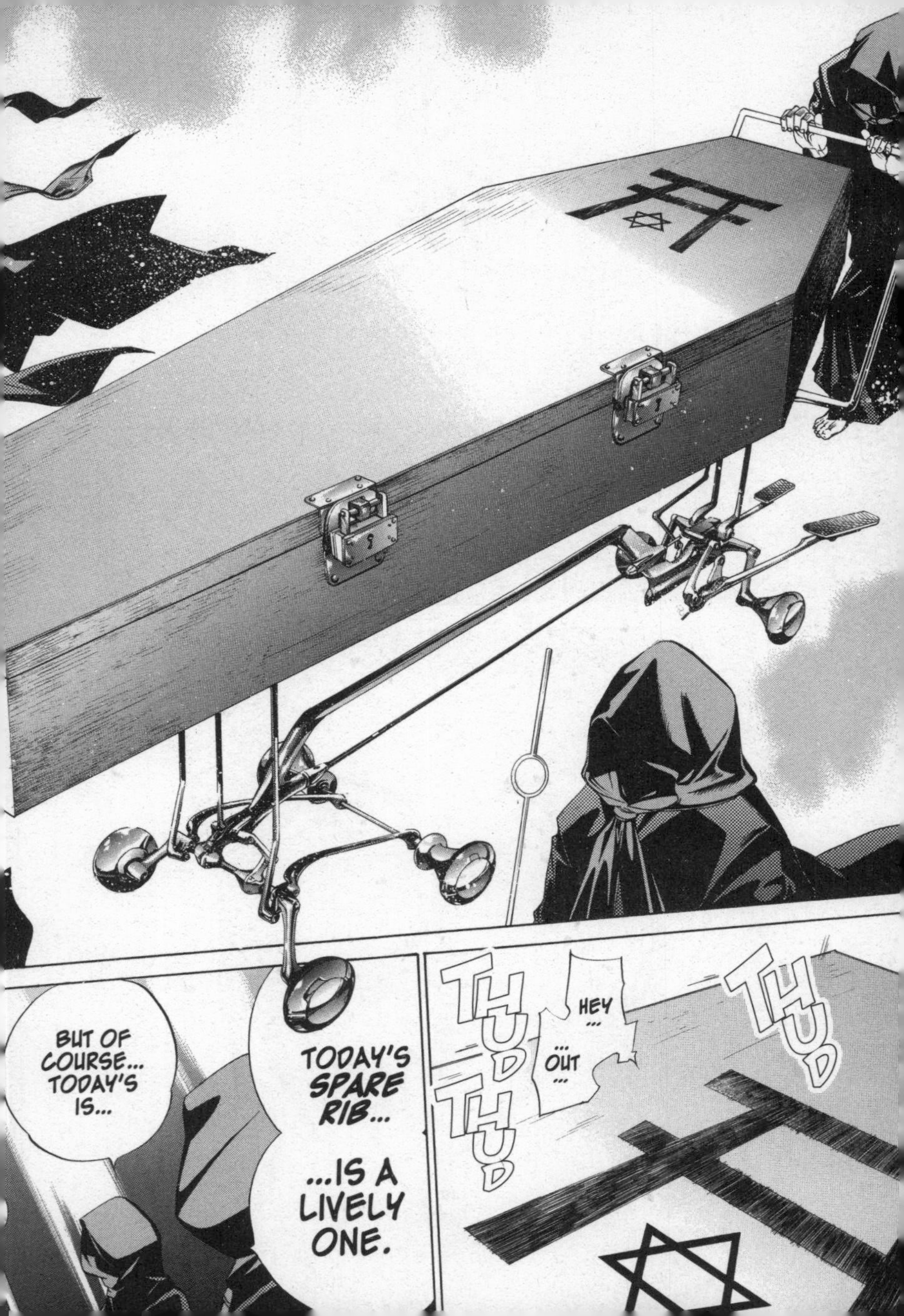
THUD
HEY...
...OUT...
THUD
THUD
BUT OF COURSE... TODAY'S IS...
TODAY'S SPARE RIB...
...IS A LIVELY ONE.

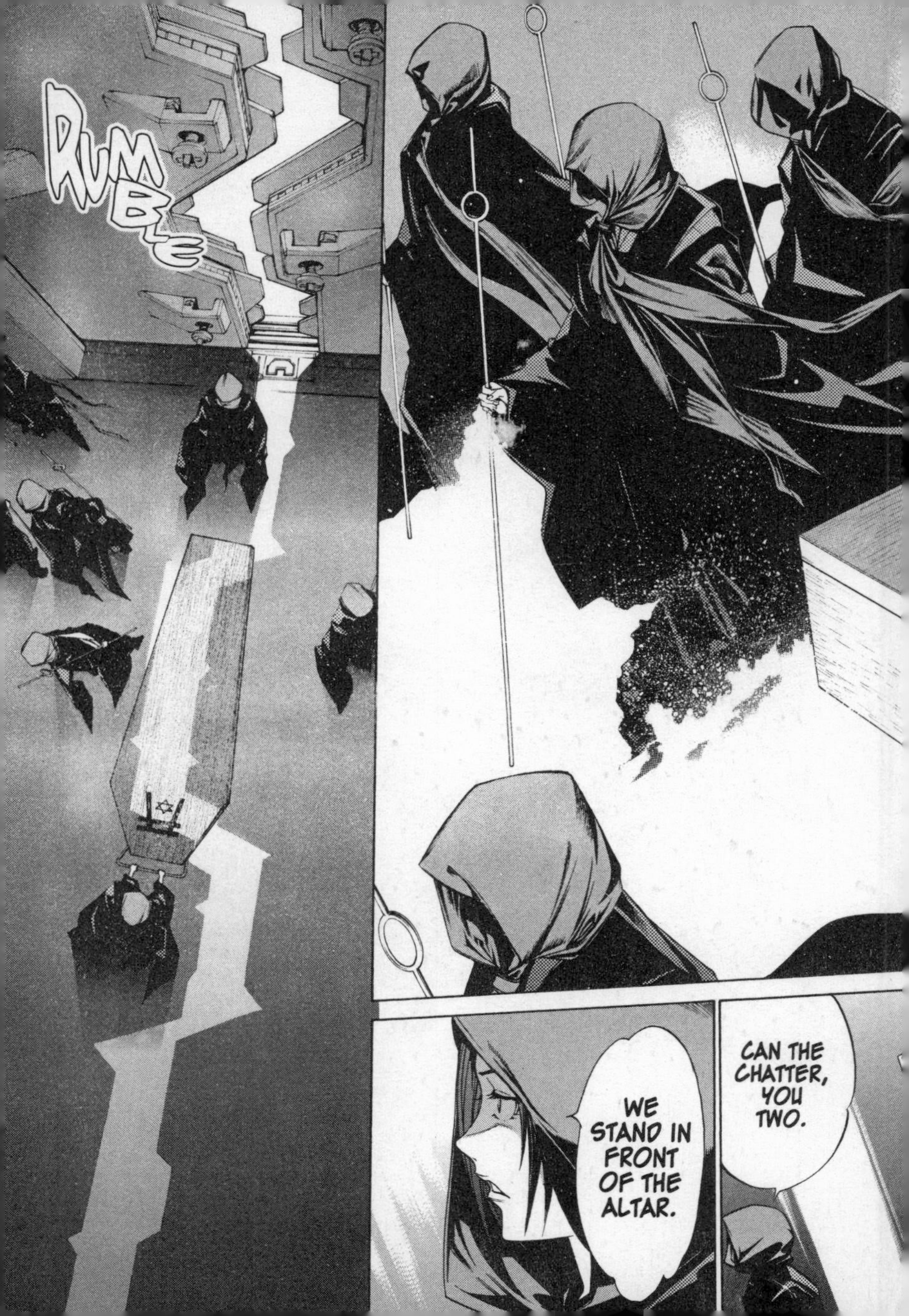
CAN THE CHATTER, YOU TWO.
WE STAND IN FRONT OF THE ALTAR.
RUMBLE

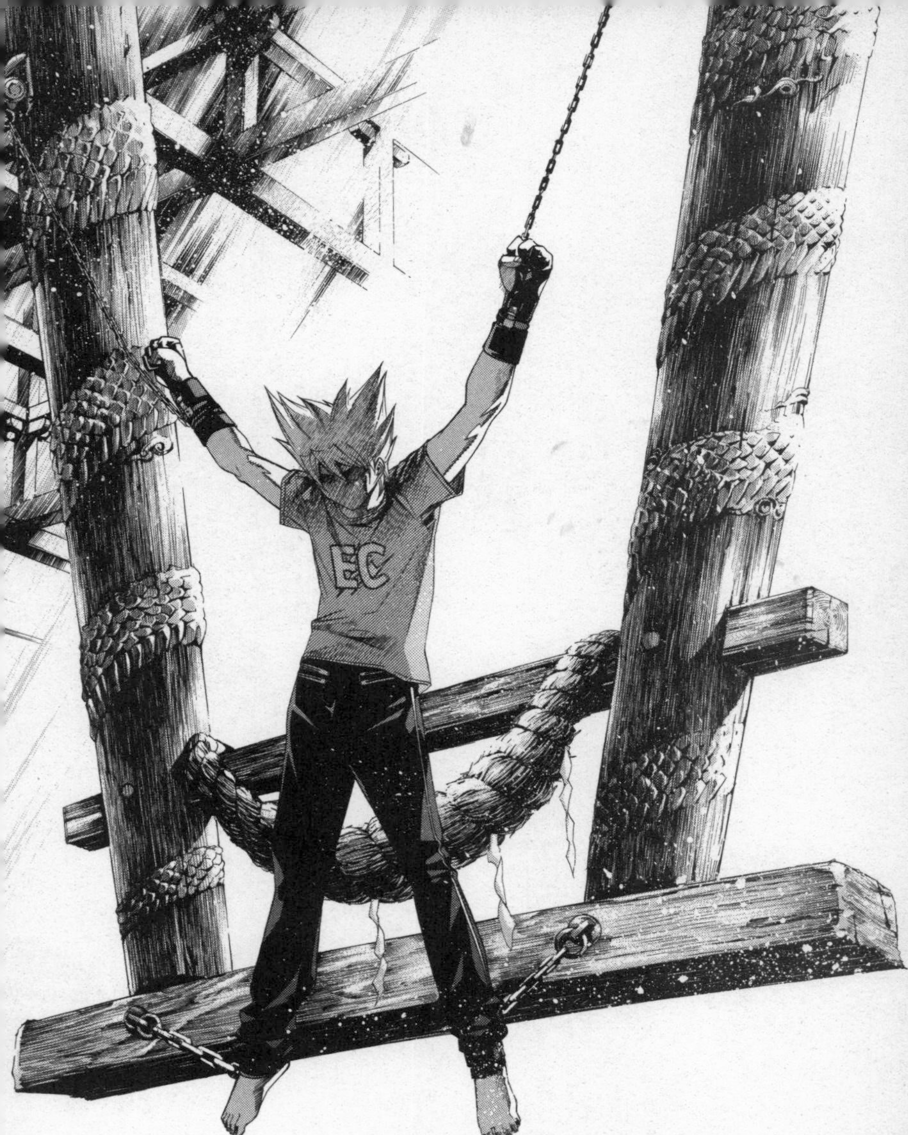
EC

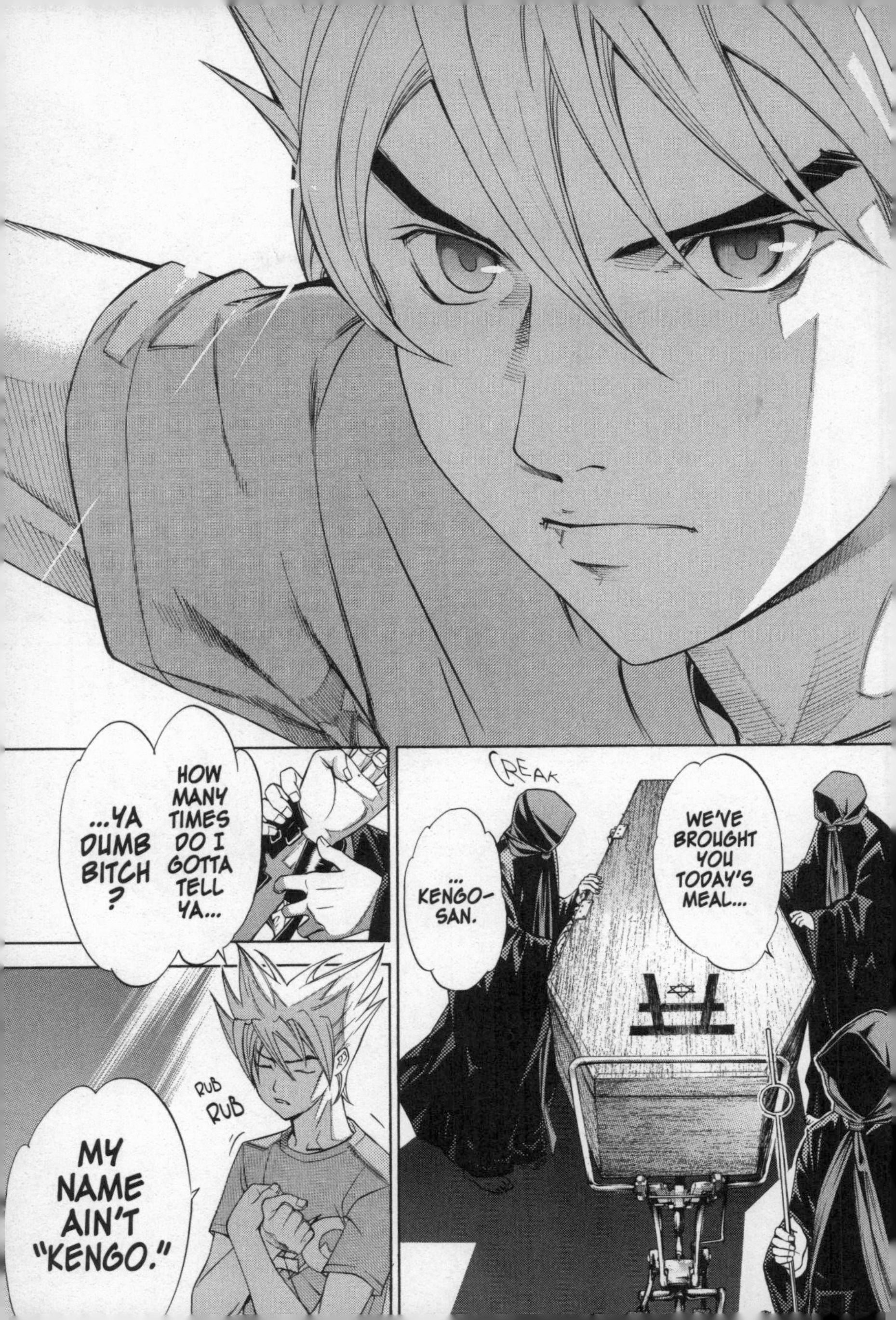
CREAK
WE'VE BROUGHT YOU TODAY'S MEAL...
...KENGO-SAN.
HOW MANY TIMES DO I GOTTA TELL YA...
...YA DUMB BITCH?
RUB RUB
MY NAME AIN'T "KENGO."

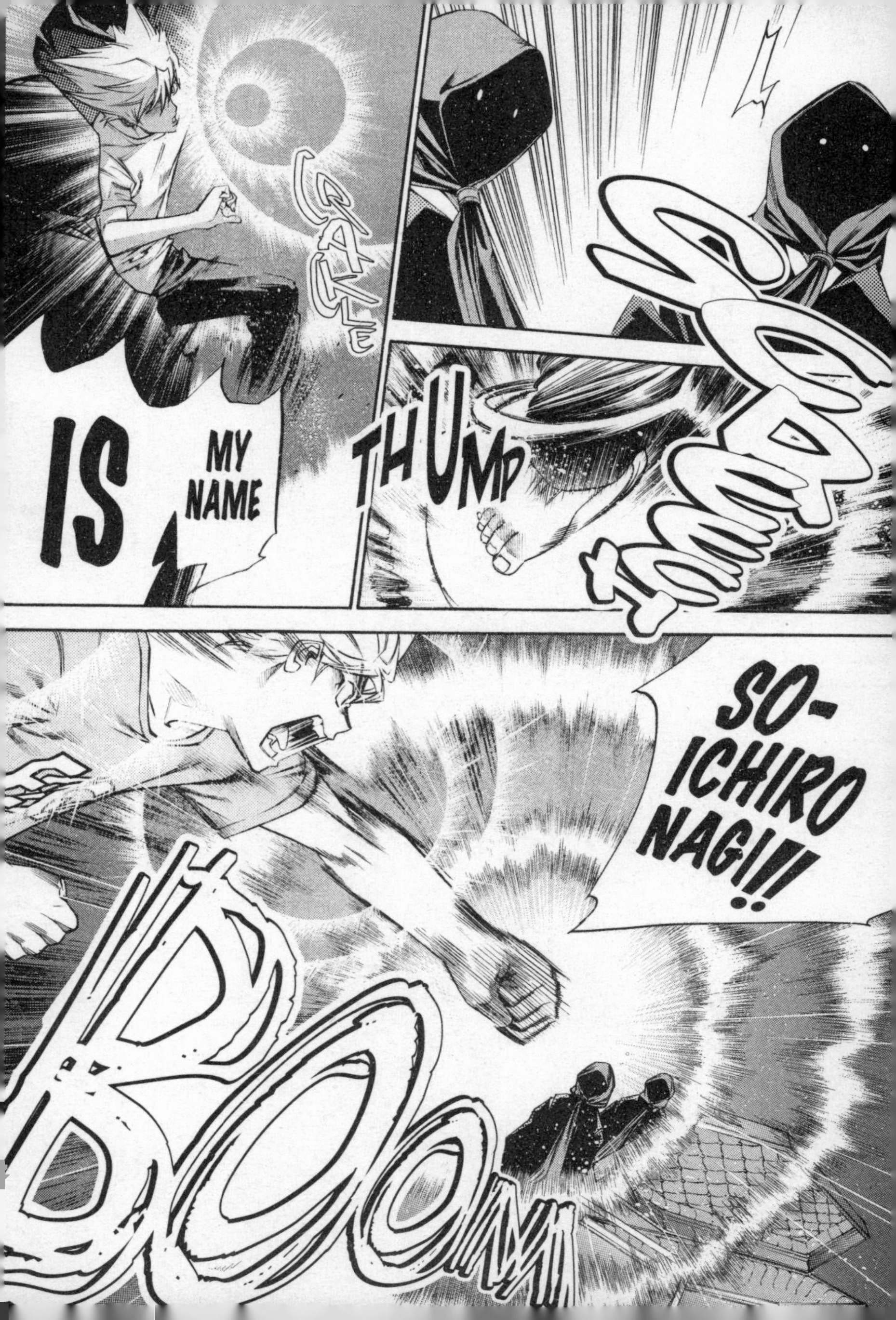
THUMP
CRACKLE
MY NAME
IS
SO-ICHIRO NAGI!!
BOOM

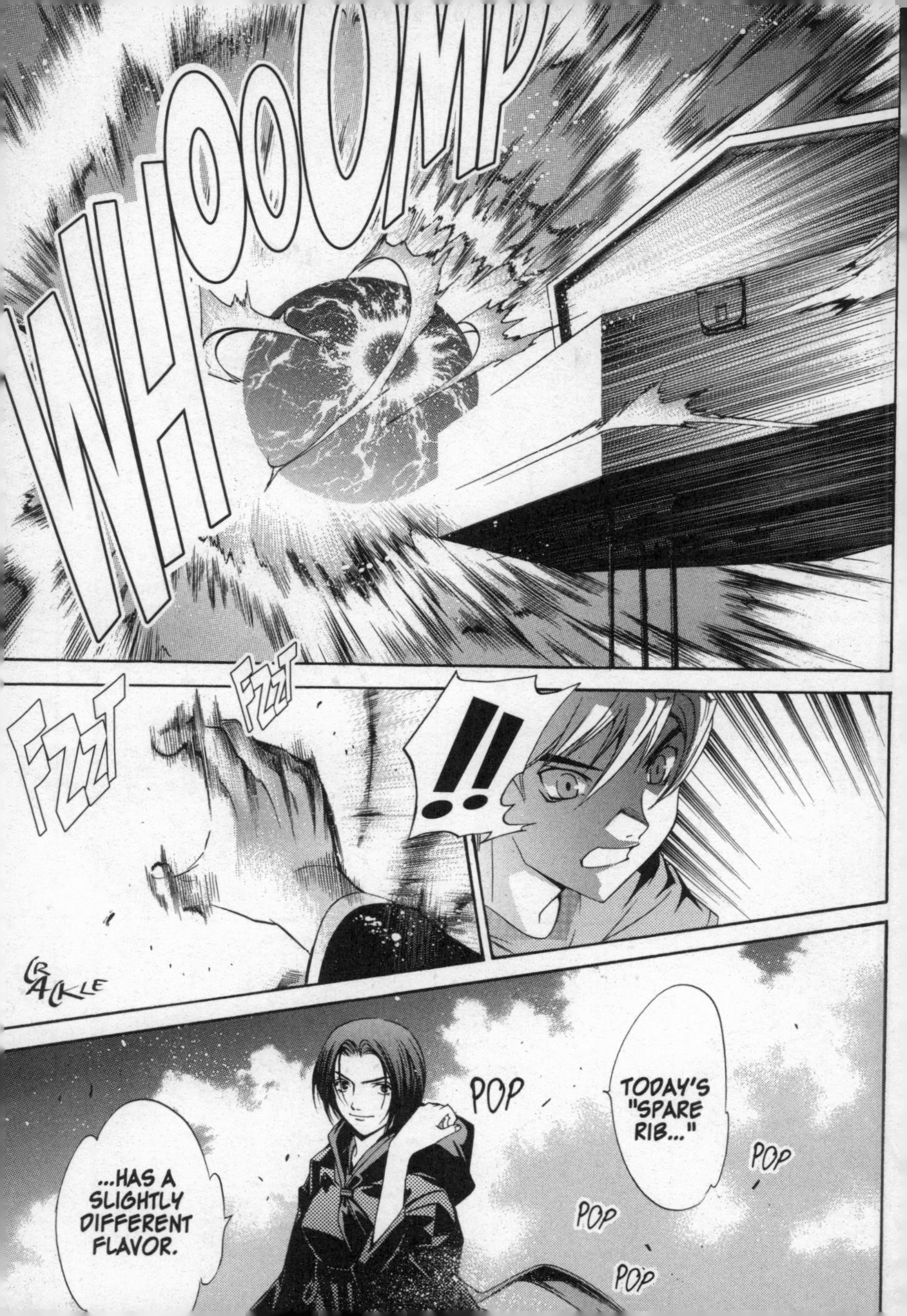
WHOOOMP
FZZT
FZZT
!!
CRACKLE
TODAY'S "SPARE RIB..."
POP
...HAS A SLIGHTLY DIFFERENT FLAVOR.
POP
POP
POP

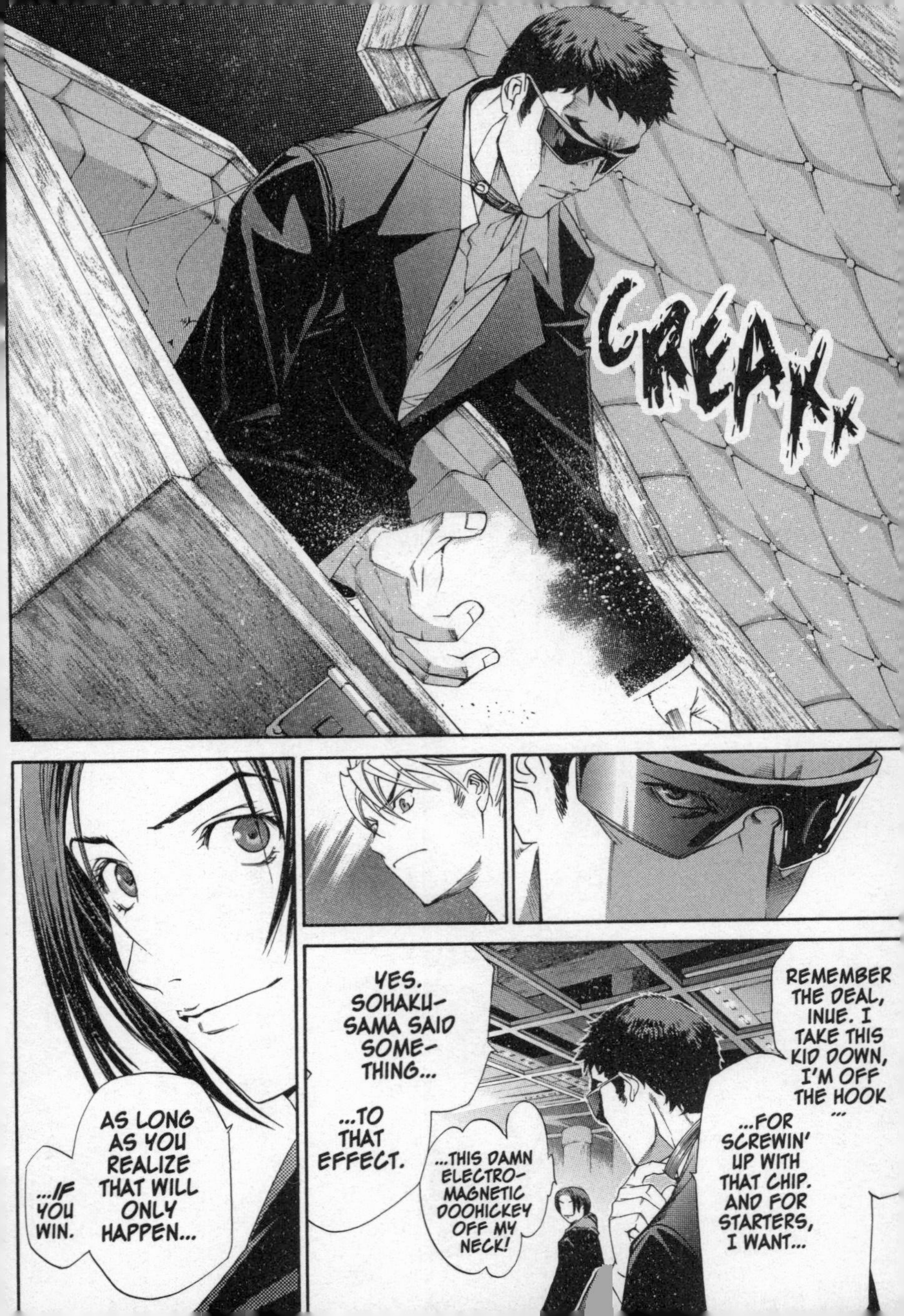
CREAK
REMEMBER THE DEAL, INUE. I TAKE THIS KID DOWN, I'M OFF THE HOOK...
...FOR SCREWIN' UP WITH THAT CHIP. AND FOR STARTERS, I WANT...
...THIS DAMN ELECTRO-MAGNETIC DOOHICKEY OFF MY NECK!
YES. SOHAKU-SAMA SAID SOME-THING...
...TO THAT EFFECT.
AS LONG AS YOU REALIZE THAT WILL ONLY HAPPEN...
...IF YOU WIN.

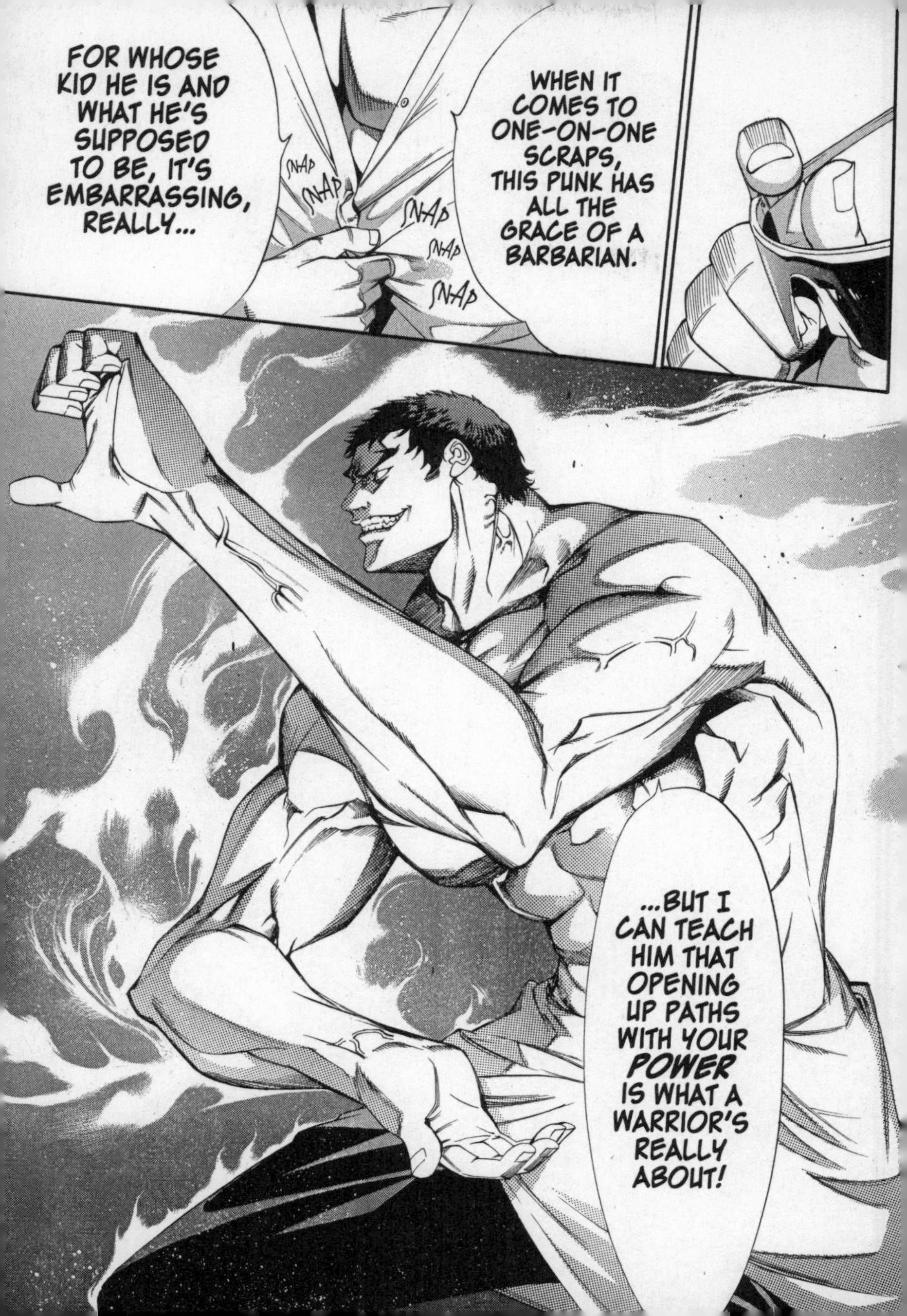
WHEN IT COMES TO ONE-ON-ONE SCRAPS, THIS PUNK HAS ALL THE GRACE OF A BARBARIAN.
FOR WHOSE KID HE IS AND WHAT HE'S SUPPOSED TO BE, IT'S EMBARRASSING, REALLY...
SNAP
SNAP
SNAP
SNAP
SNAP
...BUT I CAN TEACH HIM THAT OPENING UP PATHS WITH YOUR POWER IS WHAT A WARRIOR'S REALLY ABOUT!

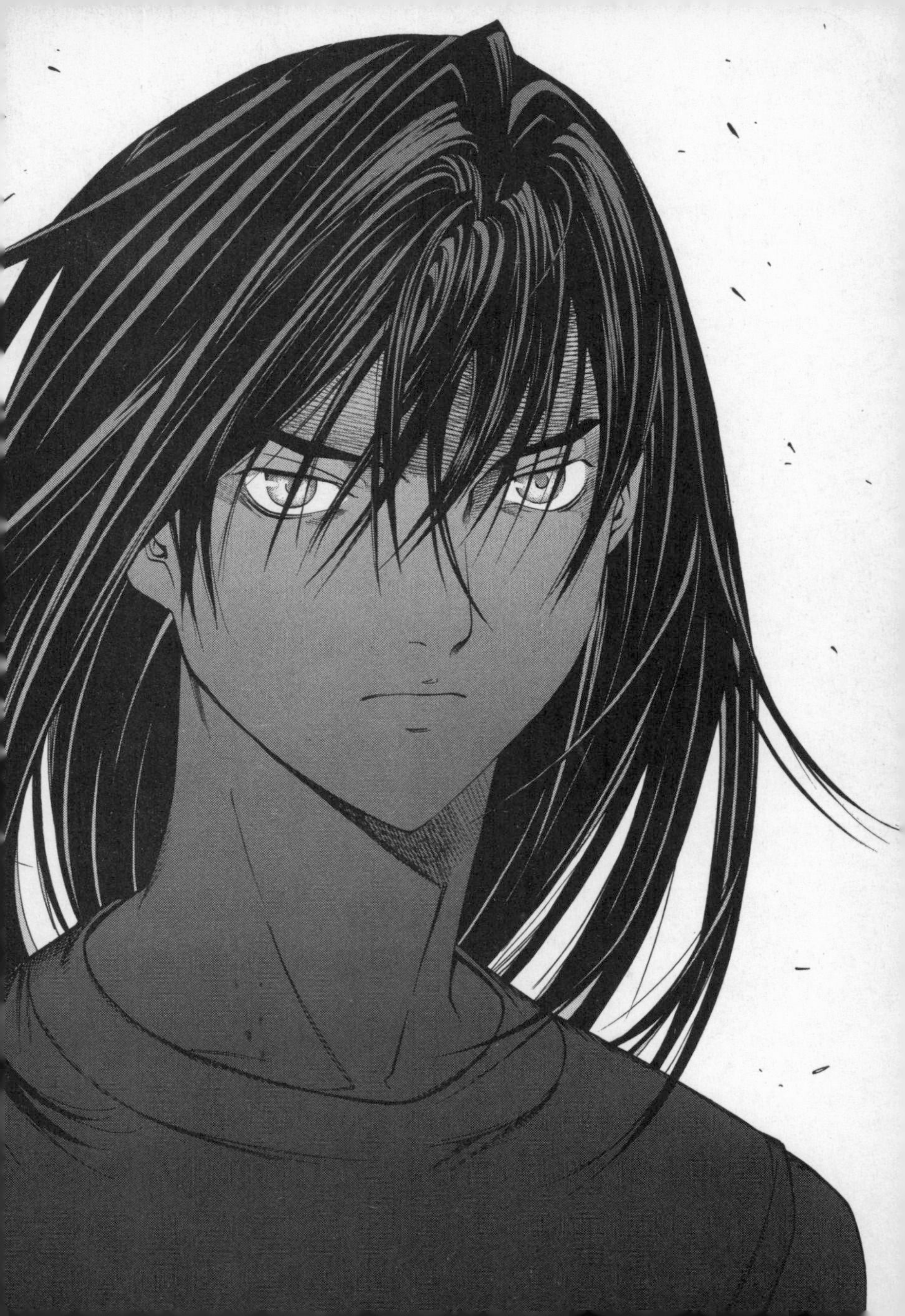

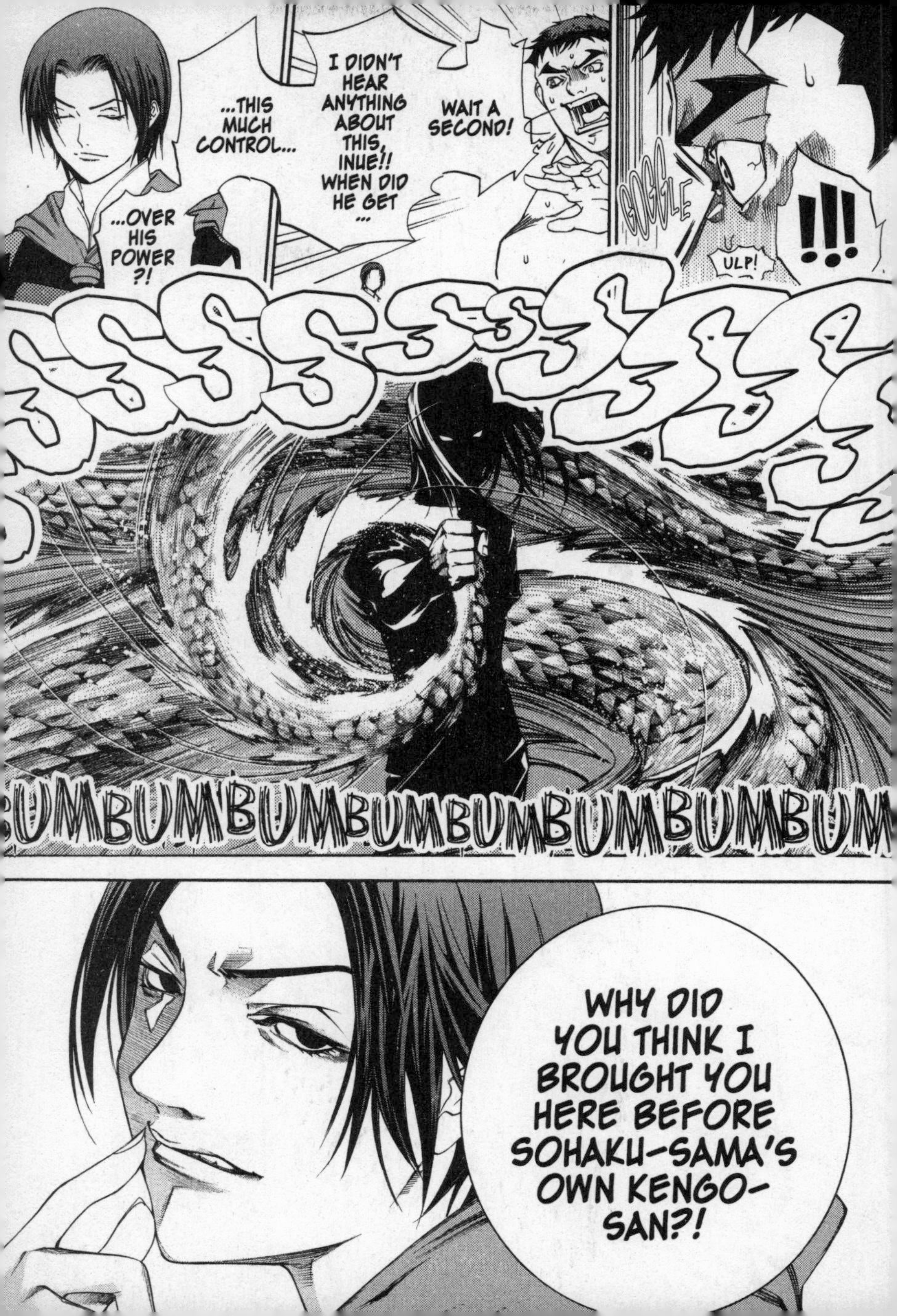
GOGGLE
!!!
ULP!
WAIT A SECOND!
I DIDN'T HEAR ANYTHING ABOUT THIS, INUE!! WHEN DID HE GET ...
...THIS MUCH CONTROL...
...OVER HIS POWER?!
SSSSSSSSSS
BUMBUMBUMBUMBUMBUMBUMBUMBUM
WHY DID YOU THINK I BROUGHT YOU HERE BEFORE SOHAKU-SAMA'S OWN KENGO-SAN?!

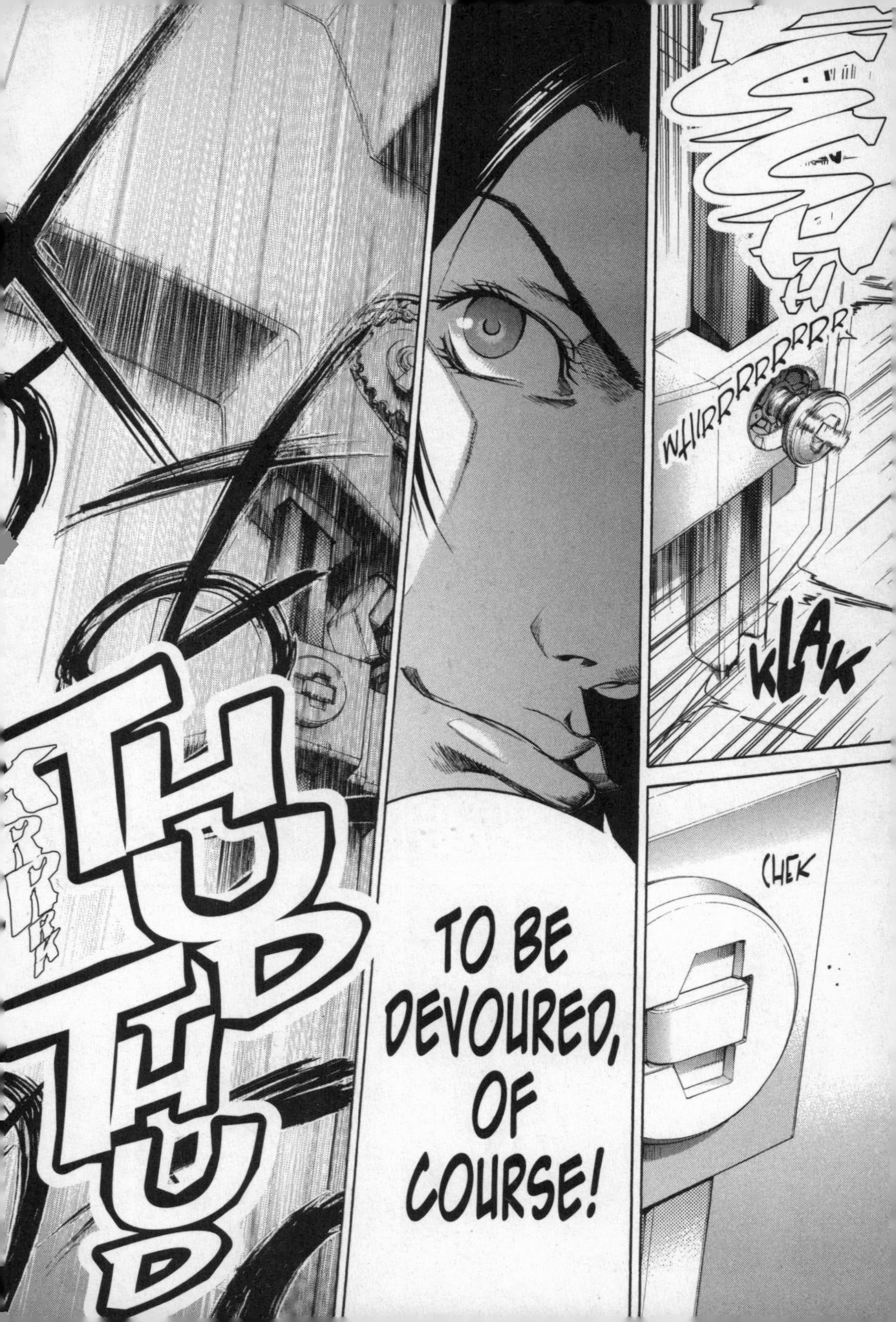
WHIRRRRRRRRR
KLAK
CHEK
TO BE DEVOURED, OF COURSE!
THUD THUD

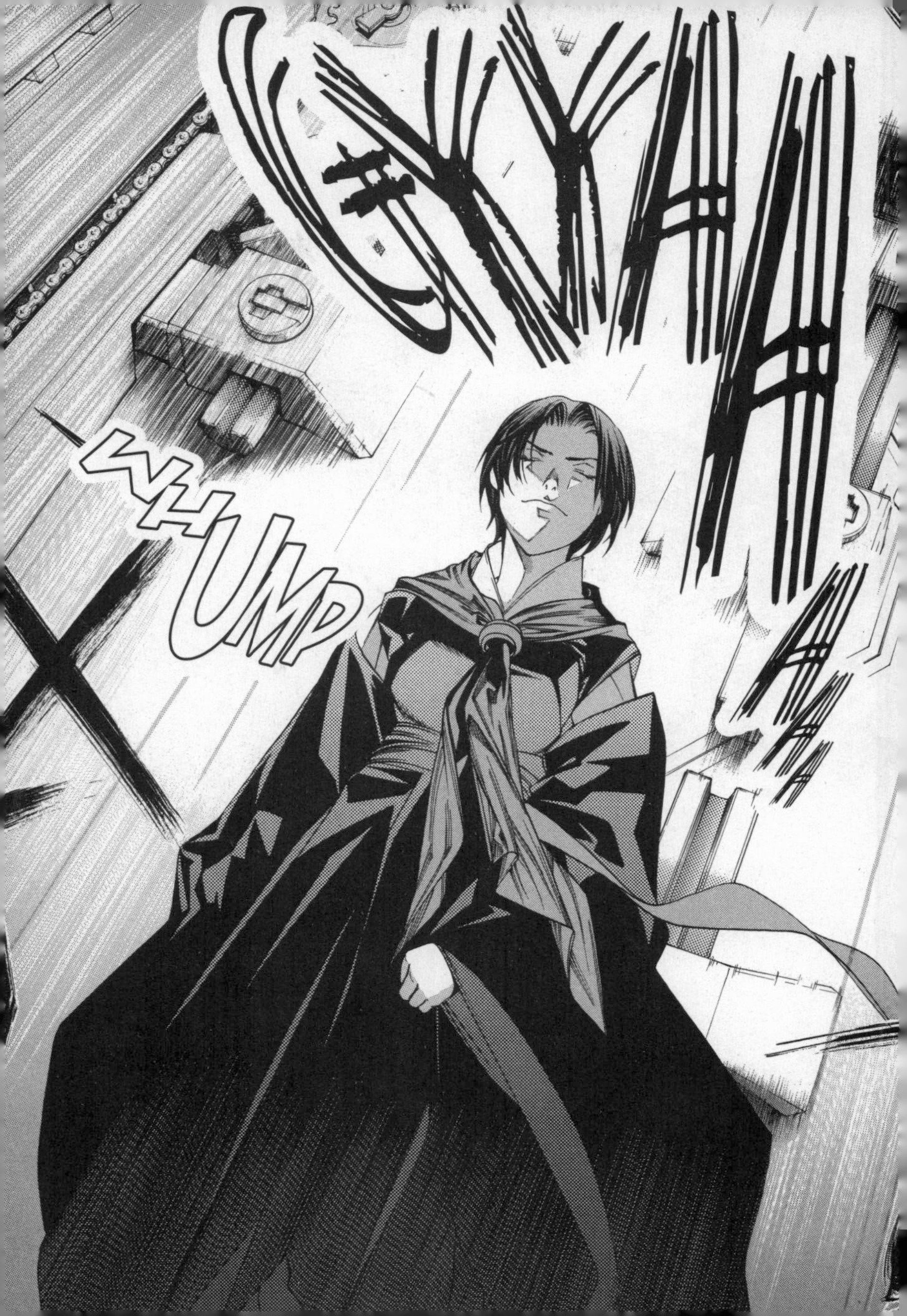
GYYAAAAAAAA
WHUMP

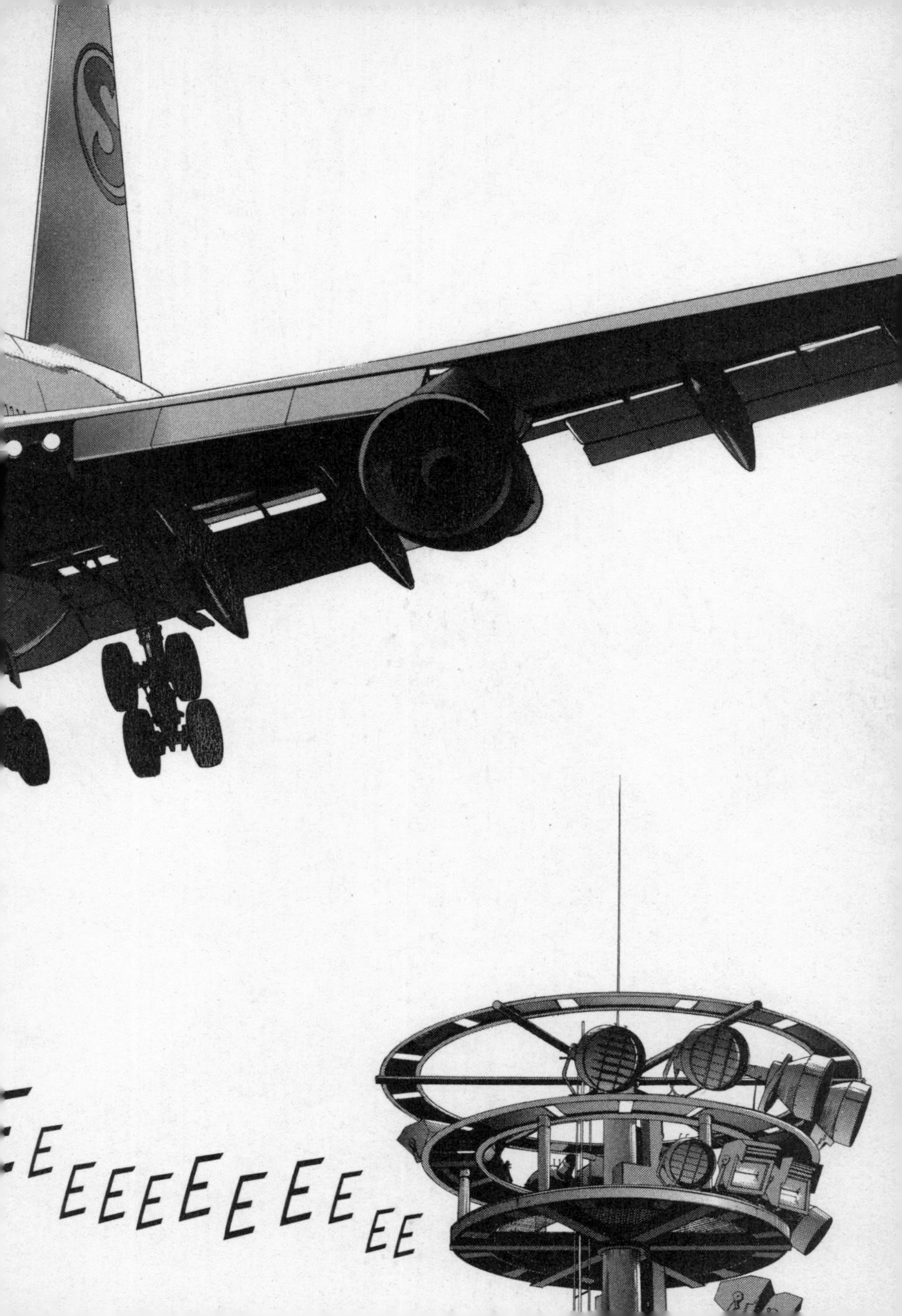
EEEEEEEEEEEE

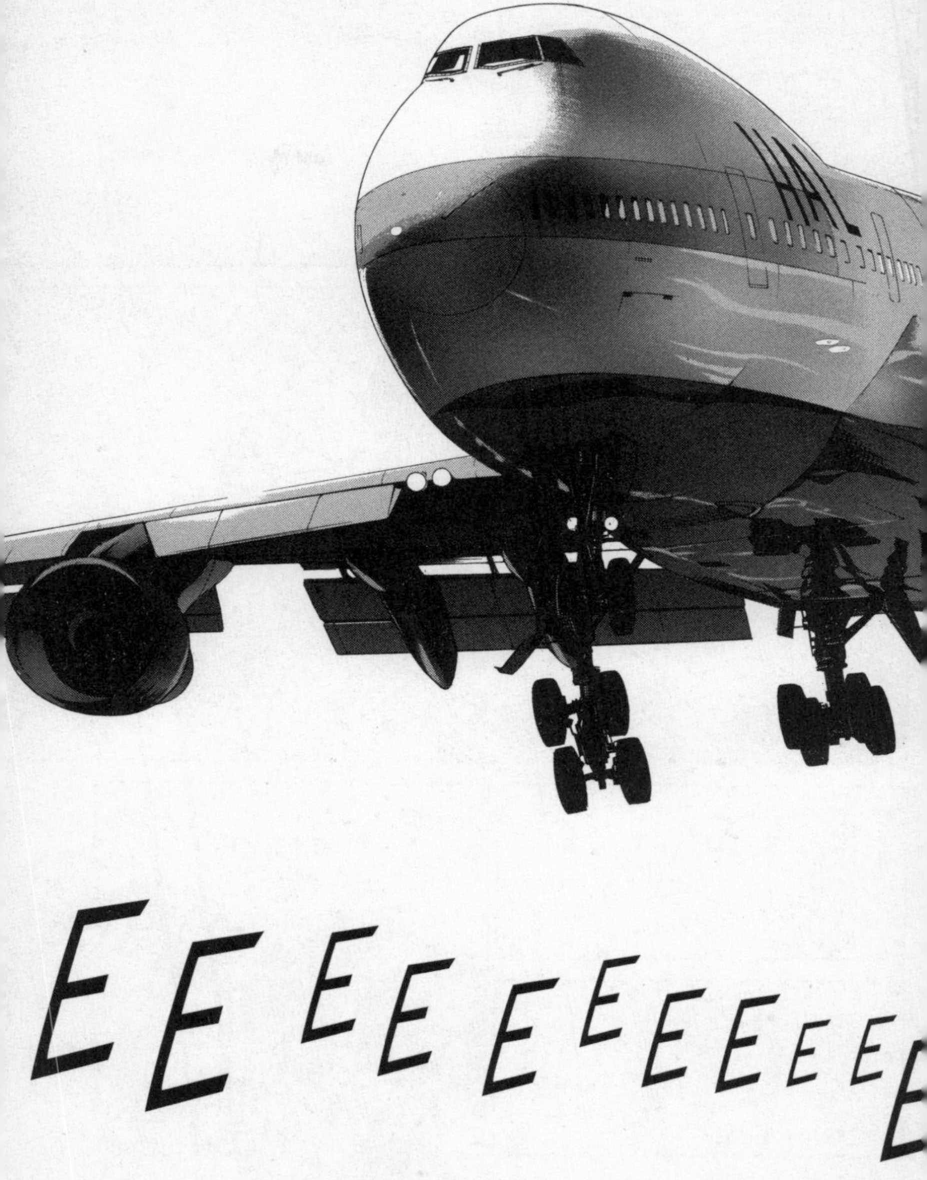
HAL
EEEEEEEEEEE

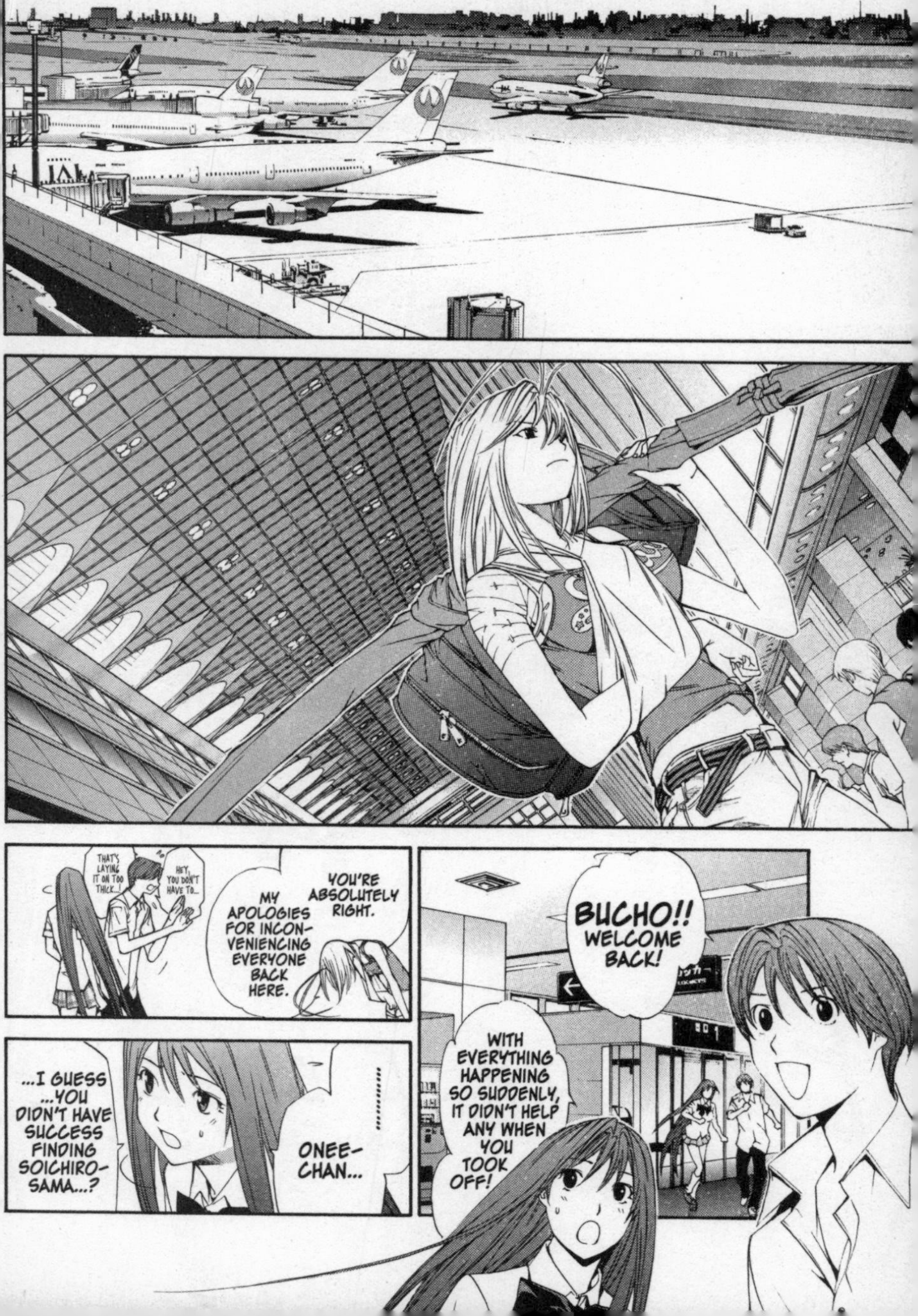
BUCHO!! WELCOME BACK!
WITH EVERYTHING HAPPENING SO SUDDENLY, IT DIDN'T HELP ANY WHEN YOU TOOK OFF!
YOU'RE ABSOLUTELY RIGHT.
MY APOLOGIES FOR INCONVENIENCING EVERYONE BACK HERE.
HEY, YOU DON'T HAVE TO...
THAT'S LAYING IT ON TOO THICK...!
....
ONEE-CHAN...
...I GUESS ...YOU DIDN'T HAVE SUCCESS FINDING SOICHIRO-SAMA...?

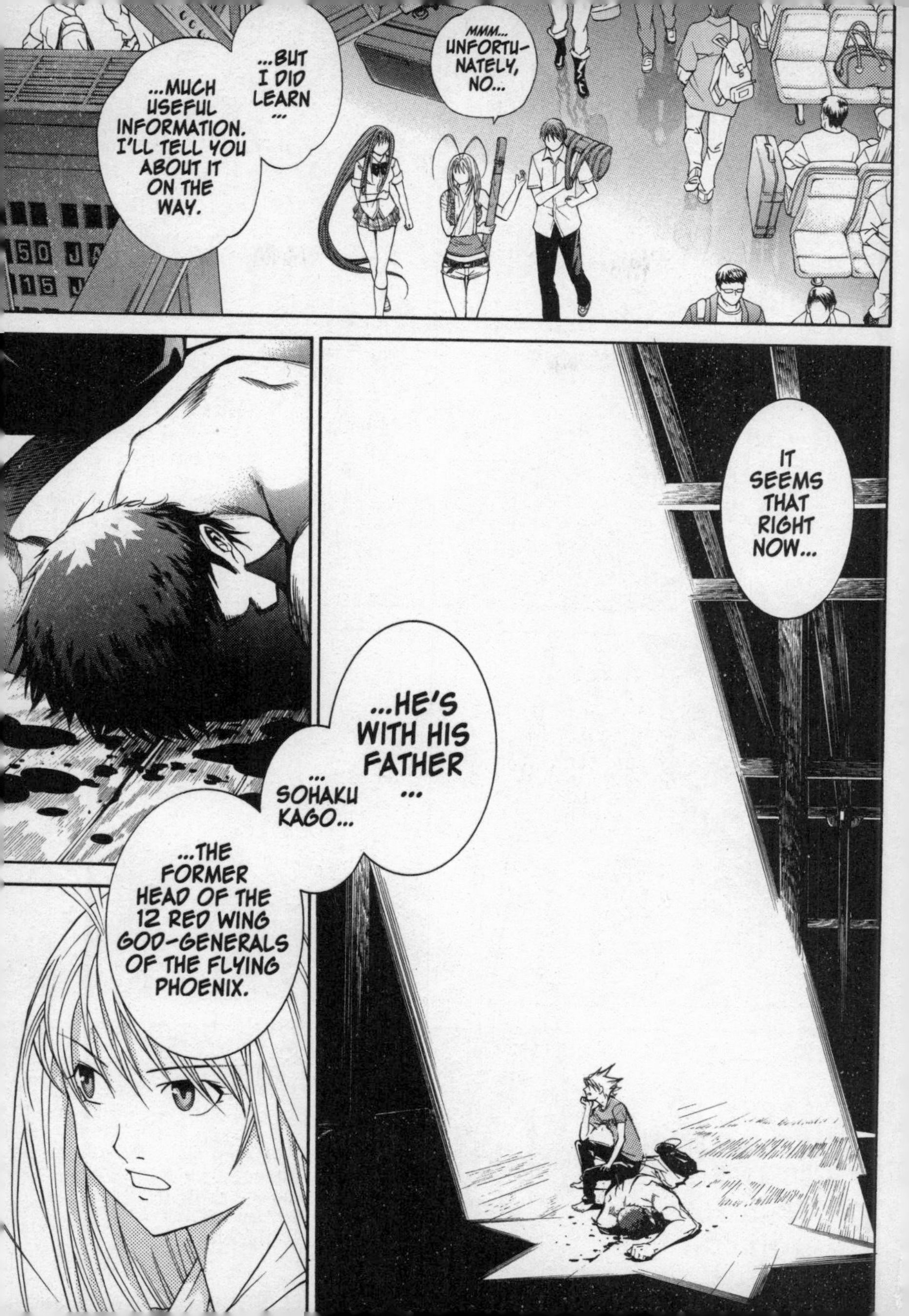
MMM... UNFORTUNATELY, NO...
...BUT I DID LEARN...
...MUCH USEFUL INFORMATION. I'LL TELL YOU ABOUT IT ON THE WAY.
IT SEEMS THAT RIGHT NOW...
...HE'S WITH HIS FATHER...
...SOHAKU KAGO...
...THE FORMER HEAD OF THE 12 RED WING GOD-GENERALS OF THE FLYING PHOENIX.

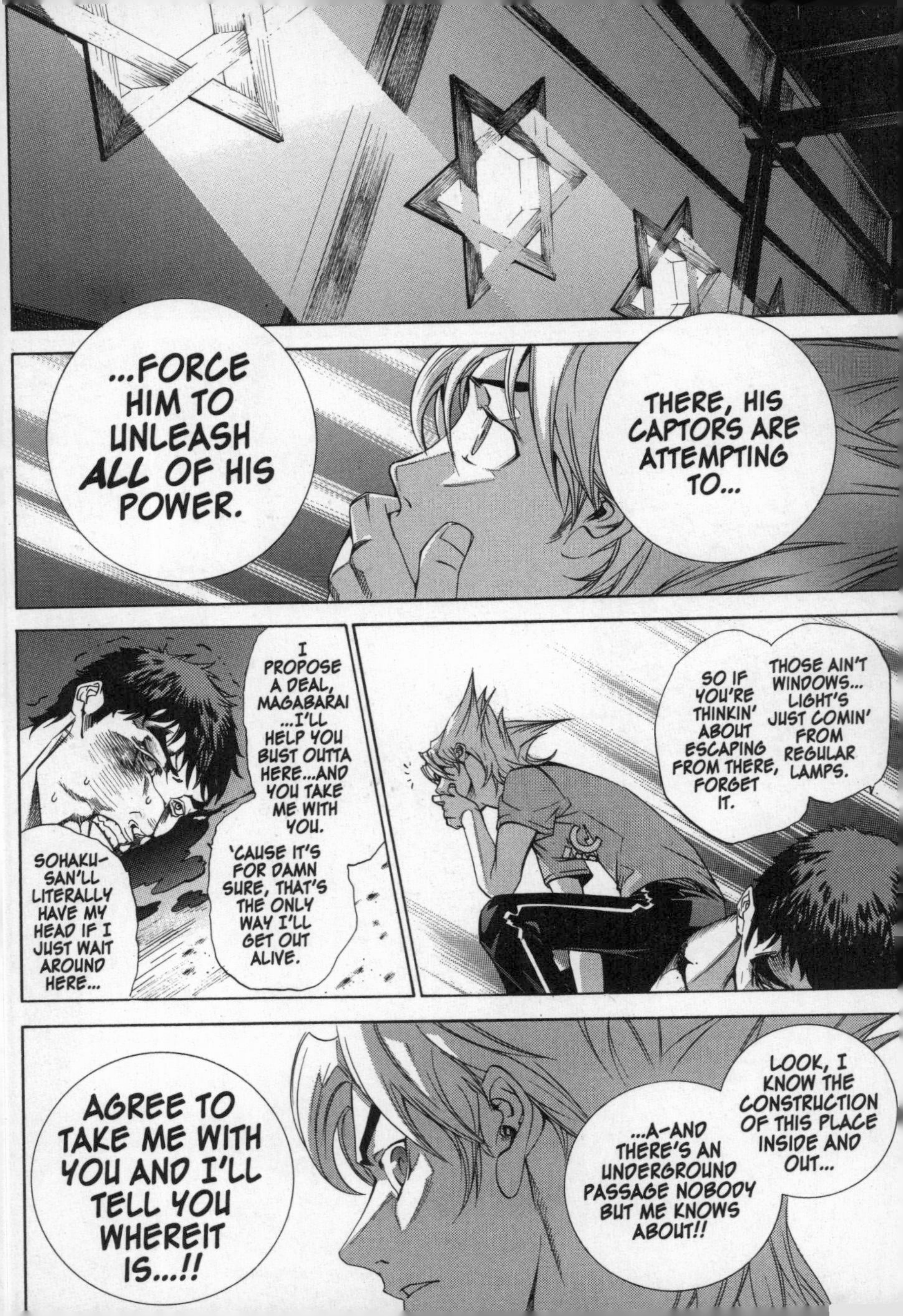
THERE, HIS CAPTORS ARE ATTEMPTING TO...
...FORCE HIM TO UNLEASH ALL OF HIS POWER.
THOSE AIN'T WINDOWS... LIGHT'S JUST COMIN' FROM REGULAR LAMPS.
SO IF YOU'RE THINKIN' ABOUT ESCAPING FROM THERE, FORGET IT.
I PROPOSE A DEAL, MAGABARAI ...I'LL HELP YOU BUST OUTTA HERE...AND YOU TAKE ME WITH YOU.
'CAUSE IT'S FOR DAMN SURE, THAT'S THE ONLY WAY I'LL GET OUT ALIVE.
SOHAKU-SAN'LL LITERALLY HAVE MY HEAD IF I JUST WAIT AROUND HERE...
LOOK, I KNOW THE CONSTRUCTION OF THIS PLACE INSIDE AND OUT...
...A-AND THERE'S AN UNDERGROUND PASSAGE NOBODY BUT ME KNOWS ABOUT!!
AGREE TO TAKE ME WITH YOU AND I'LL TELL YOU WHEREIT IS...!!

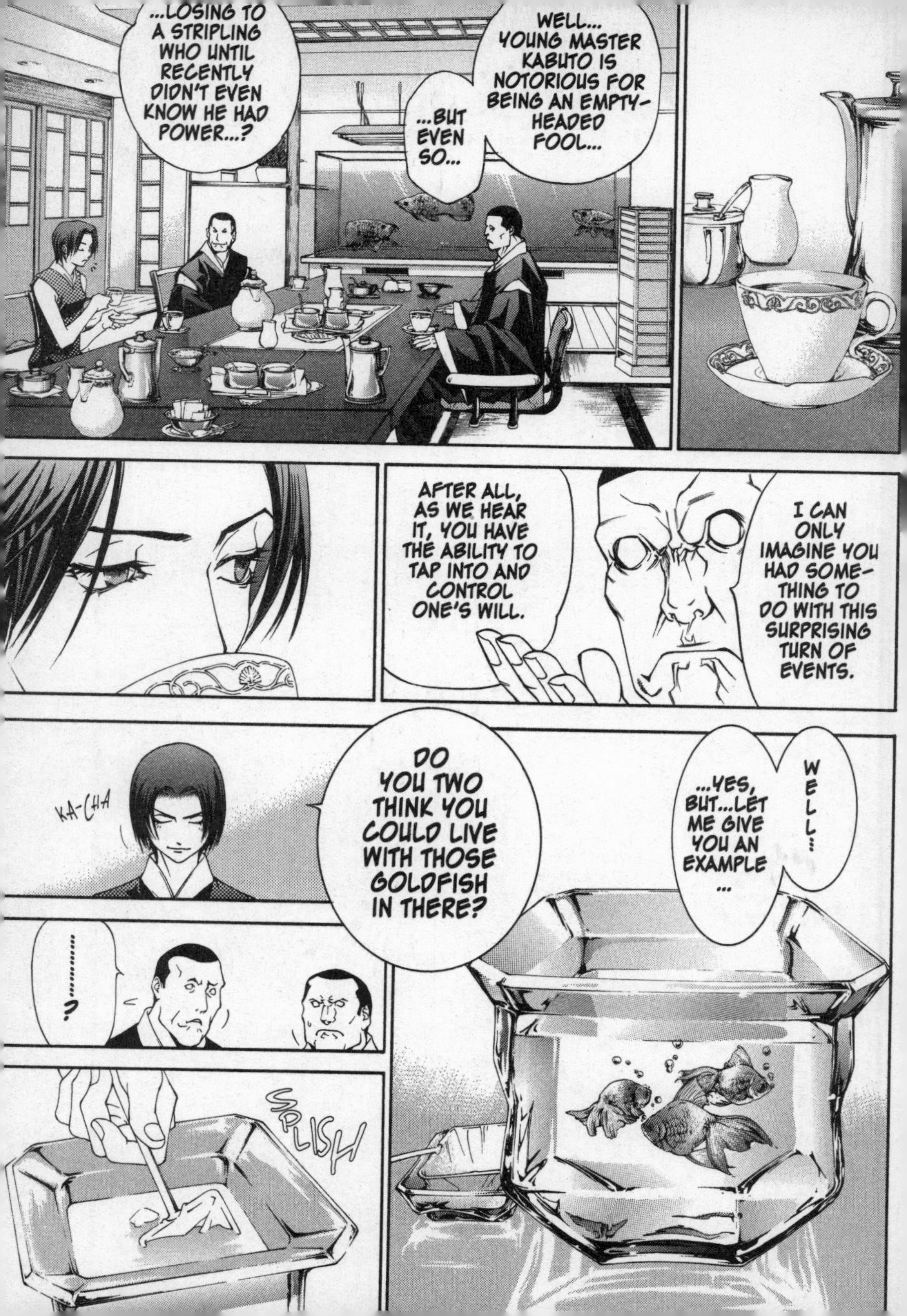
WELL... YOUNG MASTER KABUTO IS NOTORIOUS FOR BEING AN EMPTY-HEADED FOOL...
...BUT EVEN SO...
...LOSING TO A STRIPLING WHO UNTIL RECENTLY DIDN'T EVEN KNOW HE HAD POWER...?
I CAN ONLY IMAGINE YOU HAD SOME-THING TO DO WITH THIS SURPRISING TURN OF EVENTS.
AFTER ALL, AS WE HEAR IT, YOU HAVE THE ABILITY TO TAP INTO AND CONTROL ONE'S WILL.
WELL...
...YES, BUT...LET ME GIVE YOU AN EXAMPLE...
KA-CHA
DO YOU TWO THINK YOU COULD LIVE WITH THOSE GOLDFISH IN THERE?
......?
SPLISH

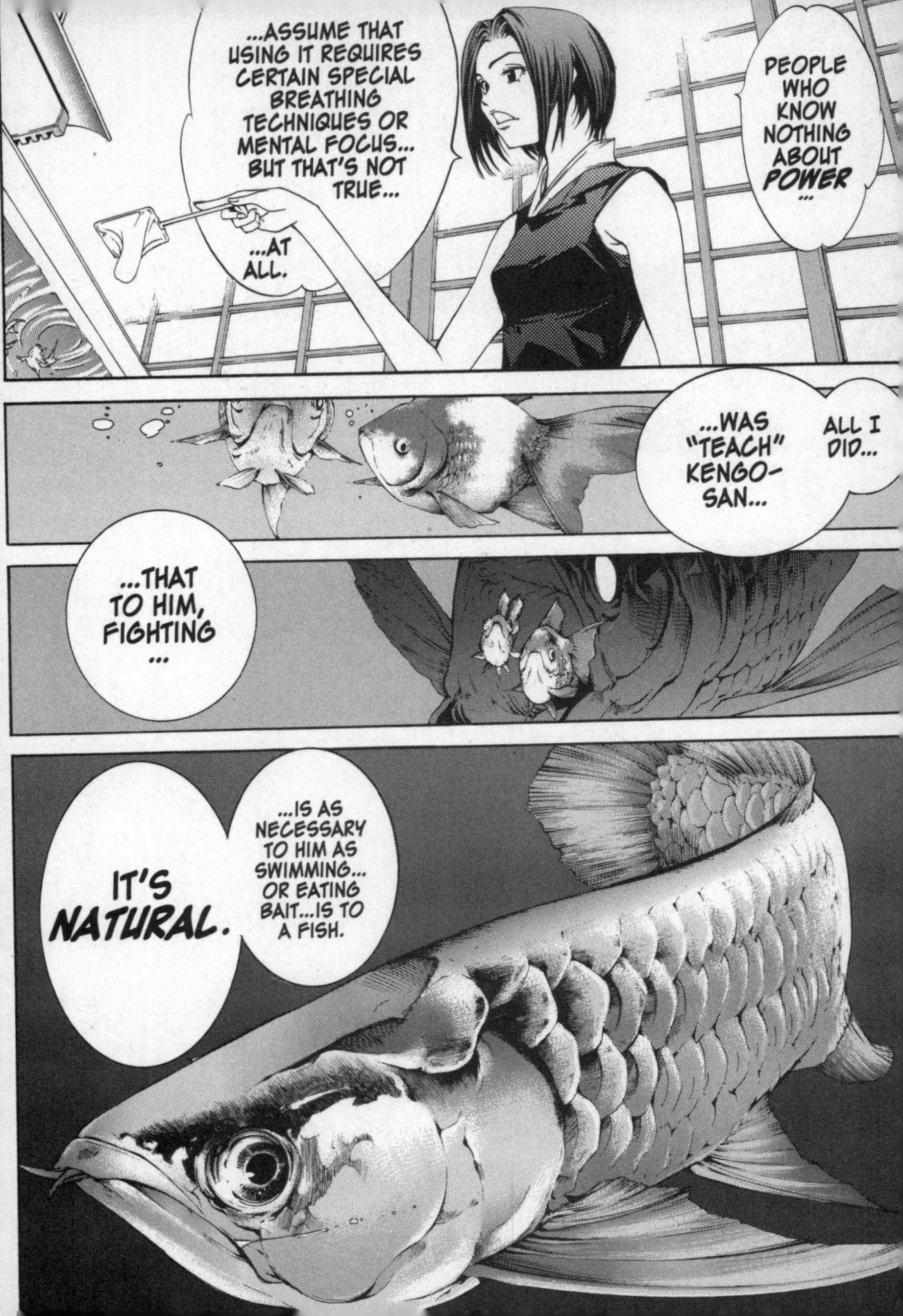
PEOPLE WHO KNOW NOTHING ABOUT *POWER* ...
...ASSUME THAT USING IT REQUIRES CERTAIN SPECIAL BREATHING TECHNIQUES OR MENTAL FOCUS... BUT THAT'S NOT TRUE...
...AT ALL.
ALL I DID...
...WAS "TEACH" KENGO-SAN...
...THAT TO HIM, FIGHTING ...
...IS AS NECESSARY TO HIM AS SWIMMING... OR EATING BAIT...IS TO A FISH.
IT'S *NATURAL*.

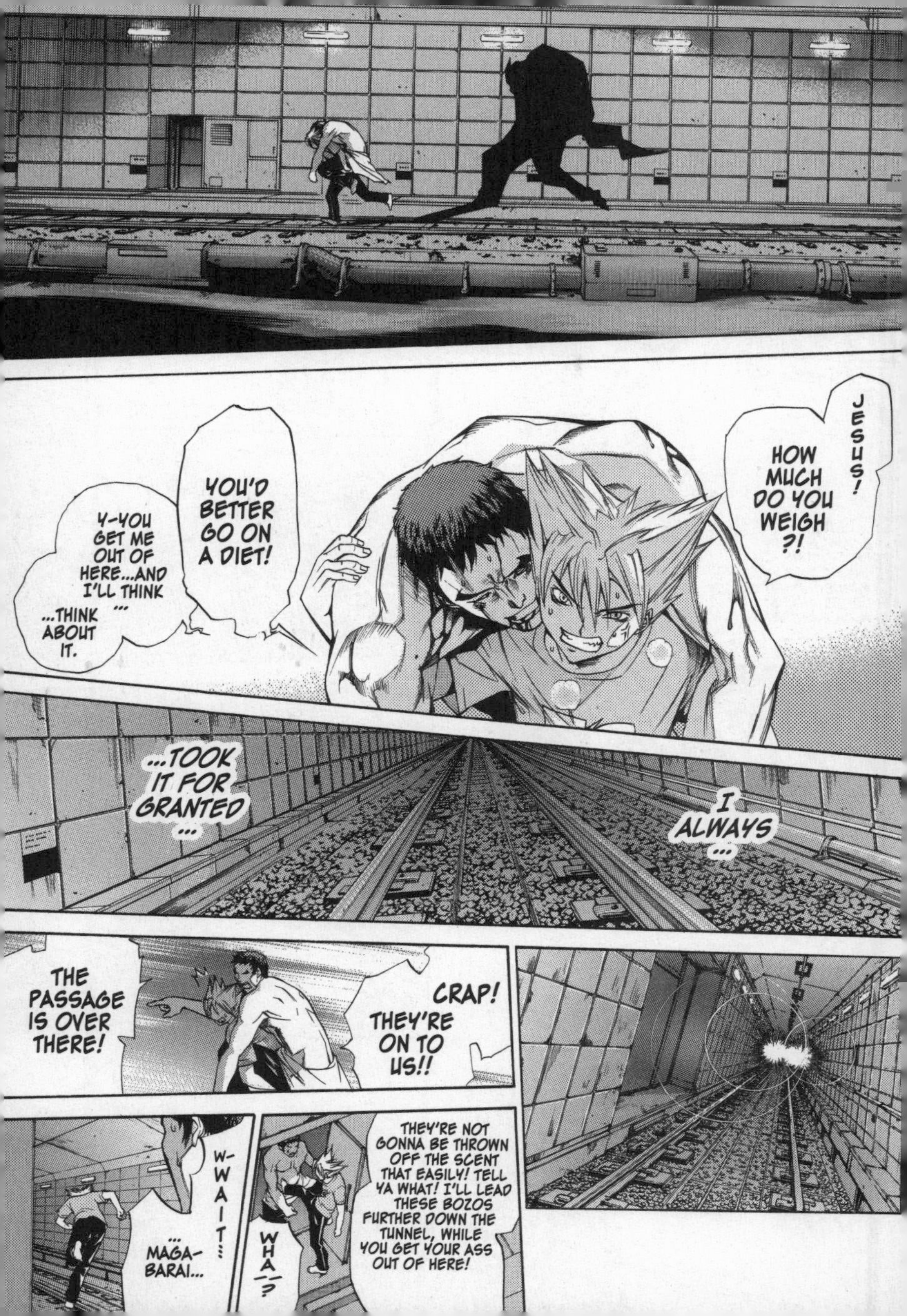
JESUS! HOW MUCH DO YOU WEIGH?!
YOU'D BETTER GO ON A DIET!
Y-YOU GET ME OUT OF HERE...AND I'LL THINK ...
...THINK ABOUT IT.
I ALWAYS ...
...TOOK IT FOR GRANTED ...
CRAP! THEY'RE ON TO US!!
THE PASSAGE IS OVER THERE!
THEY'RE NOT GONNA BE THROWN OFF THE SCENT THAT EASILY! TELL YA WHAT! I'LL LEAD THESE BOZOS FURTHER DOWN THE TUNNEL, WHILE YOU GET YOUR ASS OUT OF HERE!
WHA-?
W-WAIT... ...MAGA-BARAI...

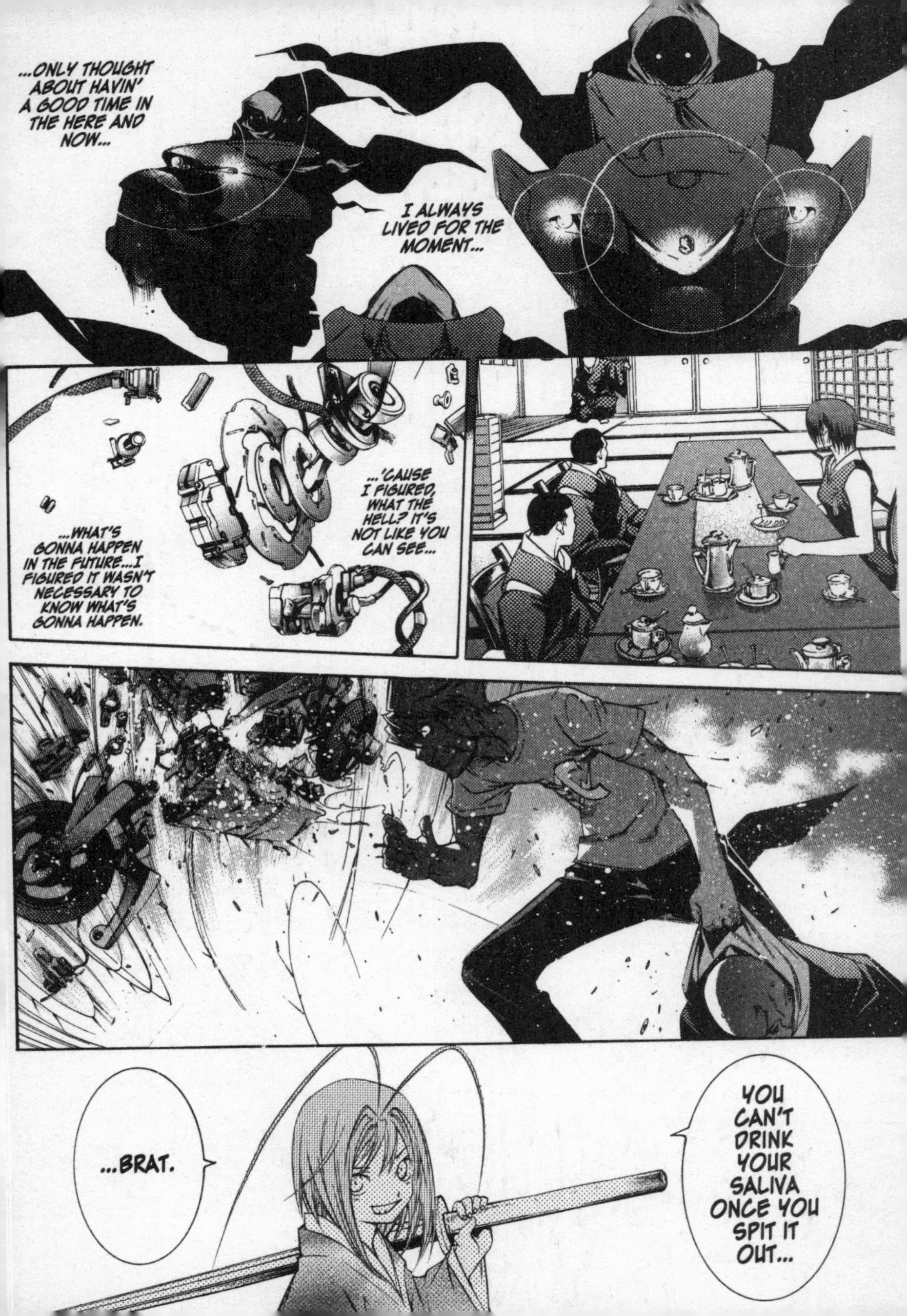
I ALWAYS LIVED FOR THE MOMENT...
...ONLY THOUGHT ABOUT HAVIN' A GOOD TIME IN THE HERE AND NOW...
...'CAUSE I FIGURED, WHAT THE HELL? IT'S NOT LIKE YOU CAN SEE...
...WHAT'S GONNA HAPPEN IN THE FUTURE...I FIGURED IT WASN'T NECESSARY TO KNOW WHAT'S GONNA HAPPEN.
YOU CAN'T DRINK YOUR SALIVA ONCE YOU SPIT IT OUT...
...BRAT.

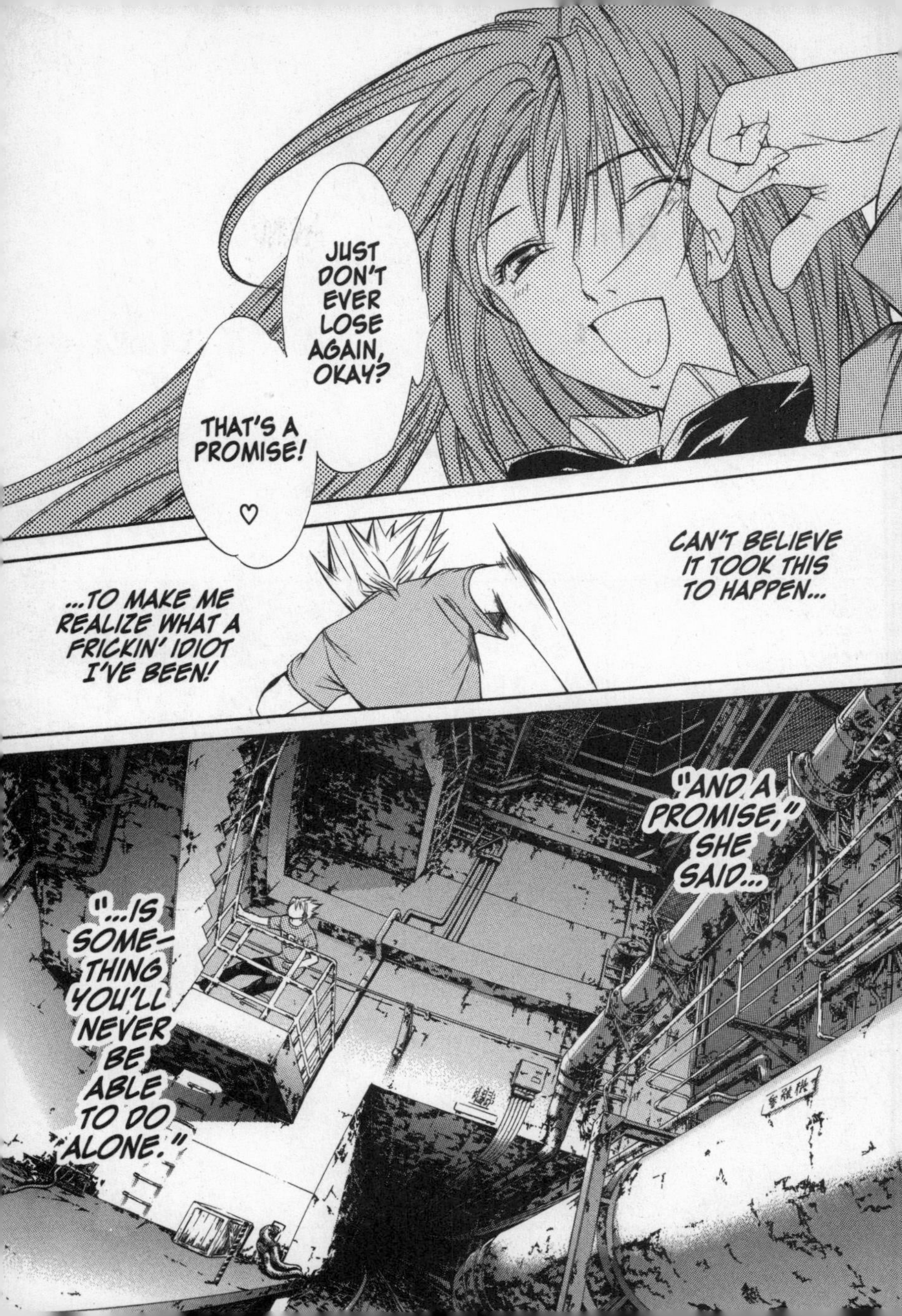
JUST DON'T EVER LOSE AGAIN, OKAY?
THAT'S A PROMISE!
♡
CAN'T BELIEVE IT TOOK THIS TO HAPPEN...
...TO MAKE ME REALIZE WHAT A FRICKIN' IDIOT I'VE BEEN!
"AND A PROMISE," SHE SAID...
"...IS SOME-THING YOU'LL NEVER BE ABLE TO DO ALONE."

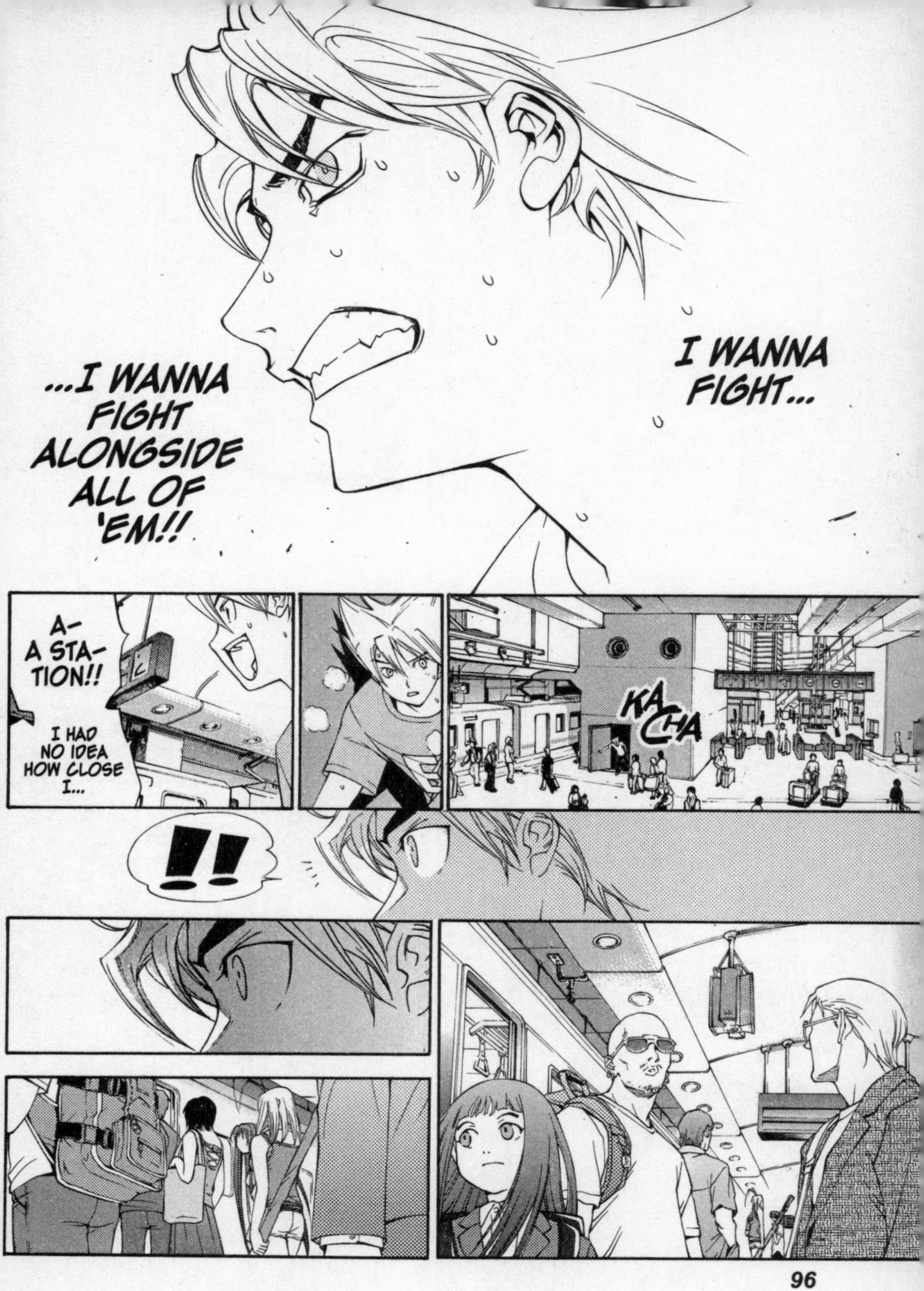
I WANNA FIGHT...
...I WANNA FIGHT ALONGSIDE ALL OF 'EM!!
KA CHA
A- A STA- TION!!
I HAD NO IDEA HOW CLOSE I...
!!

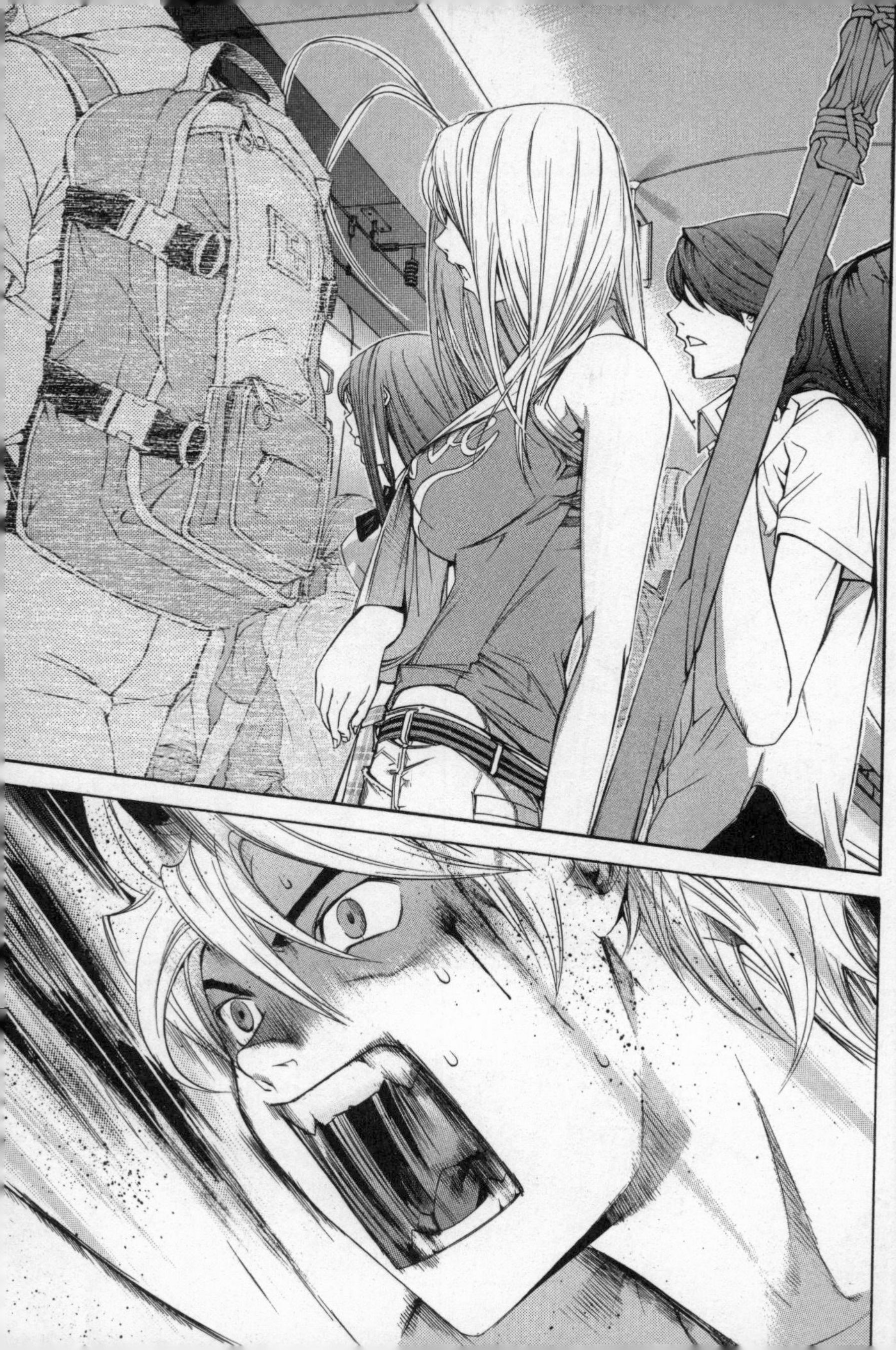

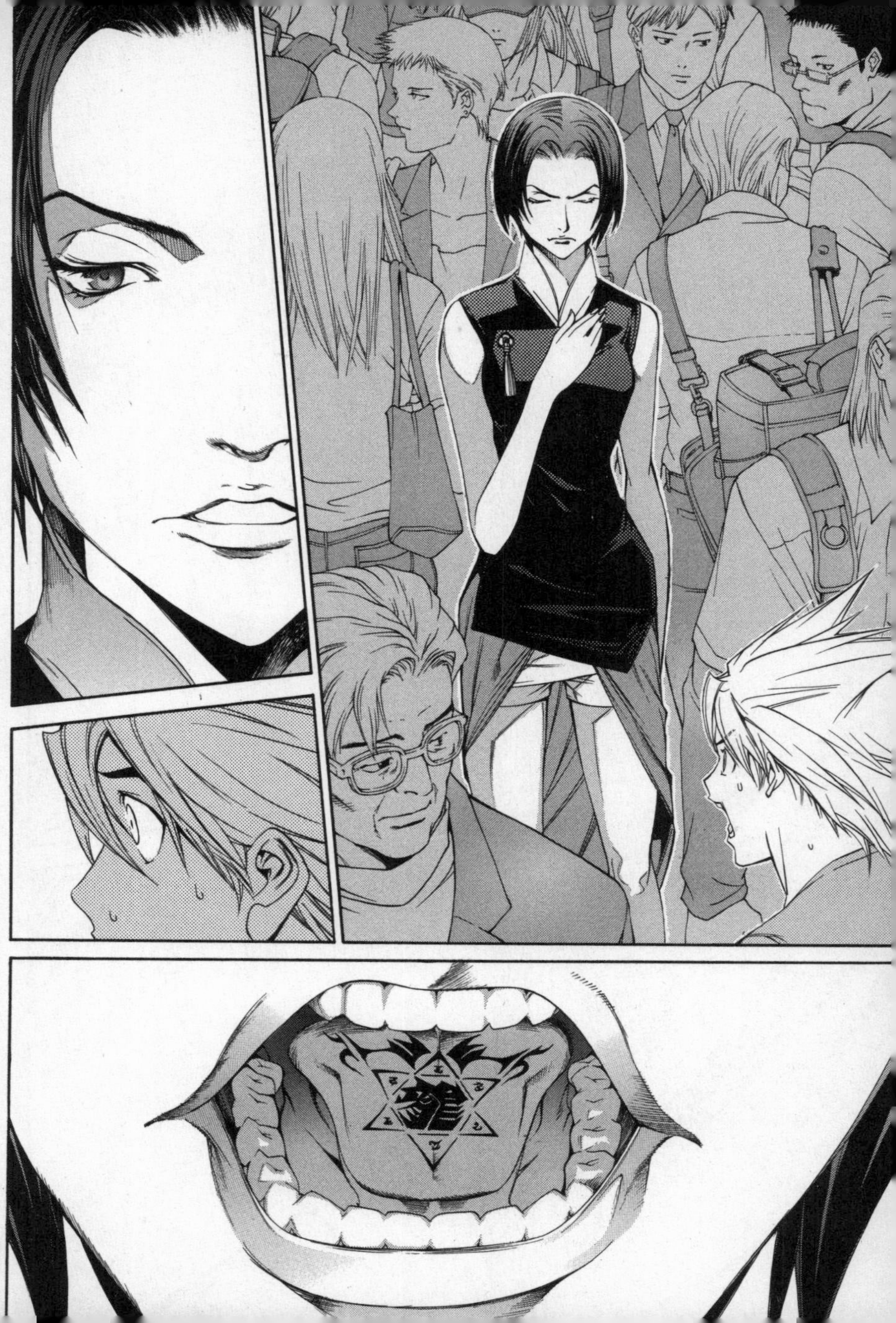

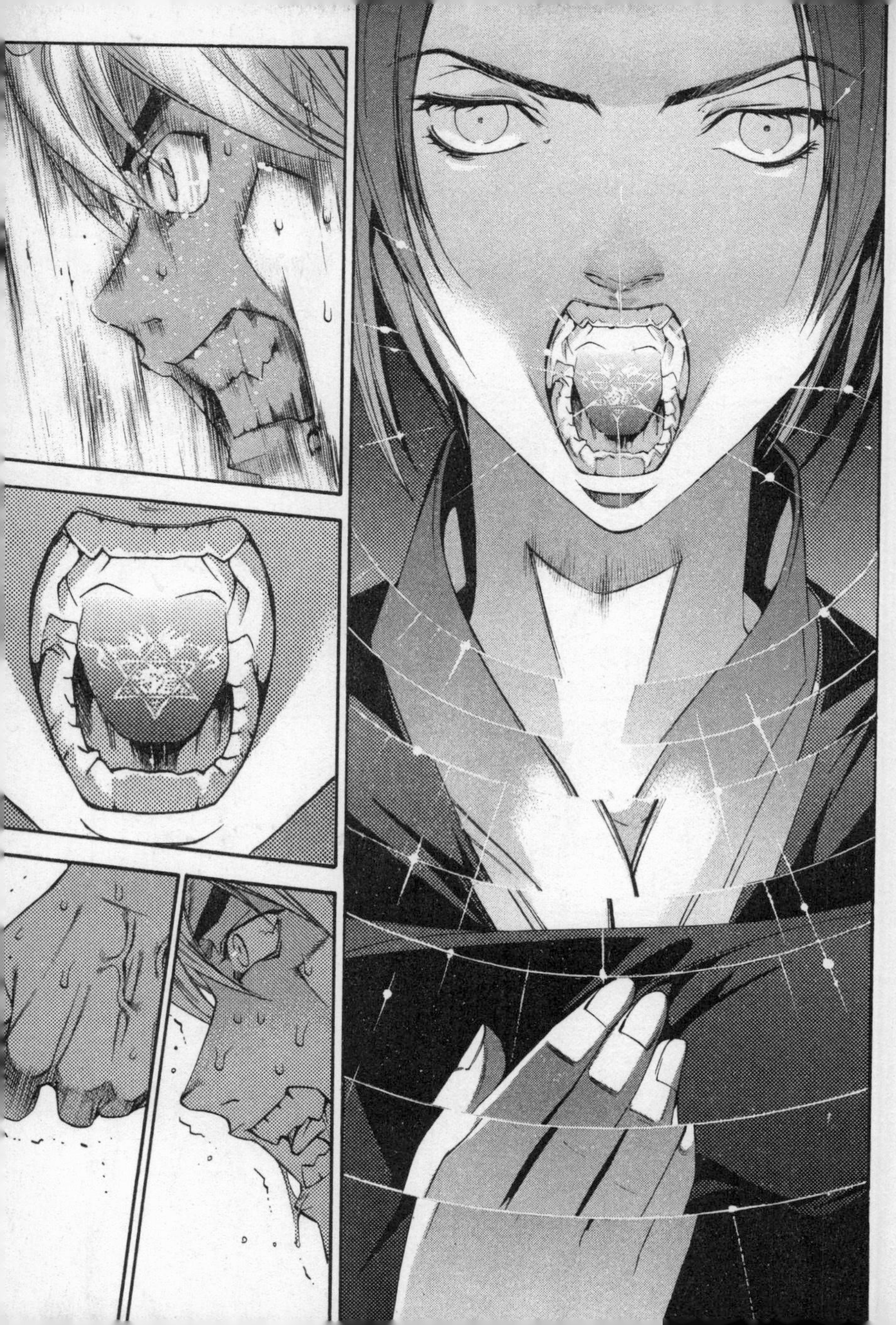

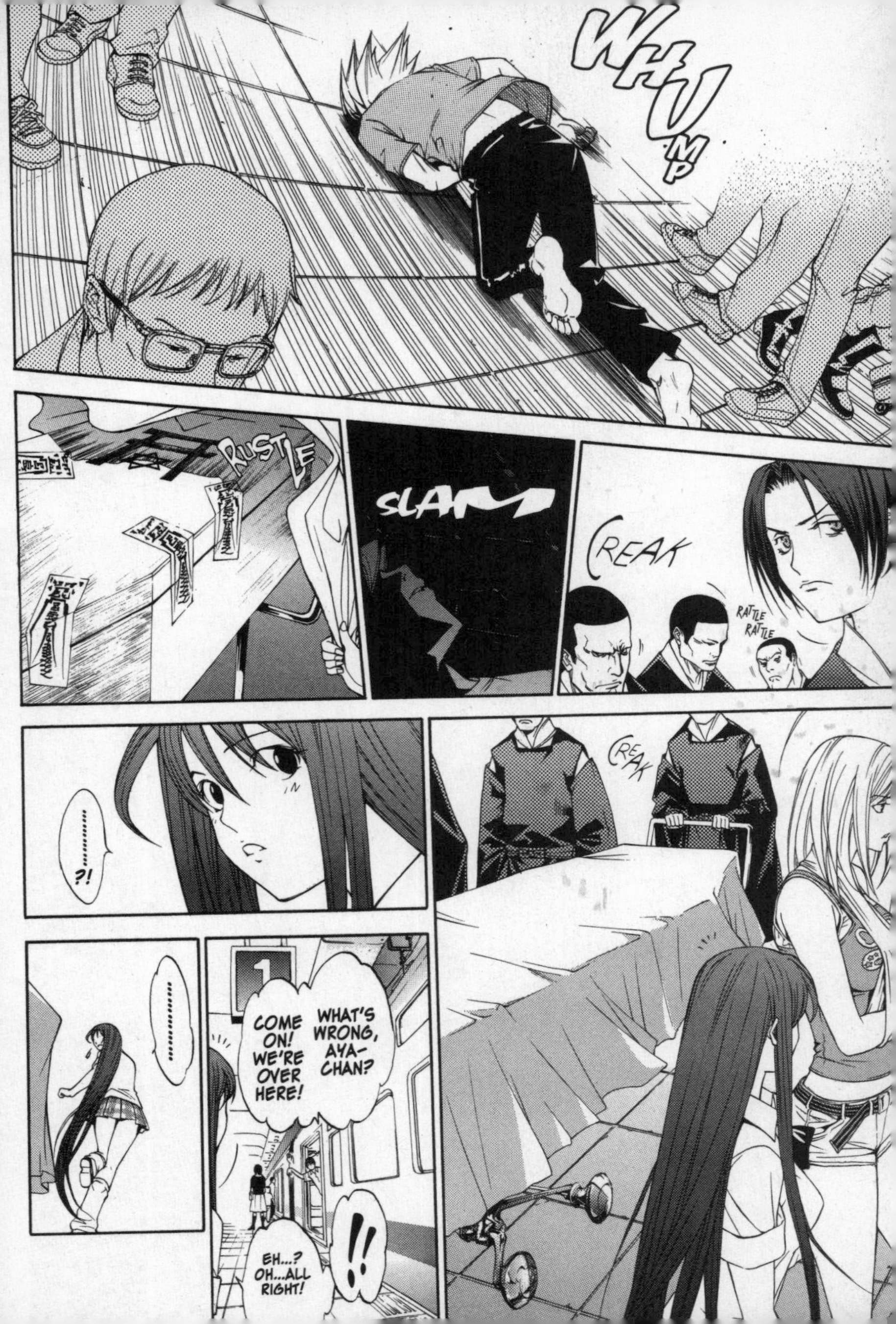
WHUMP
CREAK
RATTLE RATTLE
SLAM
RUSTLE
CREAK
......?!
WHAT'S WRONG, AYA-CHAN?
COME ON! WE'RE OVER HERE!
!!
EH...? OH...ALL RIGHT!
......

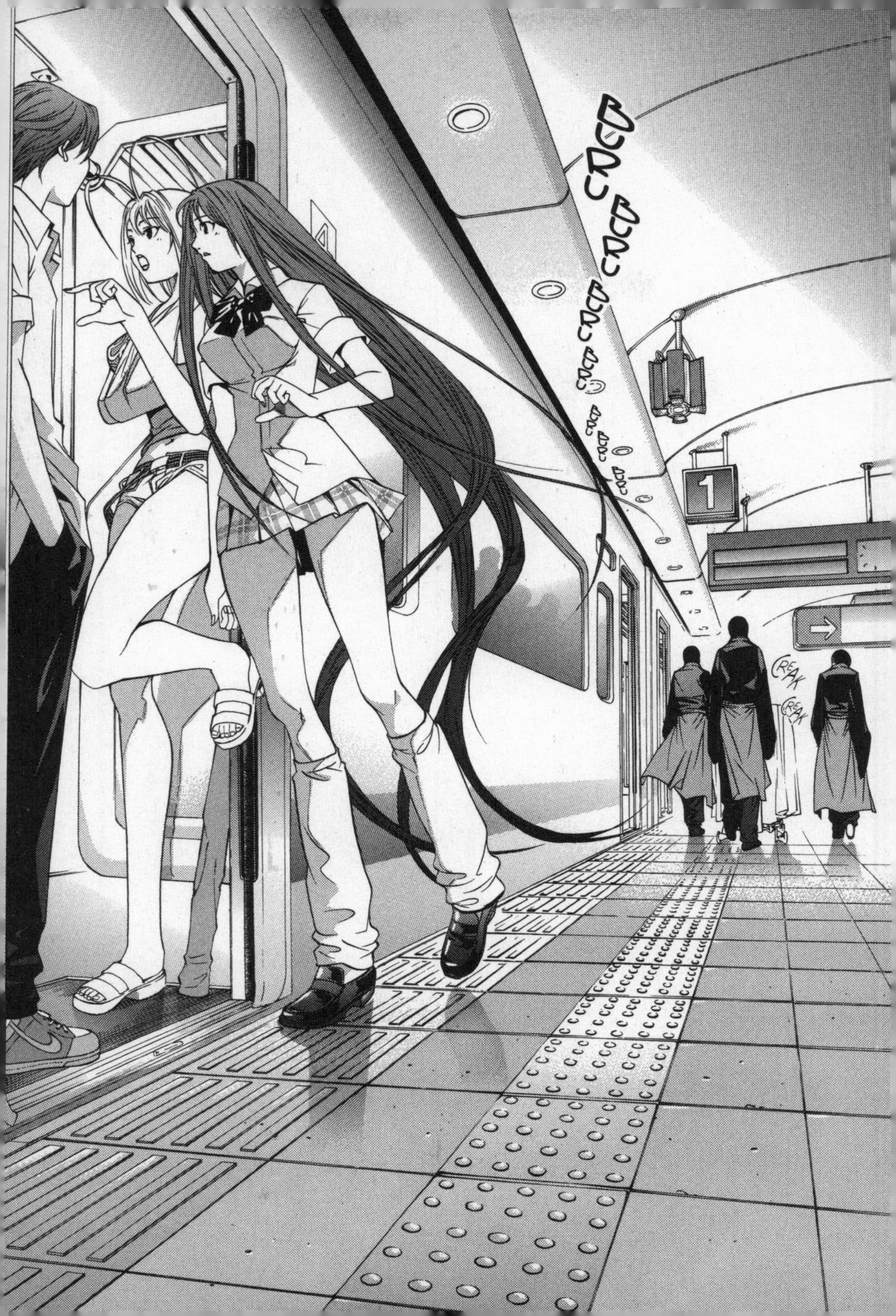
BURU BURU BURU BURU BURU BURU BURU
1
CREAK CREAK

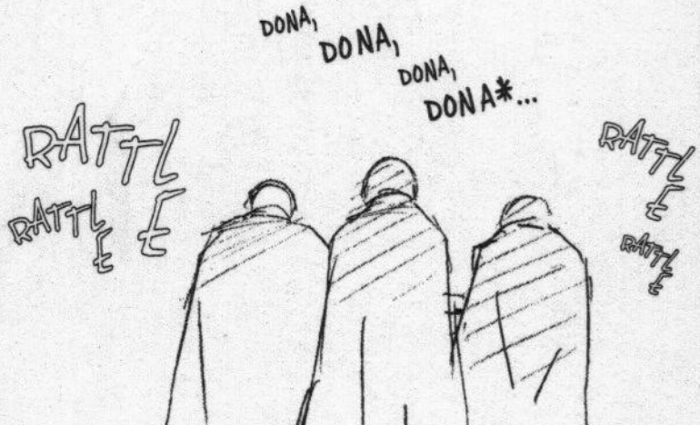
DONA, DONA, DONA, DONA*...
RATTLE
RATTLE
RATTLE
RATTLE

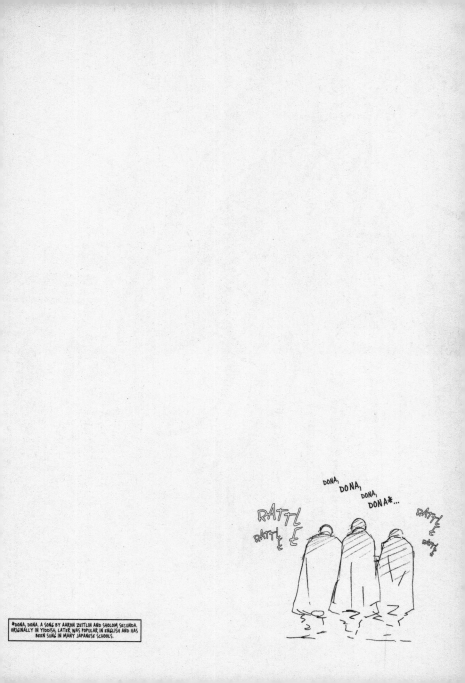

*DONA, DONA. A SONG BY AARON ZEITLIN AND SHOLOM SECUNDA. ORIGINALLY IN YIDDISH, LATER WAS POPULAR IN ENGLISH AND HAS BEEN SUNG IN MANY JAPANESE SCHOOLS.

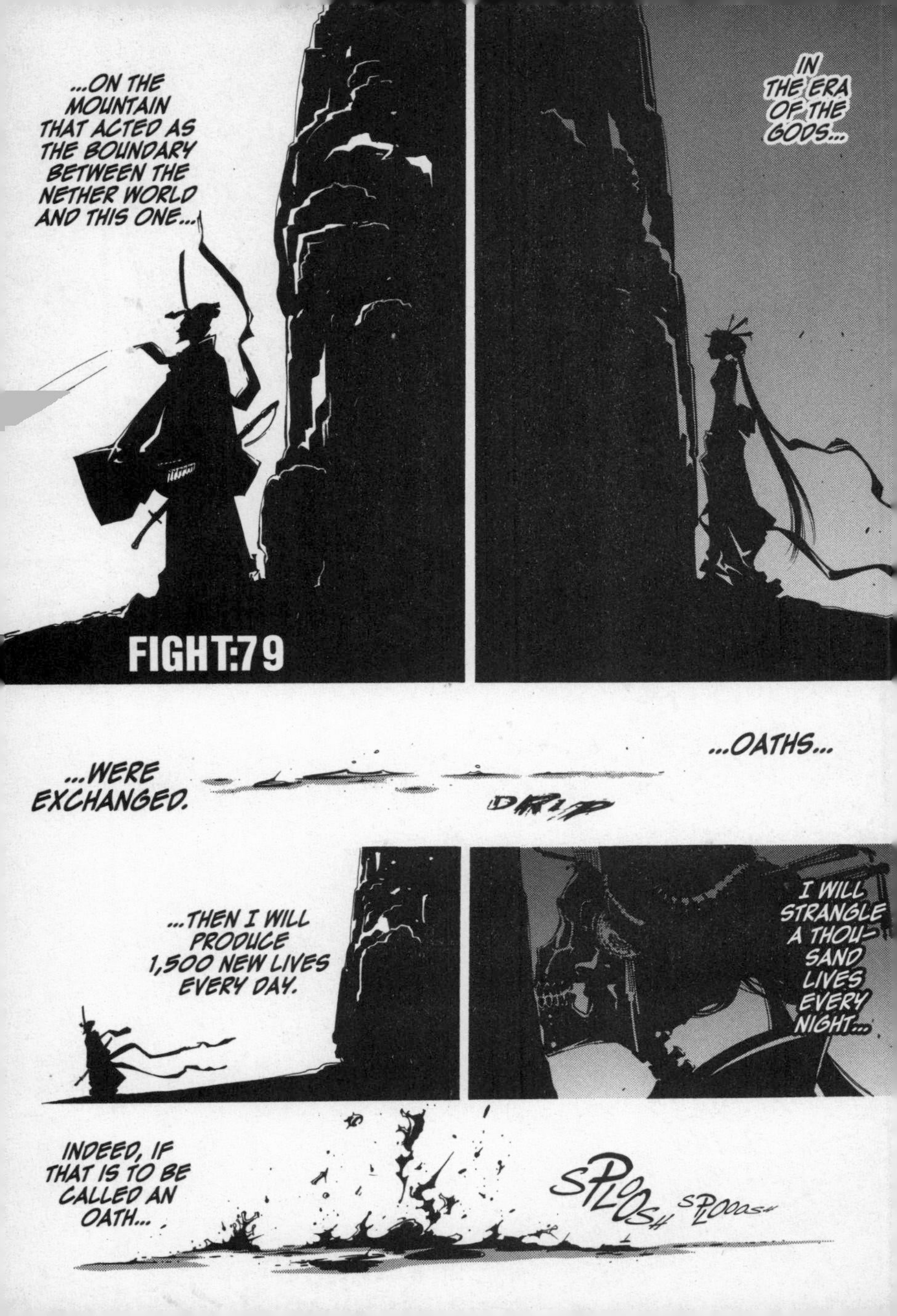
IN THE ERA OF THE GODS...
...ON THE MOUNTAIN THAT ACTED AS THE BOUNDARY BETWEEN THE NETHER WORLD AND THIS ONE...
FIGHT:79
...OATHS...
DRIP
...WERE EXCHANGED.
I WILL STRANGLE A THOUSAND LIVES EVERY NIGHT...
...THEN I WILL PRODUCE 1,500 NEW LIVES EVERY DAY.
SPLOOSH
SPLOOSH
INDEED, IF THAT IS TO BE CALLED AN OATH...

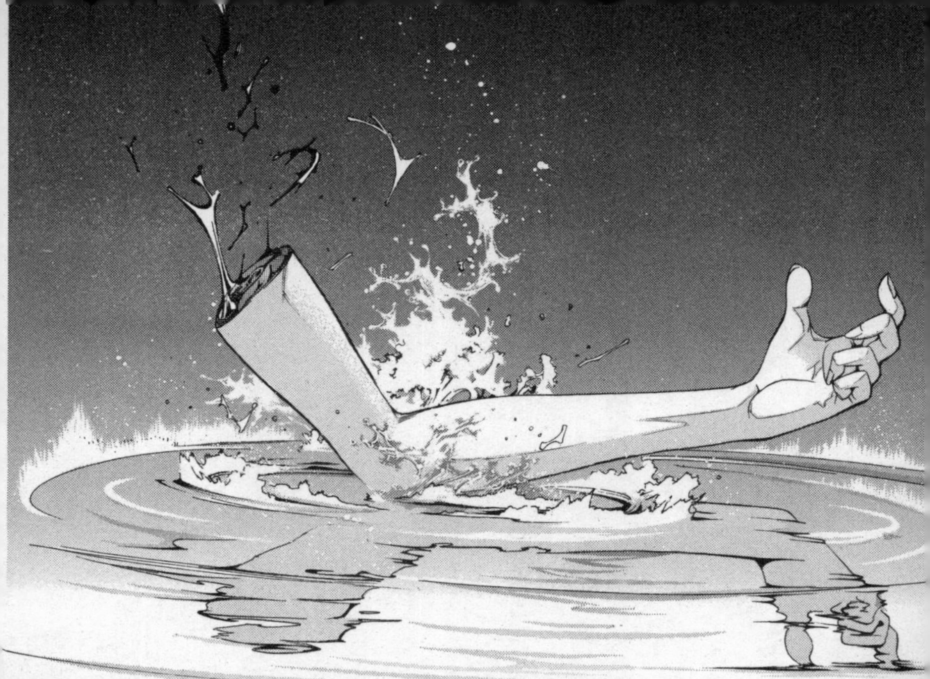
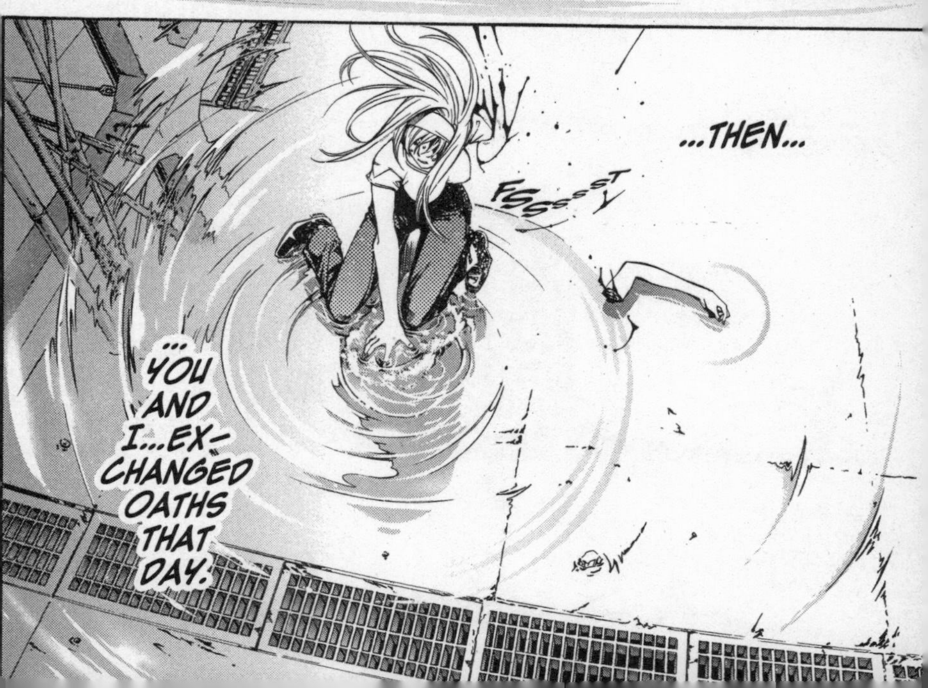
...THEN...
FSSSSSST
...YOU AND I...EX-CHANGED OATHS THAT DAY.

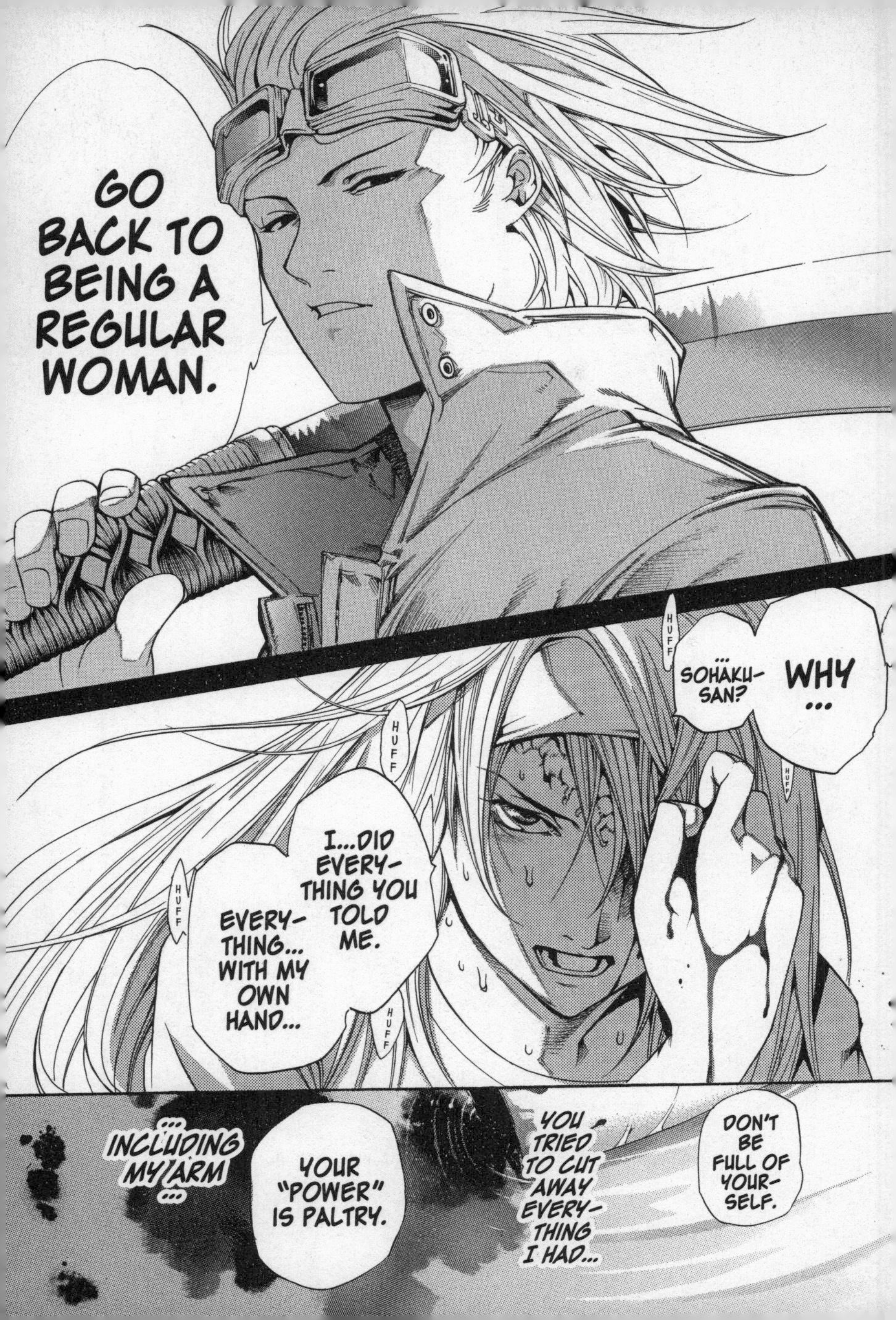
GO BACK TO BEING A REGULAR WOMAN.
HUFF
WHY ...
...SOHAKU-SAN?
HUFF
HUFF
I...DID EVERYTHING YOU TOLD ME.
HUFF
EVERYTHING... WITH MY OWN HAND...
HUFF
DON'T BE FULL OF YOURSELF.
YOU TRIED TO CUT AWAY EVERYTHING I HAD...
YOUR "POWER" IS PALTRY.
...INCLUDING MY ARM...

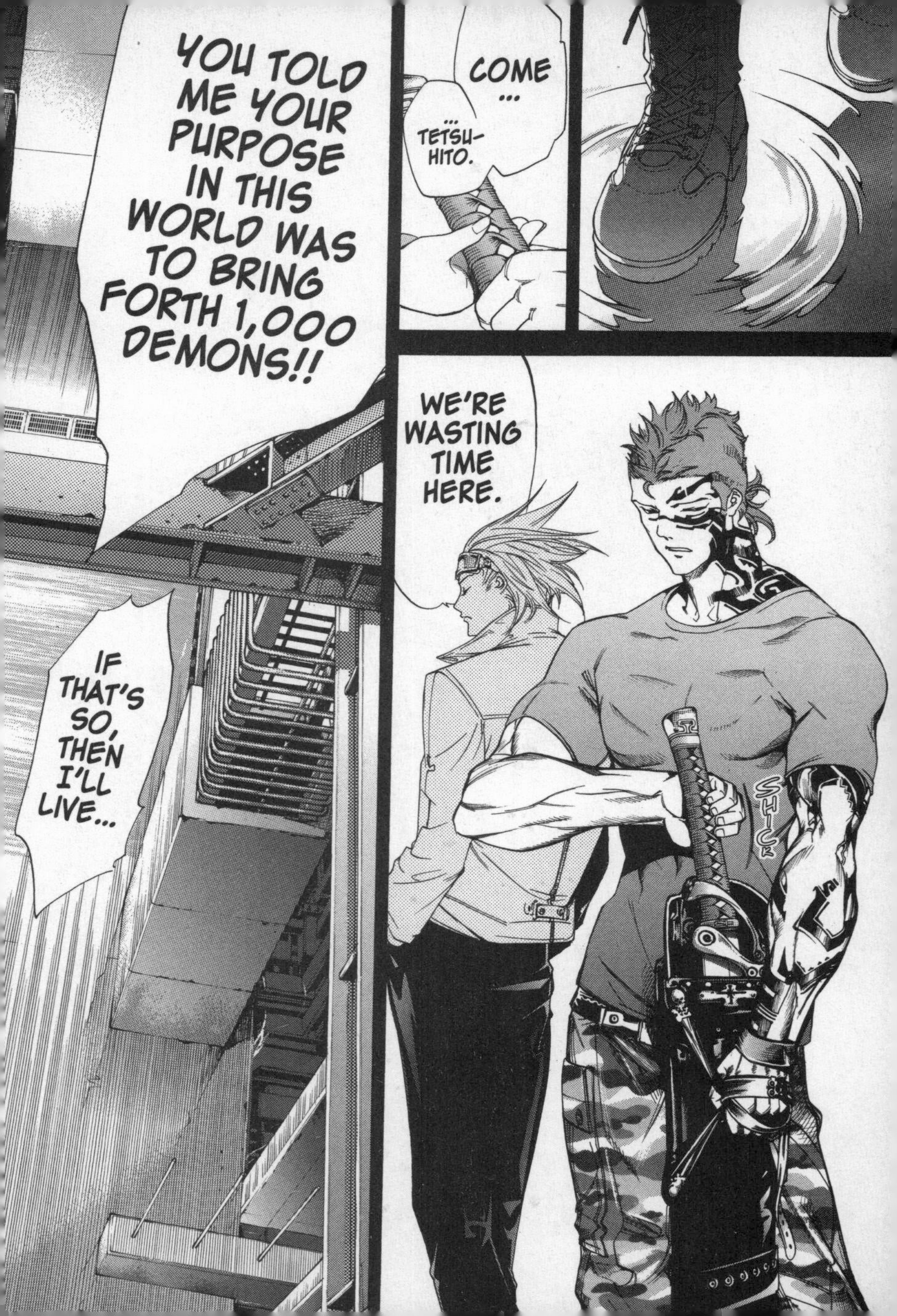
COME...
...TETSU-HITO.
WE'RE WASTING TIME HERE.
SHICK
YOU TOLD ME YOUR PURPOSE IN THIS WORLD WAS TO BRING FORTH 1,000 DEMONS!!
IF THAT'S SO, THEN I'LL LIVE...

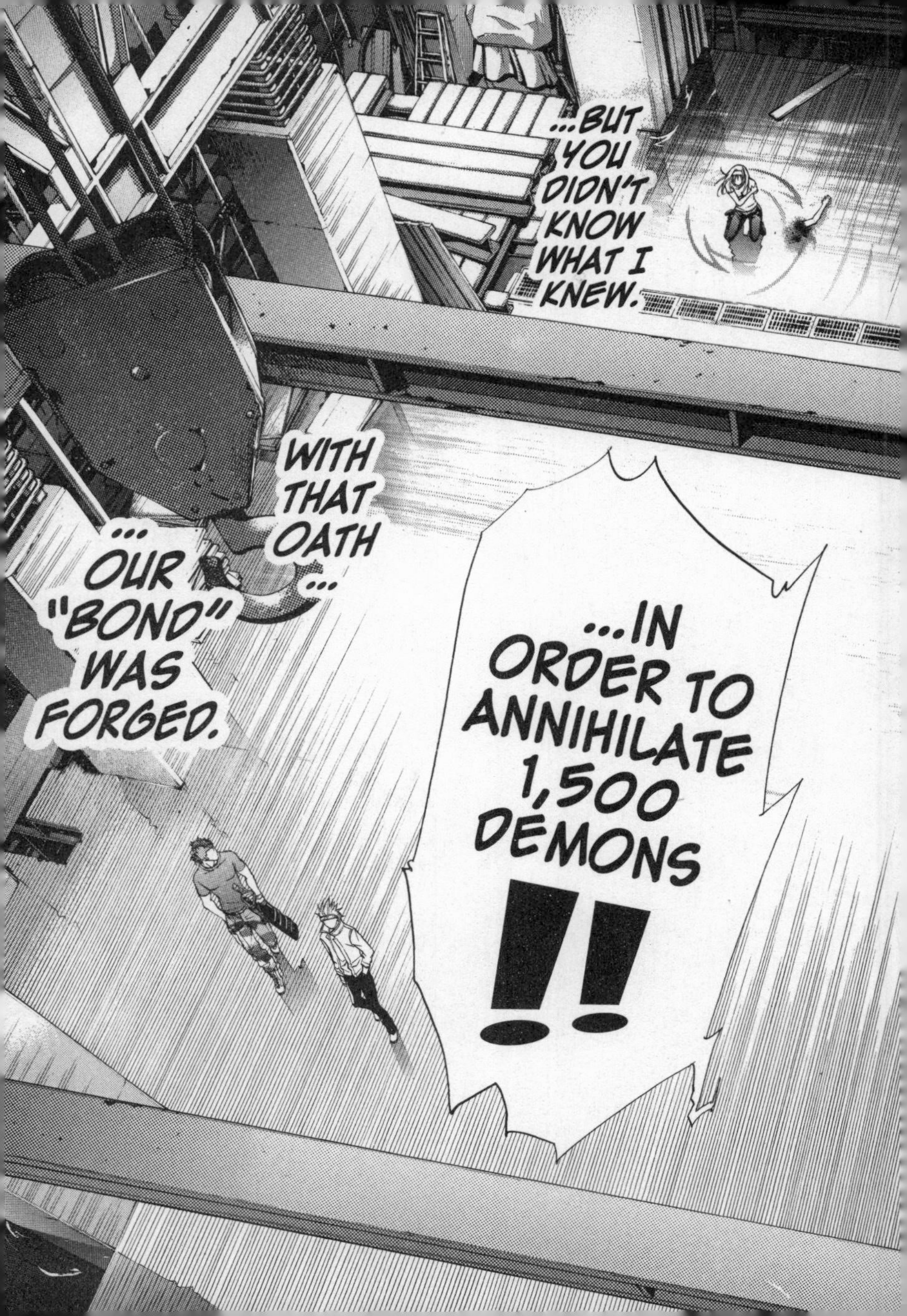
...BUT YOU DIDN'T KNOW WHAT I KNEW.
...IN ORDER TO ANNIHILATE 1,500 DEMONS!!
WITH THAT OATH...
...OUR "BOND" WAS FORGED.

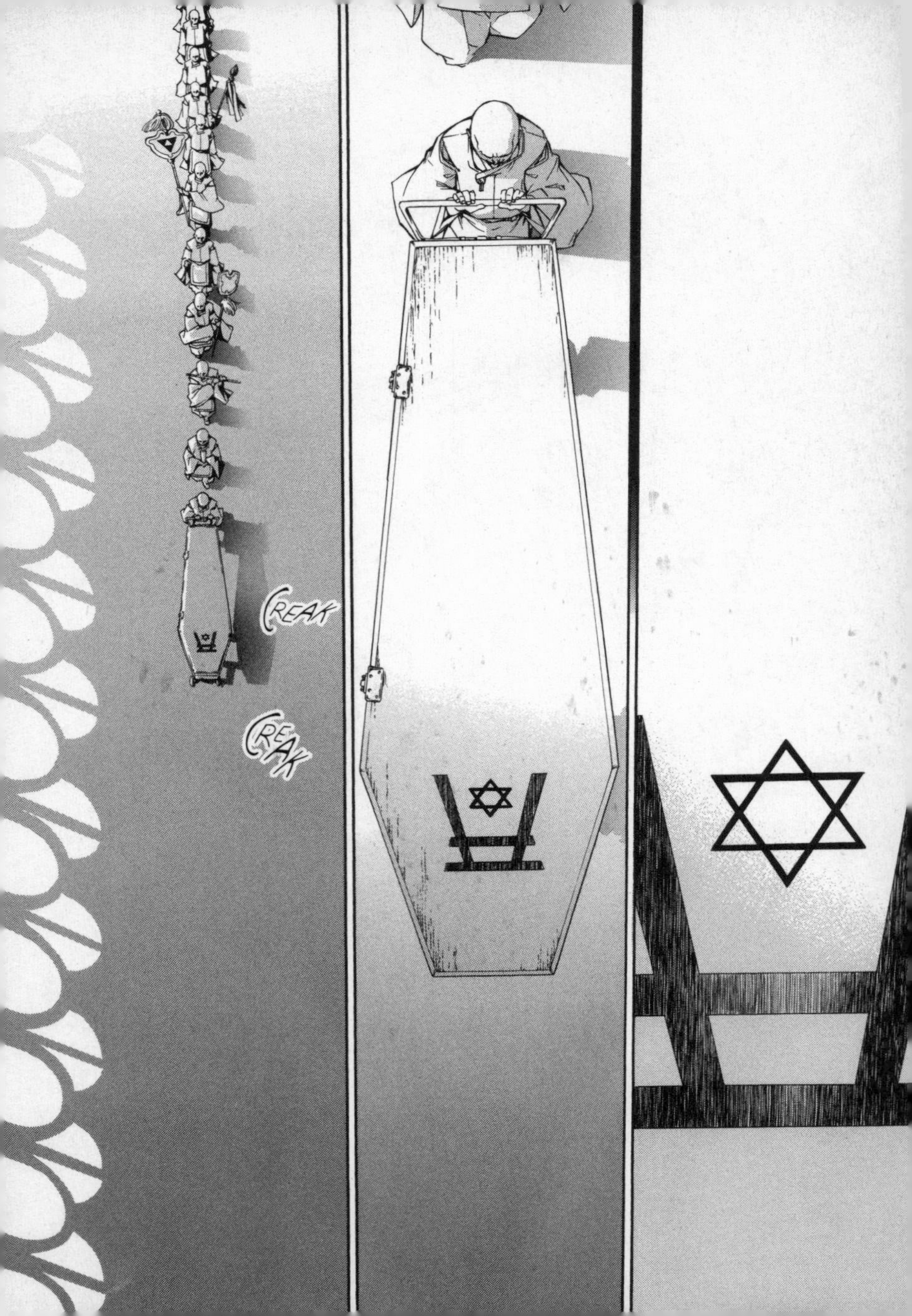
CREAK
CREAK

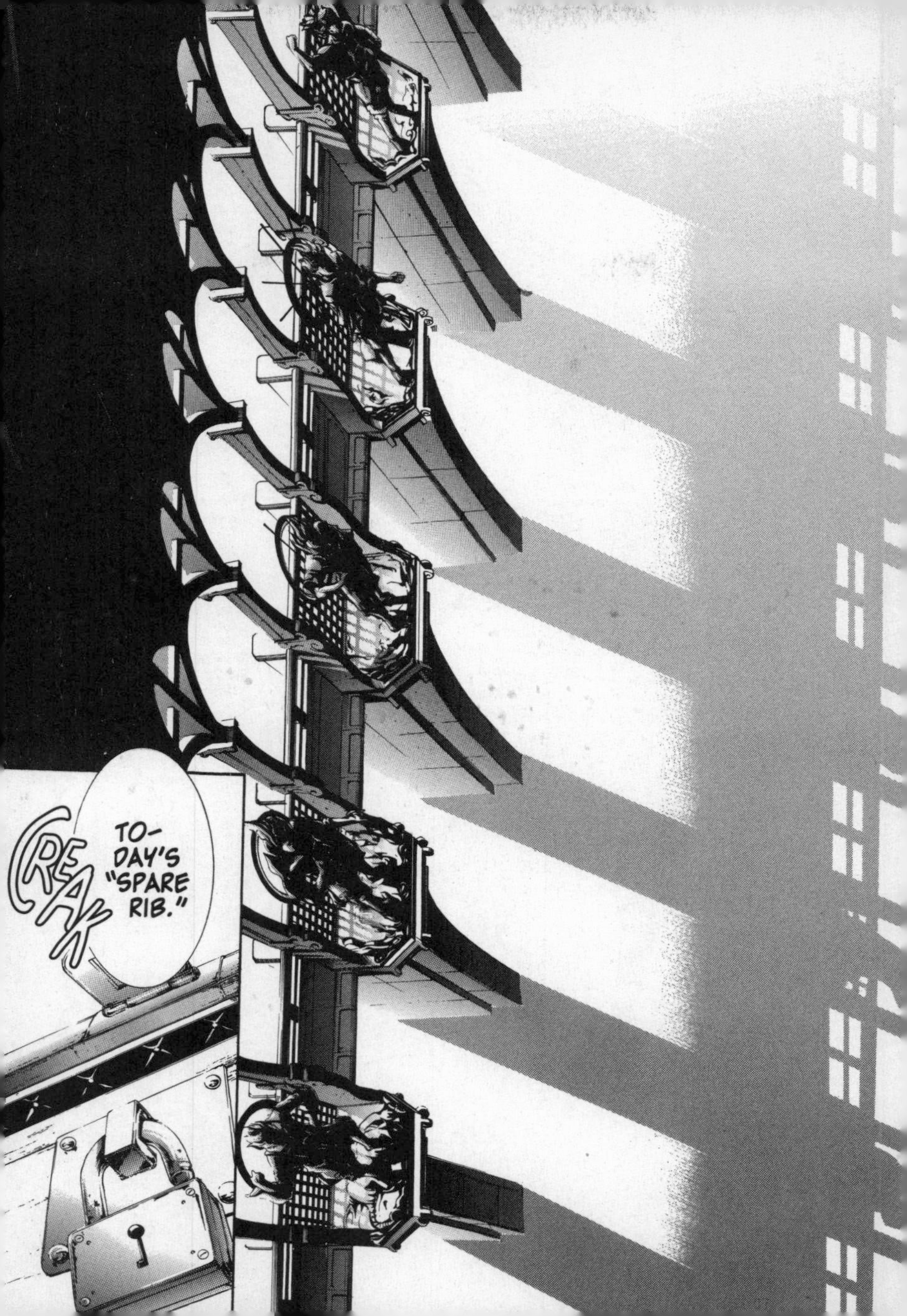
TO-DAY'S "SPARE RIB."
CREAK

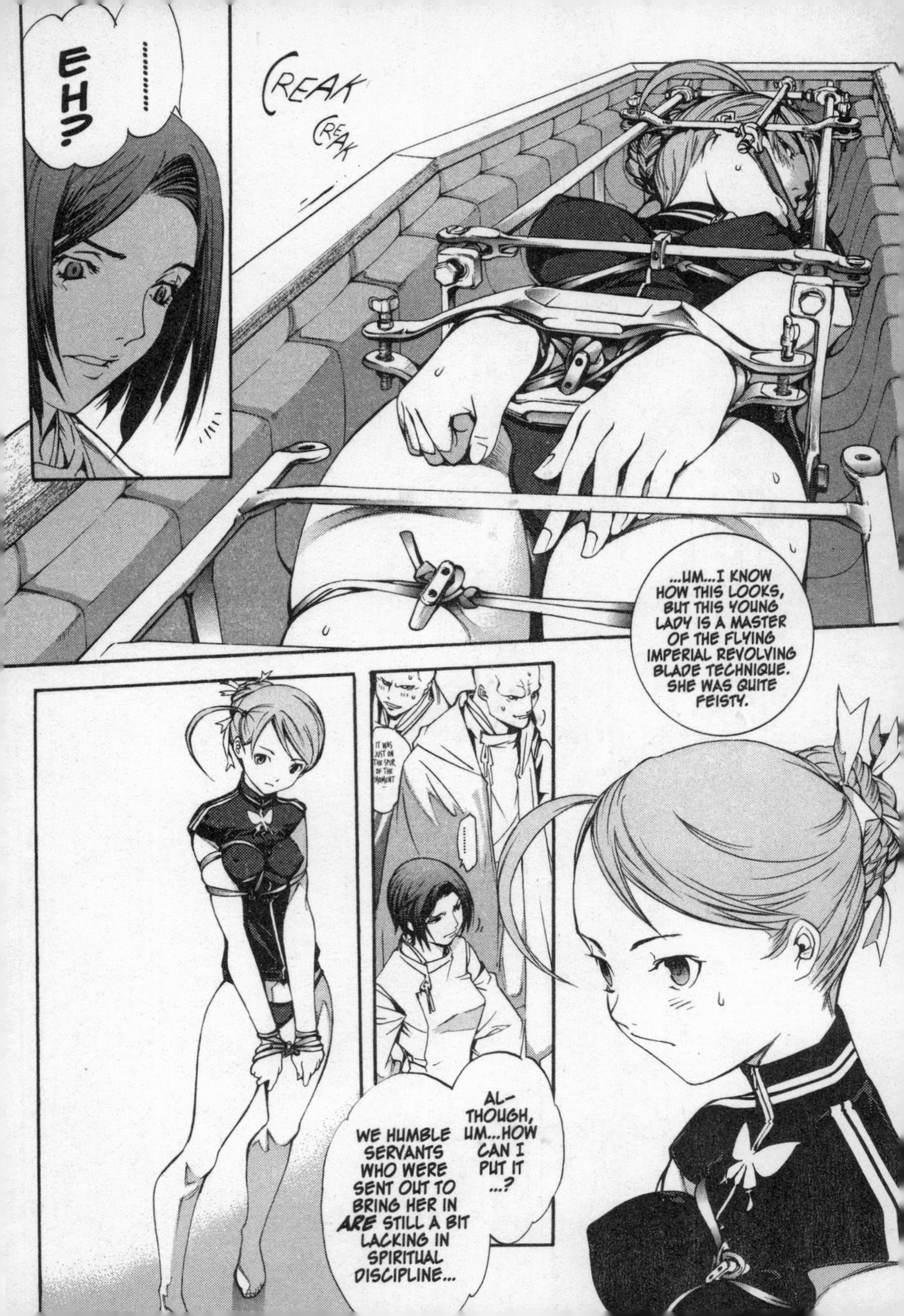
CREAK
CREAK
...UM...I KNOW HOW THIS LOOKS, BUT THIS YOUNG LADY IS A MASTER OF THE FLYING IMPERIAL REVOLVING BLADE TECHNIQUE. SHE WAS QUITE FEISTY.
......
EH?
AL-THOUGH, UM...HOW CAN I PUT IT ...?
WE HUMBLE SERVANTS WHO WERE SENT OUT TO BRING HER IN ARE STILL A BIT LACKING IN SPIRITUAL DISCIPLINE...
IT WAS JUST ON THE SPUR OF THE MOMENT
......

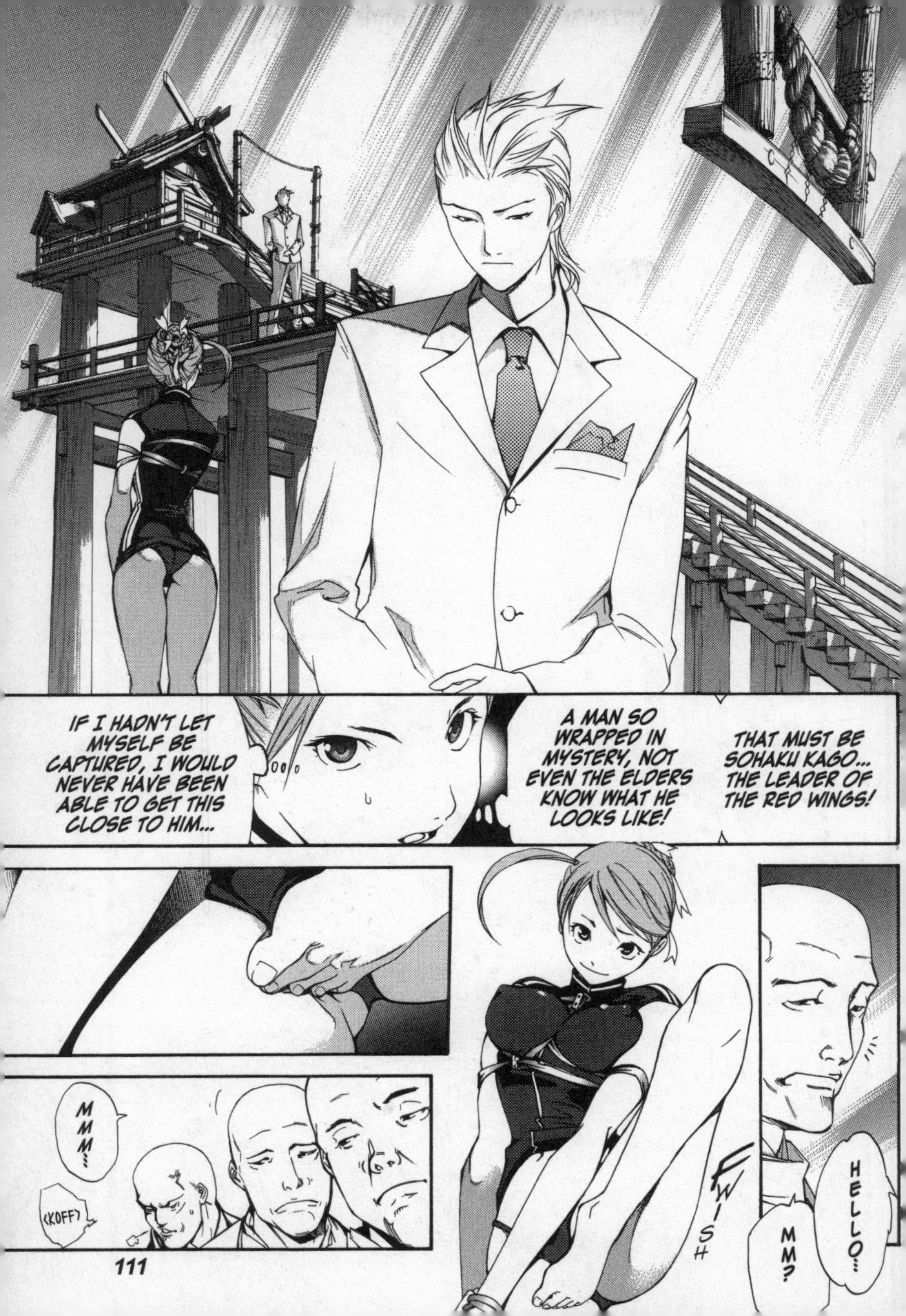
THAT MUST BE SOHAKU KAGO... THE LEADER OF THE RED WINGS!
A MAN SO WRAPPED IN MYSTERY, NOT EVEN THE ELDERS KNOW WHAT HE LOOKS LIKE!
IF I HADN'T LET MYSELF BE CAPTURED, I WOULD NEVER HAVE BEEN ABLE TO GET THIS CLOSE TO HIM...
HELLO...
MM?
FWISH
MMM...
<KOFF>

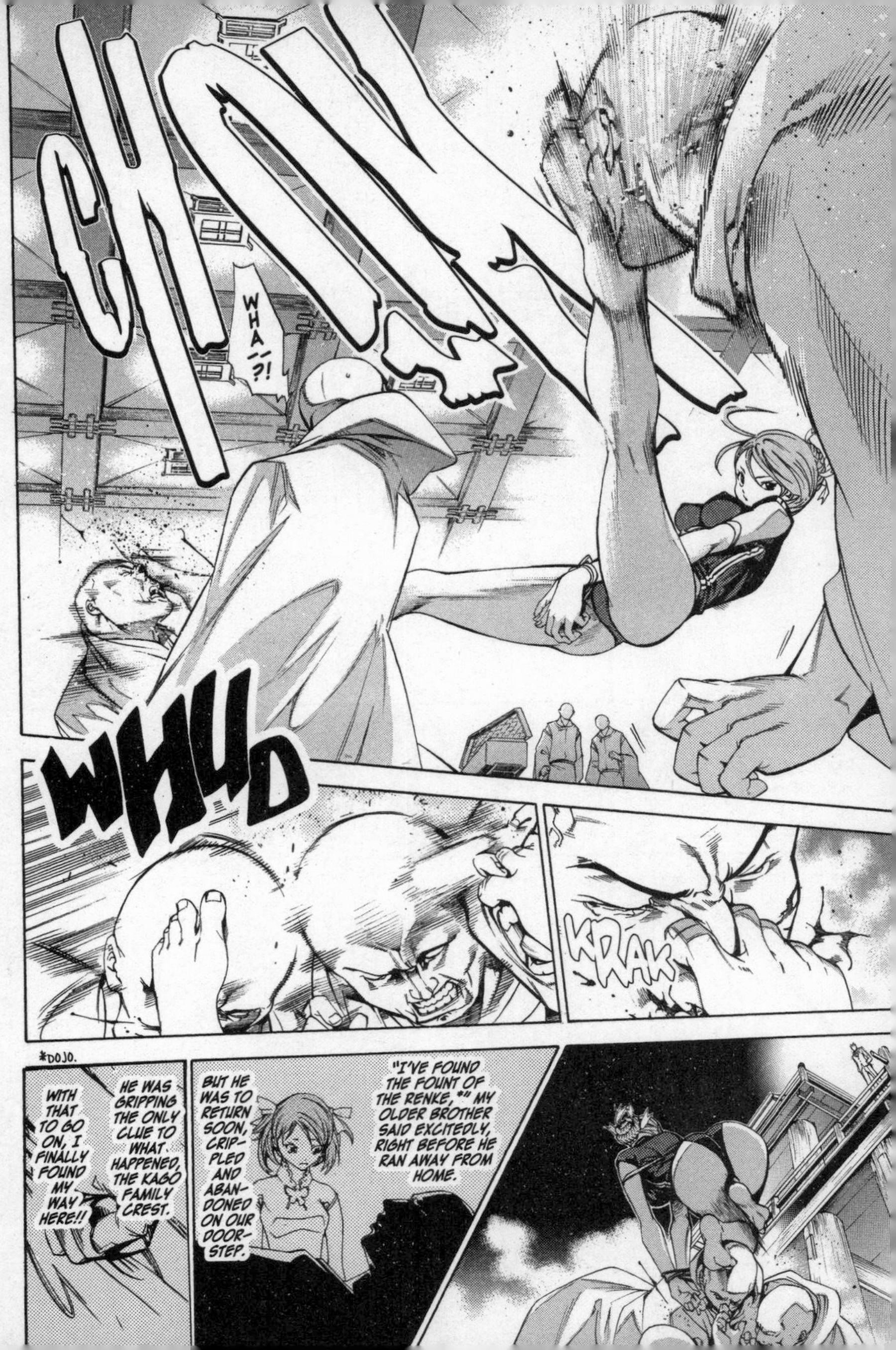
WHA—?!
KRAK
WHUD
"I'VE FOUND THE FOUNT OF THE RENKE,*" MY OLDER BROTHER SAID EXCITEDLY, RIGHT BEFORE HE RAN AWAY FROM HOME.
BUT HE WAS TO RETURN SOON, CRIPPLED AND ABANDONED ON OUR DOORSTEP.
HE WAS GRIPPING THE ONLY CLUE TO WHAT HAPPENED, THE KAGO FAMILY CREST.
WITH THAT TO GO ON, I FINALLY FOUND MY WAY HERE!!
*DOJO.

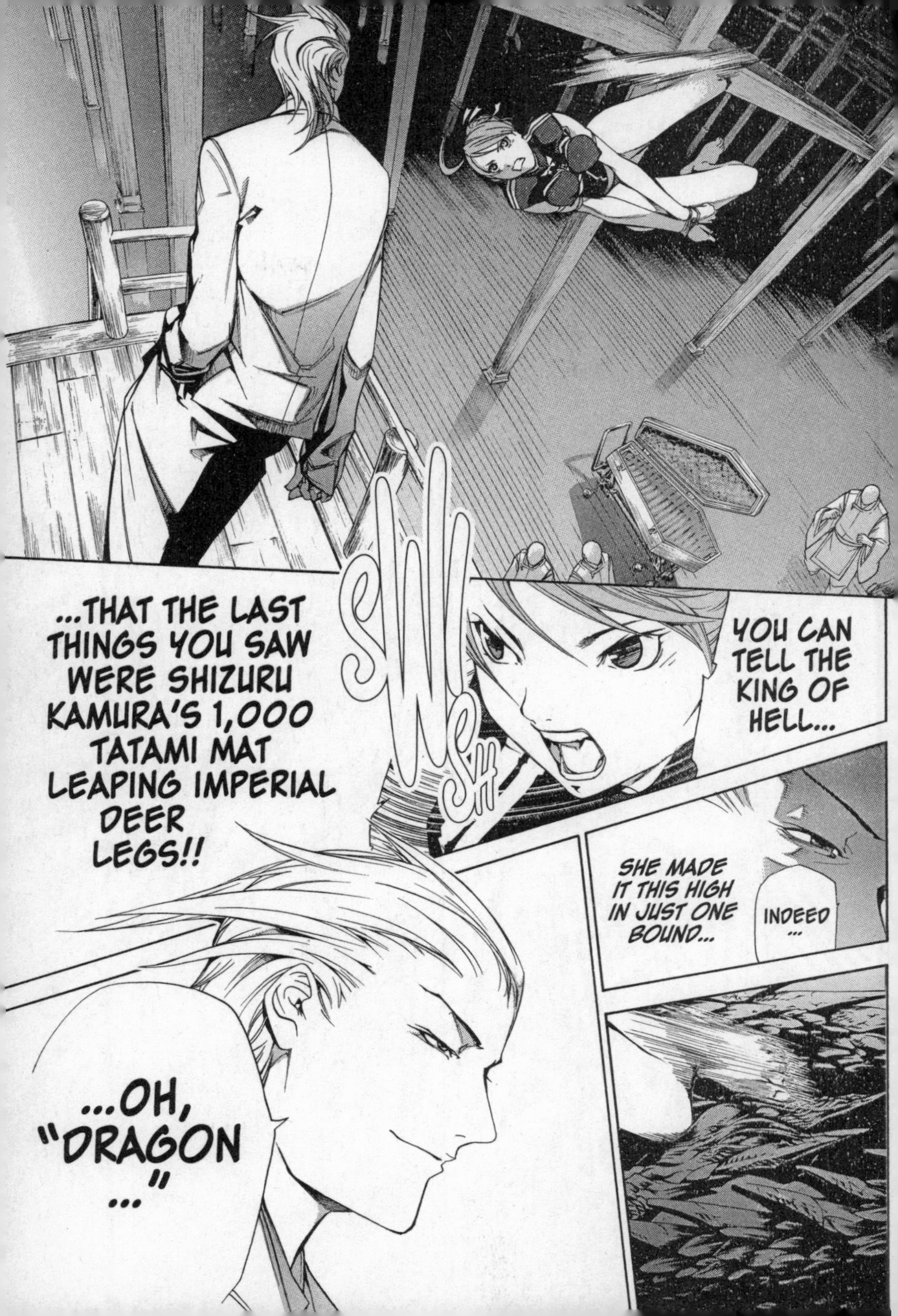
YOU CAN TELL THE KING OF HELL...
SWISH
...THAT THE LAST THINGS YOU SAW WERE SHIZURU KAMURA'S 1,000 TATAMI MAT LEAPING IMPERIAL DEER LEGS!!
SHE MADE IT THIS HIGH IN JUST ONE BOUND...
INDEED...
...OH, "DRAGON"...

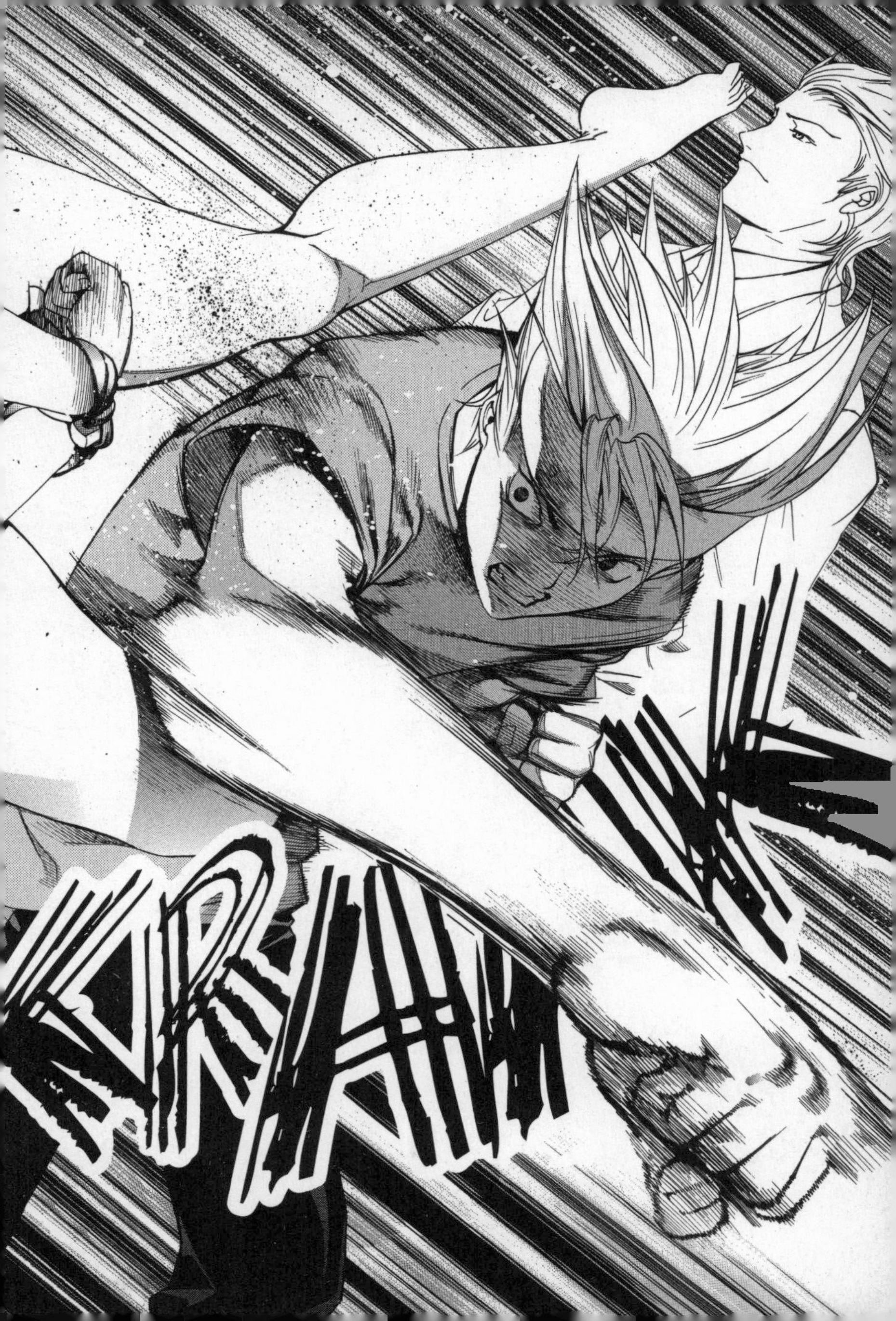

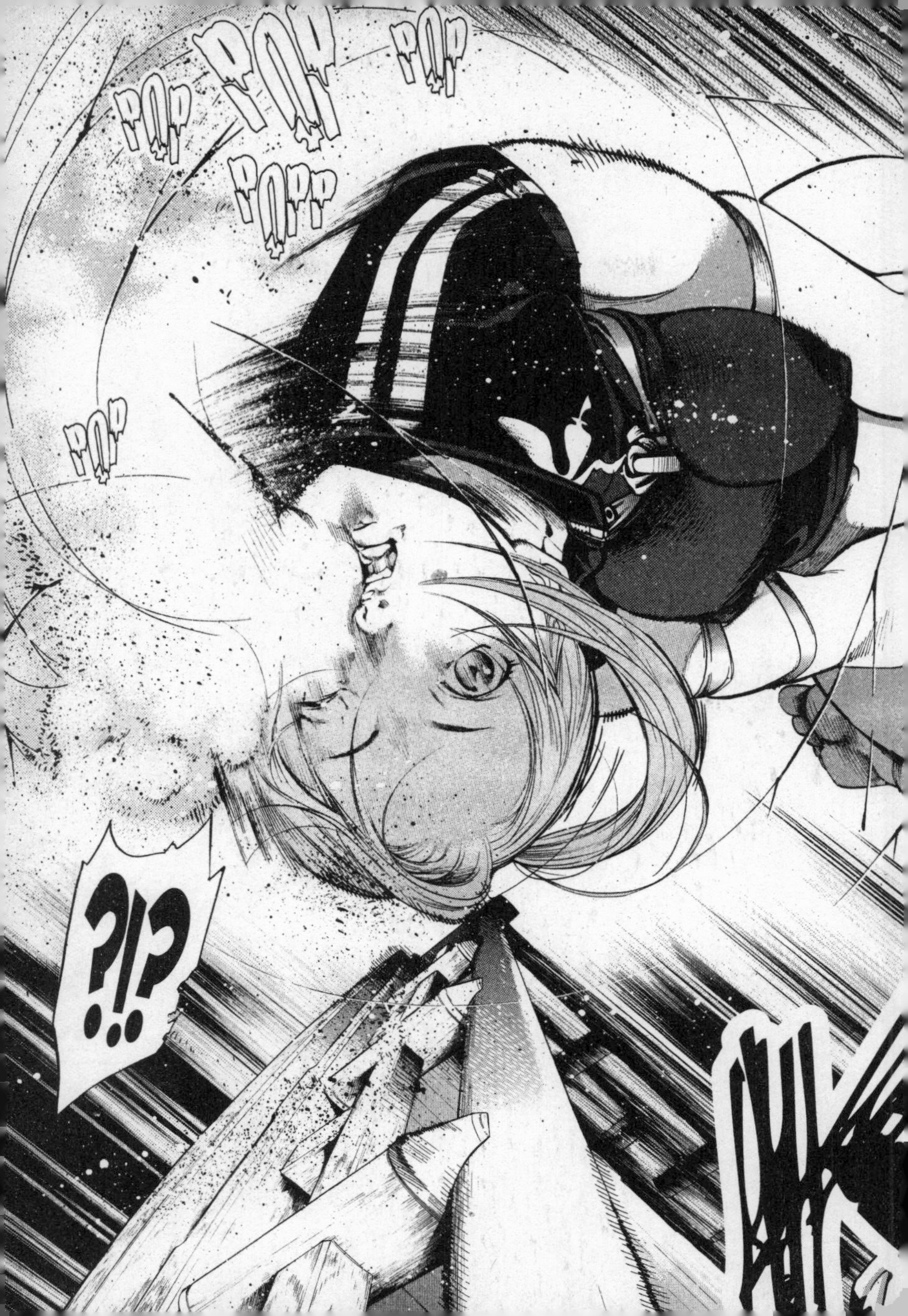
POP
POP
POP
POPP
POP
?!?

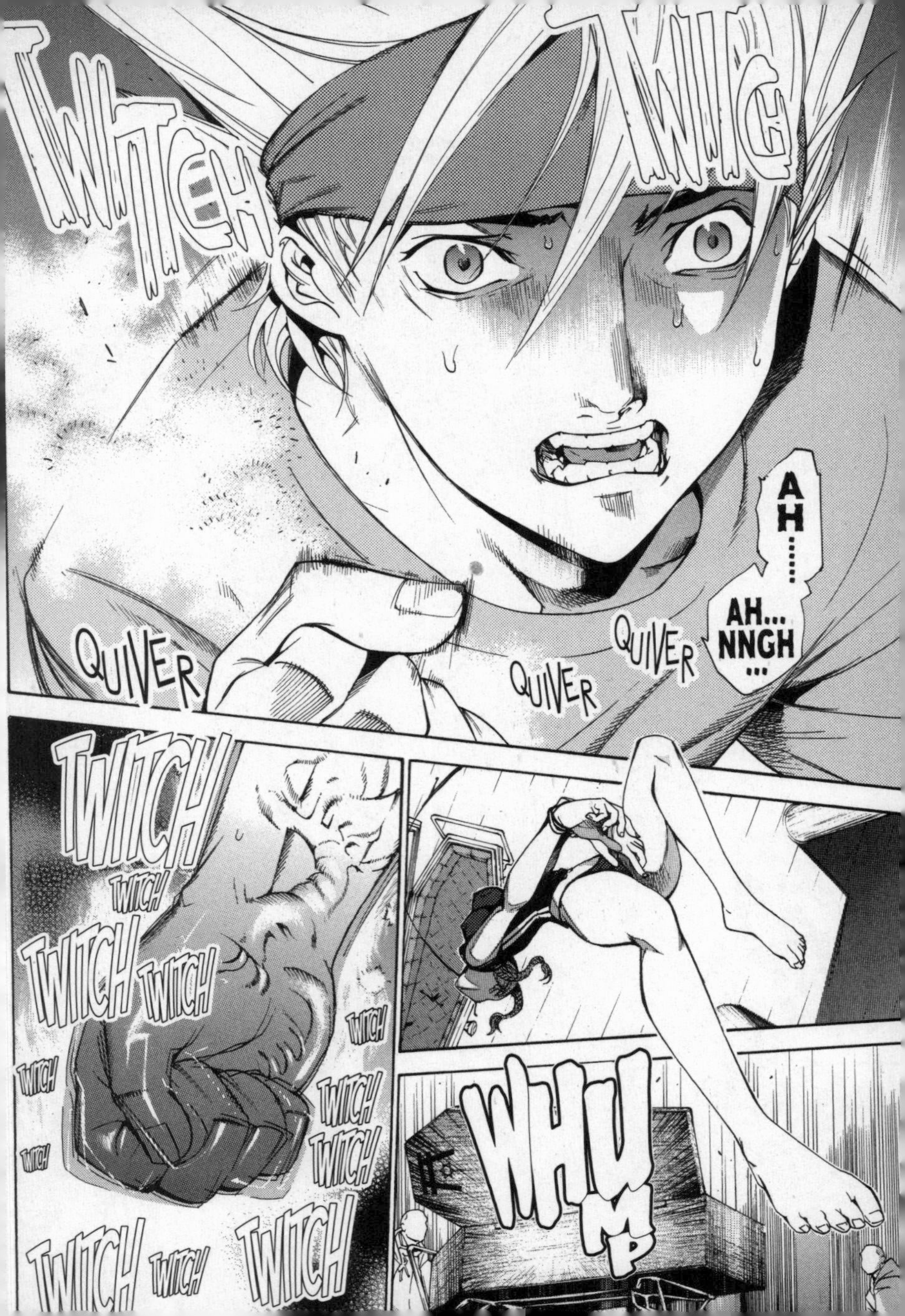
TWITCH
TWITCH
AH......
AH... NNGH ...
QUIVER
QUIVER
QUIVER
WHUMP
TWITCH
TWITCH
TWITCH
TWITCH
TWITCH
TWITCH
TWITCH
TWITCH
TWITCH
TWITCH
TWITCH
TWITCH

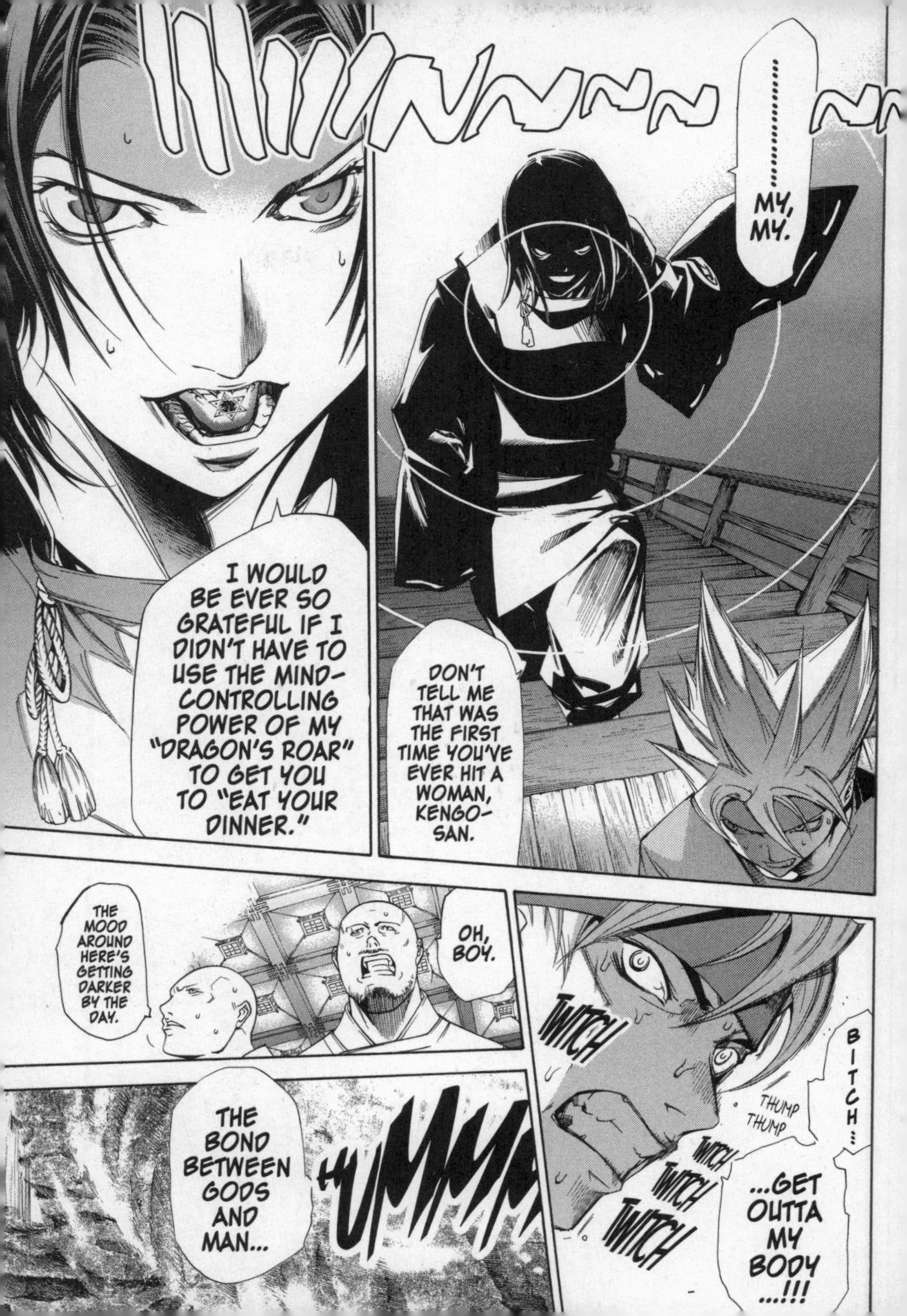
......MY, MY.
DON'T TELL ME THAT WAS THE FIRST TIME YOU'VE EVER HIT A WOMAN, KENGO-SAN.
I WOULD BE EVER SO GRATEFUL IF I DIDN'T HAVE TO USE THE MIND-CONTROLLING POWER OF MY "DRAGON'S ROAR" TO GET YOU TO "EAT YOUR DINNER."
BITCH...
THUMP THUMP
TWITCH
TWITCH
TWITCH
TWITCH
...GET OUTTA MY BODY ...!!!
OH, BOY.
THE MOOD AROUND HERE'S GETTING DARKER BY THE DAY.
THE BOND BETWEEN GODS AND MAN...

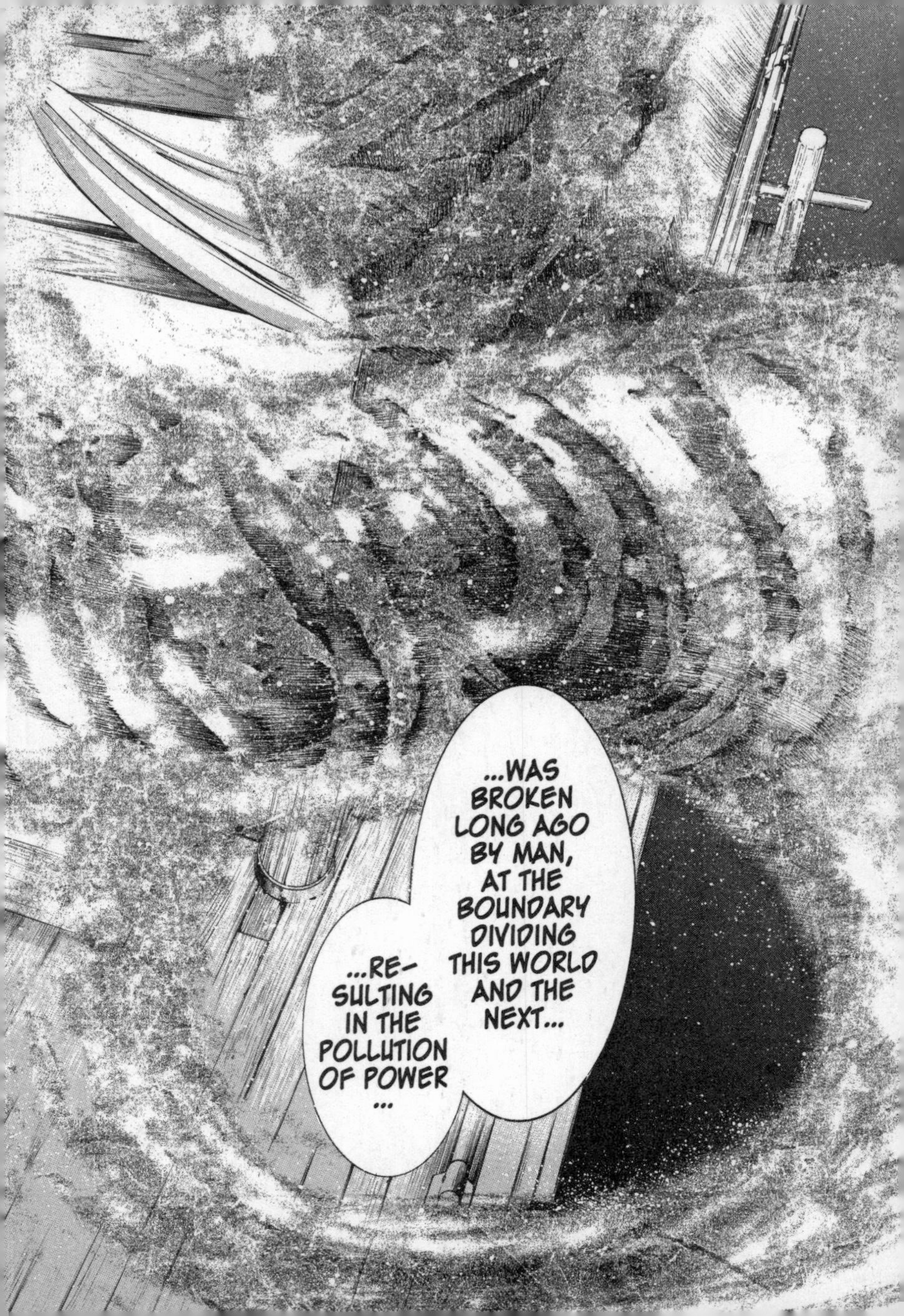
...WAS BROKEN LONG AGO BY MAN, AT THE BOUNDARY DIVIDING THIS WORLD AND THE NEXT...
...RE-SULTING IN THE POLLUTION OF POWER ...

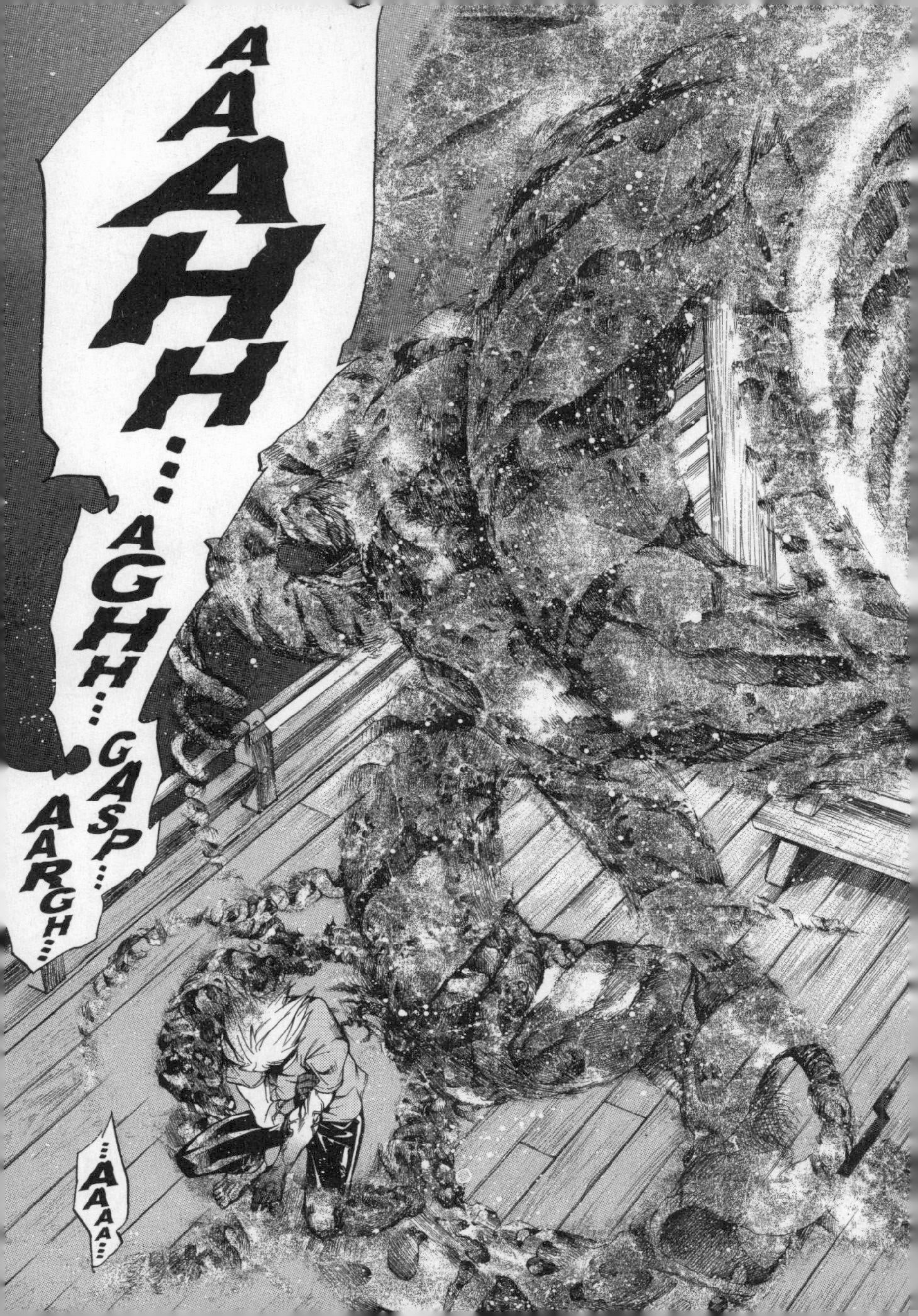

AAAHH...
AGHH...
GASP...
AARGH...
...AAAA...

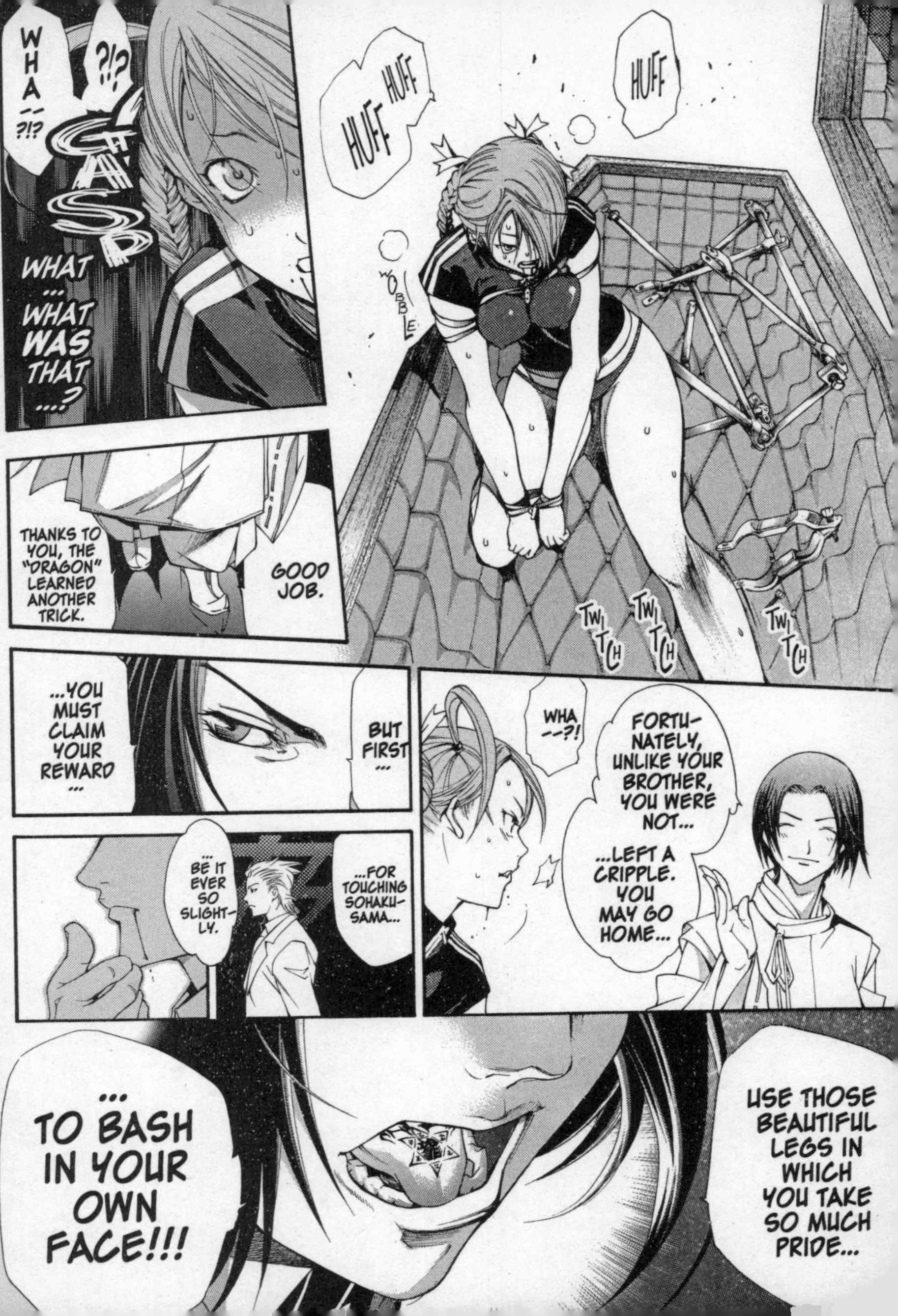
HUFF HUFF HUFF
HUFF
WOBBLE
TWITCH
TWITCH
TWITCH
?!?
WHA--?!?
GASP
WHAT... WHAT WAS THAT...?
GOOD JOB.
THANKS TO YOU, THE "DRAGON" LEARNED ANOTHER TRICK.
WHA--?!
FORTU-NATELY, UNLIKE YOUR BROTHER, YOU WERE NOT...
...LEFT A CRIPPLE. YOU MAY GO HOME...
BUT FIRST...
...YOU MUST CLAIM YOUR REWARD...
...FOR TOUCHING SOHAKU-SAMA...
...BE IT EVER SO SLIGHT-LY.
USE THOSE BEAUTIFUL LEGS IN WHICH YOU TAKE SO MUCH PRIDE...
...TO BASH IN YOUR OWN FACE!!!

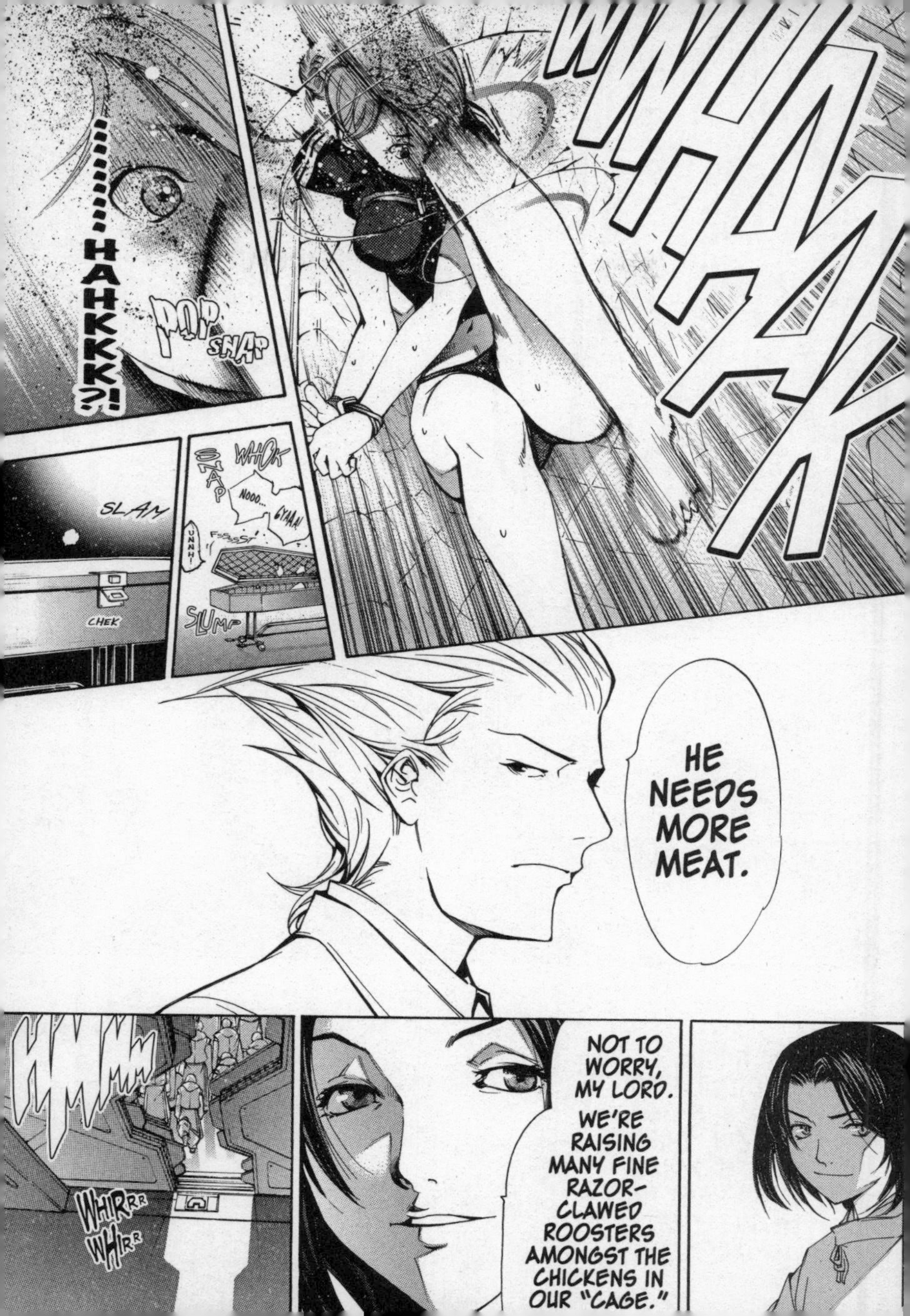
WHAAK
......HAHKKK?!
POP
SNAP
WHOK
SNAP
NOOO...
GYAAA!
UNNH!
FSSSST
SLUMP
SLAM
CHEK
HE NEEDS MORE MEAT.
NOT TO WORRY, MY LORD.
WE'RE RAISING MANY FINE RAZOR-CLAWED ROOSTERS AMONGST THE CHICKENS IN OUR "CAGE."
WHIRRR
WHIRRR

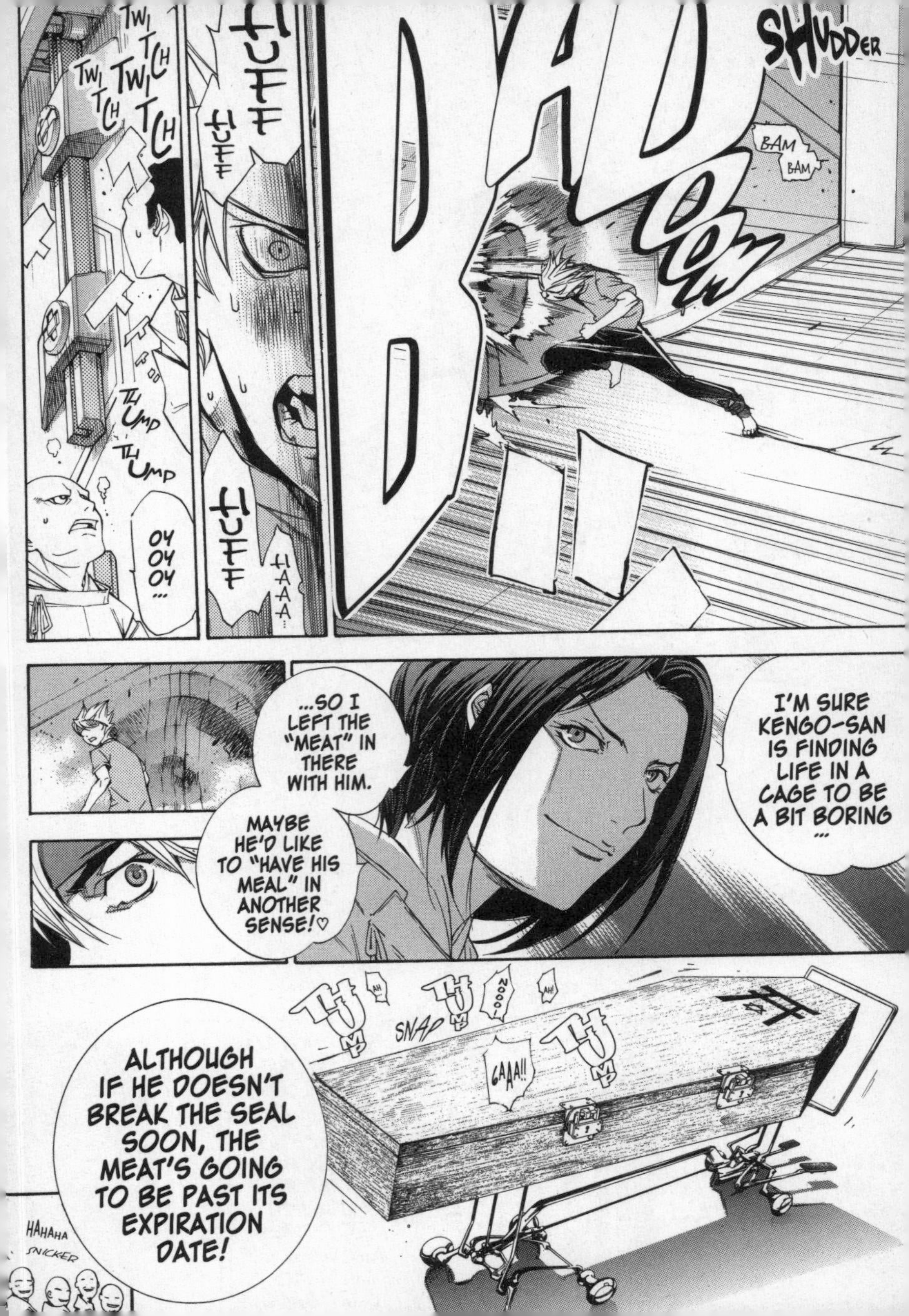
SHUDDER
BAM BAM
HUFF HUFF
HUFF HUFF
HUFF HUFF
HAAAA...
TWITCH TWITCH TWITCH
THUMP THUMP
OY OY OY ...
I'M SURE KENGO-SAN IS FINDING LIFE IN A CAGE TO BE A BIT BORING ...
...SO I LEFT THE "MEAT" IN THERE WITH HIM.
MAYBE HE'D LIKE TO "HAVE HIS MEAL" IN ANOTHER SENSE!♡
AH!
NOOO!
THUMP
AH
THUMP
SNAP
THUMP
GAAA!!
ALTHOUGH IF HE DOESN'T BREAK THE SEAL SOON, THE MEAT'S GOING TO BE PAST ITS EXPIRATION DATE!
HAHAHA
SNICKER

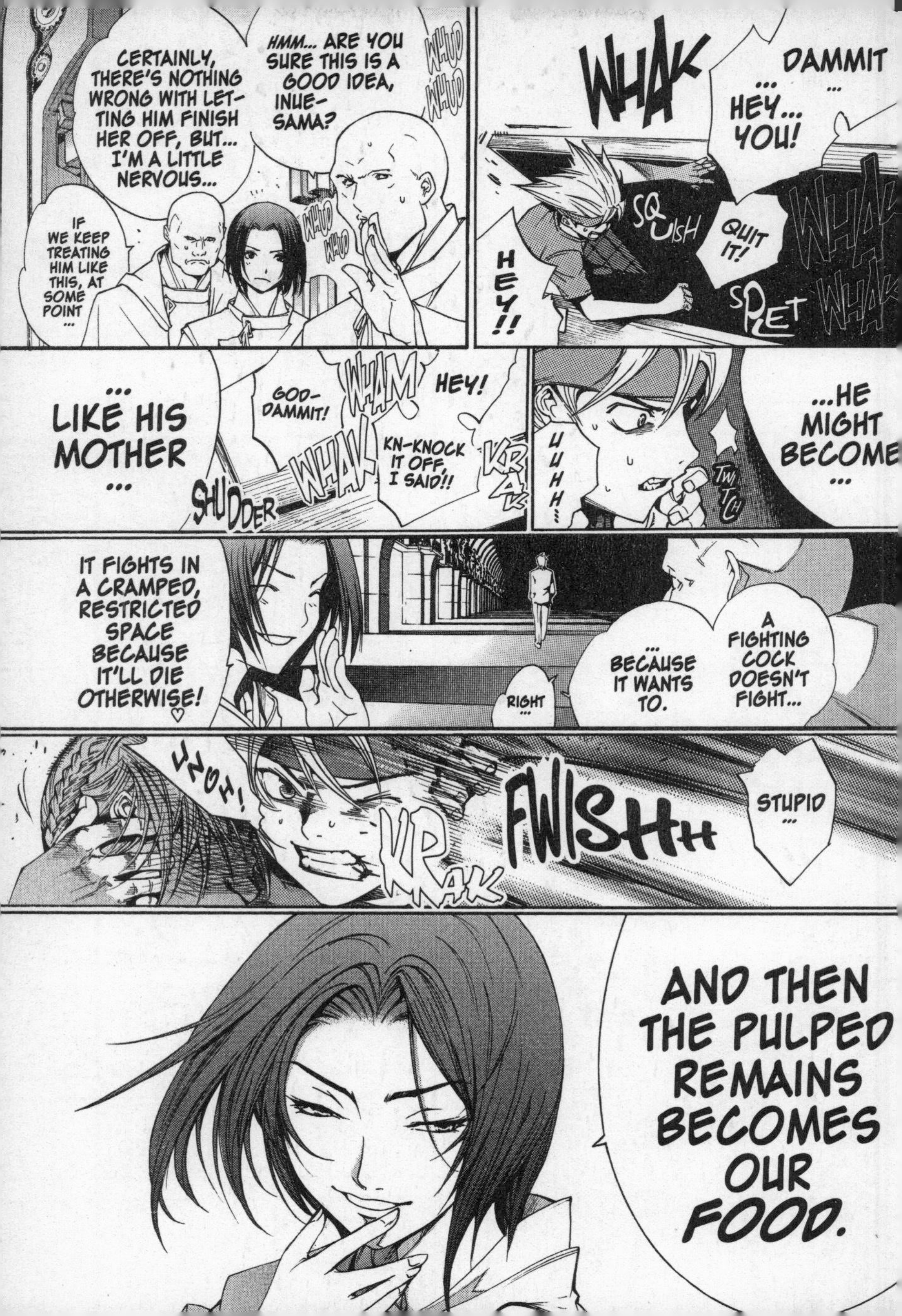
WHAK
DAMMIT... HEY... YOU!
SQUISH
QUIT IT!
WHAK
SPLET
WHAK
HEY!!
WHUD WHUD
HMM... ARE YOU SURE THIS IS A GOOD IDEA, INUE-SAMA?
CERTAINLY, THERE'S NOTHING WRONG WITH LETTING HIM FINISH HER OFF, BUT... I'M A LITTLE NERVOUS...
WHUD WHUD
IF WE KEEP TREATING HIM LIKE THIS, AT SOME POINT...
...HE MIGHT BECOME...
TWITCH
UUHH..
HEY!
KRAK
WHAM
GOD-DAMMIT!
KN-KNOCK IT OFF, I SAID!!
WHAK
...LIKE HIS MOTHER...
SHUDDER
A FIGHTING COCK DOESN'T FIGHT...
...BECAUSE IT WANTS TO.
RIGHT...
IT FIGHTS IN A CRAMPED, RESTRICTED SPACE BECAUSE IT'LL DIE OTHERWISE!♡
STUPID...
FWISHH
KRAK
AND THEN THE PULPED REMAINS BECOMES OUR FOOD.

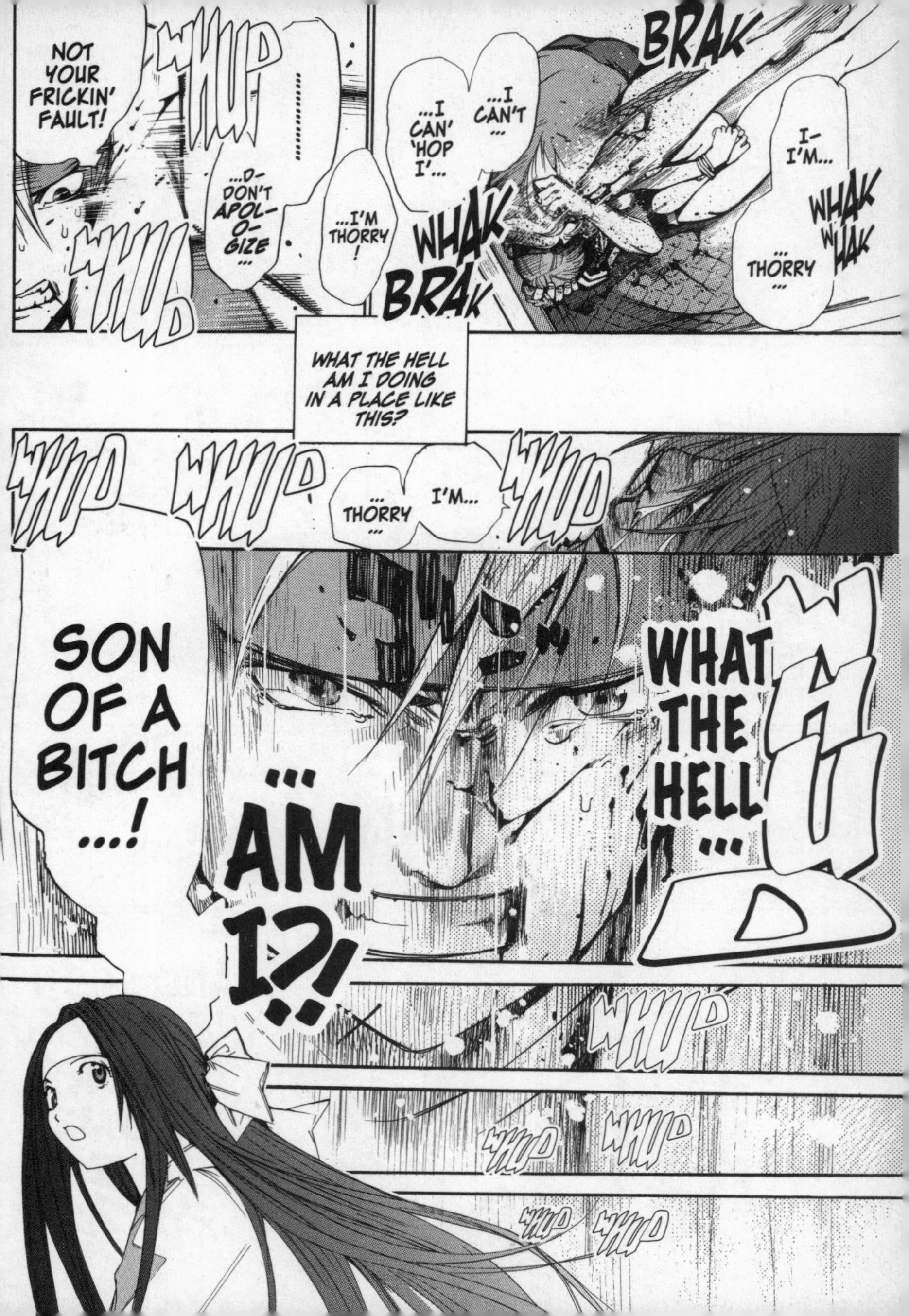
I-
I'M...
WHAK
WHAK
... THORRY ...
BRAK
...I CAN'T ...
...I CAN' 'HOP I'...
WHAK
BRAK
...I'M THORRY !
......
...D-DON'T APOLO-O-GIZE ...
WHUD
NOT YOUR FRICKIN' FAULT!
WHUD
WHAT THE HELL AM I DOING IN A PLACE LIKE THIS?
WHUD
I'M...
... THORRY ...
WHUD
WHUD
WHUD
WHAT THE HELL ...
... AM I?!
SON OF A BITCH ...!
WHUD
WHUD
WHUD
WHUD
WHUD

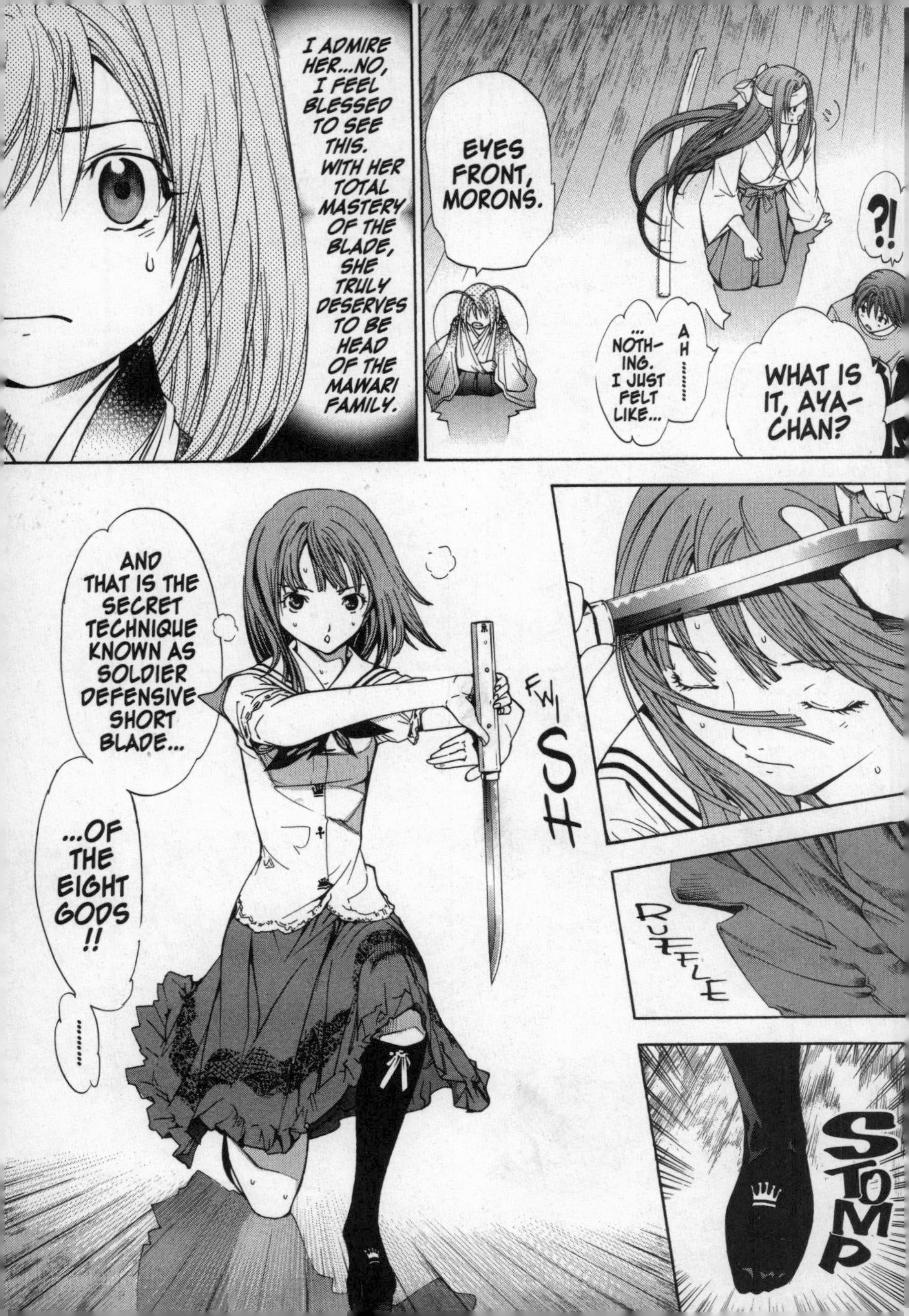
?!
WHAT IS IT, AYA-CHAN?
AH......
...NOTHING. I JUST FELT LIKE...
EYES FRONT, MORONS.
I ADMIRE HER...NO, I FEEL BLESSED TO SEE THIS. WITH HER TOTAL MASTERY OF THE BLADE, SHE TRULY DESERVES TO BE HEAD OF THE MAWARI FAMILY.
RUFFLE
STOMP
FWISH
AND THAT IS THE SECRET TECHNIQUE KNOWN AS SOLDIER DEFENSIVE SHORT BLADE...
...OF THE EIGHT GODS!!
......

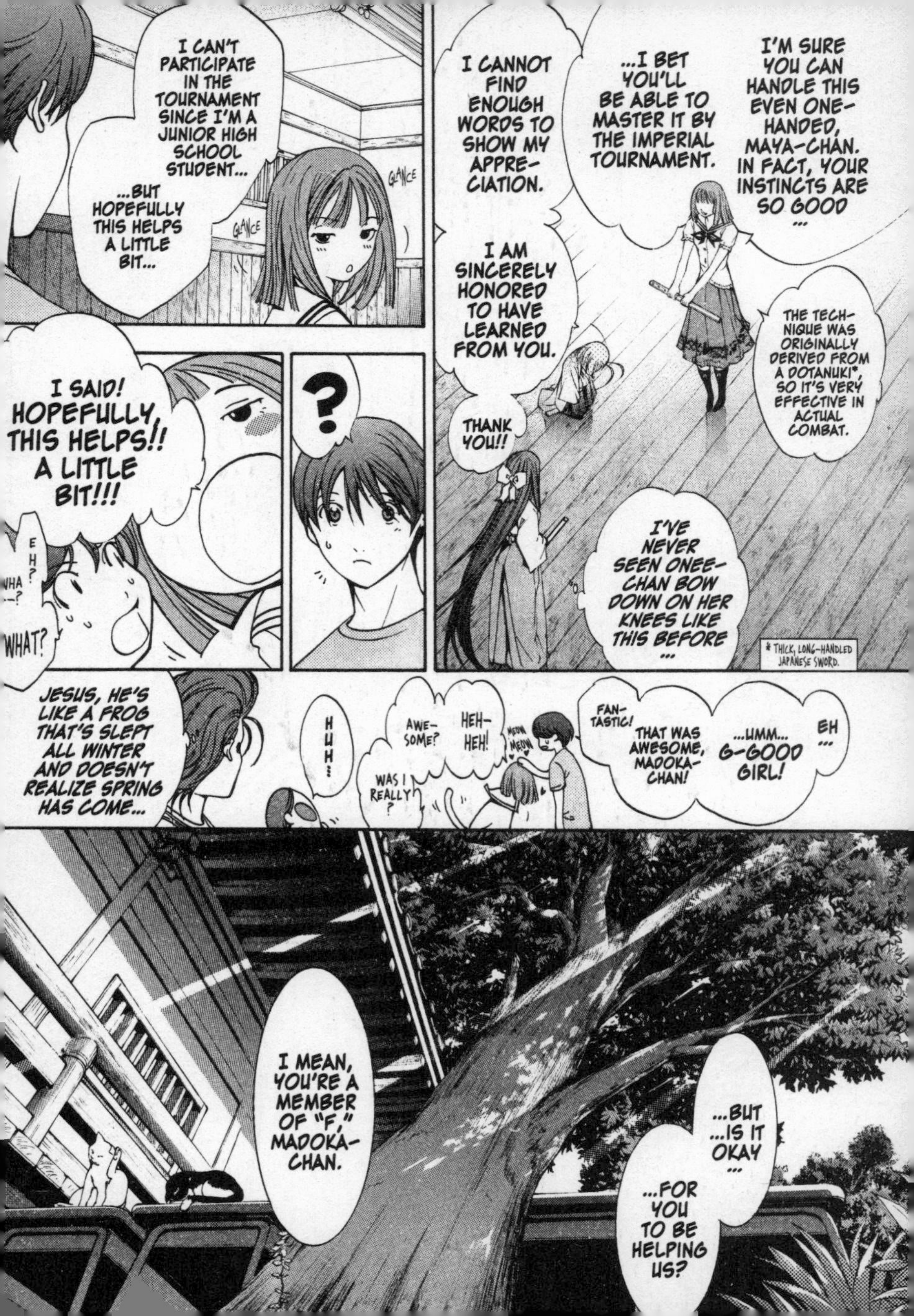
I'M SURE YOU CAN HANDLE THIS EVEN ONE-HANDED, MAYA-CHAN. IN FACT, YOUR INSTINCTS ARE SO GOOD ...
...I BET YOU'LL BE ABLE TO MASTER IT BY THE IMPERIAL TOURNAMENT.
I CANNOT FIND ENOUGH WORDS TO SHOW MY APPRE-CIATION.
I AM SINCERELY HONORED TO HAVE LEARNED FROM YOU.
THE TECH-NIQUE WAS ORIGINALLY DERIVED FROM A DOTANUKI*, SO IT'S VERY EFFECTIVE IN ACTUAL COMBAT.
THANK YOU!!
I'VE NEVER SEEN ONEE-CHAN BOW DOWN ON HER KNEES LIKE THIS BEFORE ...
* THICK, LONG-HANDLED JAPANESE SWORD.
I CAN'T PARTICIPATE IN THE TOURNAMENT SINCE I'M A JUNIOR HIGH SCHOOL STUDENT...
GLANCE
GLANCE
...BUT HOPEFULLY THIS HELPS A LITTLE BIT...
?
I SAID! HOPEFULLY, THIS HELPS!! A LITTLE BIT!!!
EH?
WHA--?
WHAT?
EH ...
...UMM... G-GOOD GIRL!
THAT WAS AWESOME, MADOKA-CHAN!
FAN-TASTIC!
MEOW MEOW
HEH-HEH!
AWE-SOME?
WAS I REALLY?
HUH?
JESUS, HE'S LIKE A FROG THAT'S SLEPT ALL WINTER AND DOESN'T REALIZE SPRING HAS COME...
...BUT ...IS IT OKAY ...
...FOR YOU TO BE HELPING US?
I MEAN, YOU'RE A MEMBER OF "F," MADOKA-CHAN.

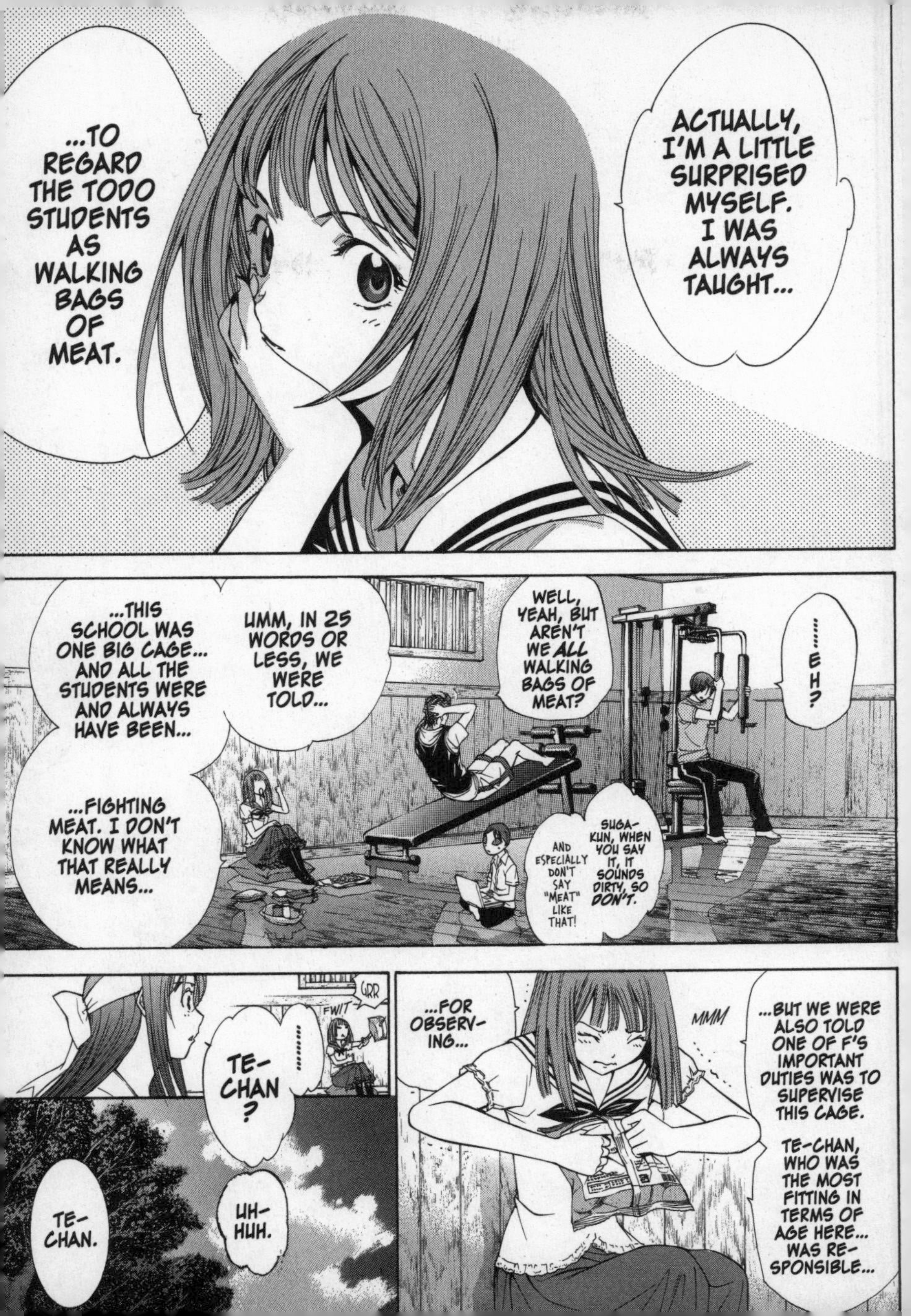
ACTUALLY, I'M A LITTLE SURPRISED MYSELF. I WAS ALWAYS TAUGHT...
...TO REGARD THE TODO STUDENTS AS WALKING BAGS OF MEAT.
......EH?
WELL, YEAH, BUT AREN'T WE *ALL* WALKING BAGS OF MEAT?
SUGA-KUN, WHEN YOU SAY IT, IT SOUNDS DIRTY, SO *DON'T*.
AND ESPECIALLY DON'T SAY "MEAT" LIKE THAT!
UMM, IN 25 WORDS OR LESS, WE WERE TOLD...
...THIS SCHOOL WAS ONE BIG CAGE... AND ALL THE STUDENTS WERE AND ALWAYS HAVE BEEN...
...FIGHTING MEAT. I DON'T KNOW WHAT THAT REALLY MEANS...
...BUT WE WERE ALSO TOLD ONE OF F'S IMPORTANT DUTIES WAS TO SUPERVISE THIS CAGE.
MMM
TE-CHAN, WHO WAS THE MOST FITTING IN TERMS OF AGE HERE... WAS RESPONSIBLE...
...FOR OBSERVING...
GRR
FWIT
......
TE-CHAN?
UH-HUH.
TE-CHAN.

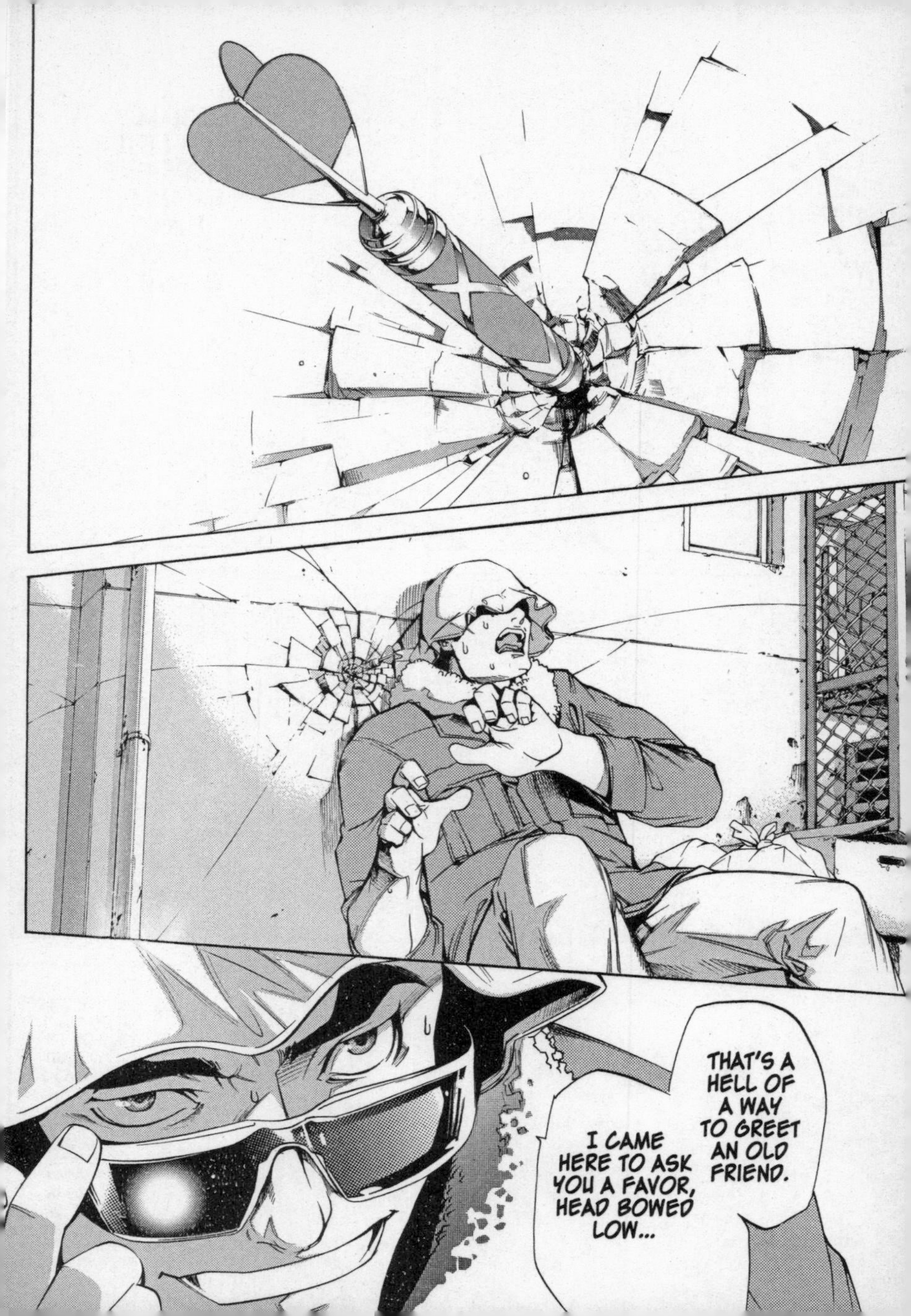
THAT'S A HELL OF A WAY TO GREET AN OLD FRIEND.
I CAME HERE TO ASK YOU A FAVOR, HEAD BOWED LOW...

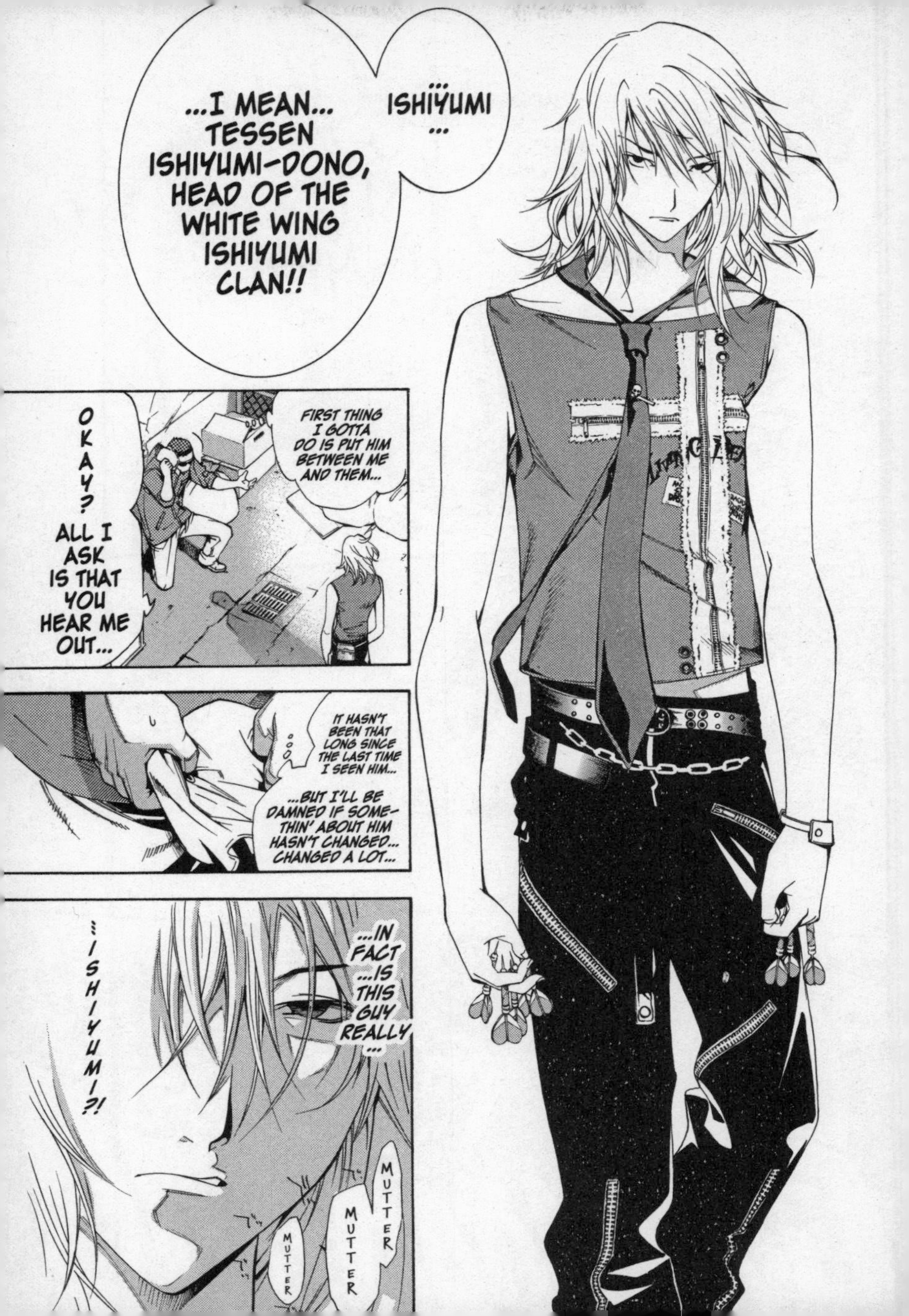
ISHIYUMI...
...I MEAN... TESSEN ISHIYUMI-DONO, HEAD OF THE WHITE WING ISHIYUMI CLAN!!
FIRST THING I GOTTA DO IS PUT HIM BETWEEN ME AND THEM...
OKAY? ALL I ASK IS THAT YOU HEAR ME OUT...
...
IT HASN'T BEEN THAT LONG SINCE THE LAST TIME I SEEN HIM...
...BUT I'LL BE DAMNED IF SOMETHIN' ABOUT HIM HASN'T CHANGED... CHANGED A LOT...
...IN FACT ...IS THIS GUY REALLY...
...ISHIYUMI?!
MUTTER MUTTER
MUTTER

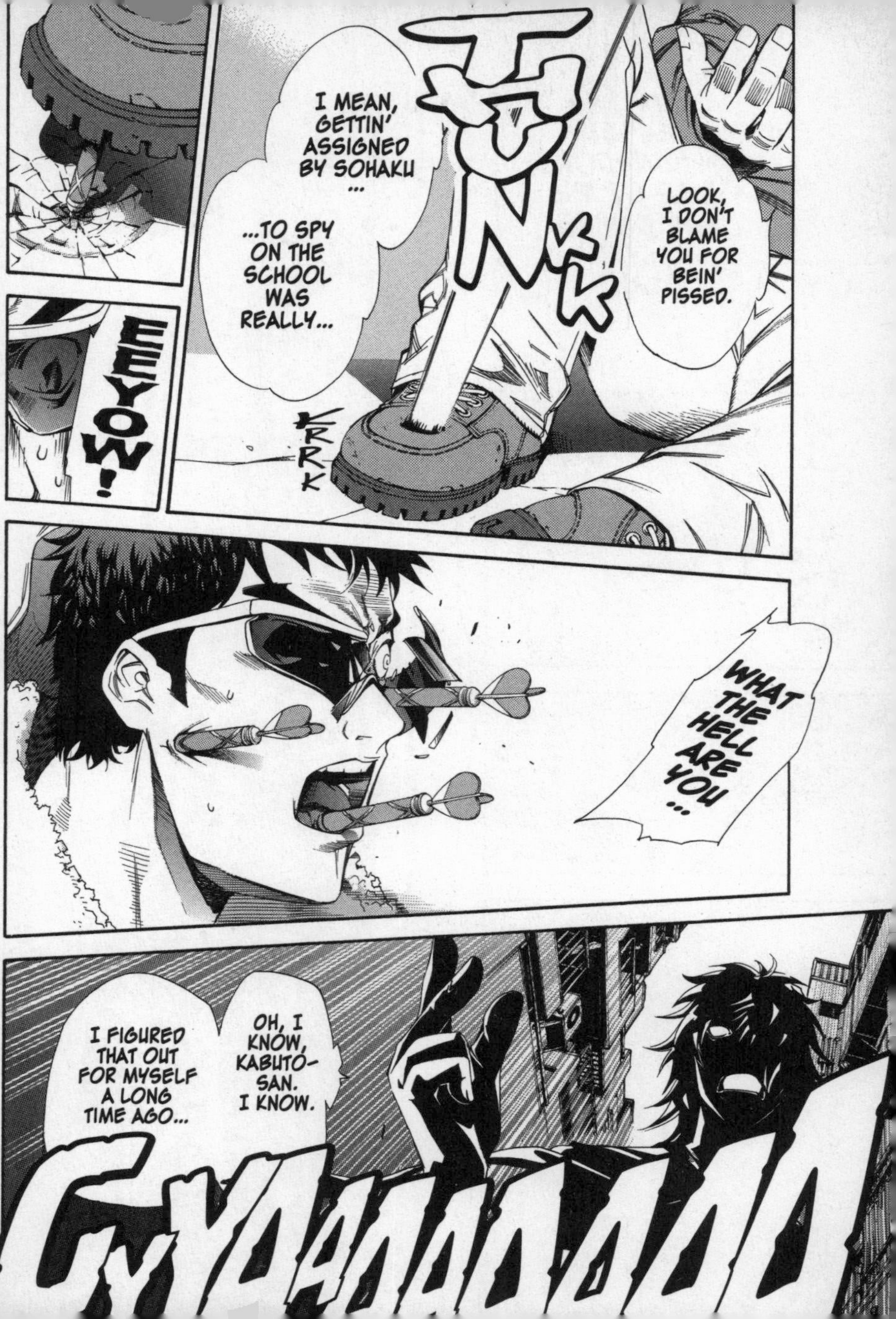
LOOK, I DON'T BLAME YOU FOR BEIN' PISSED.
I MEAN, GETTIN' ASSIGNED BY SOHAKU ...
...TO SPY ON THE SCHOOL WAS REALLY...
JUNK
KRRK
EEYOW!
WHAT THE HELL ARE YOU ...
OH, I KNOW, KABUTO-SAN. I KNOW.
I FIGURED THAT OUT FOR MYSELF A LONG TIME AGO...
GYAAAAAA

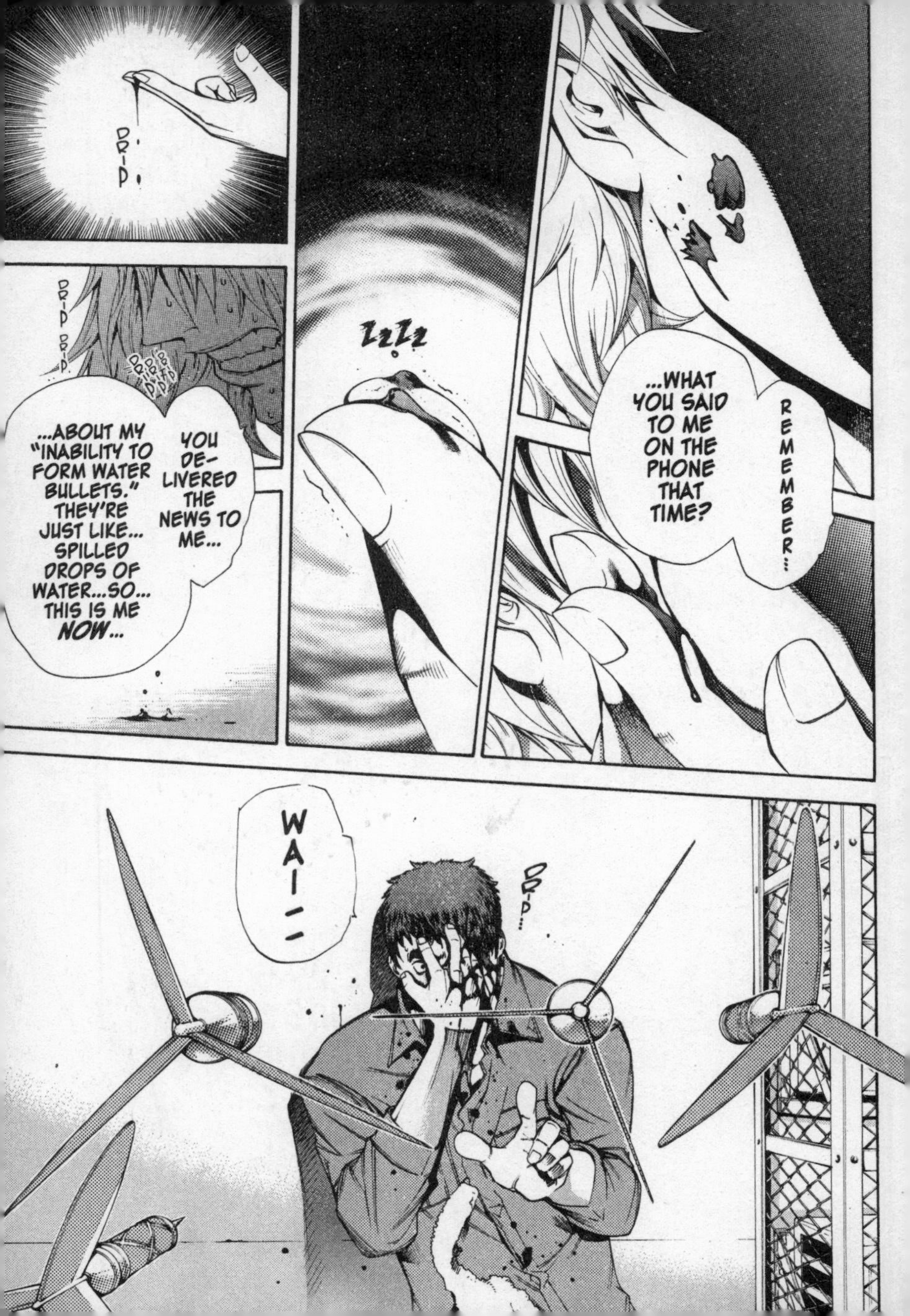
REMEMBER...
...WHAT YOU SAID TO ME ON THE PHONE THAT TIME?
ZZZZ
DRIP DRIP
DRIP DRIP...
DRIP DRIP DRIP
YOU DELIVERED THE NEWS TO ME...
...ABOUT MY "INABILITY TO FORM WATER BULLETS." THEY'RE JUST LIKE... SPILLED DROPS OF WATER...SO... THIS IS ME *NOW*...
WAI--
DRIP...

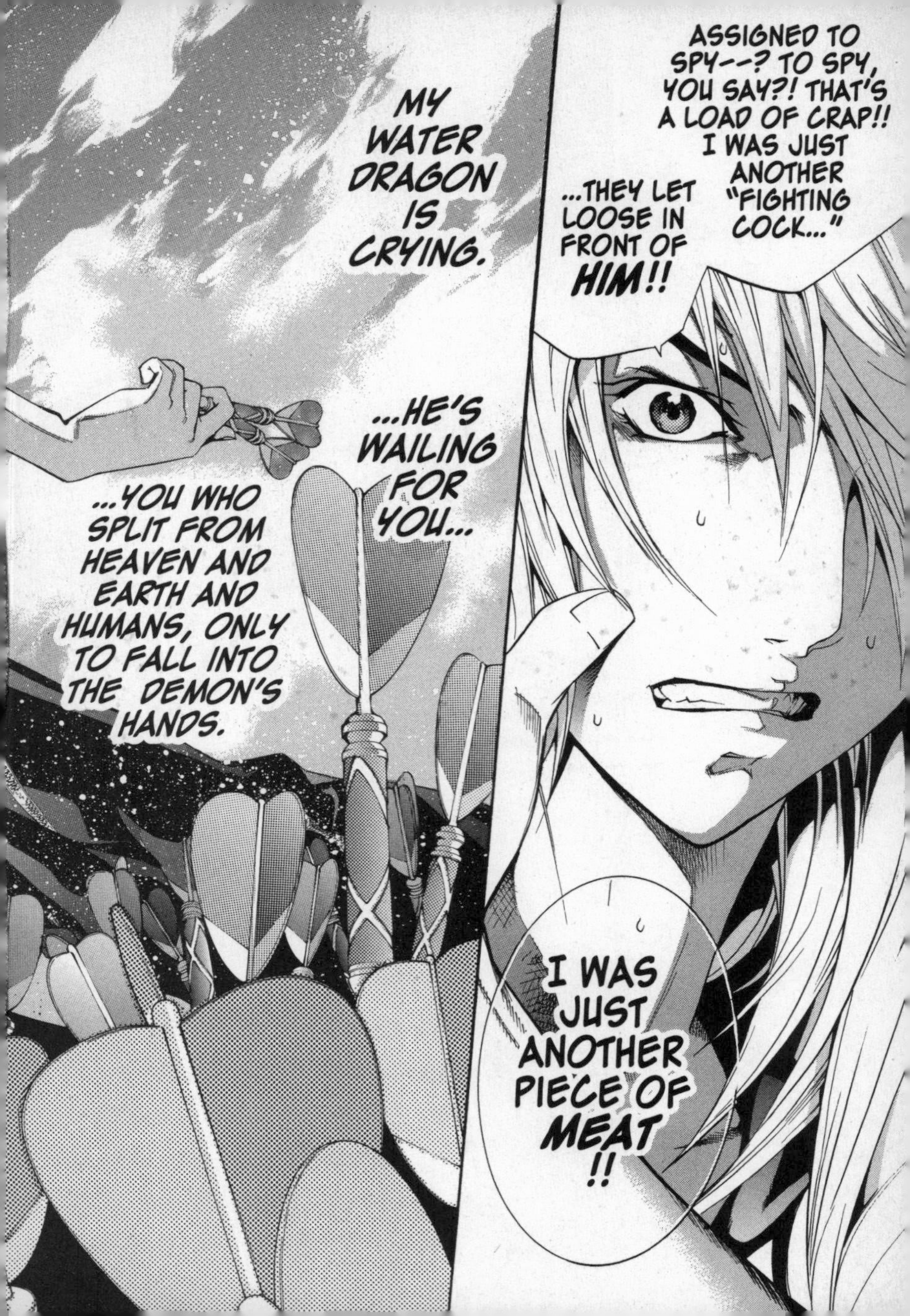
ASSIGNED TO SPY--? TO SPY, YOU SAY?! THAT'S A LOAD OF CRAP!! I WAS JUST ANOTHER "FIGHTING COCK..."
...THEY LET LOOSE IN FRONT OF HIM!!
I WAS JUST ANOTHER PIECE OF MEAT !!
MY WATER DRAGON IS CRYING.
...HE'S WAILING FOR YOU...
...YOU WHO SPLIT FROM HEAVEN AND EARTH AND HUMANS, ONLY TO FALL INTO THE DEMON'S HANDS.

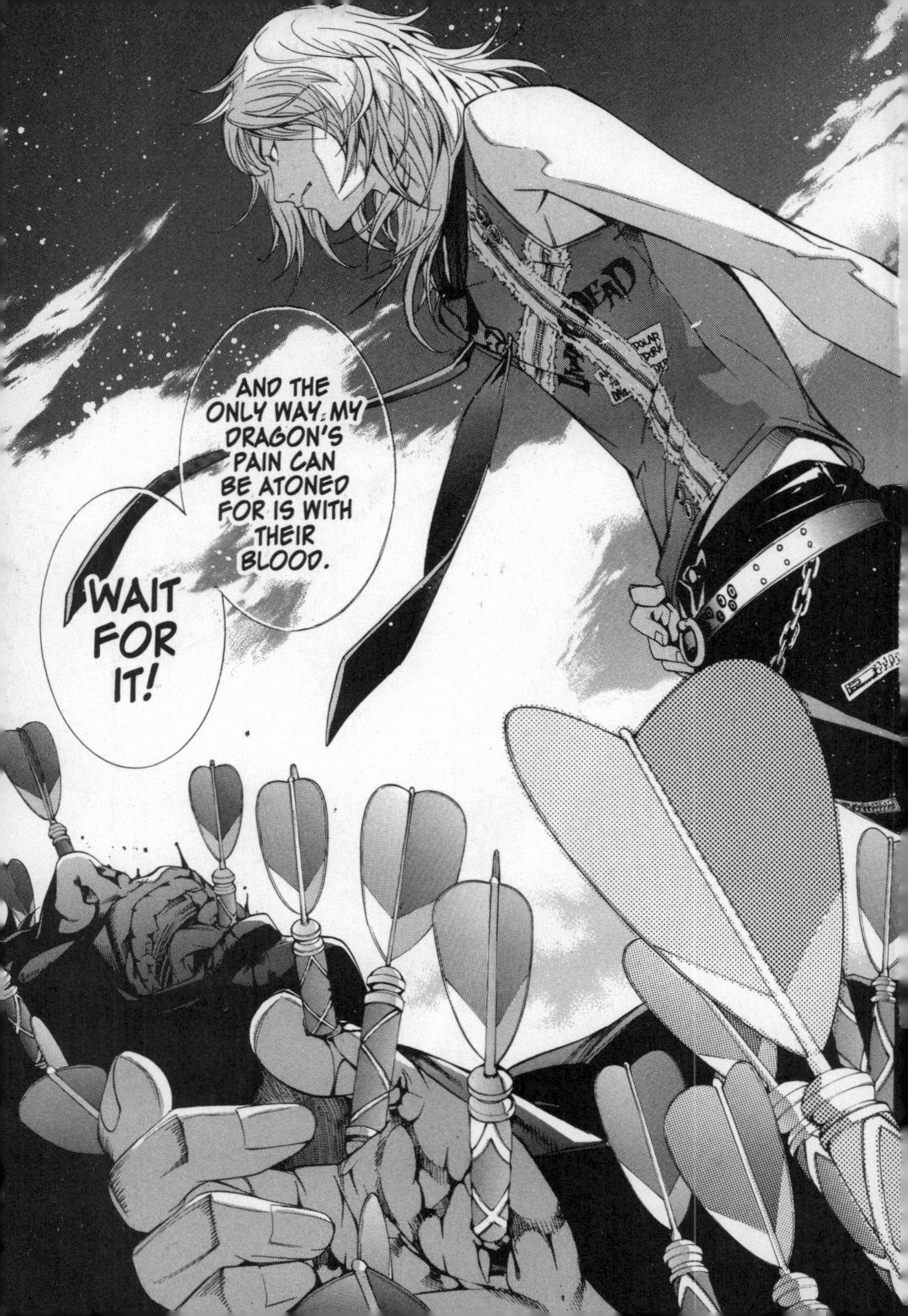
AND THE ONLY WAY MY DRAGON'S PAIN CAN BE ATONED FOR IS WITH THEIR BLOOD.
WAIT FOR IT!

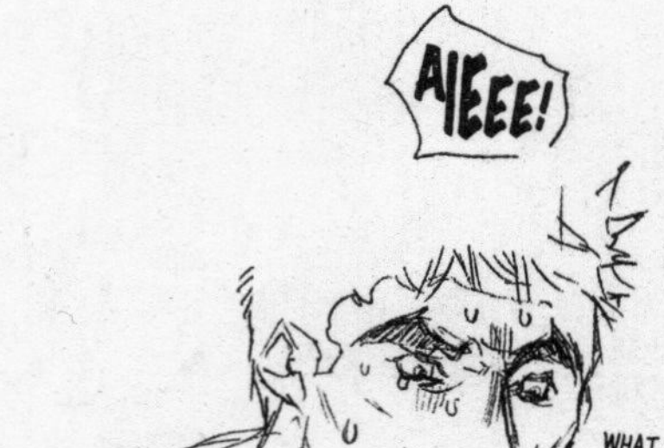
AIEEE!
WHAT DID I DO TO DESERVE THIS?!

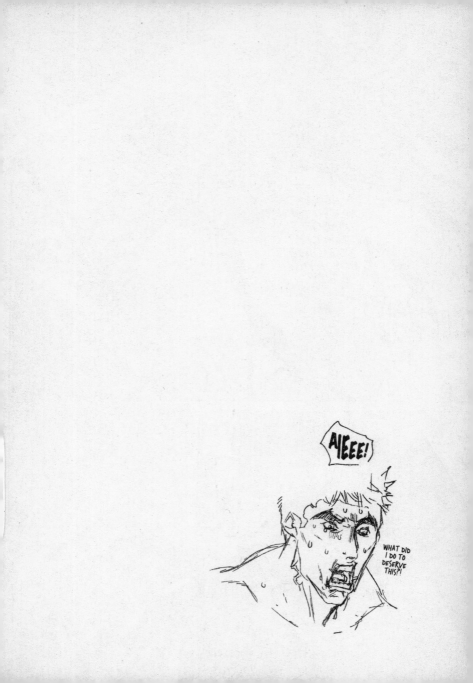

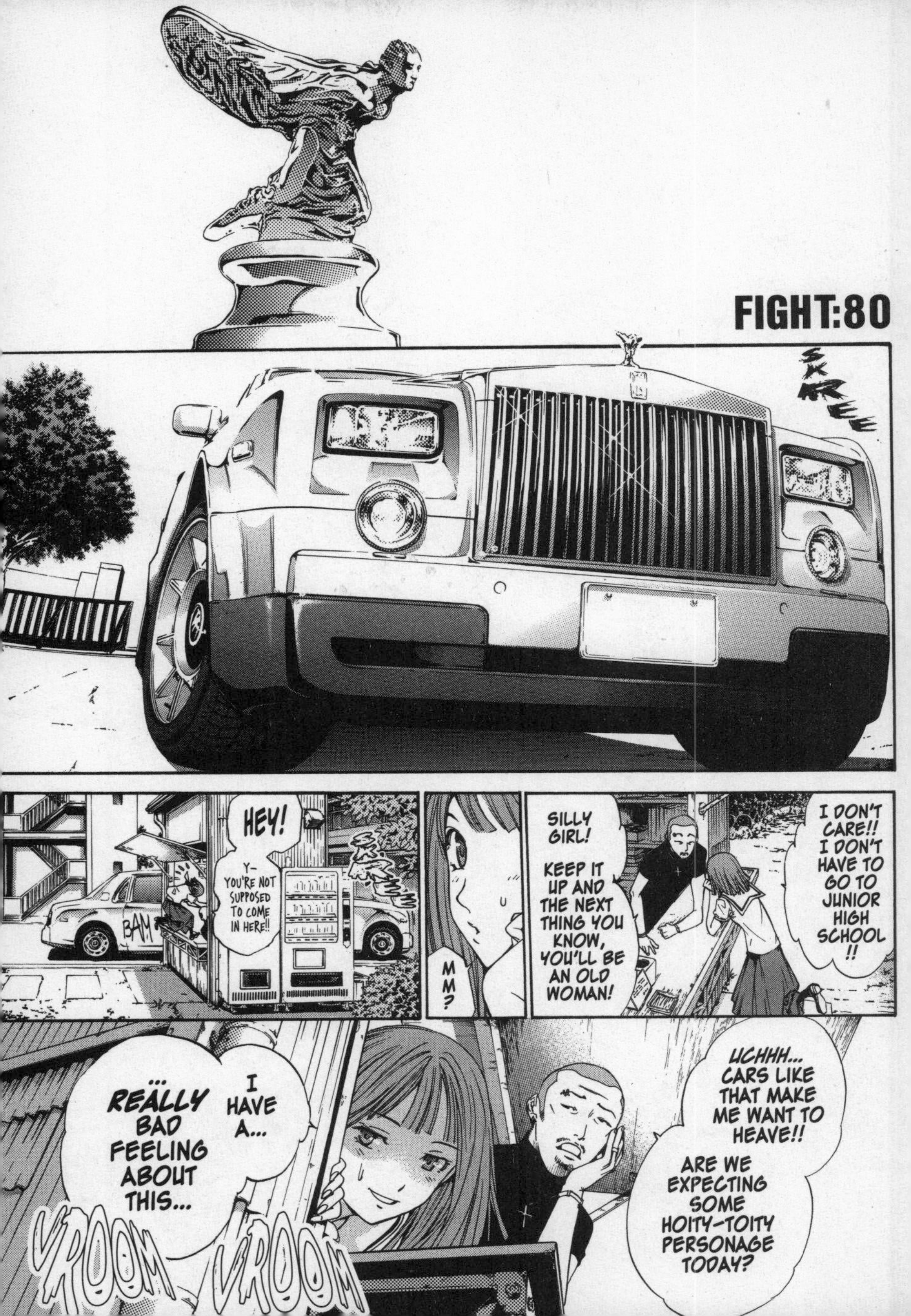
FIGHT:80
SKREE
I DON'T CARE!! I DON'T HAVE TO GO TO JUNIOR HIGH SCHOOL!!
SILLY GIRL! KEEP IT UP AND THE NEXT THING YOU KNOW, YOU'LL BE AN OLD WOMAN!
MM?
HEY!
Y-YOU'RE NOT SUPPOSED TO COME IN HERE!!
BAM
UCHHH... CARS LIKE THAT MAKE ME WANT TO HEAVE!!
ARE WE EXPECTING SOME HOITY-TOITY PERSONAGE TODAY?
I HAVE A...
...REALLY BAD FEELING ABOUT THIS...
VROOM VROOM

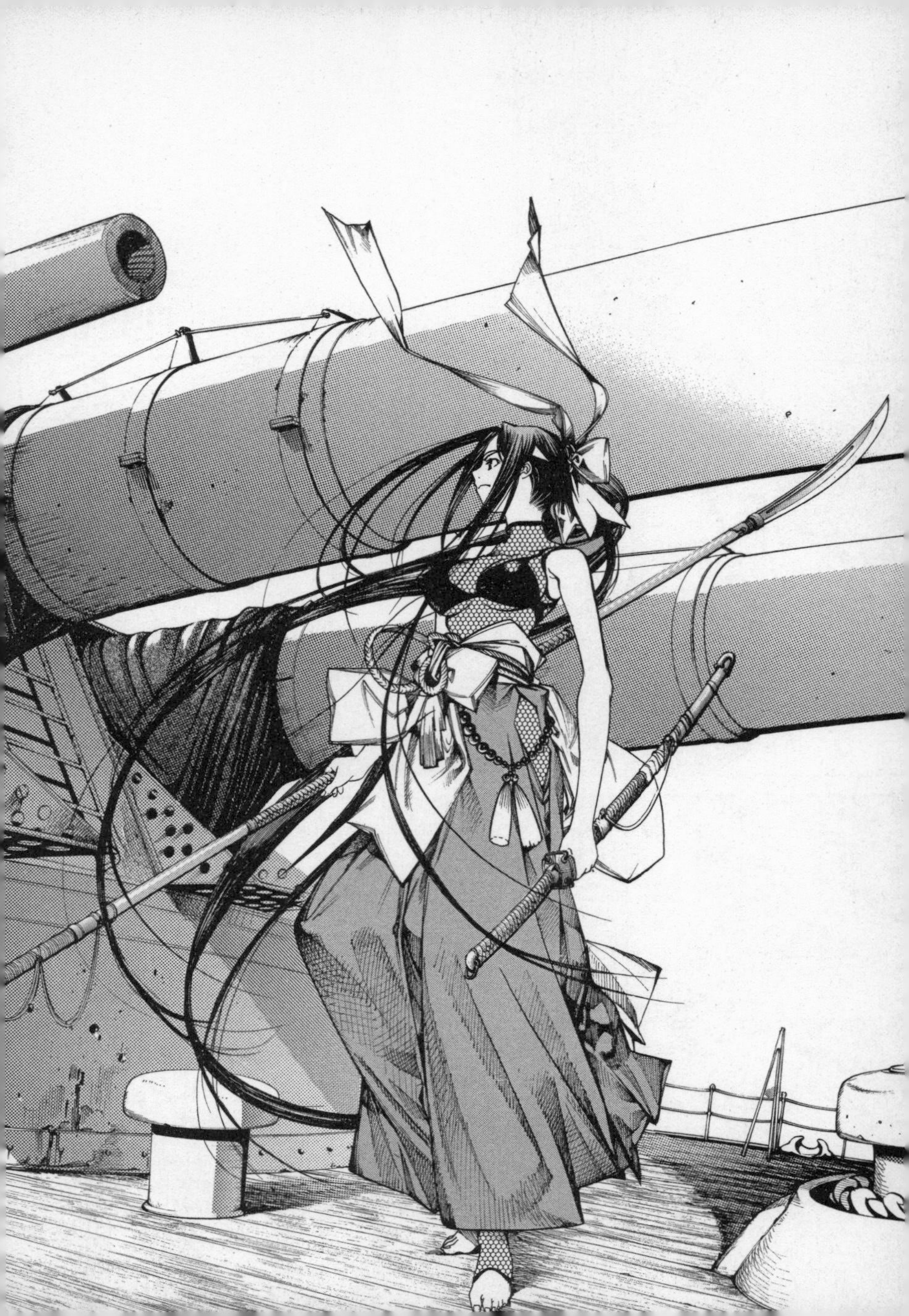

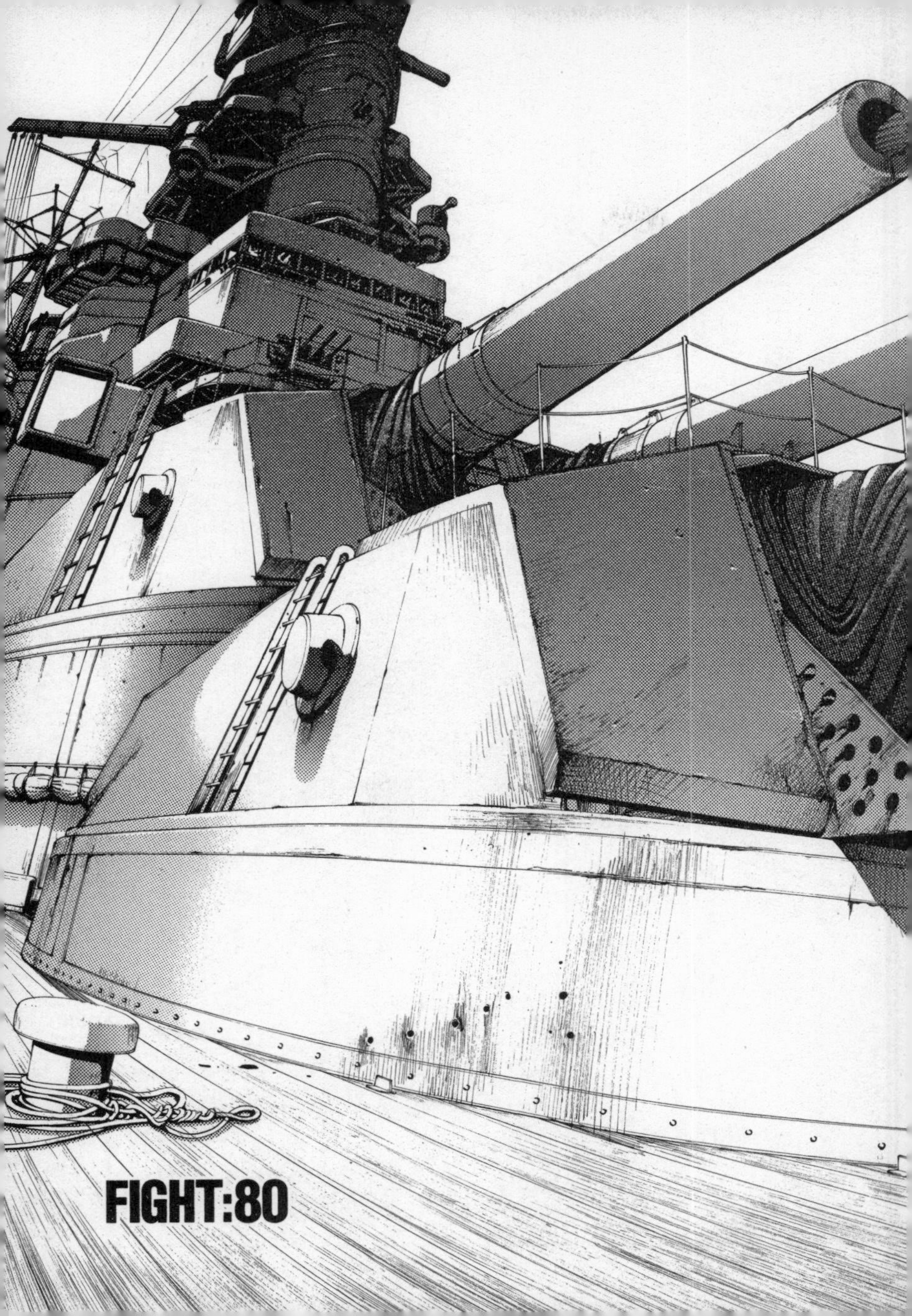
FIGHT:80

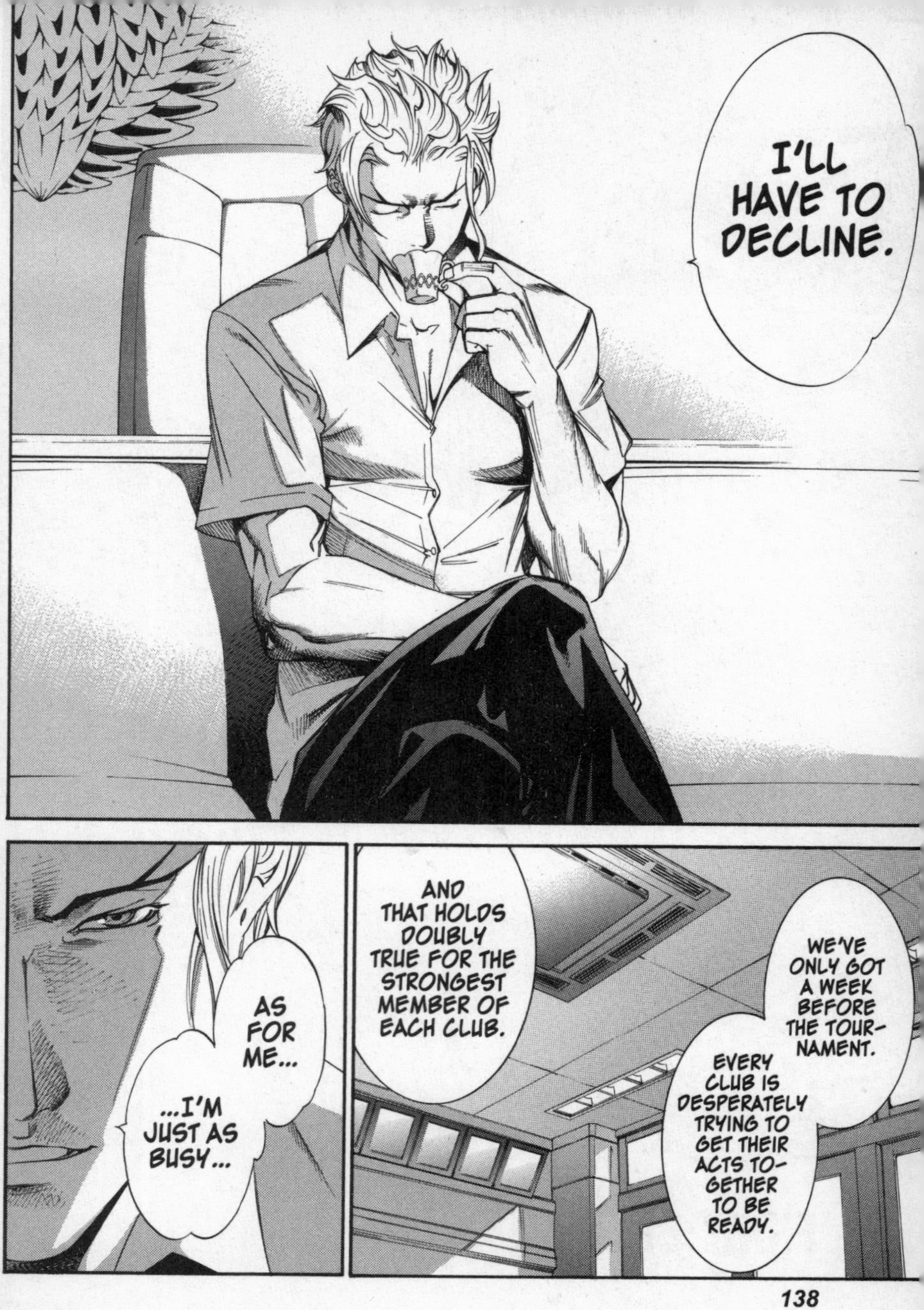
I'LL HAVE TO DECLINE.
WE'VE ONLY GOT A WEEK BEFORE THE TOUR-NAMENT.
EVERY CLUB IS DESPERATELY TRYING TO GET THEIR ACTS TO-GETHER TO BE READY.
AND THAT HOLDS DOUBLY TRUE FOR THE STRONGEST MEMBER OF EACH CLUB.
AS FOR ME...
...I'M JUST AS BUSY...

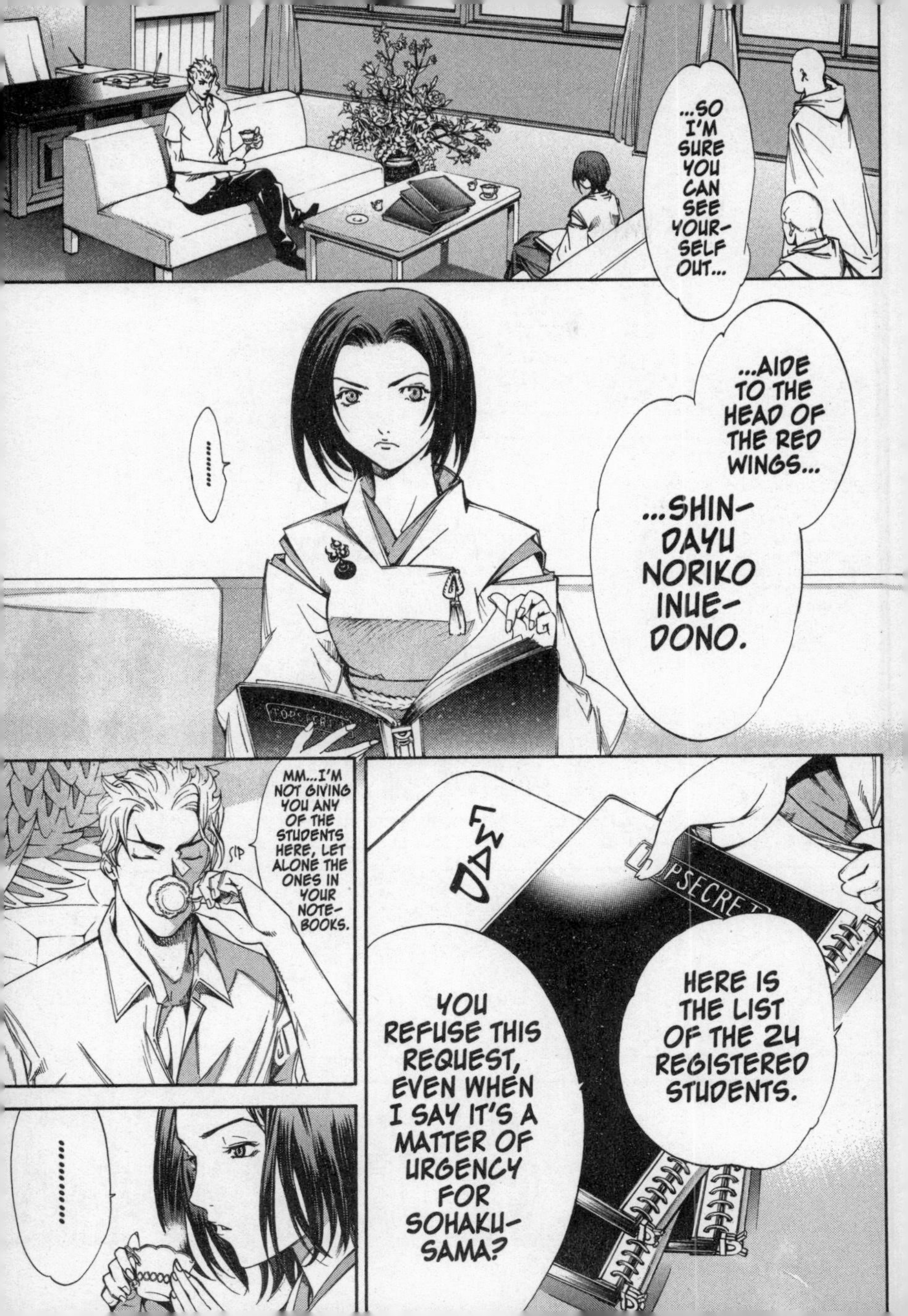
...SO I'M SURE YOU CAN SEE YOURSELF OUT...
...AIDE TO THE HEAD OF THE RED WINGS...
...SHIN-DAYU NORIKO INUE-DONO.
......
HERE IS THE LIST OF THE 24 REGISTERED STUDENTS.
YOU REFUSE THIS REQUEST, EVEN WHEN I SAY IT'S A MATTER OF URGENCY FOR SOHAKU-SAMA?
MM...I'M NOT GIVING YOU ANY OF THE STUDENTS HERE, LET ALONE THE ONES IN YOUR NOTE-BOOKS.
SIP
......

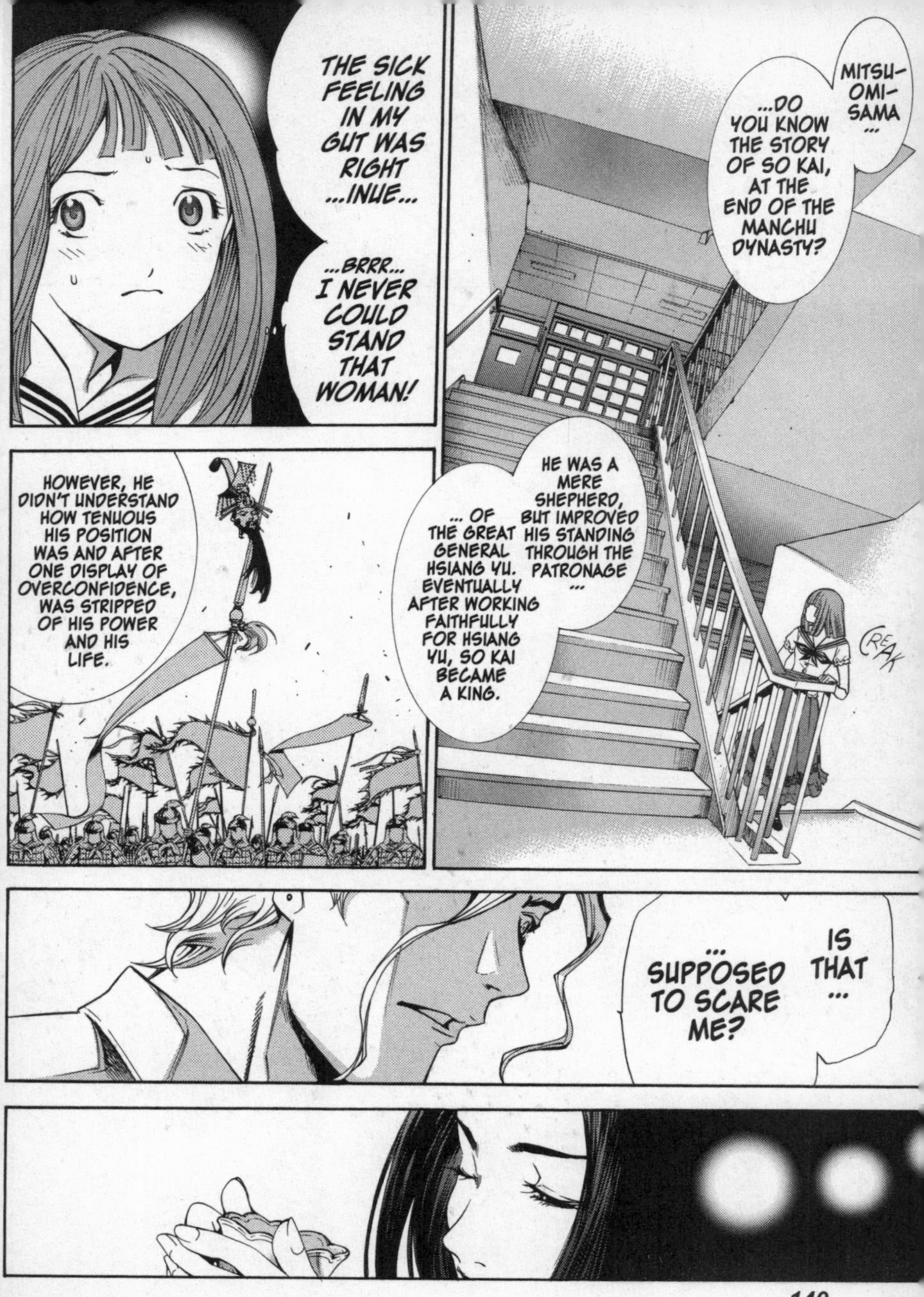
MITSU-OMI-SAMA...
...DO YOU KNOW THE STORY OF SO KAI, AT THE END OF THE MANCHU DYNASTY?
HE WAS A MERE SHEPHERD, BUT IMPROVED HIS STANDING THROUGH THE PATRONAGE...
... OF THE GREAT GENERAL HSIANG YU. EVENTUALLY AFTER WORKING FAITHFULLY FOR HSIANG YU, SO KAI BECAME A KING.
CREAK
THE SICK FEELING IN MY GUT WAS RIGHT ...INUE...
...BRRR... I NEVER COULD STAND THAT WOMAN!
HOWEVER, HE DIDN'T UNDERSTAND HOW TENUOUS HIS POSITION WAS AND AFTER ONE DISPLAY OF OVERCONFIDENCE, WAS STRIPPED OF HIS POWER AND HIS LIFE.
IS THAT ...
... SUPPOSED TO SCARE ME?

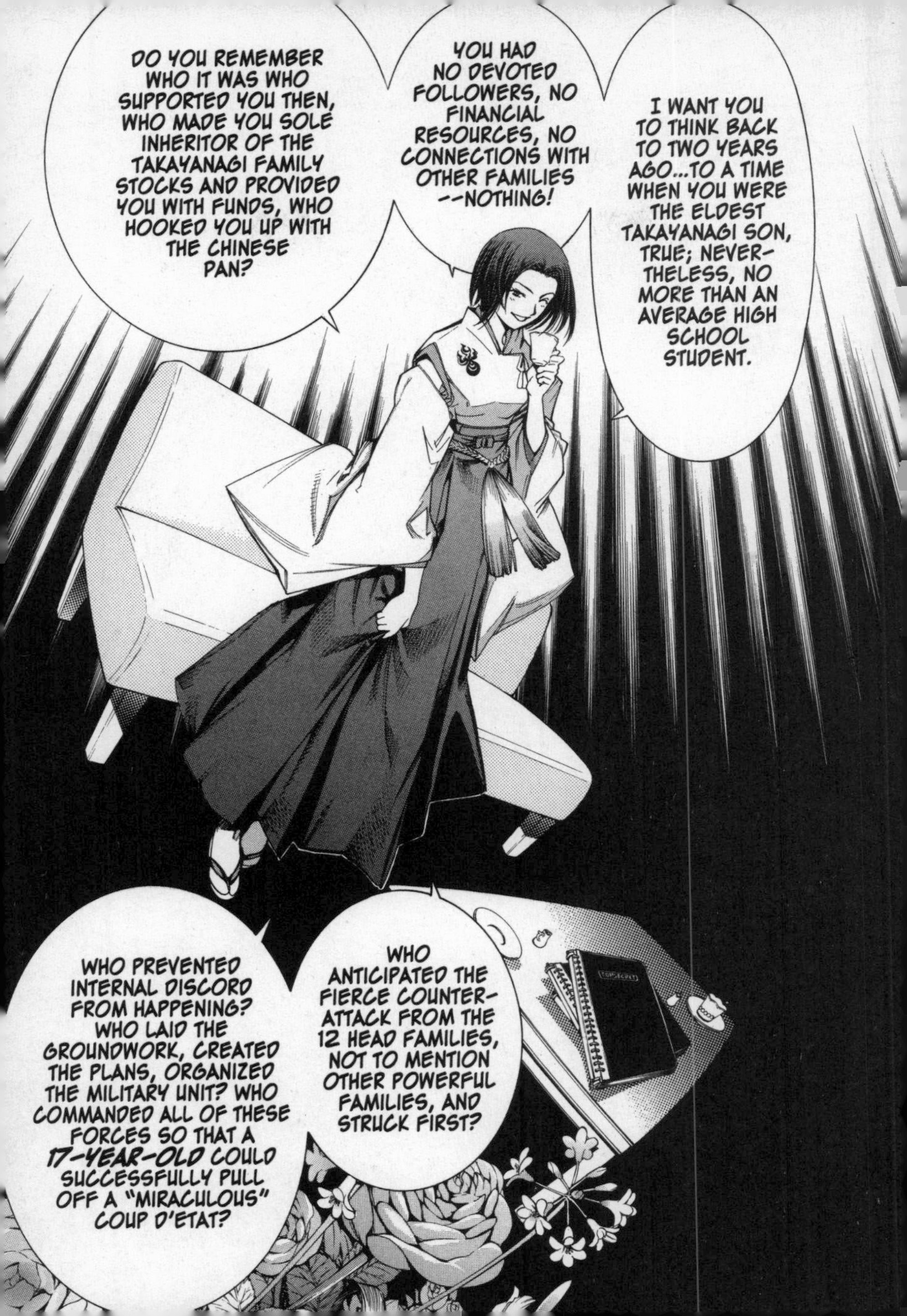
I WANT YOU TO THINK BACK TO TWO YEARS AGO...TO A TIME WHEN YOU WERE THE ELDEST TAKAYANAGI SON, TRUE; NEVER-THELESS, NO MORE THAN AN AVERAGE HIGH SCHOOL STUDENT.
YOU HAD NO DEVOTED FOLLOWERS, NO FINANCIAL RESOURCES, NO CONNECTIONS WITH OTHER FAMILIES --NOTHING!
DO YOU REMEMBER WHO IT WAS WHO SUPPORTED YOU THEN, WHO MADE YOU SOLE INHERITOR OF THE TAKAYANAGI FAMILY STOCKS AND PROVIDED YOU WITH FUNDS, WHO HOOKED YOU UP WITH THE CHINESE PAN?
WHO ANTICIPATED THE FIERCE COUNTER-ATTACK FROM THE 12 HEAD FAMILIES, NOT TO MENTION OTHER POWERFUL FAMILIES, AND STRUCK FIRST?
WHO PREVENTED INTERNAL DISCORD FROM HAPPENING? WHO LAID THE GROUNDWORK, CREATED THE PLANS, ORGANIZED THE MILITARY UNIT? WHO COMMANDED ALL OF THESE FORCES SO THAT A 17-YEAR-OLD COULD SUCCESSFULLY PULL OFF A "MIRACULOUS" COUP D'ETAT?

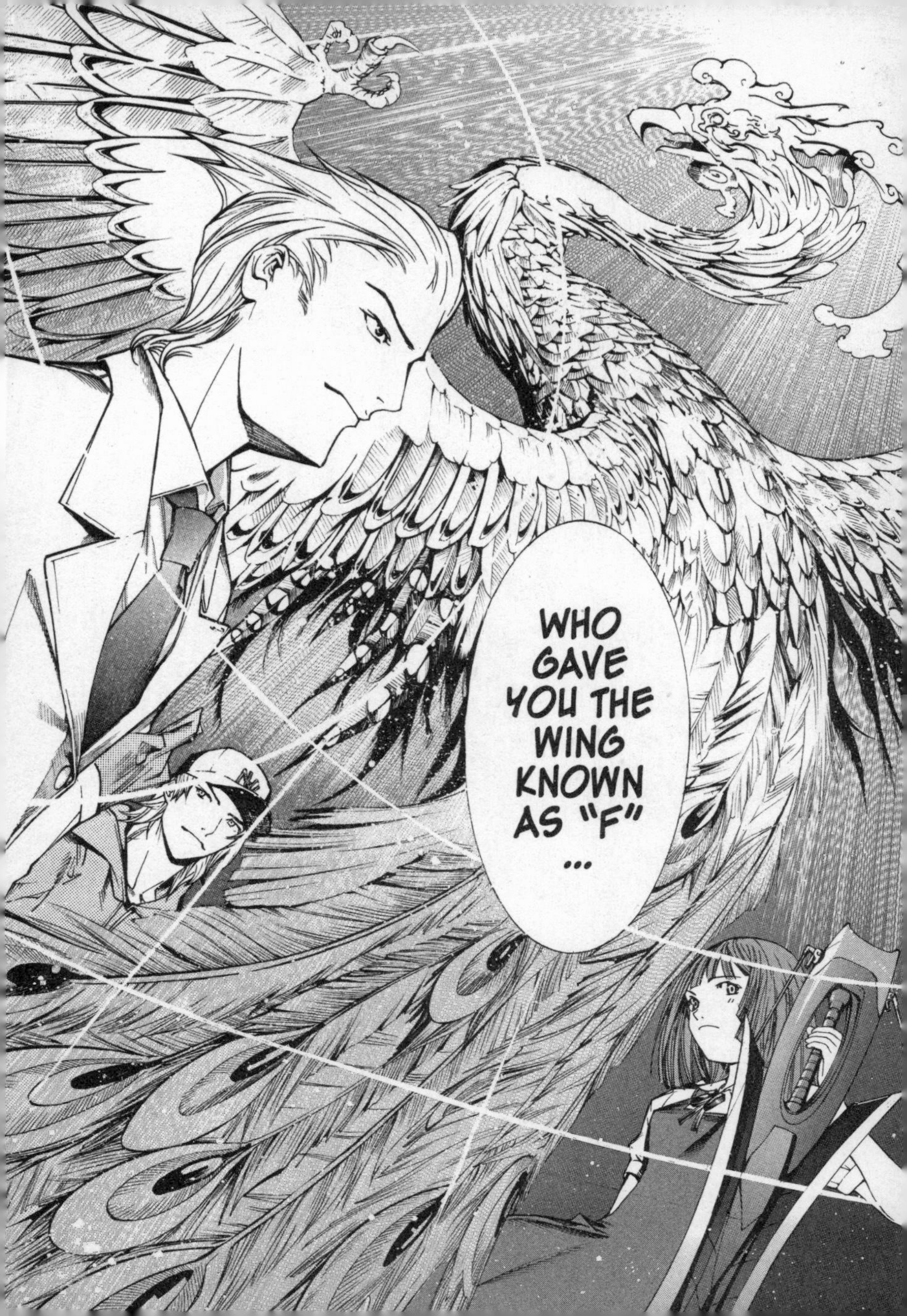
WHO GAVE YOU THE WING KNOWN AS "F" ...

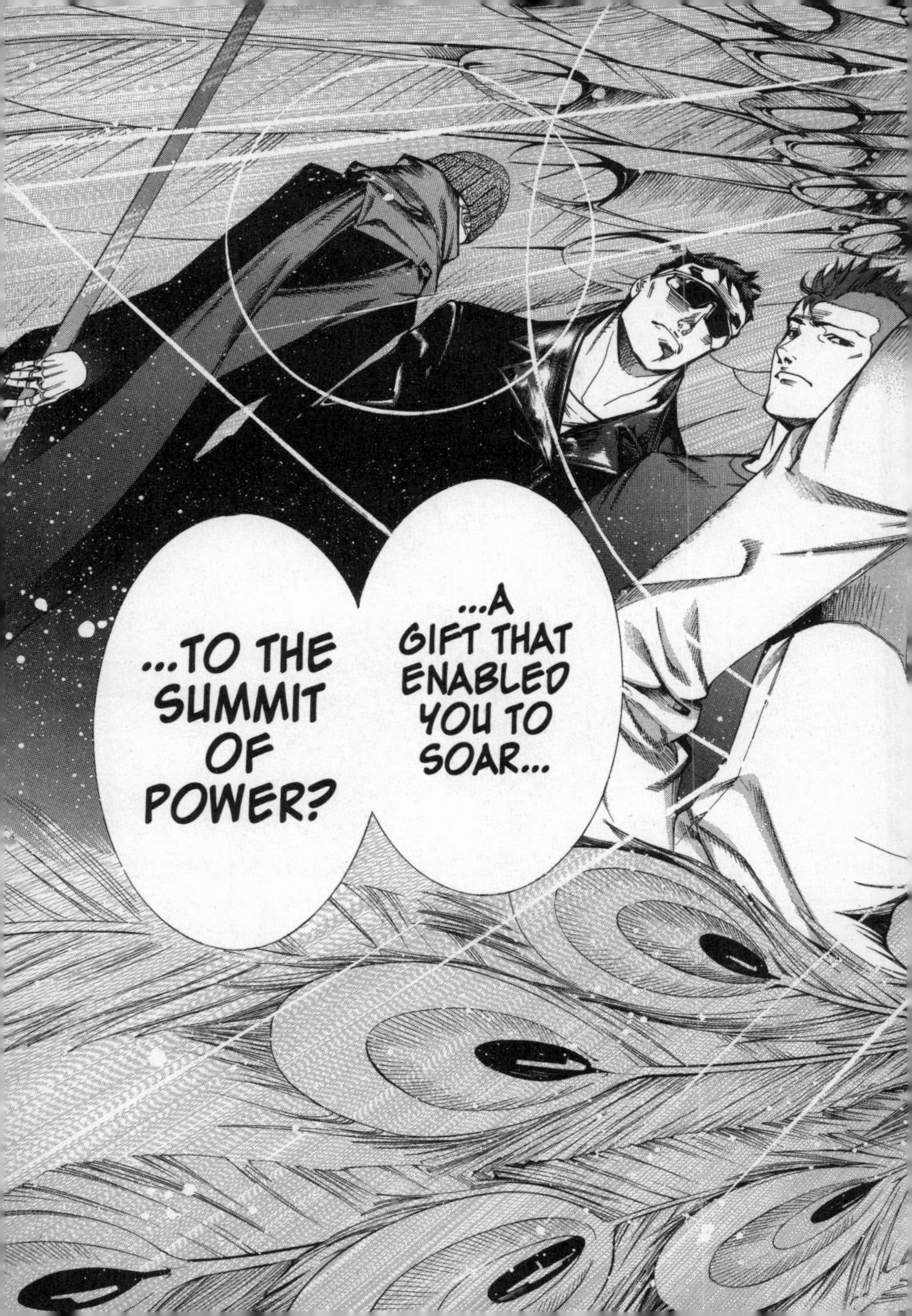
...A GIFT THAT ENABLED YOU TO SOAR...
...TO THE SUMMIT OF POWER?

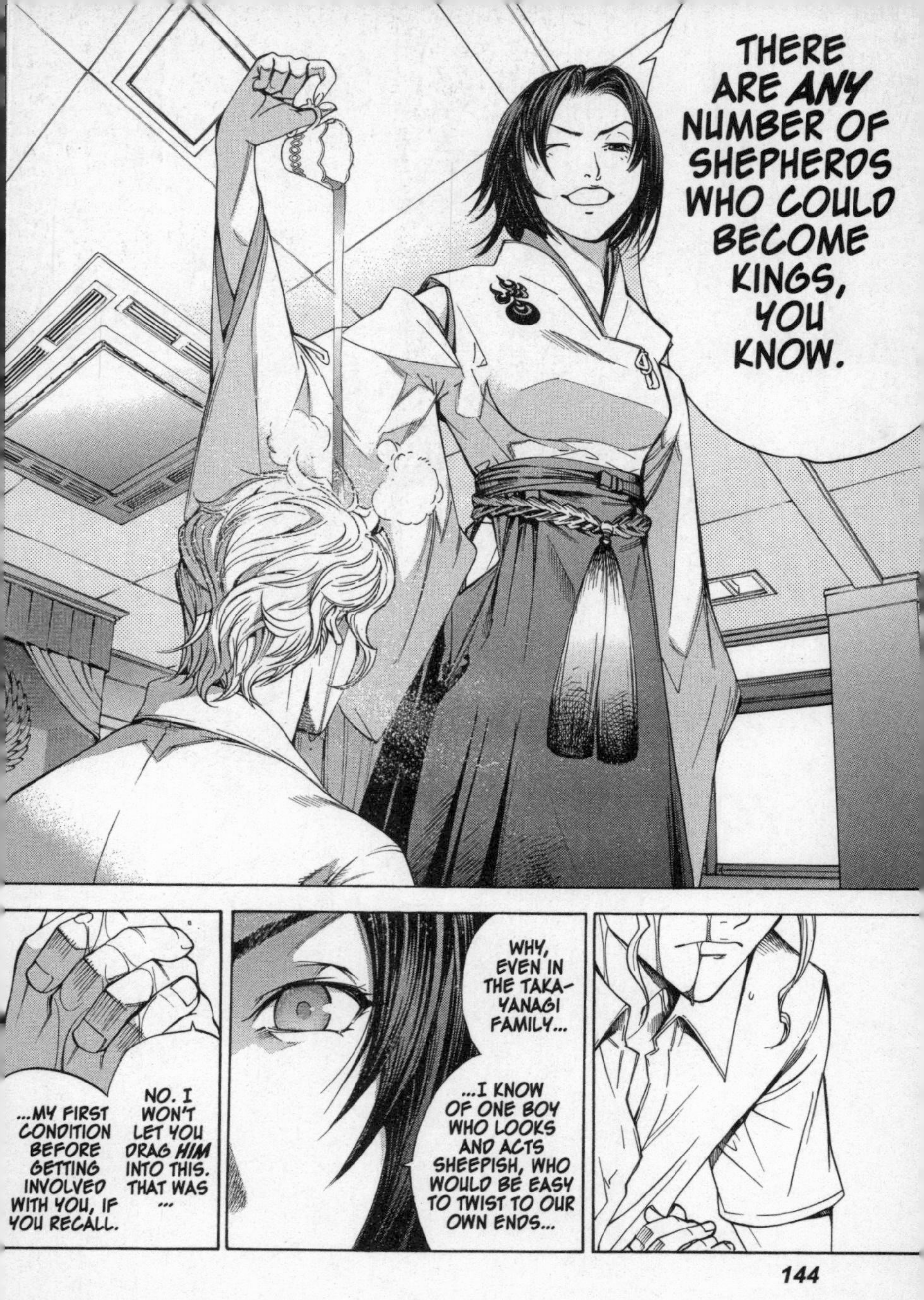
THERE ARE **ANY** NUMBER OF SHEPHERDS WHO COULD BECOME KINGS, YOU KNOW.
WHY, EVEN IN THE TAKA-YANAGI FAMILY...
...I KNOW OF ONE BOY WHO LOOKS AND ACTS SHEEPISH, WHO WOULD BE EASY TO TWIST TO OUR OWN ENDS...
NO. I WON'T LET YOU DRAG **HIM** INTO THIS. THAT WAS ...
...MY FIRST CONDITION BEFORE GETTING INVOLVED WITH YOU, IF YOU RECALL.

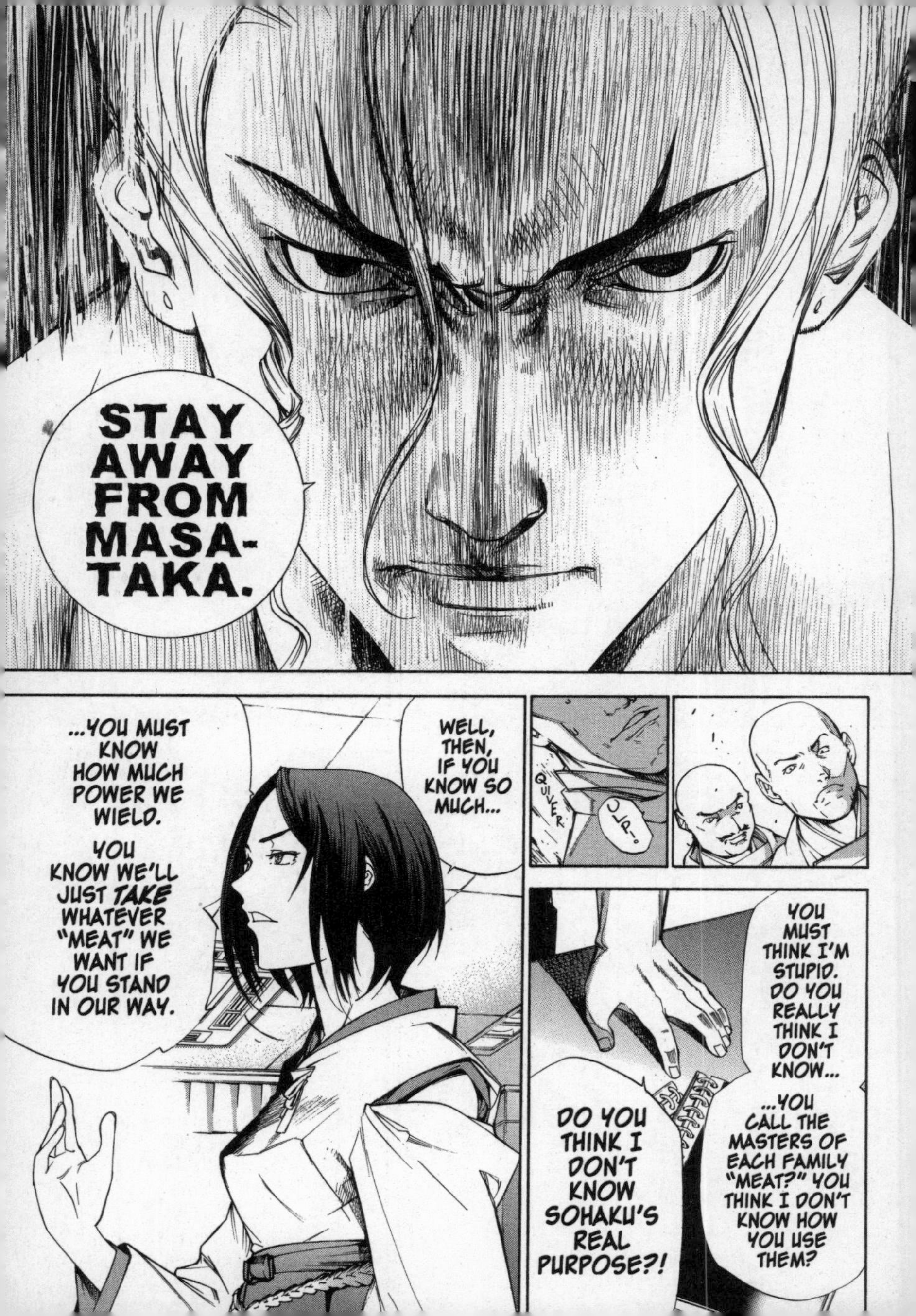
STAY AWAY FROM MASA-TAKA.
QUIVER
ULP!
YOU MUST THINK I'M STUPID. DO YOU REALLY THINK I DON'T KNOW...
...YOU CALL THE MASTERS OF EACH FAMILY "MEAT?" YOU THINK I DON'T KNOW HOW YOU USE THEM?
DO YOU THINK I DON'T KNOW SOHAKU'S REAL PURPOSE?!
WELL, THEN, IF YOU KNOW SO MUCH...
...YOU MUST KNOW HOW MUCH POWER WE WIELD.
YOU KNOW WE'LL JUST *TAKE* WHATEVER "MEAT" WE WANT IF YOU STAND IN OUR WAY.

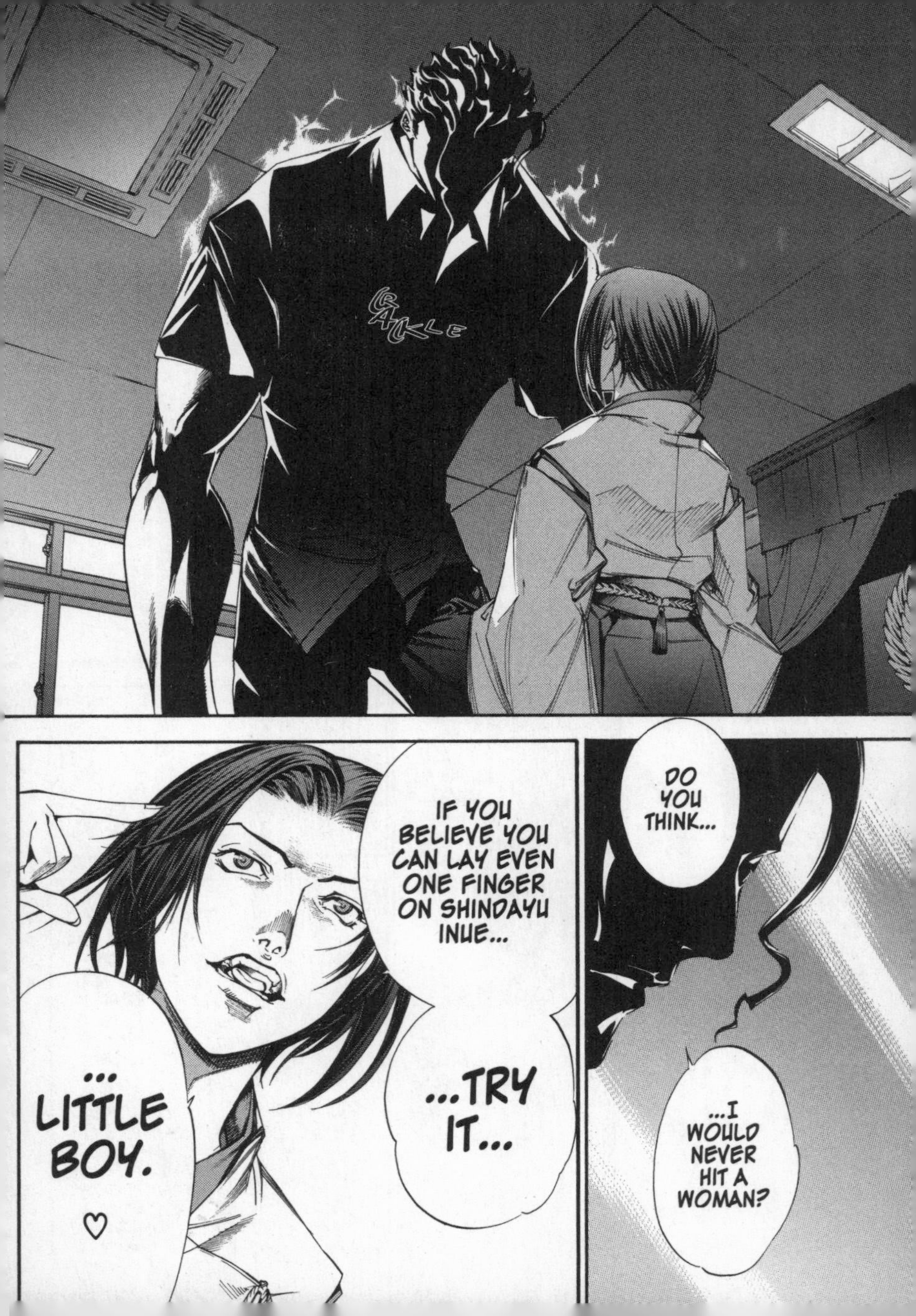
CRACKLE
DO YOU THINK...
...I WOULD NEVER HIT A WOMAN?
IF YOU BELIEVE YOU CAN LAY EVEN ONE FINGER ON SHINDAYU INUE...
...TRY IT...
... LITTLE BOY. ♡

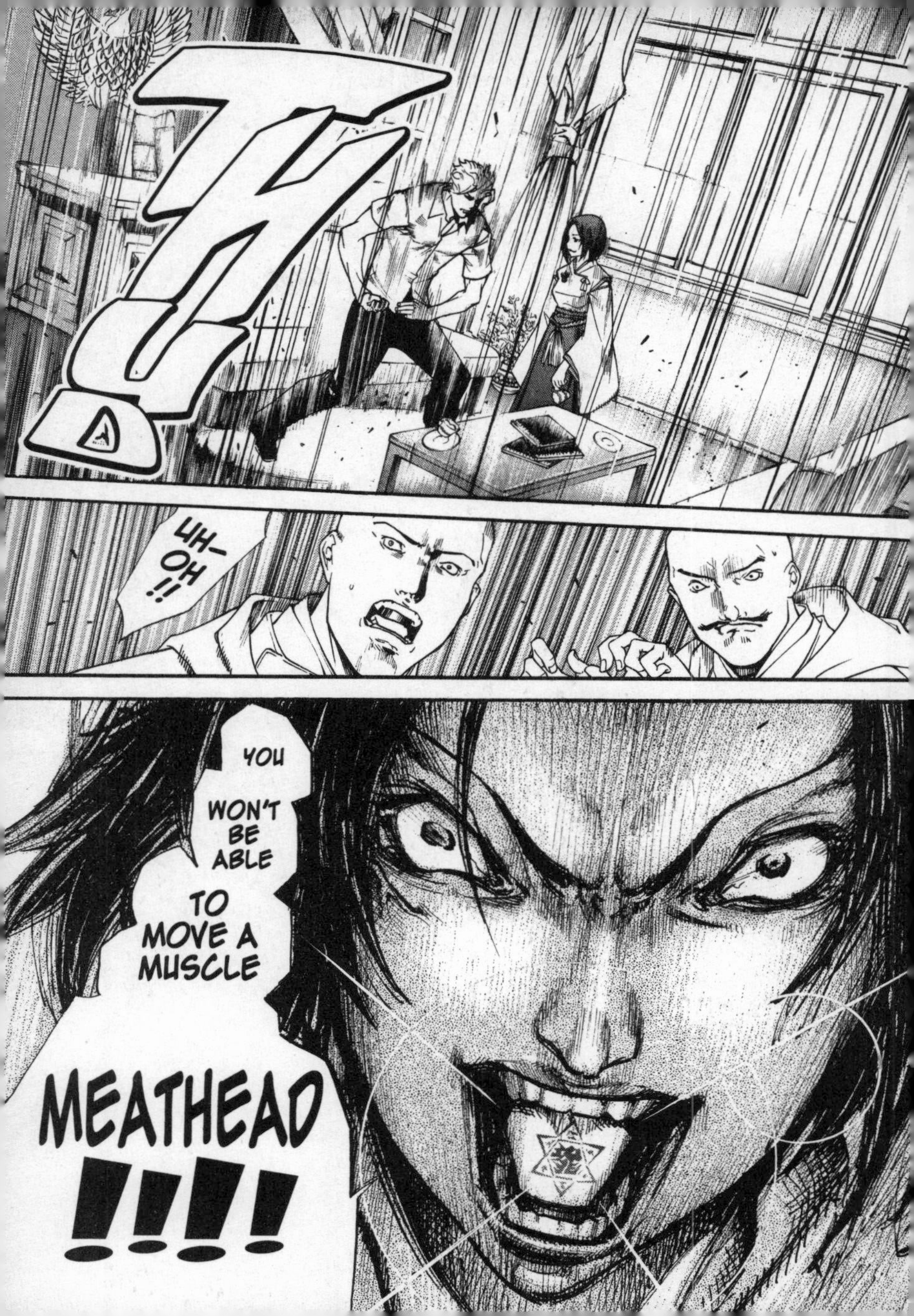
ZU
UH-OH!!
YOU WON'T BE ABLE TO MOVE A MUSCLE
MEATHEAD!!!!

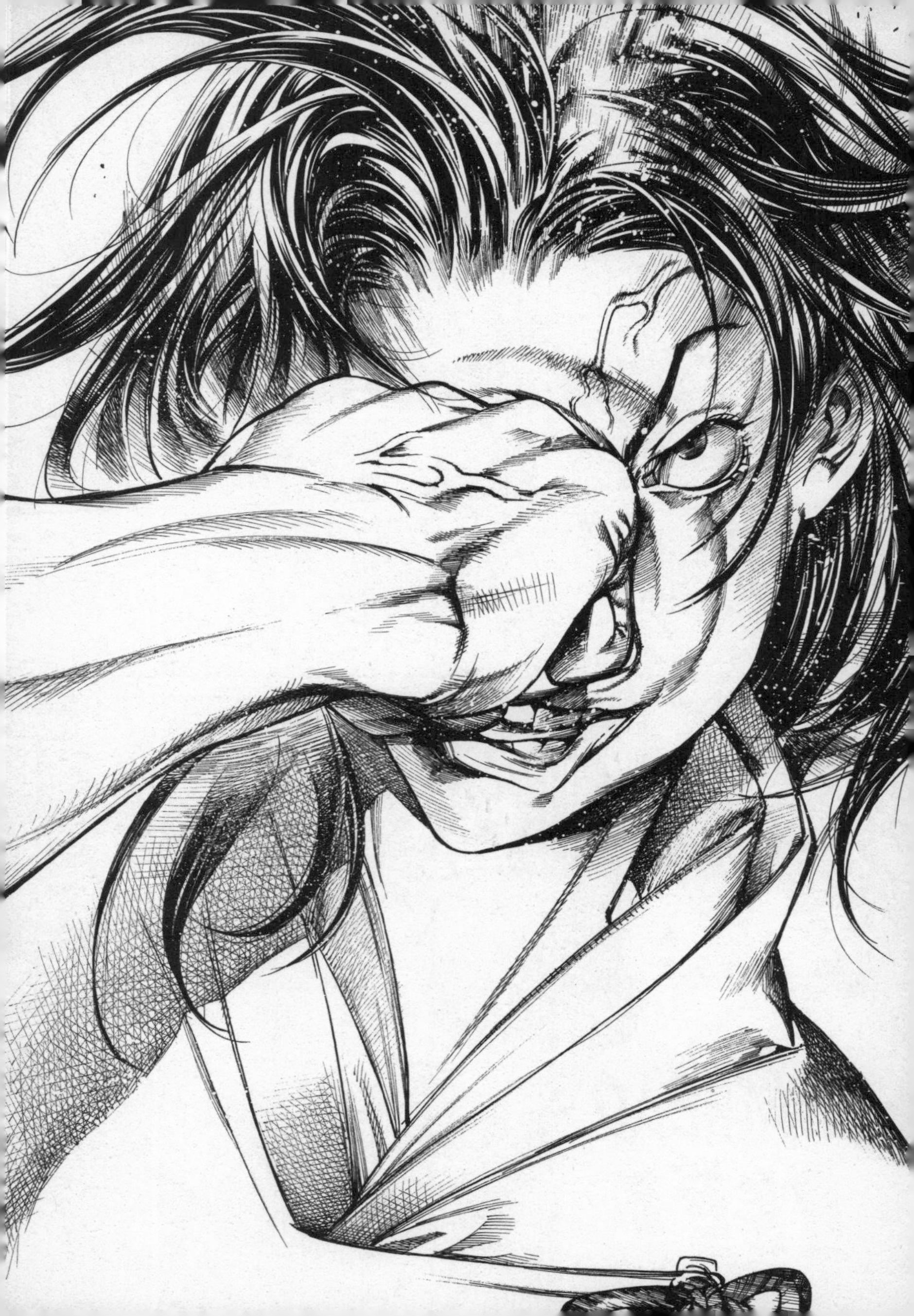

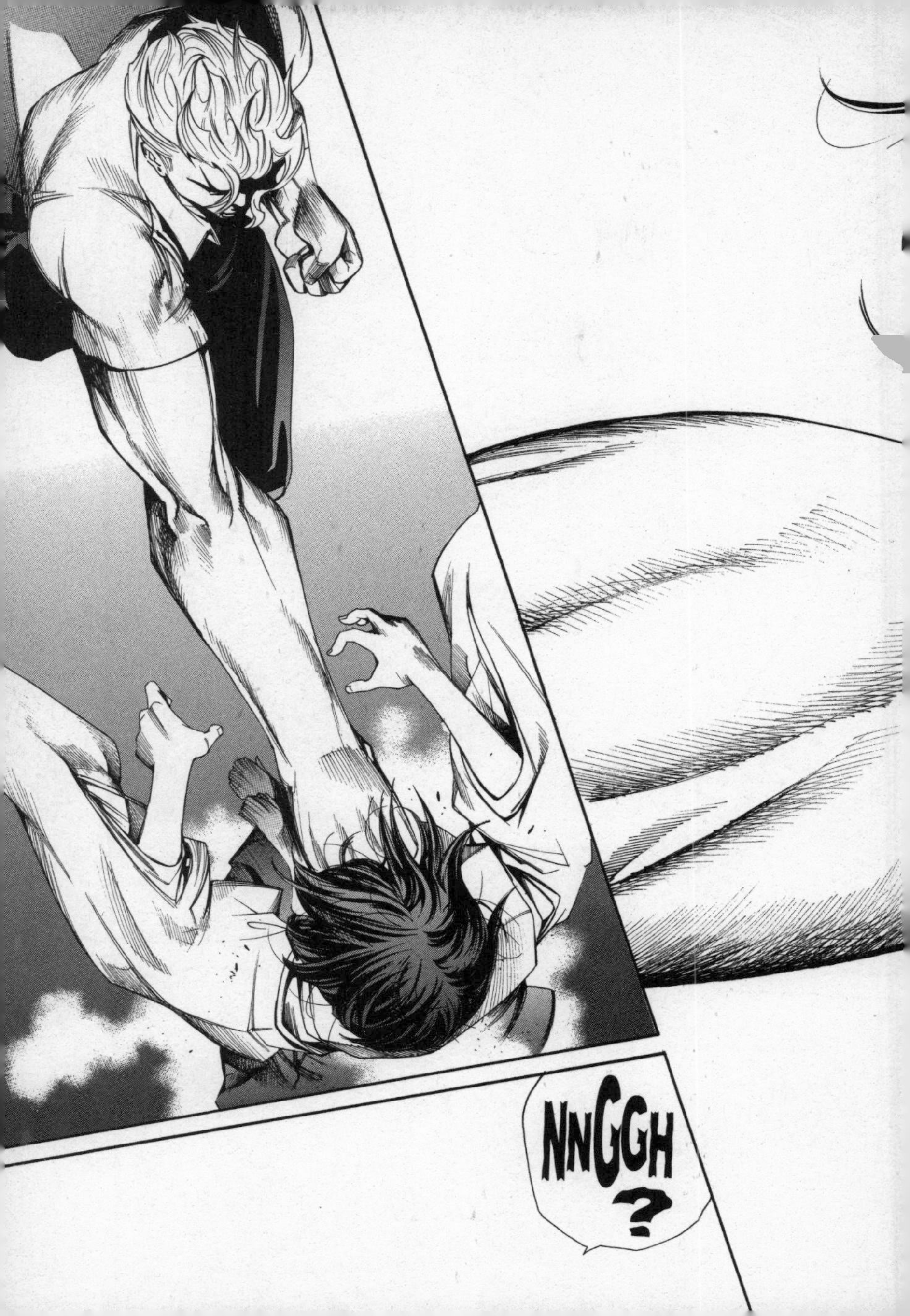
NNGGH ?

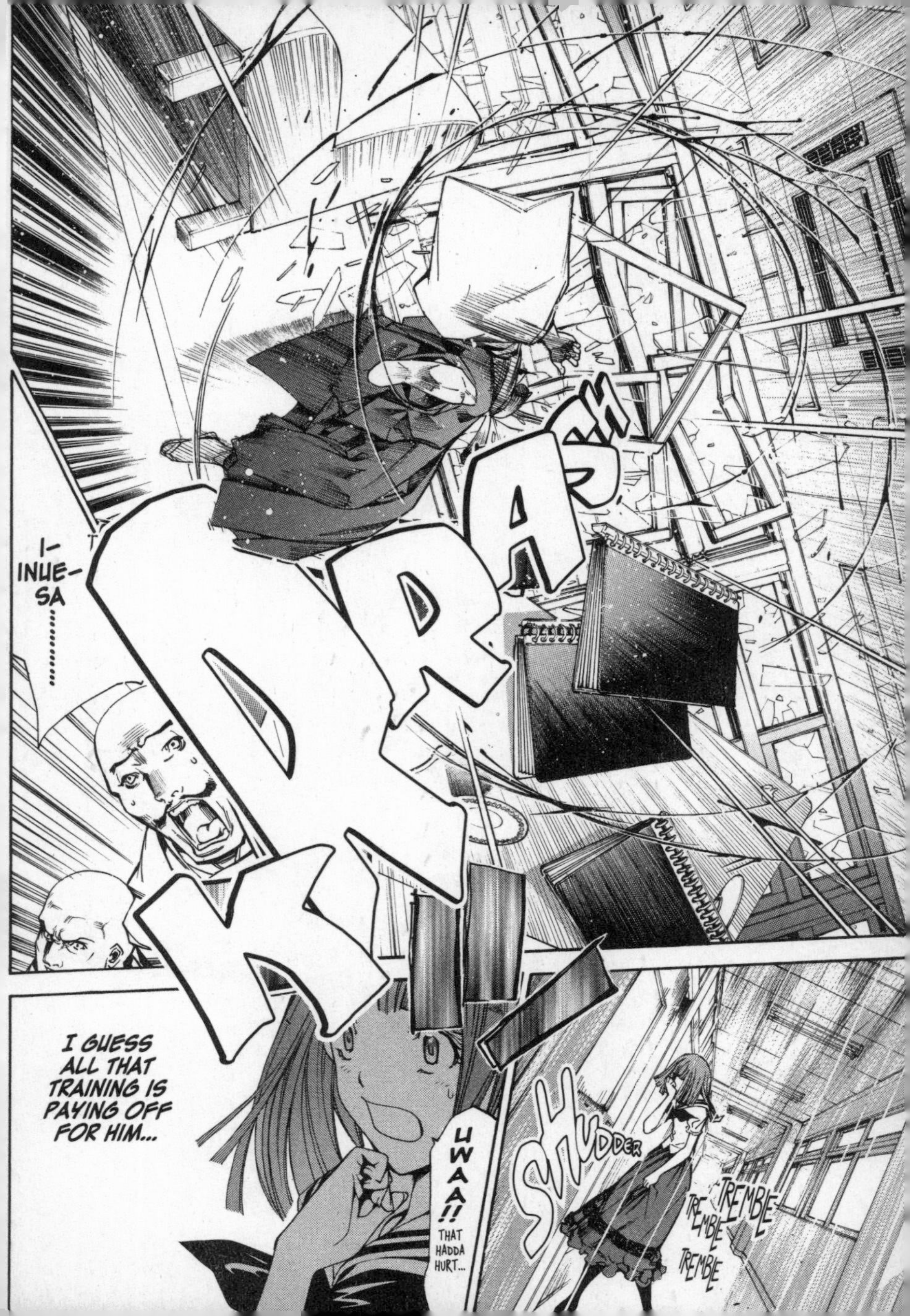
I-INUE-SA......
SHUDDER
TREMBLE
TREMBLE
TREMBLE
UWAAA!!
THAT HADDA HURT...
I GUESS ALL THAT TRAINING IS PAYING OFF FOR HIM...

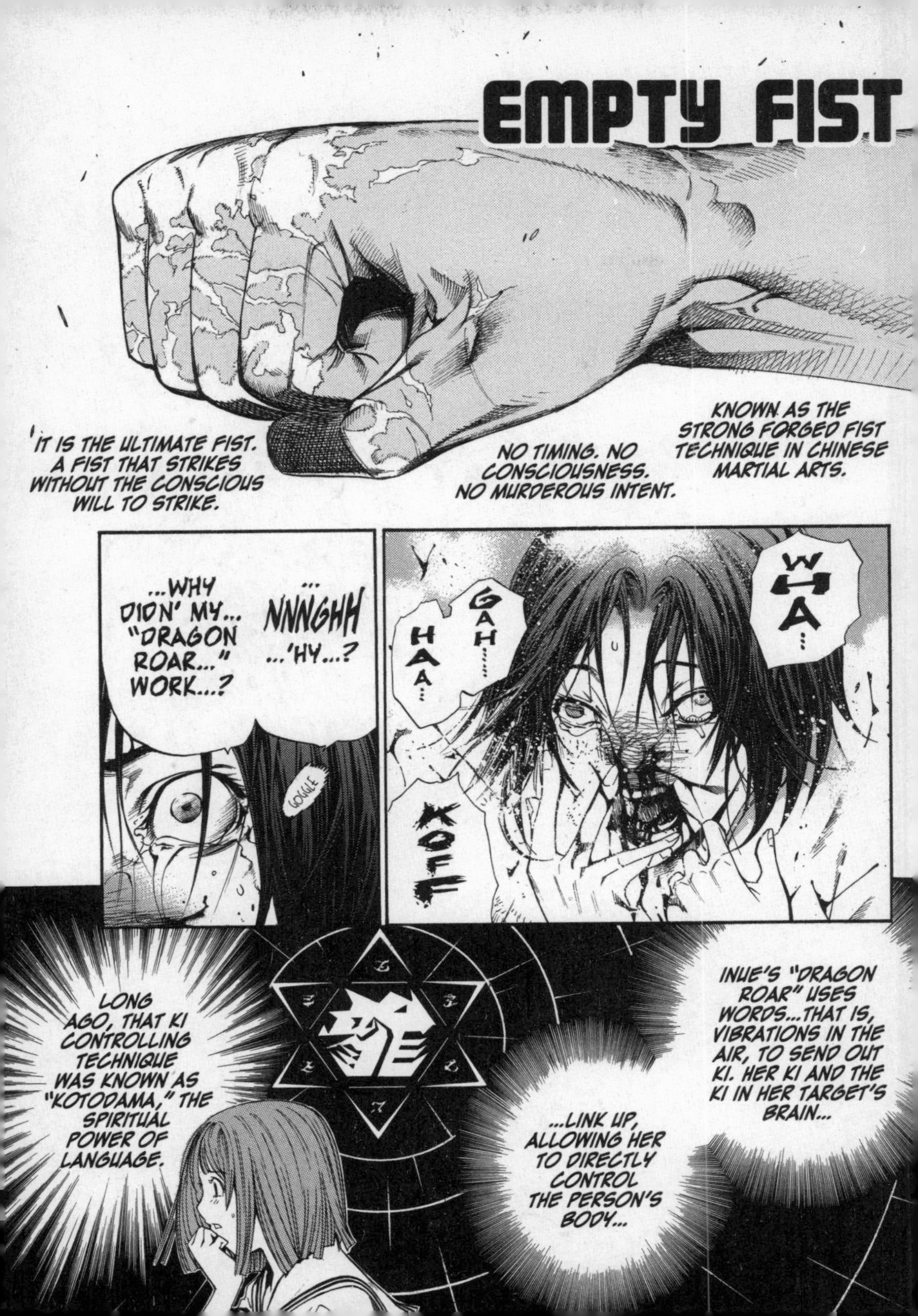
EMPTY FIST
KNOWN AS THE STRONG FORGED FIST TECHNIQUE IN CHINESE MARTIAL ARTS.
NO TIMING. NO CONSCIOUSNESS. NO MURDEROUS INTENT.
'IT IS THE ULTIMATE FIST. A FIST THAT STRIKES WITHOUT THE CONSCIOUS WILL TO STRIKE.
WHA...
GAH...
HAA...
KOFF
... NNNGHH ...'HY...?
...WHY DIDN' MY... "DRAGON ROAR..." WORK...?
GOGGLE
INUE'S "DRAGON ROAR" USES WORDS...THAT IS, VIBRATIONS IN THE AIR, TO SEND OUT KI. HER KI AND THE KI IN HER TARGET'S BRAIN...
...LINK UP, ALLOWING HER TO DIRECTLY CONTROL THE PERSON'S BODY...
LONG AGO, THAT KI CONTROLLING TECHNIQUE WAS KNOWN AS "KOTODAMA," THE SPIRITUAL POWER OF LANGUAGE.

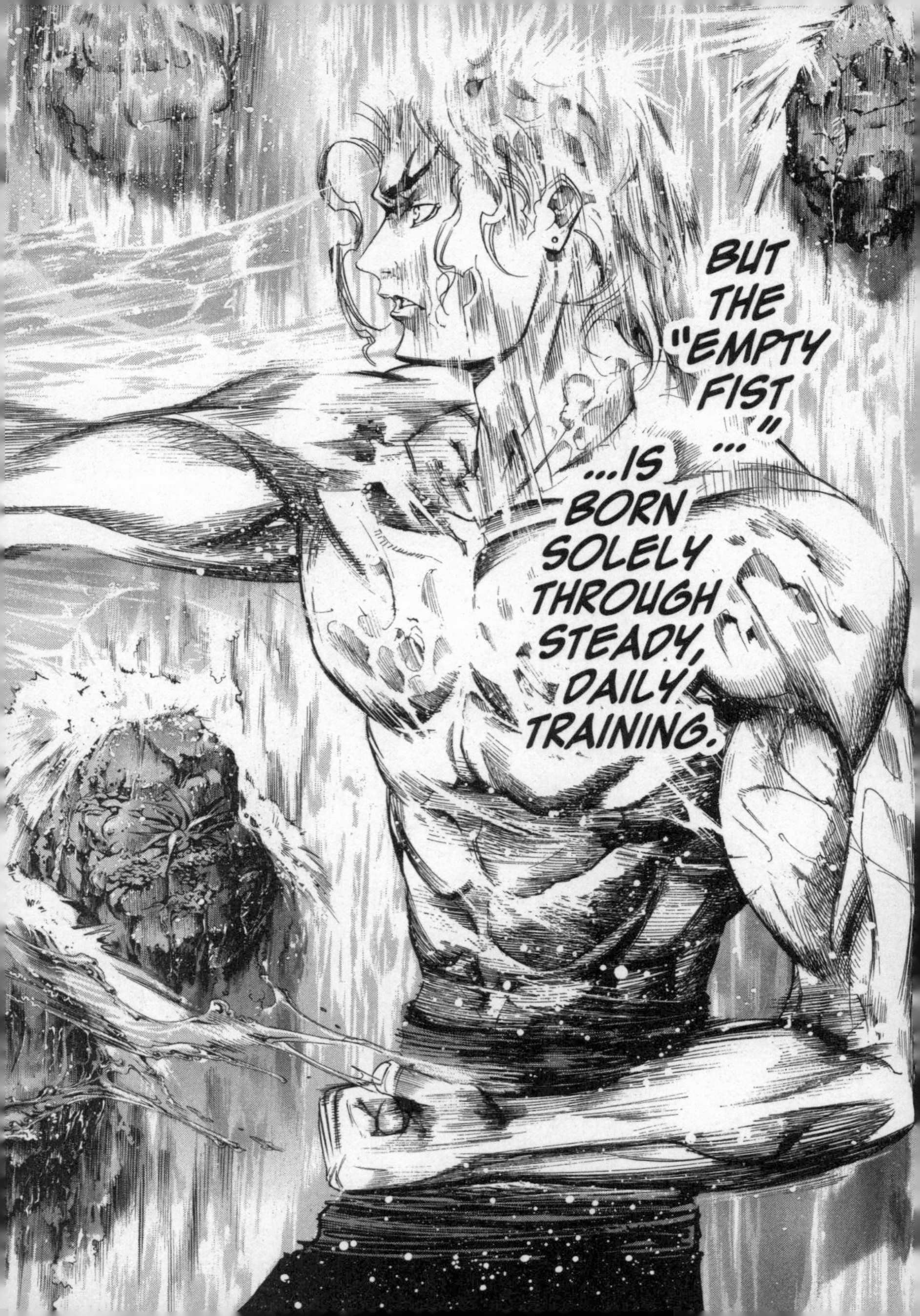
BUT THE "EMPTY FIST"...
...IS BORN SOLELY THROUGH STEADY, DAILY TRAINING.

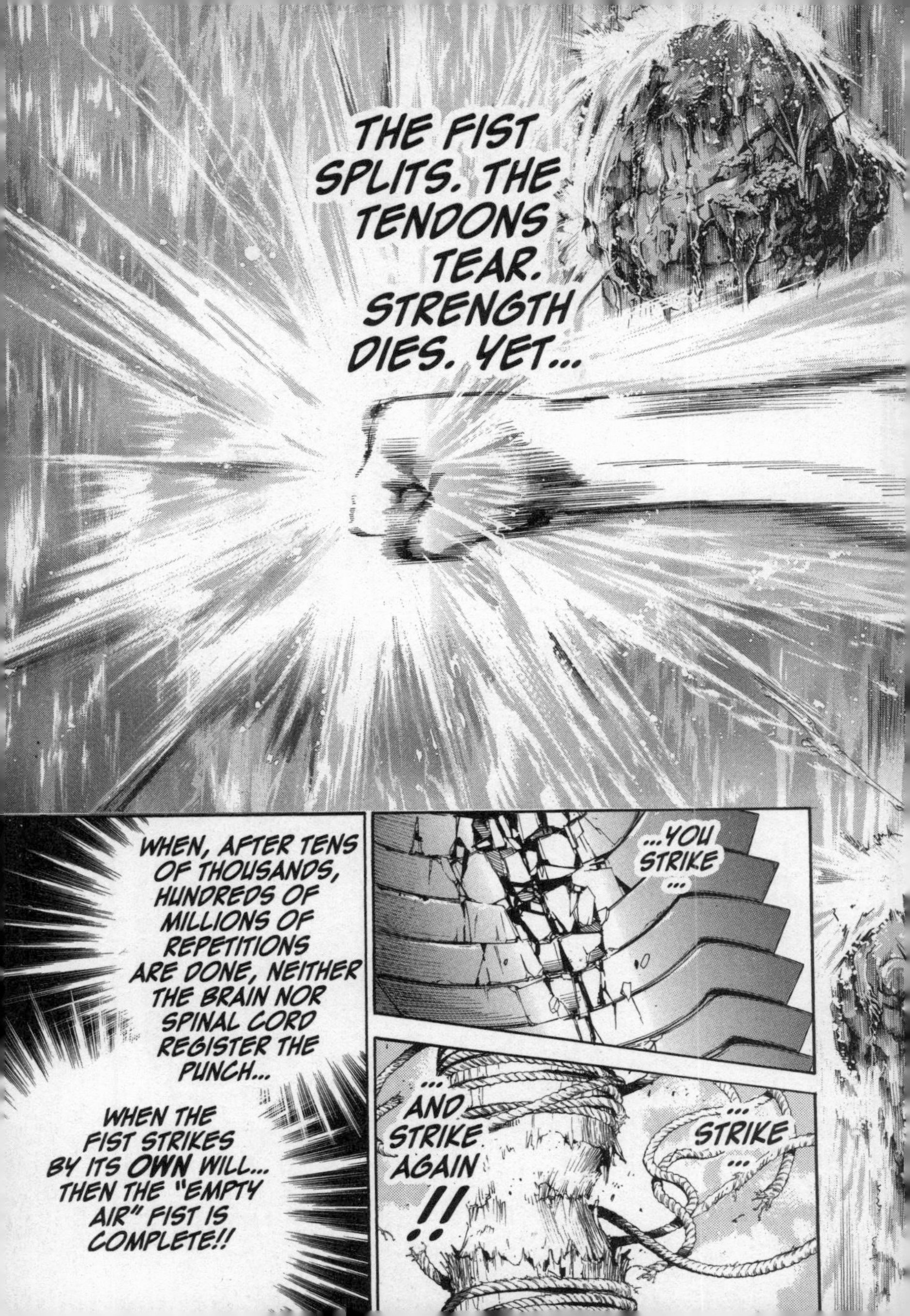
THE FIST SPLITS. THE TENDONS TEAR. STRENGTH DIES. YET...
...YOU STRIKE ...
... STRIKE ...
... AND STRIKE AGAIN !!
WHEN, AFTER TENS OF THOUSANDS, HUNDREDS OF MILLIONS OF REPETITIONS ARE DONE, NEITHER THE BRAIN NOR SPINAL CORD REGISTER THE PUNCH...
WHEN THE FIST STRIKES BY ITS **OWN** WILL... THEN THE "EMPTY AIR" FIST IS COMPLETE!!

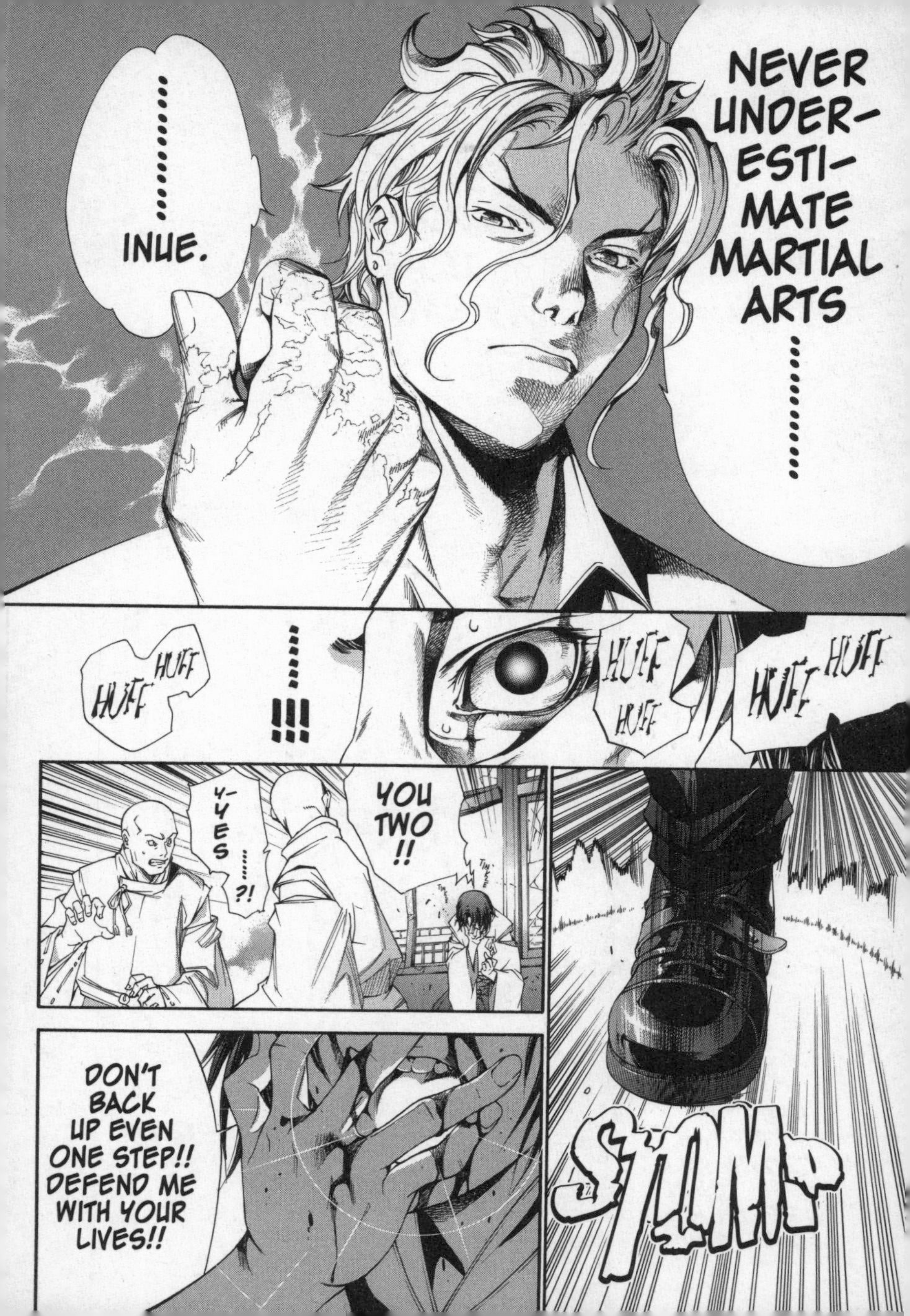
NEVER UNDER-ESTIMATE MARTIAL ARTS ....
.... INUE.
HUFF HUFF
HUFF HUFF
......!!!
HUFF HUFF
STOMP
YOU TWO!!
Y-YES ......?!
DON'T BACK UP EVEN ONE STEP!! DEFEND ME WITH YOUR LIVES!!

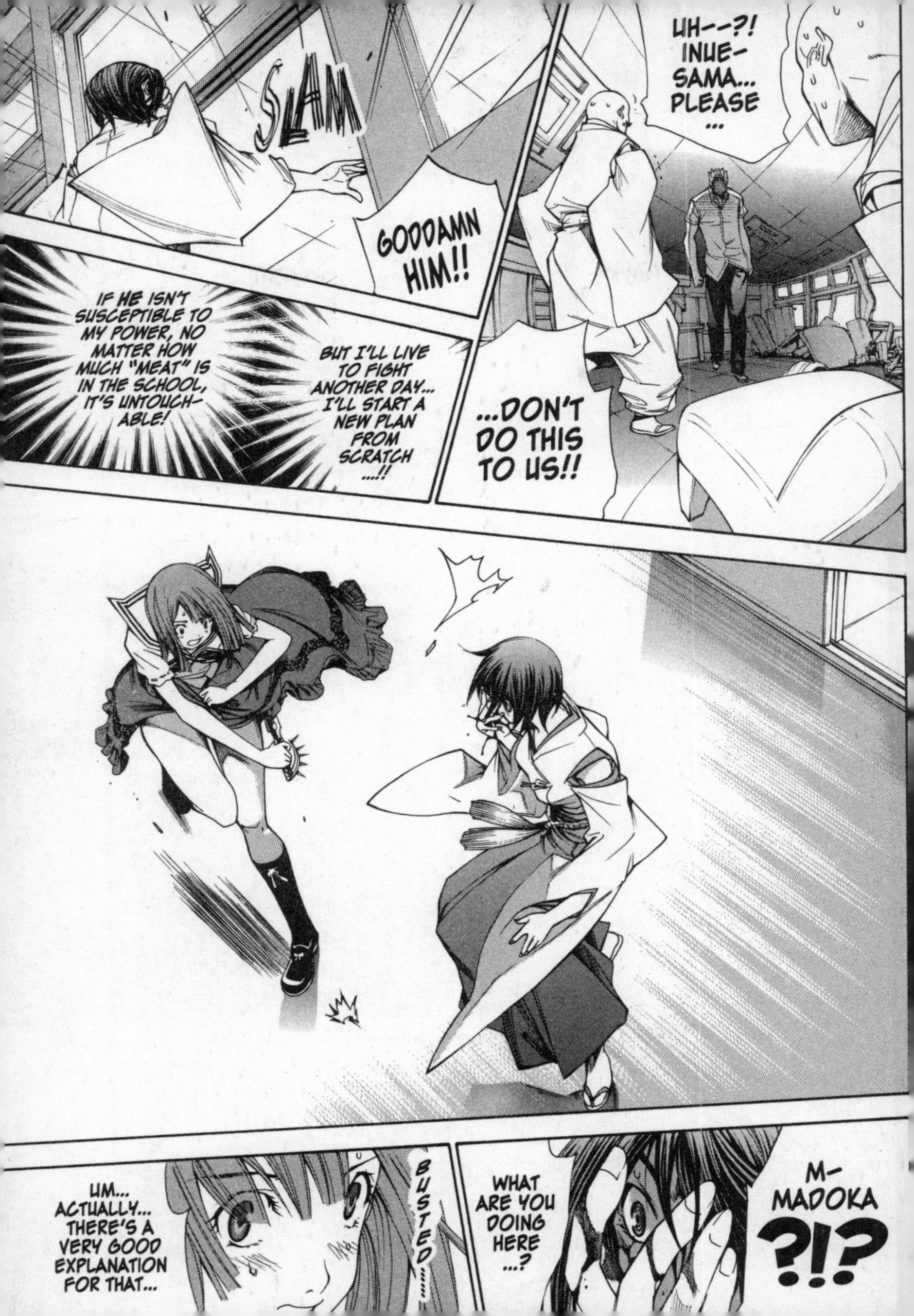
UH--?! INUE-SAMA... PLEASE ...
...DON'T DO THIS TO US!!
SLAM
GODDAMN HIM!!
IF HE ISN'T SUSCEPTIBLE TO MY POWER, NO MATTER HOW MUCH "MEAT" IS IN THE SCHOOL, IT'S UNTOUCHABLE!
BUT I'LL LIVE TO FIGHT ANOTHER DAY... I'LL START A NEW PLAN FROM SCRATCH ...!!
M-MADOKA ?!?
WHAT ARE YOU DOING HERE ...?
BUSTED.....
UM... ACTUALLY... THERE'S A VERY GOOD EXPLANATION FOR THAT...

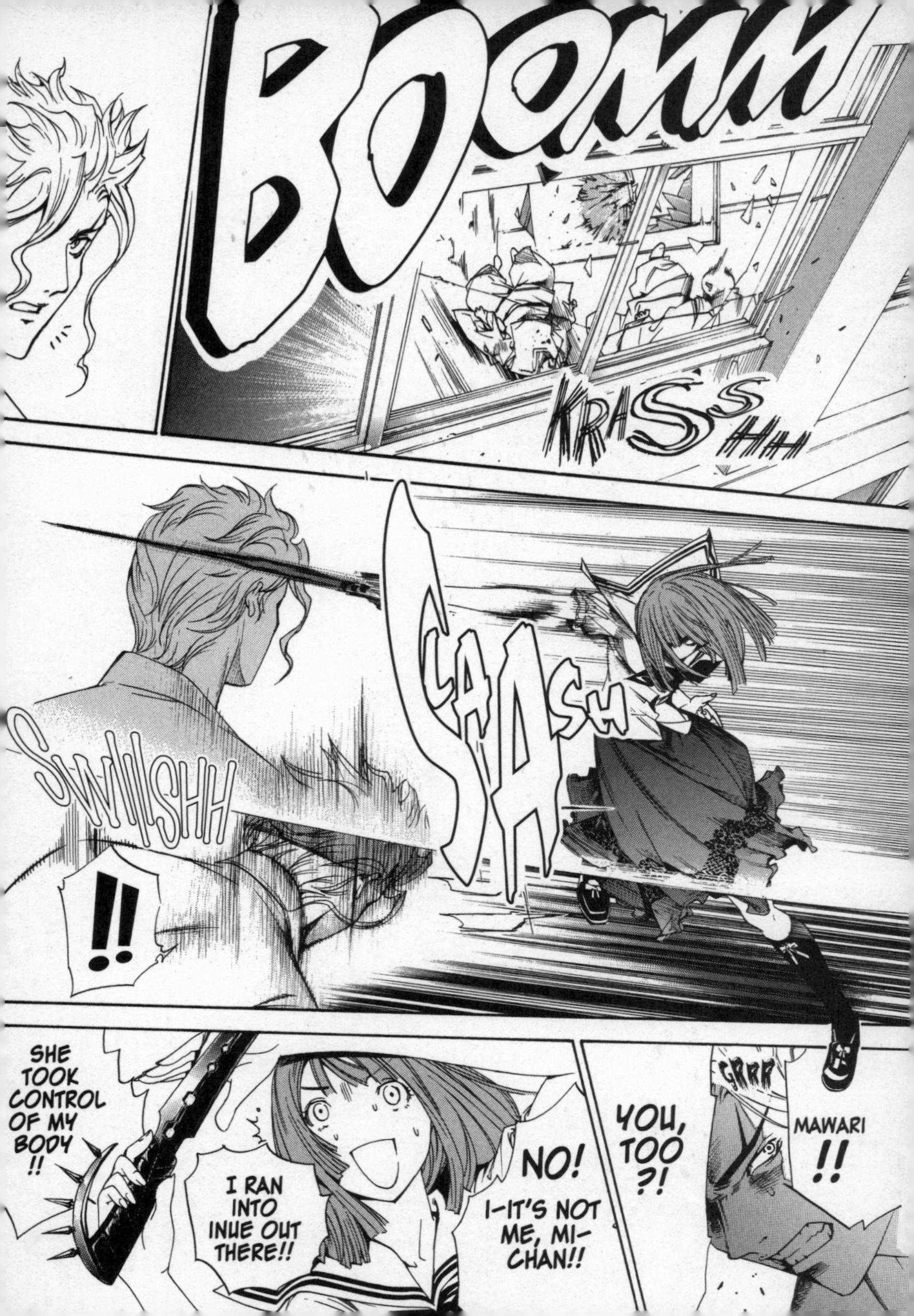
BOOM
KRASSHH
SLAASH
SWIISHH
!!
MAWARI !!
GRRR
YOU, TOO?!
NO!
I-IT'S NOT ME, MI-CHAN!!
I RAN INTO INUE OUT THERE!!
SHE TOOK CONTROL OF MY BODY!!

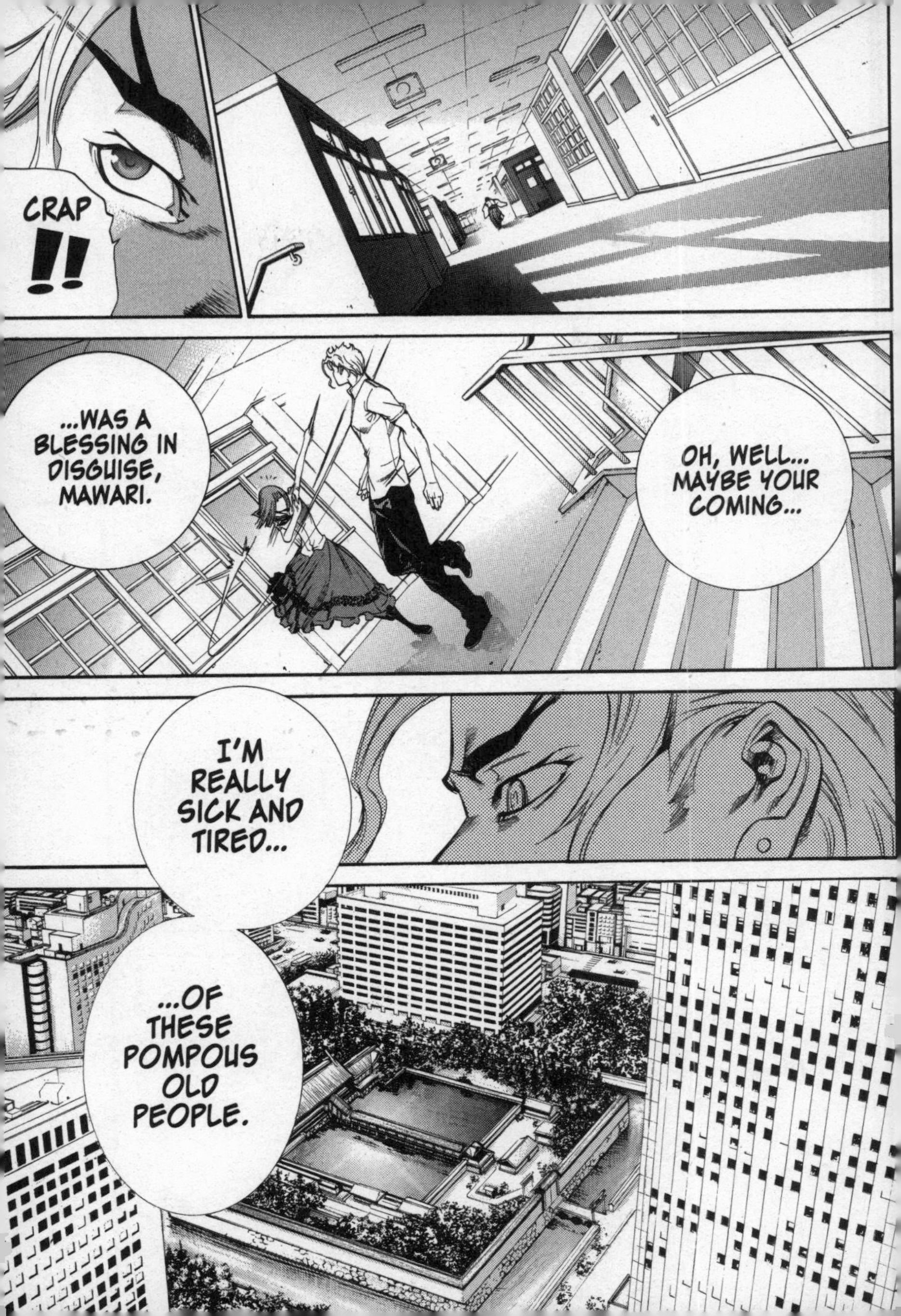
CRAP!!
OH, WELL... MAYBE YOUR COMING...
...WAS A BLESSING IN DISGUISE, MAWARI.
I'M REALLY SICK AND TIRED...
...OF THESE POMPOUS OLD PEOPLE.

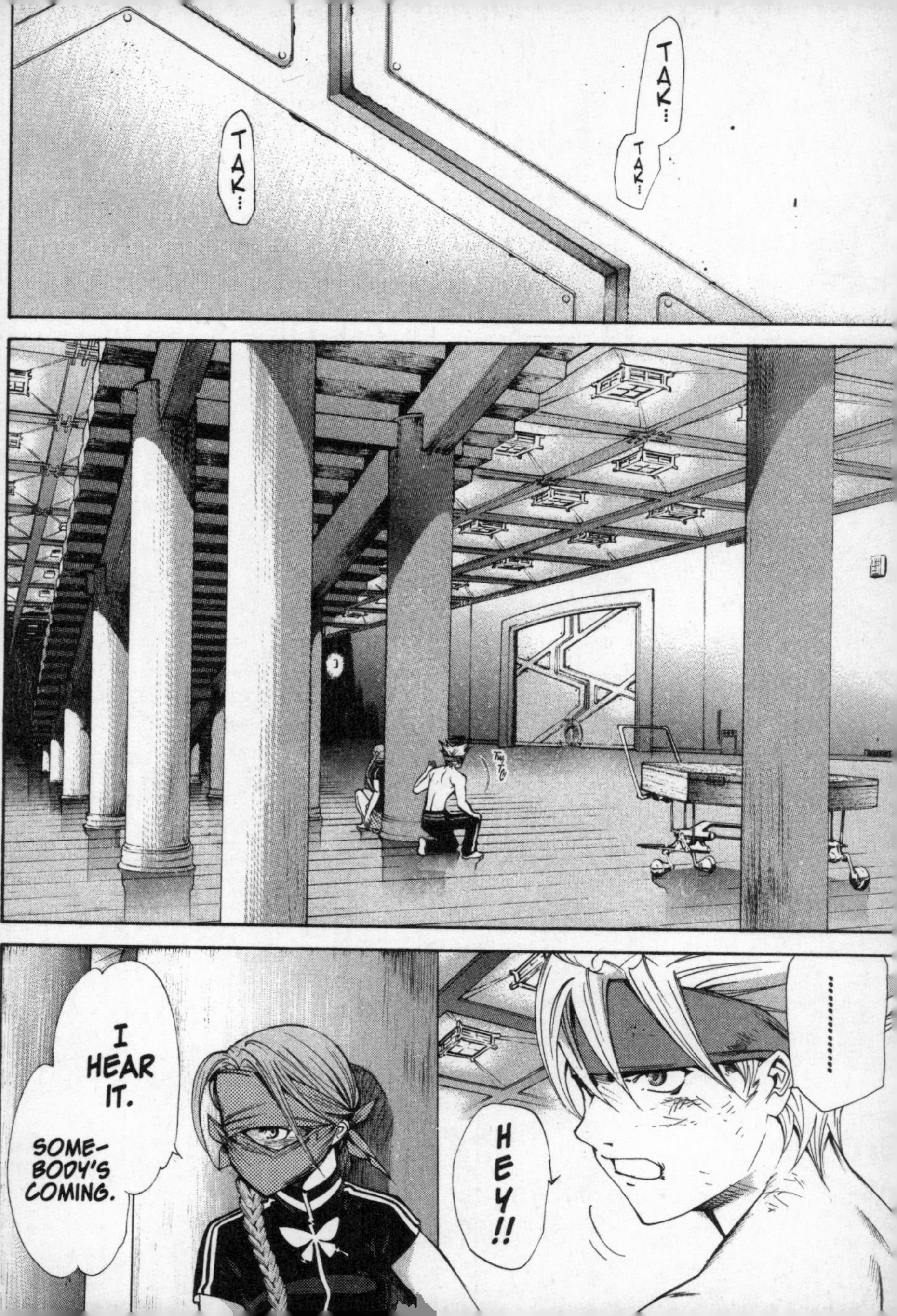
TAK... TAK...
TAK...
......
HEY!!
I HEAR IT.
SOMEBODY'S COMING.

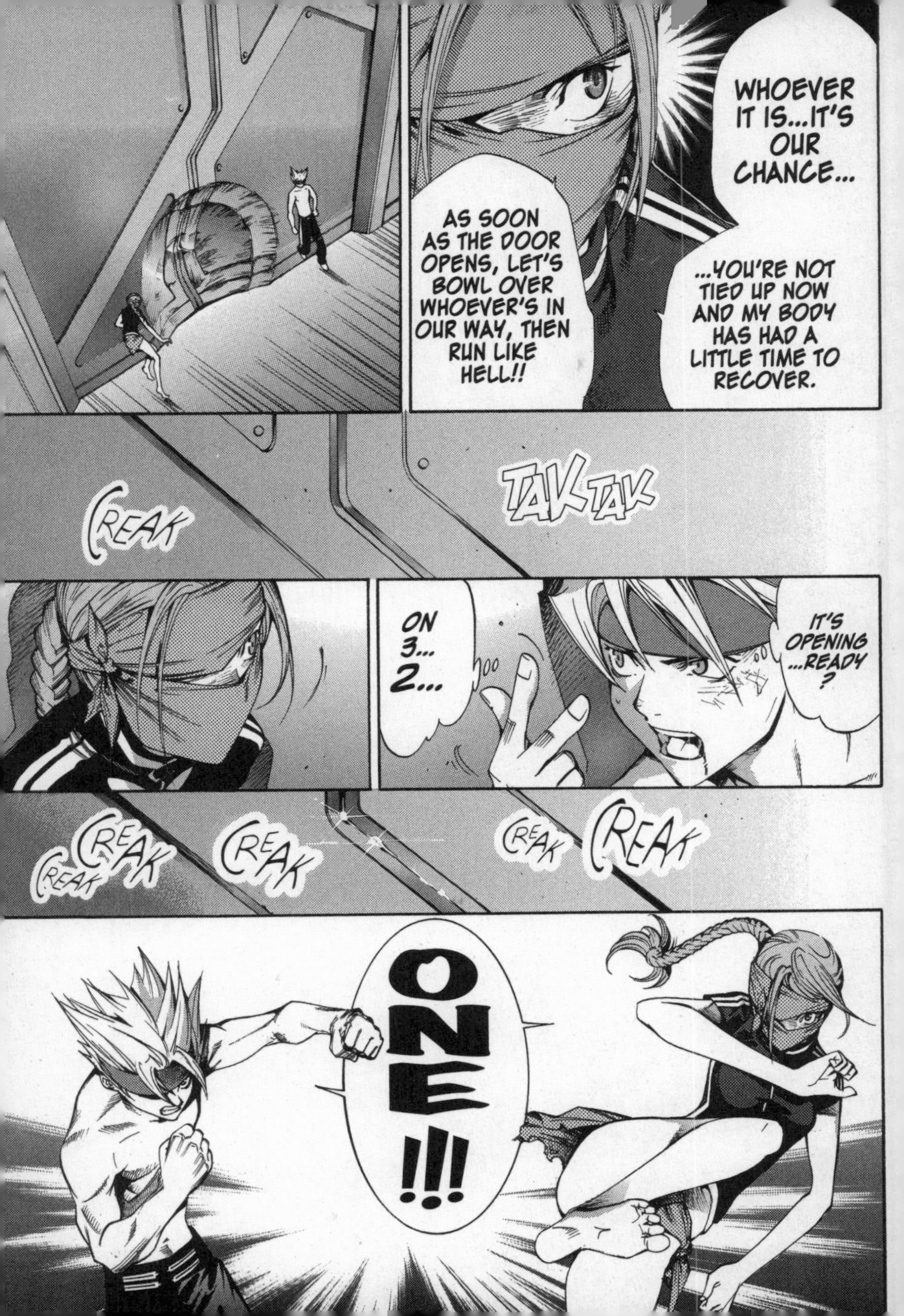
WHOEVER IT IS...IT'S OUR CHANCE...
...YOU'RE NOT TIED UP NOW AND MY BODY HAS HAD A LITTLE TIME TO RECOVER.
AS SOON AS THE DOOR OPENS, LET'S BOWL OVER WHOEVER'S IN OUR WAY, THEN RUN LIKE HELL!!
TAK TAK
CREAK
IT'S OPENING ...READY?
ON 3... 2...
CREAK
CREAK
CREAK
CREAK
CREAK
ONE!!!

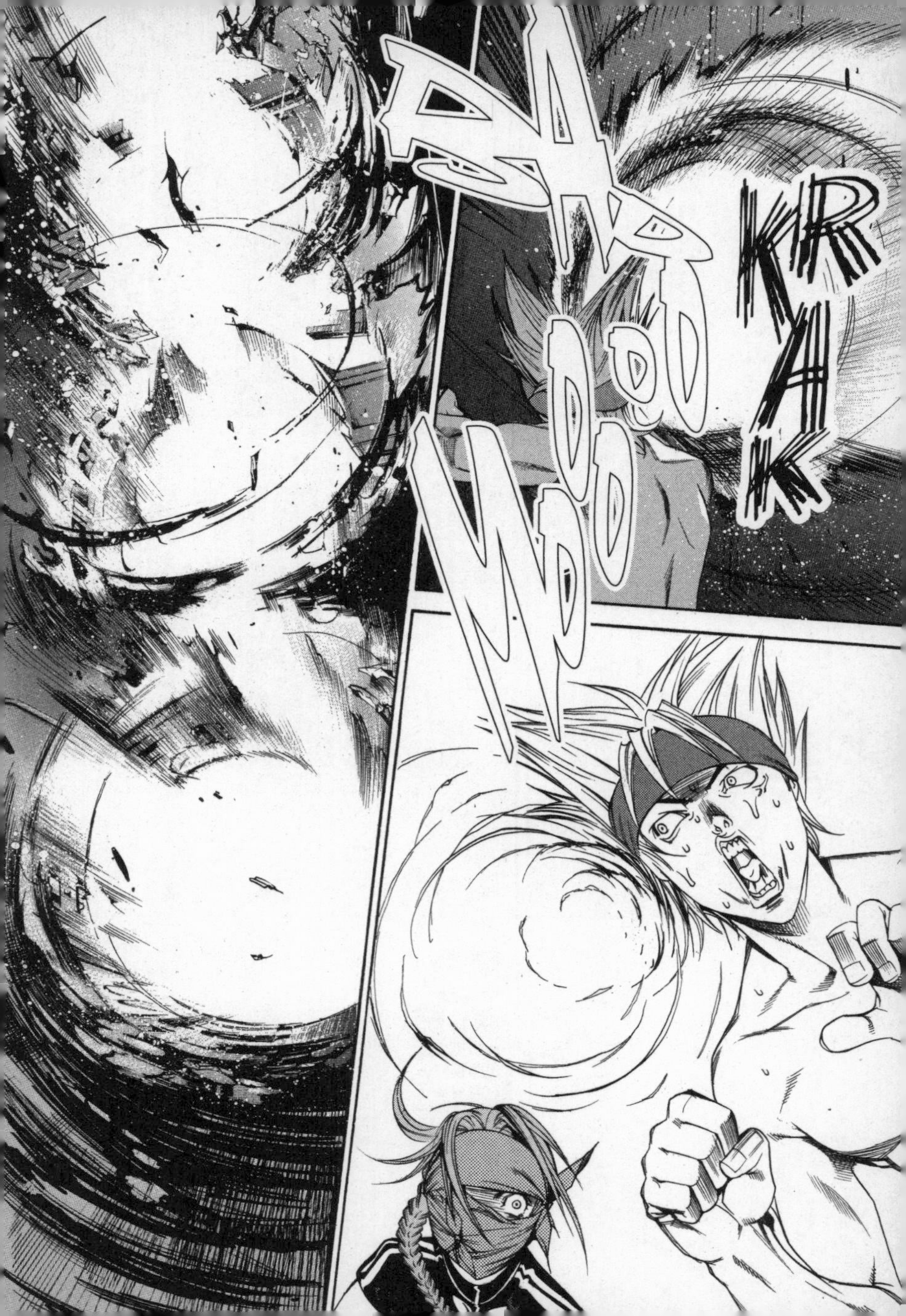
KRAK

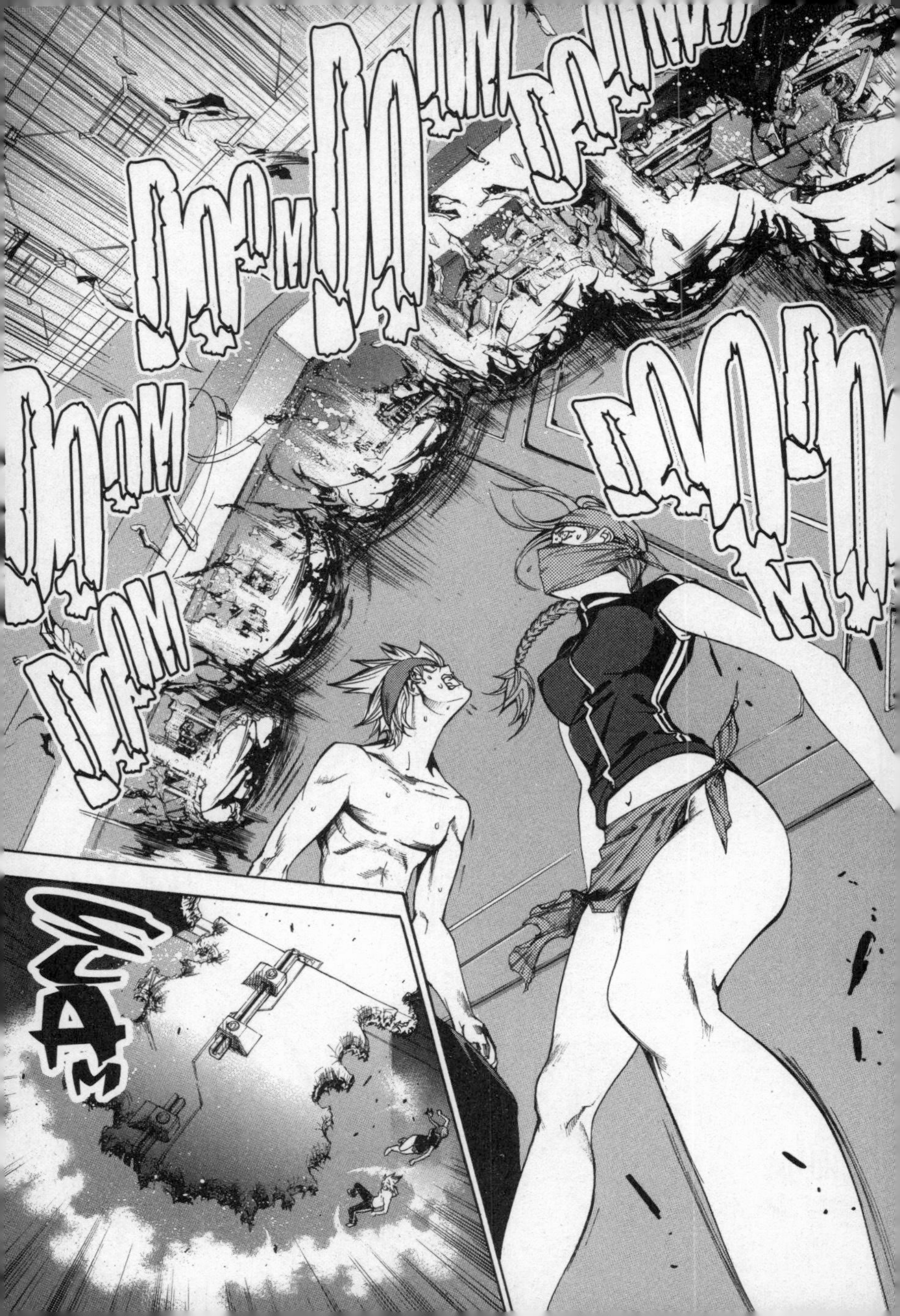
DOOOM
DOOM
DOOM
DOOM
DOOM
SLAM

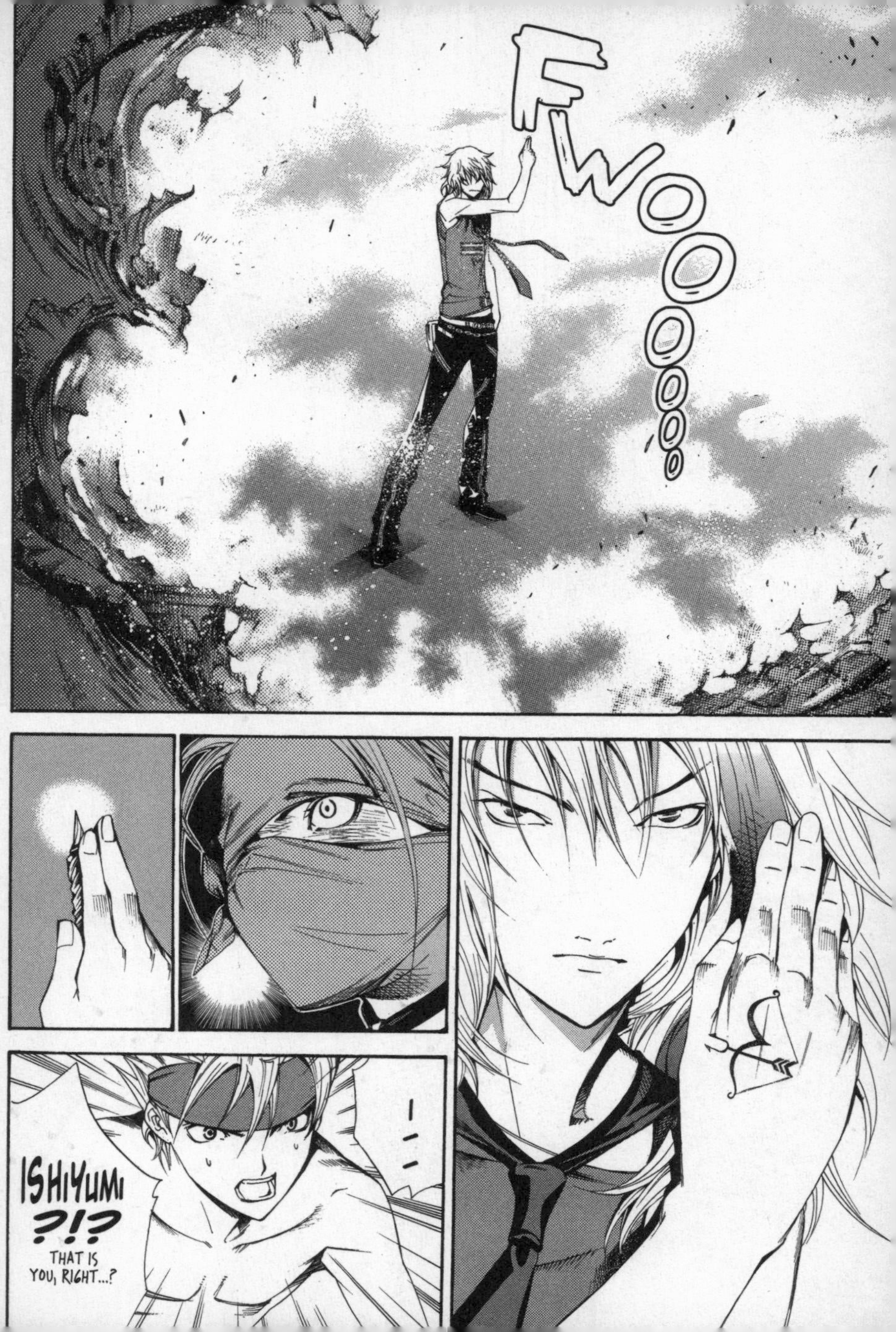
FWOOOOOOO
!
ISHIYUMI ?!?
THAT IS YOU, RIGHT...?

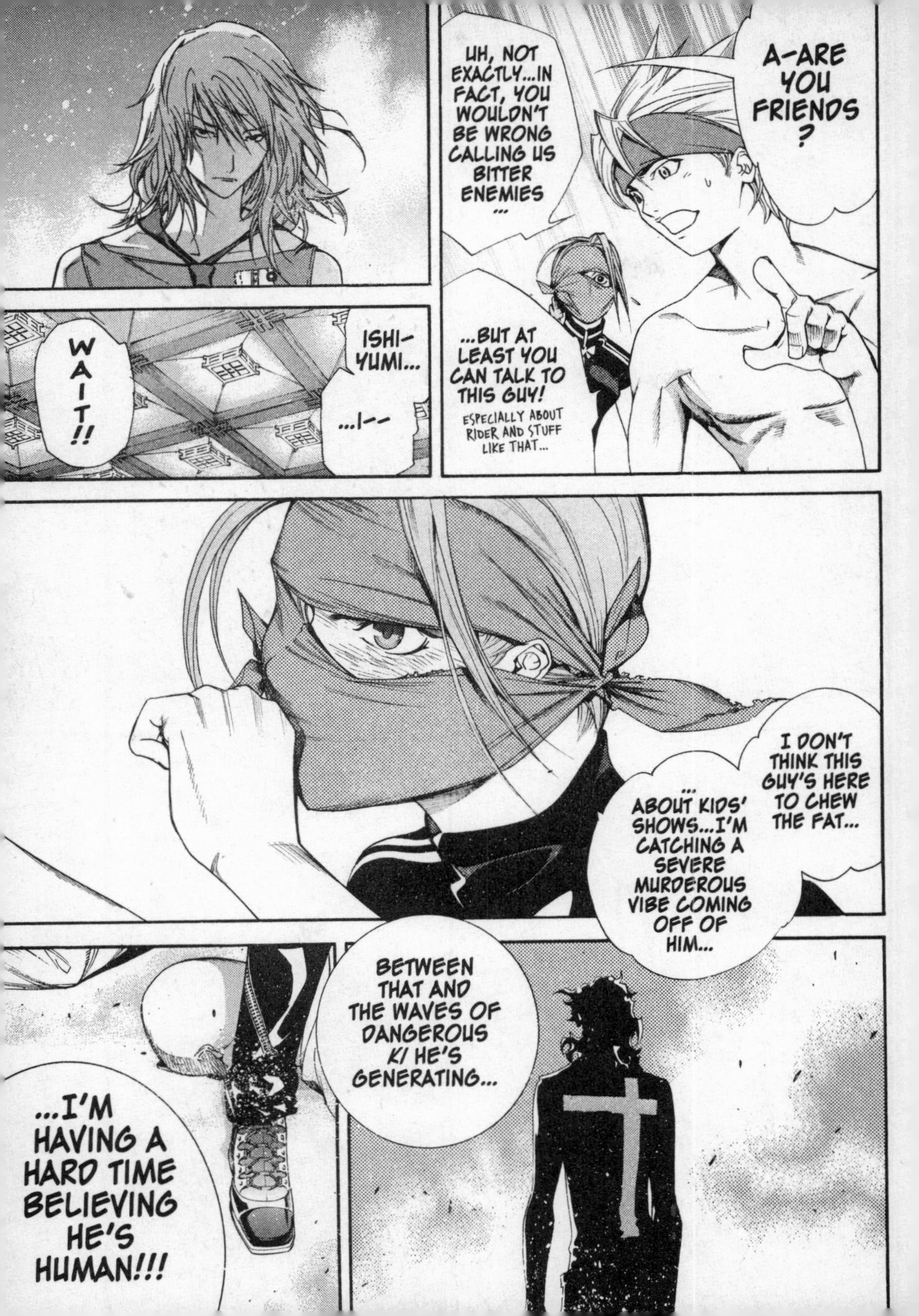
A-ARE YOU FRIENDS?
UH, NOT EXACTLY...IN FACT, YOU WOULDN'T BE WRONG CALLING US BITTER ENEMIES...
...BUT AT LEAST YOU CAN TALK TO THIS GUY!
ESPECIALLY ABOUT RIDER AND STUFF LIKE THAT...
ISHI-YUMI...
...I--
WAIT!!
I DON'T THINK THIS GUY'S HERE TO CHEW THE FAT...
... ABOUT KIDS' SHOWS...I'M CATCHING A SEVERE MURDEROUS VIBE COMING OFF OF HIM...
BETWEEN THAT AND THE WAVES OF DANGEROUS KI HE'S GENERATING...
...I'M HAVING A HARD TIME BELIEVING HE'S HUMAN!!!

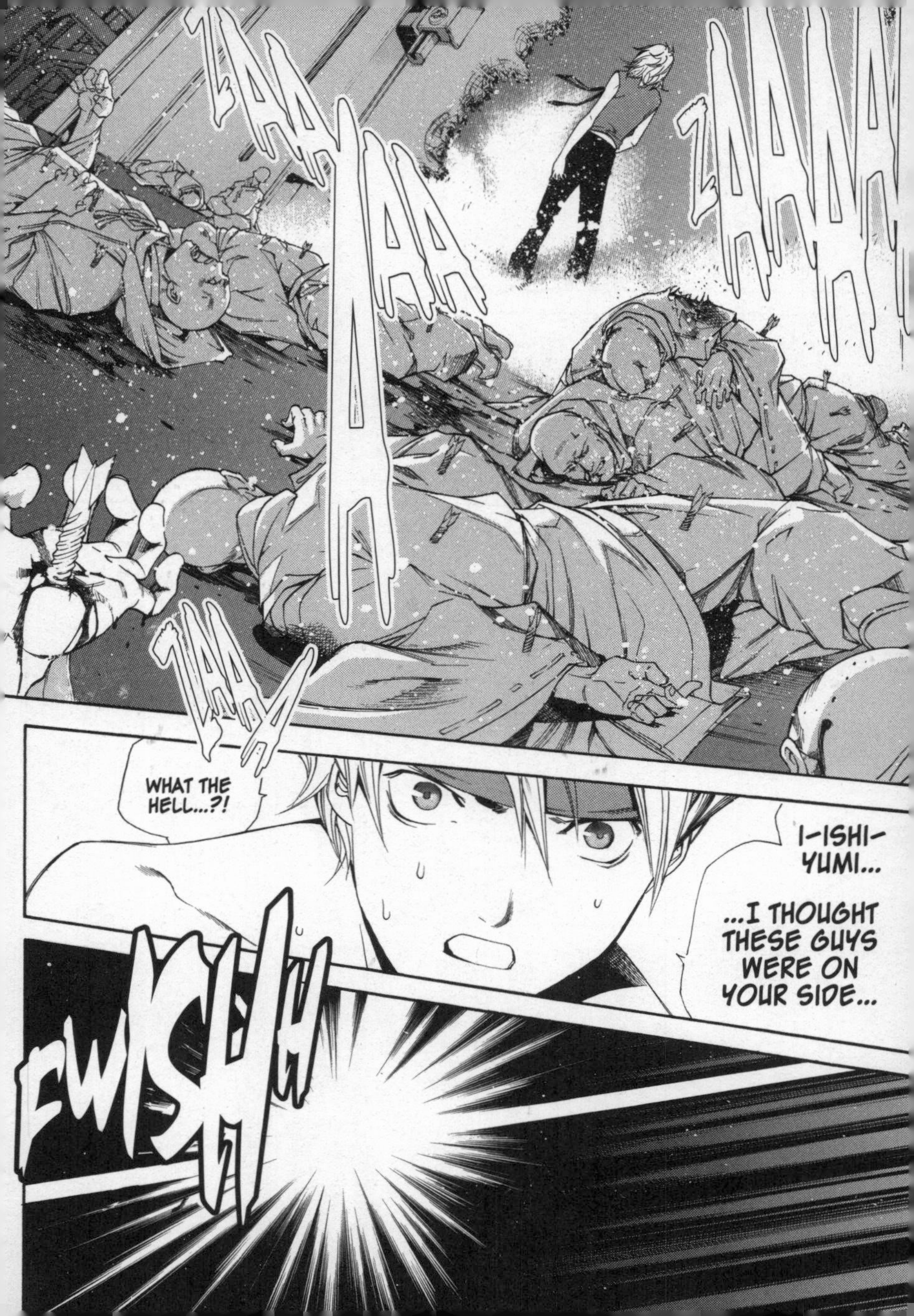
ZAAAAA
ZAAAAAA
ZAAA
WHAT THE HELL...?!
I-ISHI-YUMI...
...I THOUGHT THESE GUYS WERE ON YOUR SIDE...
CWISHH

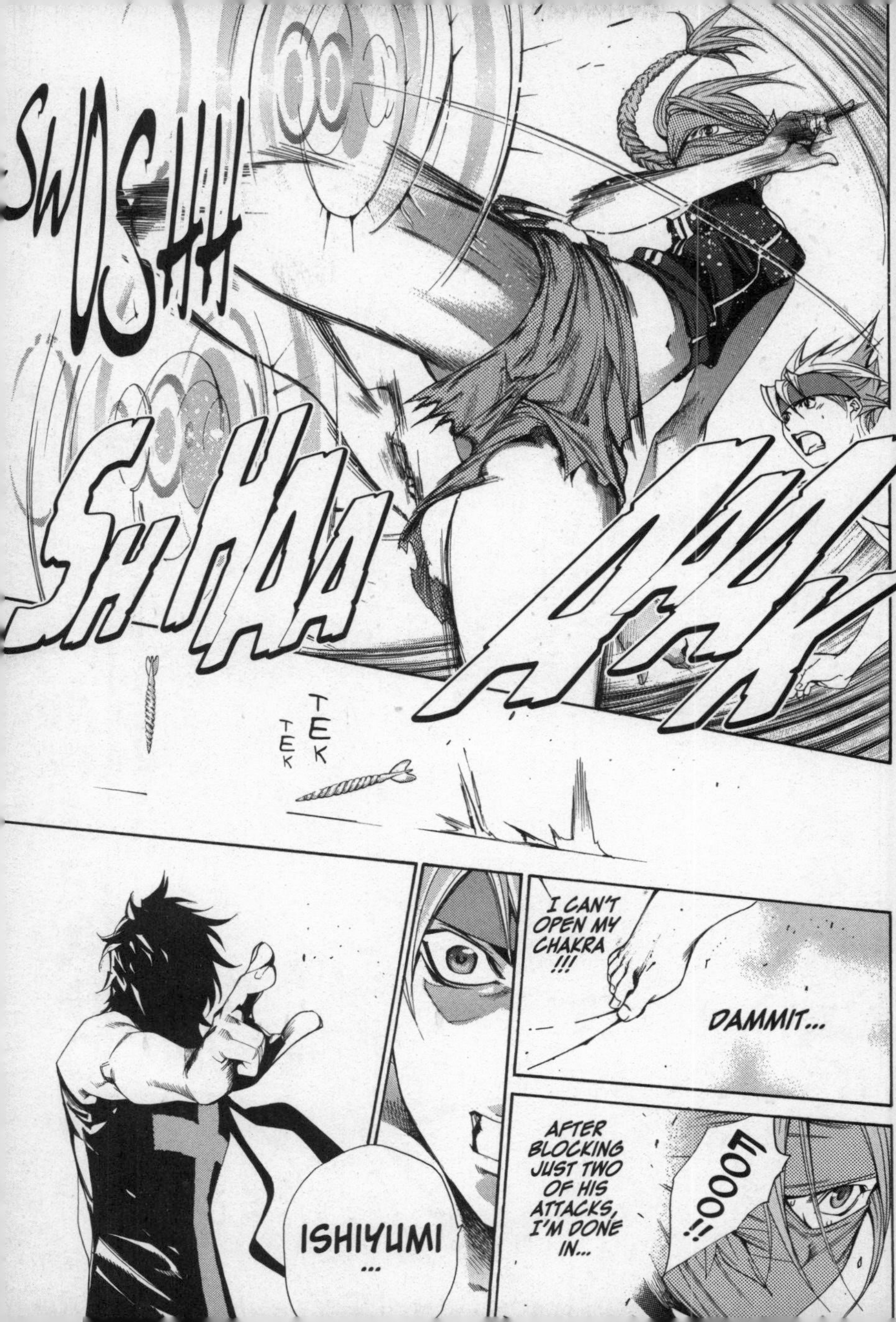
SWOSHHH
TEK TEK
I CAN'T OPEN MY CHAKRA !!!
DAMMIT...
AFTER BLOCKING JUST TWO OF HIS ATTACKS, I'M DONE IN...
...
ISHIYUMI ...

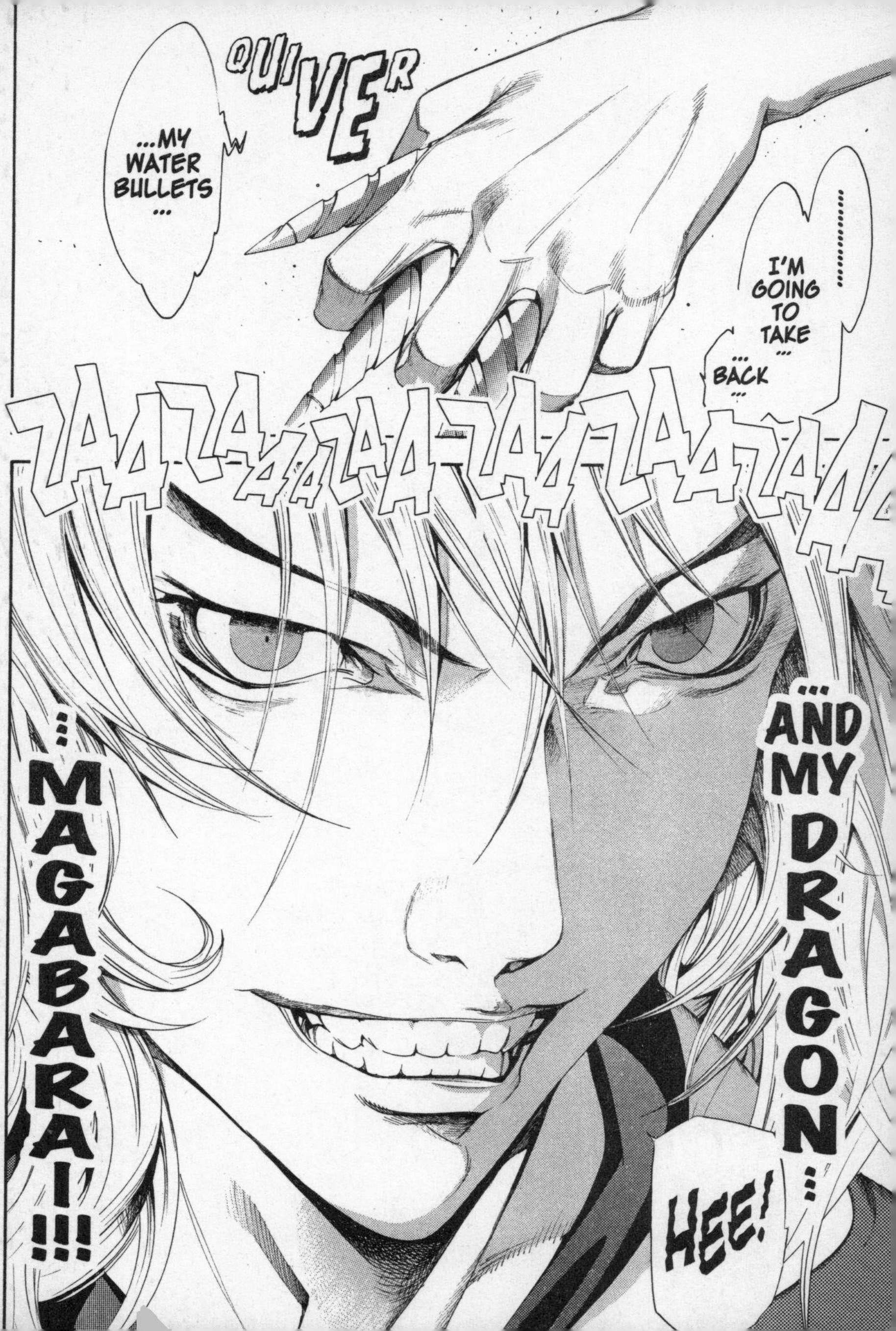
....
I'M GOING TO TAKE ... BACK ...
...MY WATER BULLETS ...
QUIVER
ZAA ZAA ZAA ZAA ZAA ZAA ZAA ZAA ZAA
...AND MY DRAGON...
HEE!
...MAGABARAI!!!

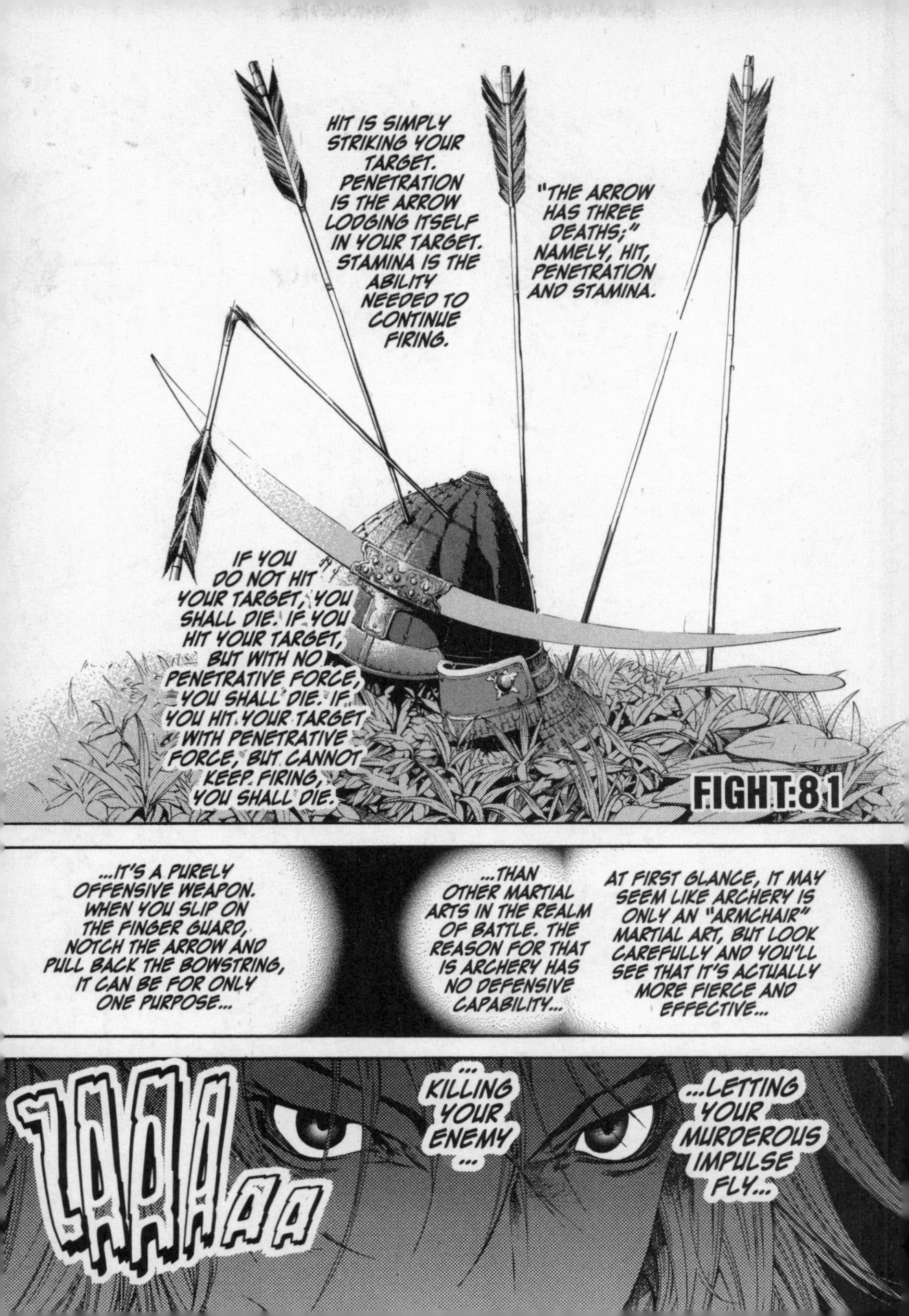
"THE ARROW HAS THREE DEATHS;" NAMELY, HIT, PENETRATION AND STAMINA.
HIT IS SIMPLY STRIKING YOUR TARGET. PENETRATION IS THE ARROW LODGING ITSELF IN YOUR TARGET. STAMINA IS THE ABILITY NEEDED TO CONTINUE FIRING.
IF YOU DO NOT HIT YOUR TARGET, YOU SHALL DIE. IF YOU HIT YOUR TARGET, BUT WITH NO PENETRATIVE FORCE, YOU SHALL DIE. IF YOU HIT YOUR TARGET WITH PENETRATIVE FORCE, BUT CANNOT KEEP FIRING, YOU SHALL DIE.
FIGHT:81
AT FIRST GLANCE, IT MAY SEEM LIKE ARCHERY IS ONLY AN "ARMCHAIR" MARTIAL ART, BUT LOOK CAREFULLY AND YOU'LL SEE THAT IT'S ACTUALLY MORE FIERCE AND EFFECTIVE...
...THAN OTHER MARTIAL ARTS IN THE REALM OF BATTLE. THE REASON FOR THAT IS ARCHERY HAS NO DEFENSIVE CAPABILITY...
...IT'S A PURELY OFFENSIVE WEAPON. WHEN YOU SLIP ON THE FINGER GUARD, NOTCH THE ARROW AND PULL BACK THE BOWSTRING, IT CAN BE FOR ONLY ONE PURPOSE...
...LETTING YOUR MURDEROUS IMPULSE FLY...
...KILLING YOUR ENEMY...

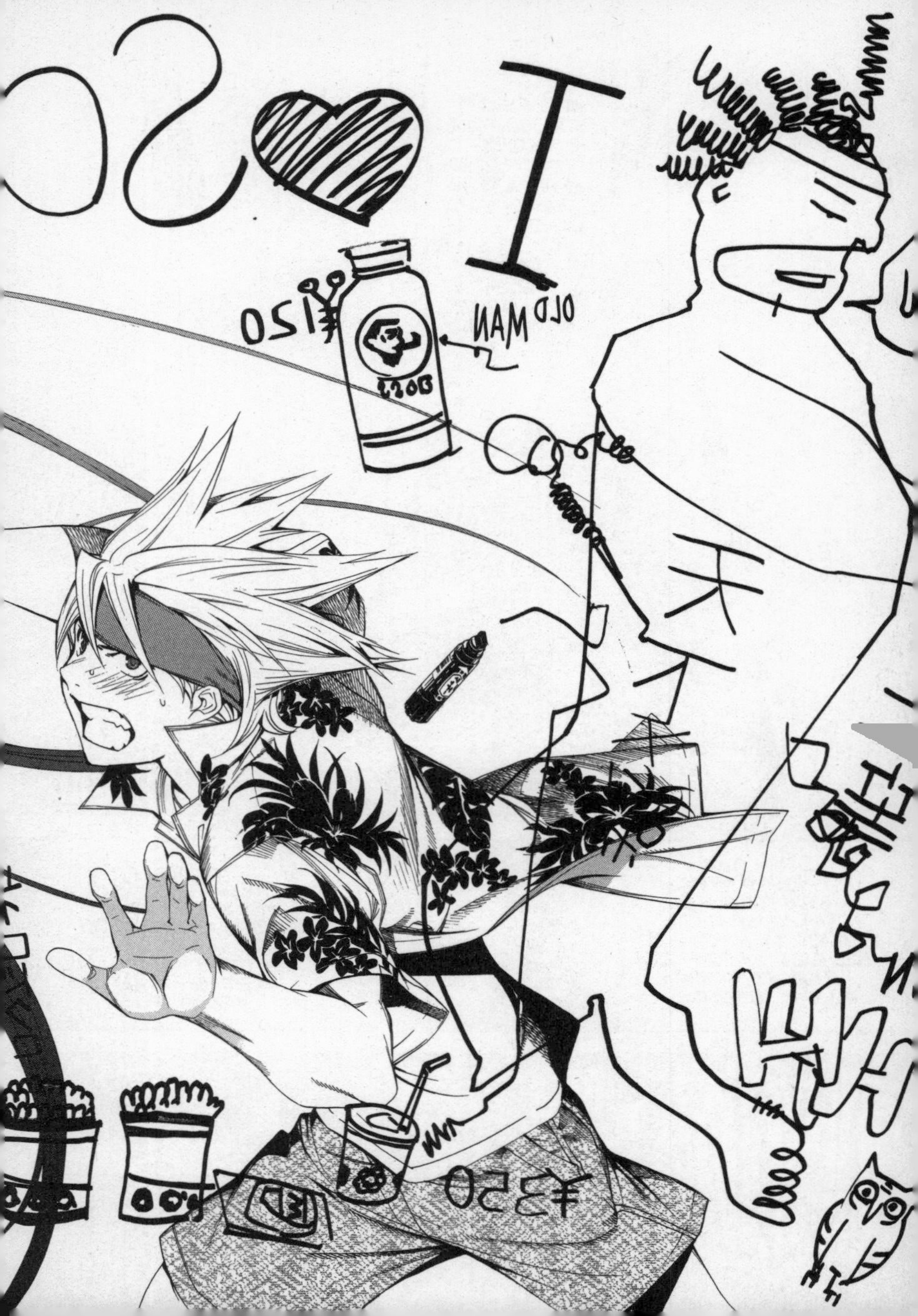
OLD MAN
120
¥350

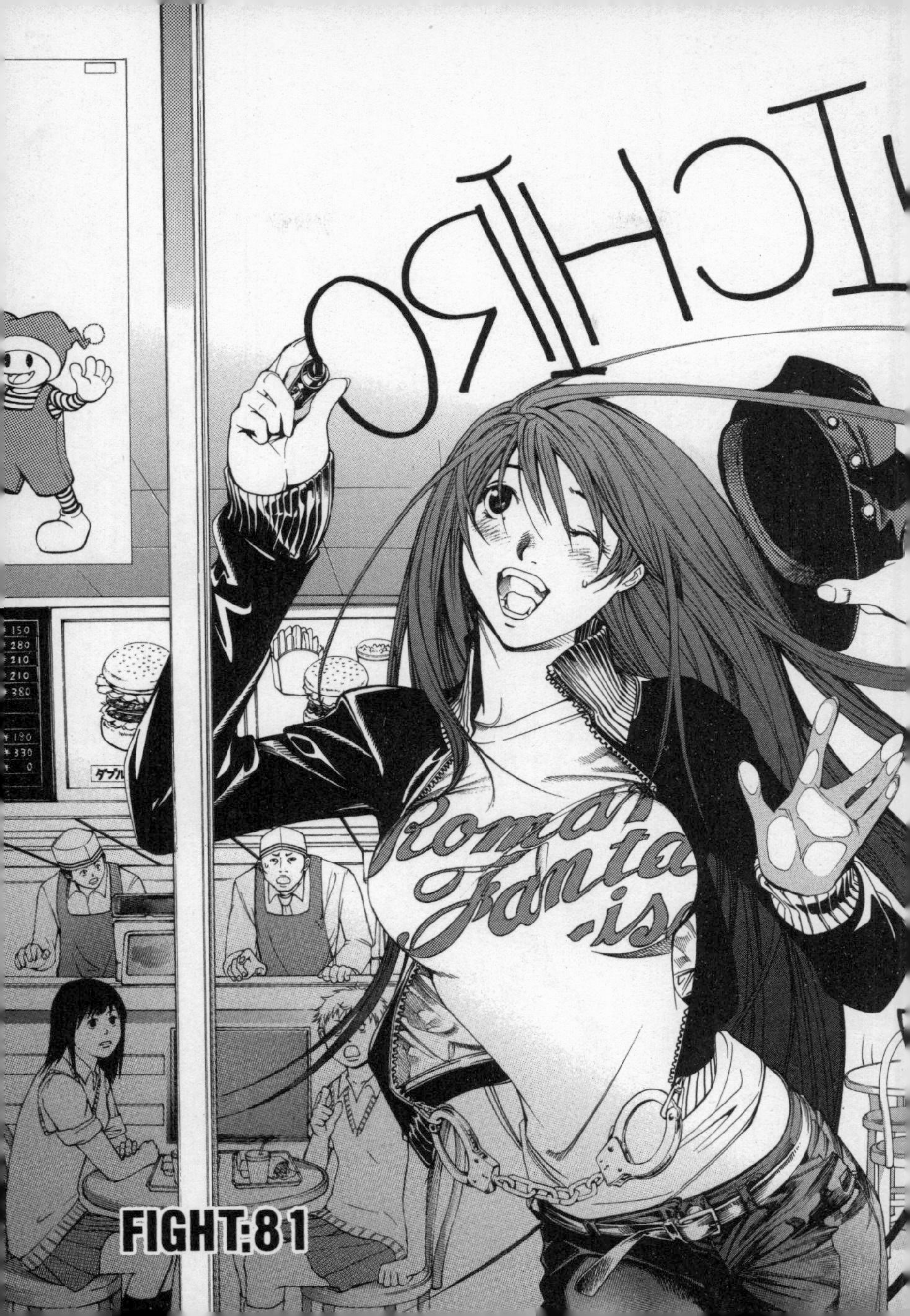
ICHIRO
FIGHT:81

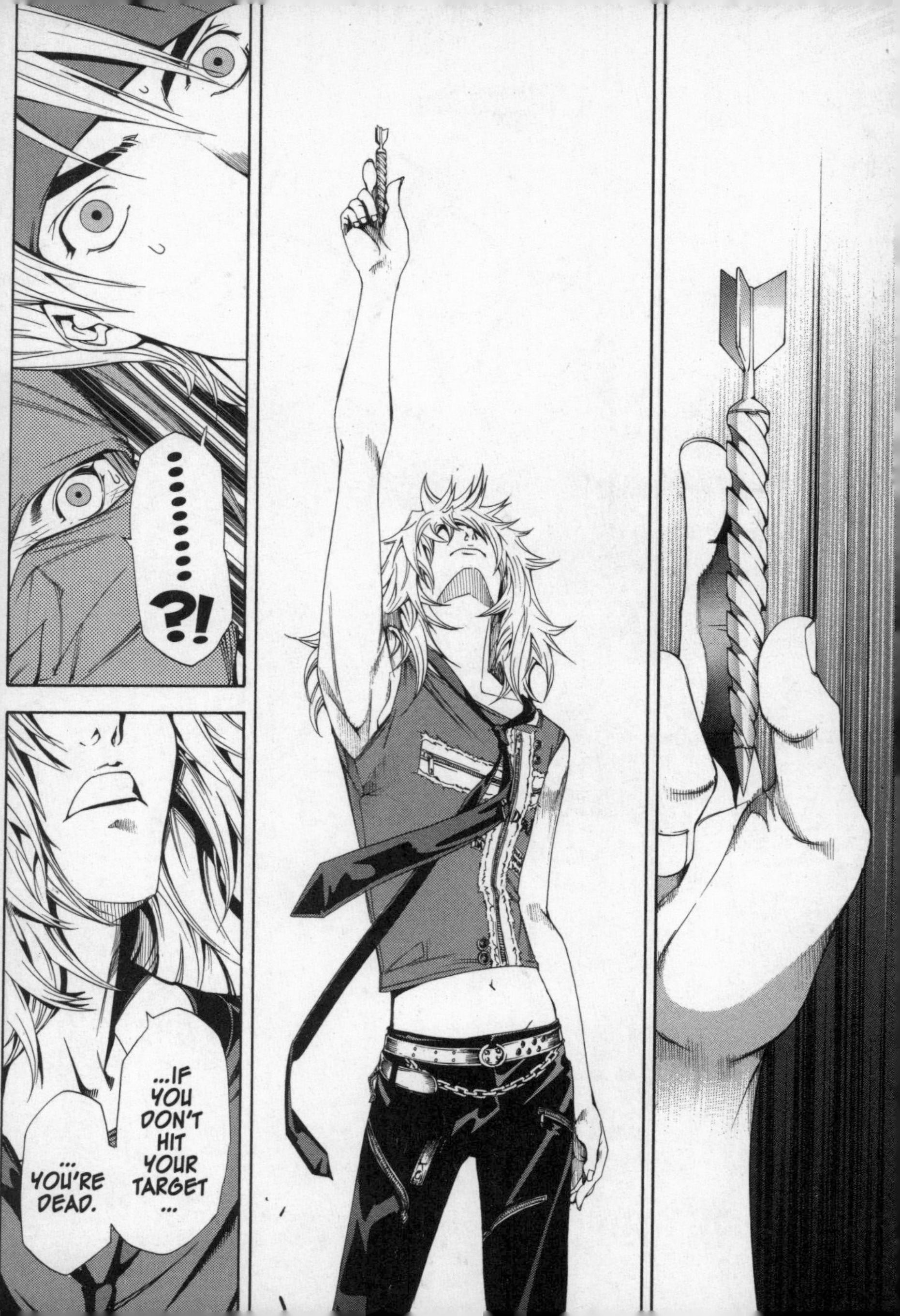
......?!
...IF YOU DON'T HIT YOUR TARGET ...
... YOU'RE DEAD.

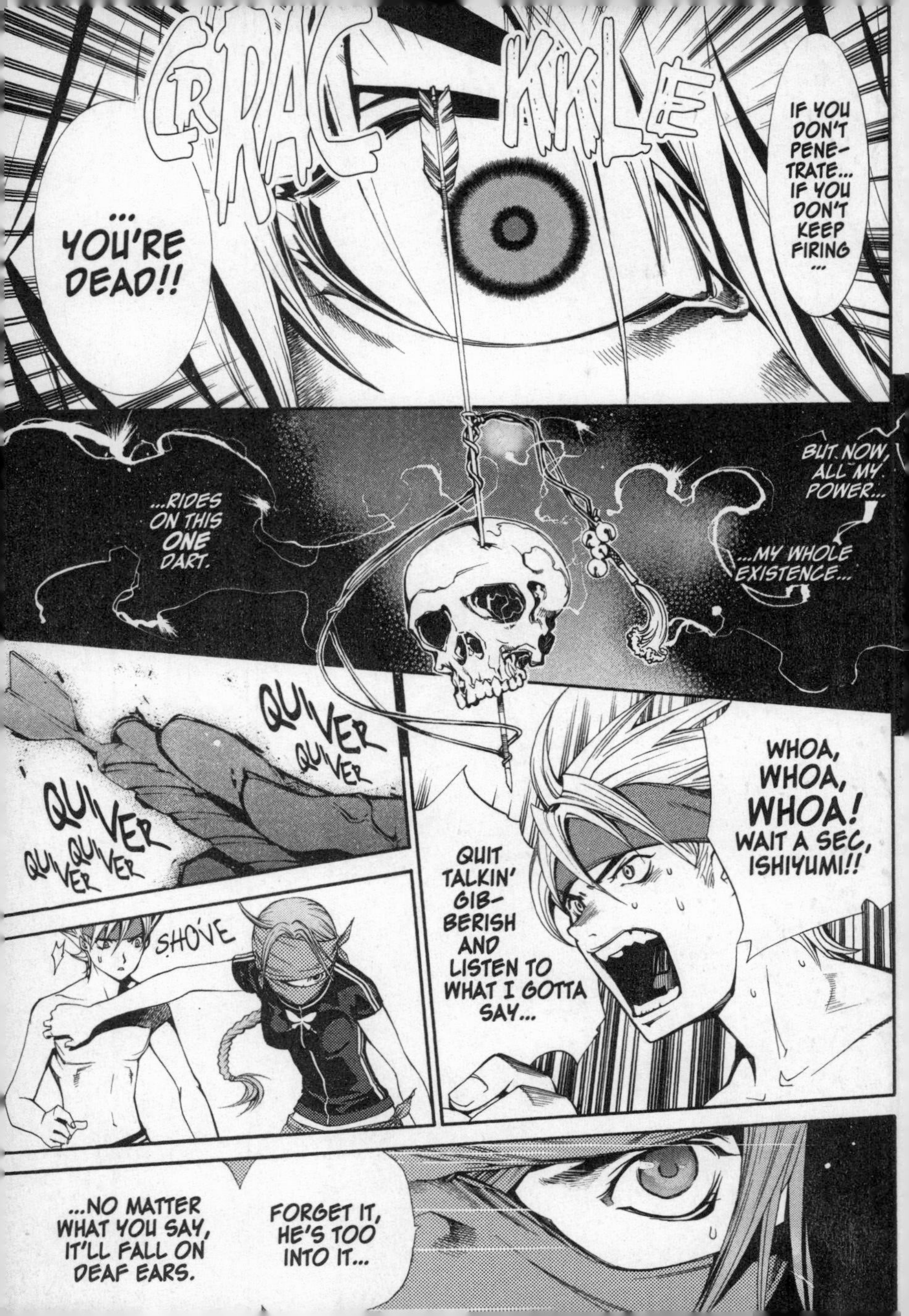
IF YOU DON'T PENE-TRATE... IF YOU DON'T KEEP FIRING ...
CRRACKKLE
... YOU'RE DEAD!!
BUT NOW, ALL MY POWER...
...MY WHOLE EXISTENCE...
...RIDES ON THIS ONE DART.
WHOA, WHOA, WHOA! WAIT A SEC, ISHIYUMI!!
QUIT TALKIN' GIB-BERISH AND LISTEN TO WHAT I GOTTA SAY...
QUIVER QUIVER
QUIVER QUIVER QUIVER
SHOVE
FORGET IT, HE'S TOO INTO IT...
...NO MATTER WHAT YOU SAY, IT'LL FALL ON DEAF EARS.

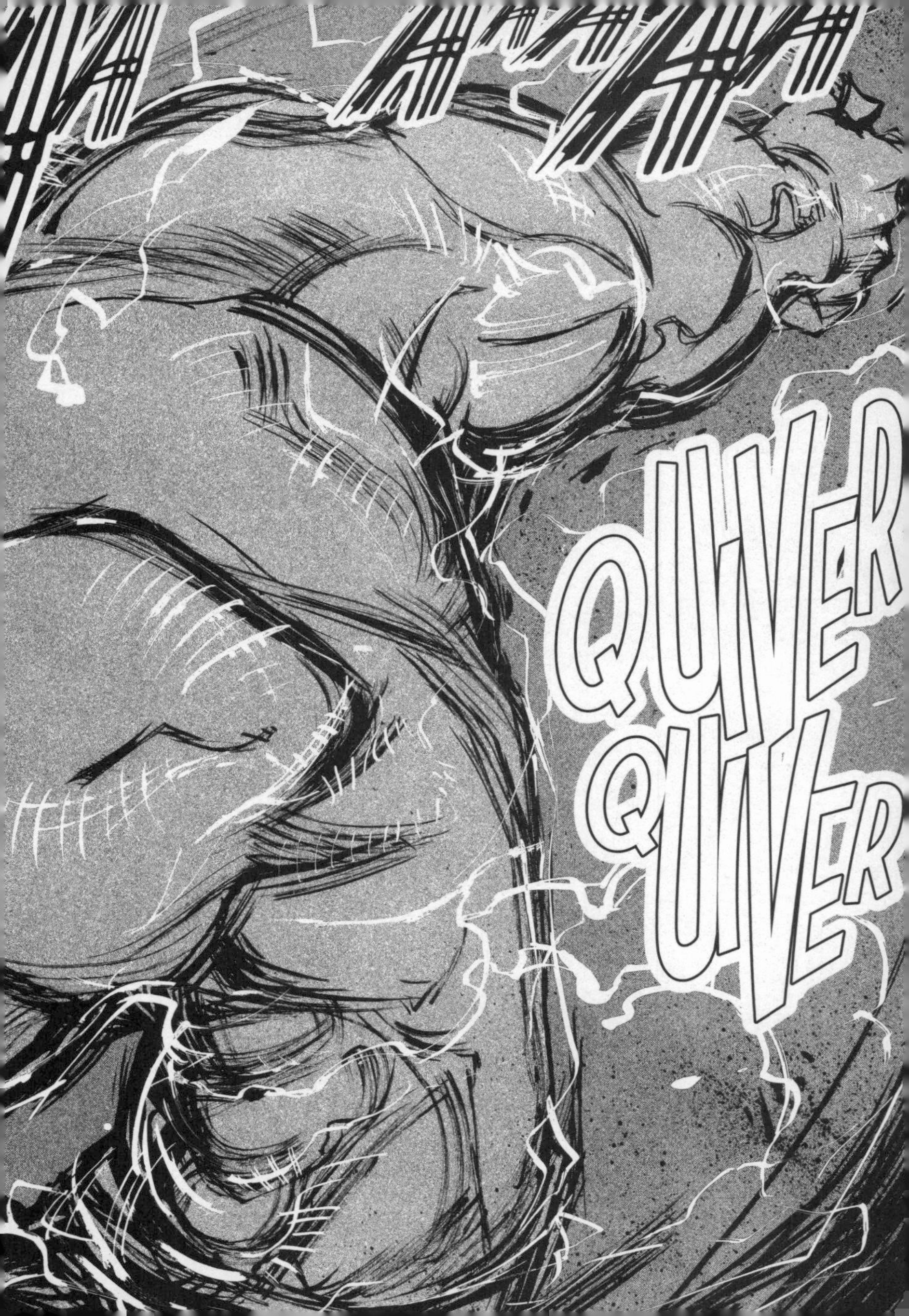
QUIVER
QUIVER

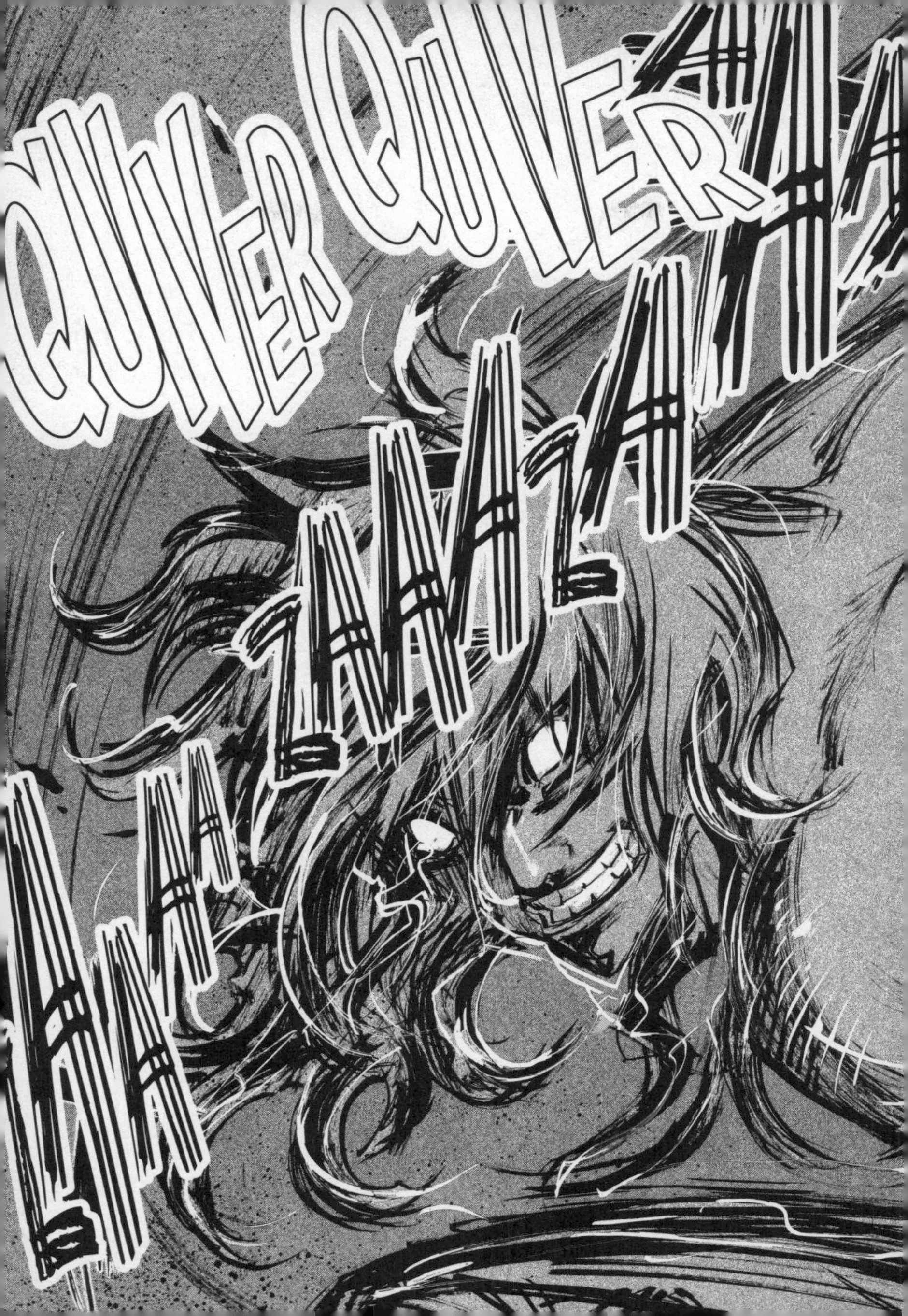
QUIVER QUIVER
HAHAHAHA

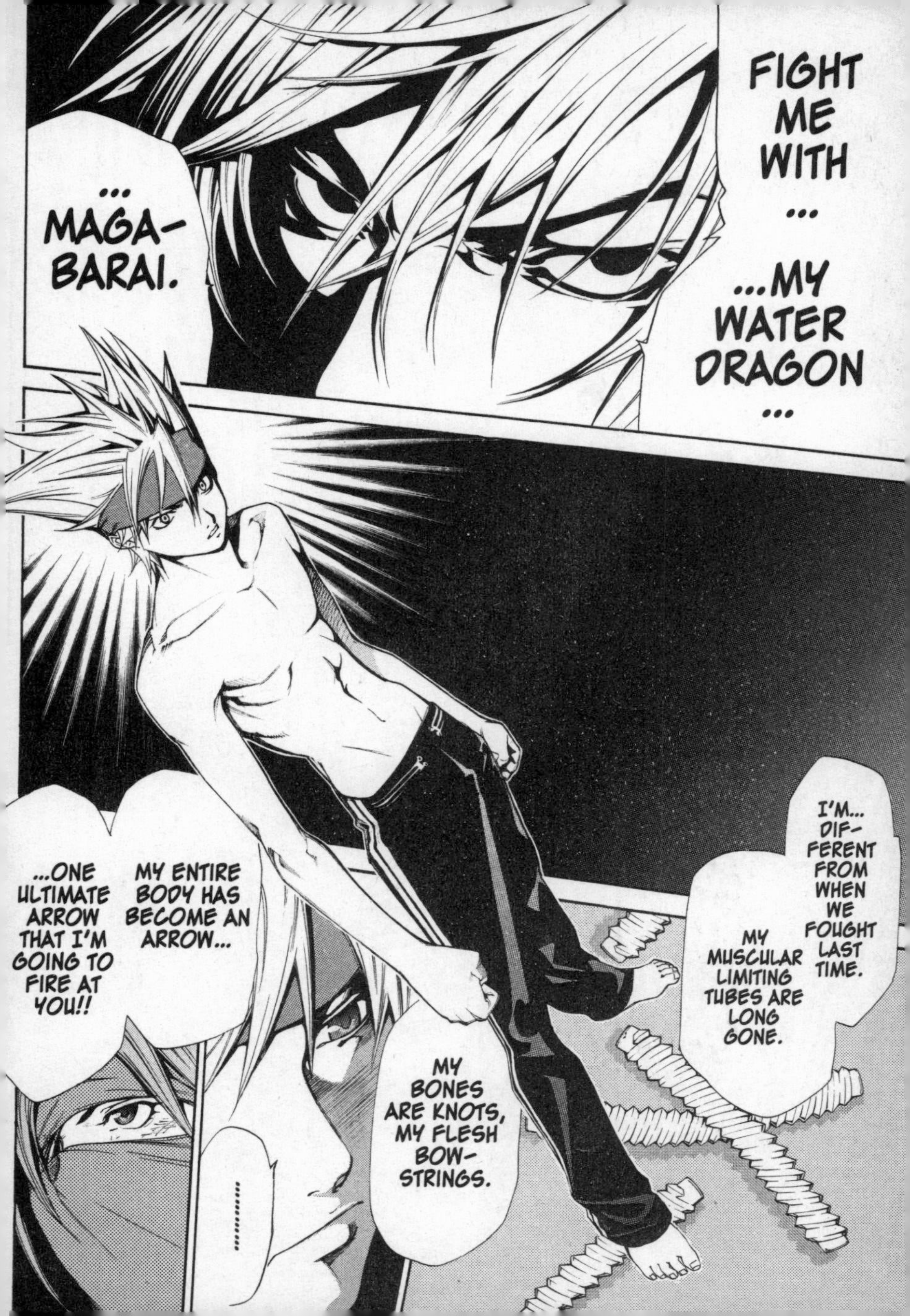
FIGHT ME WITH ...
...MY WATER DRAGON ...
... MAGA-BARAI.
I'M... DIF-FERENT FROM WHEN WE FOUGHT LAST TIME.
MY MUSCULAR LIMITING TUBES ARE LONG GONE.
MY BONES ARE KNOTS, MY FLESH BOW-STRINGS.
MY ENTIRE BODY HAS BECOME AN ARROW...
...ONE ULTIMATE ARROW THAT I'M GOING TO FIRE AT YOU!!
......

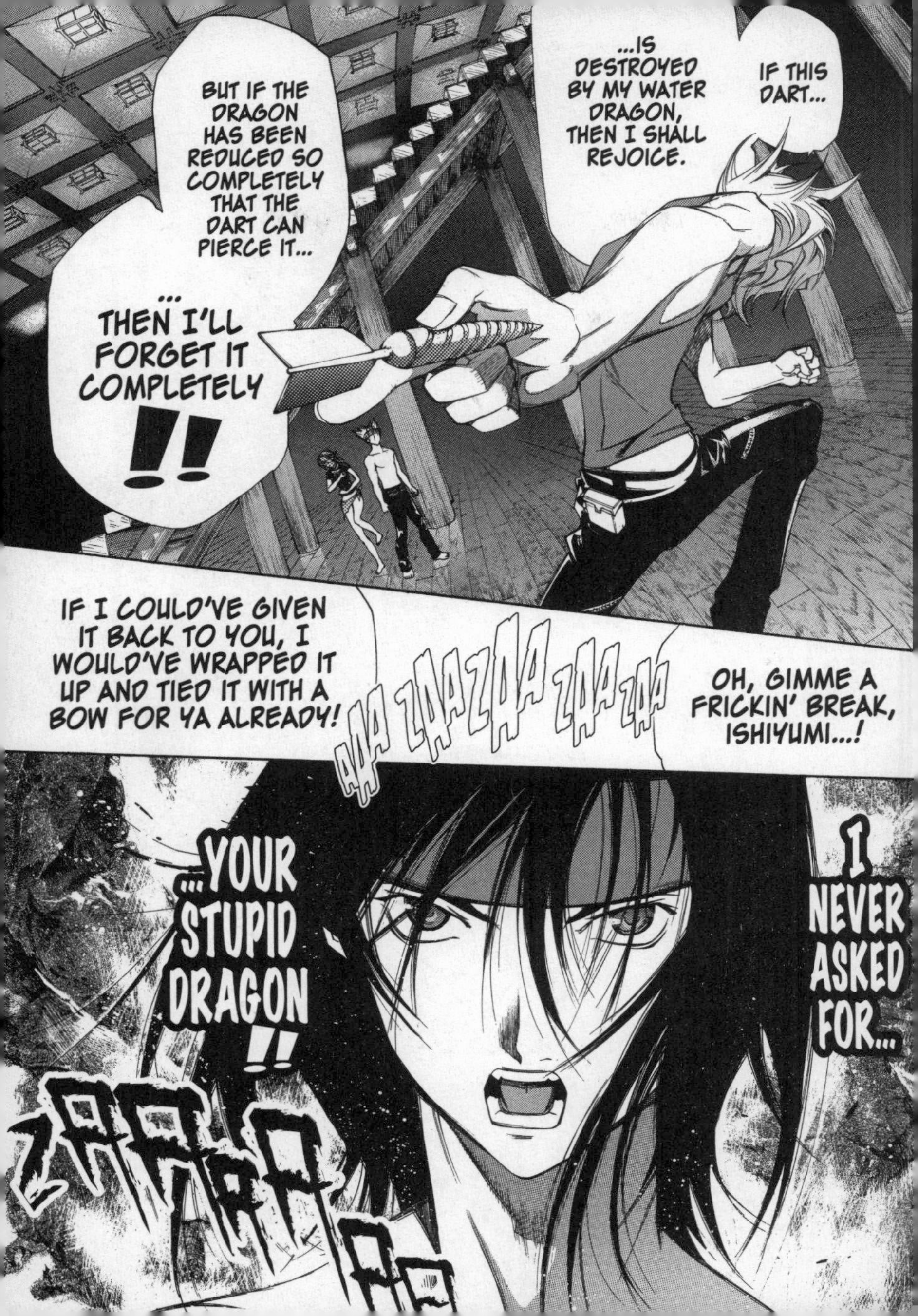
IF THIS DART...
...IS DESTROYED BY MY WATER DRAGON, THEN I SHALL REJOICE.
BUT IF THE DRAGON HAS BEEN REDUCED SO COMPLETELY THAT THE DART CAN PIERCE IT...
...THEN I'LL FORGET IT COMPLETELY!!
OH, GIMME A FRICKIN' BREAK, ISHIYUMI...!
AAA ZAA ZAA ZAA ZAA
IF I COULD'VE GIVEN IT BACK TO YOU, I WOULD'VE WRAPPED IT UP AND TIED IT WITH A BOW FOR YA ALREADY!
I NEVER ASKED FOR...
...YOUR STUPID DRAGON!!
ZAAAA

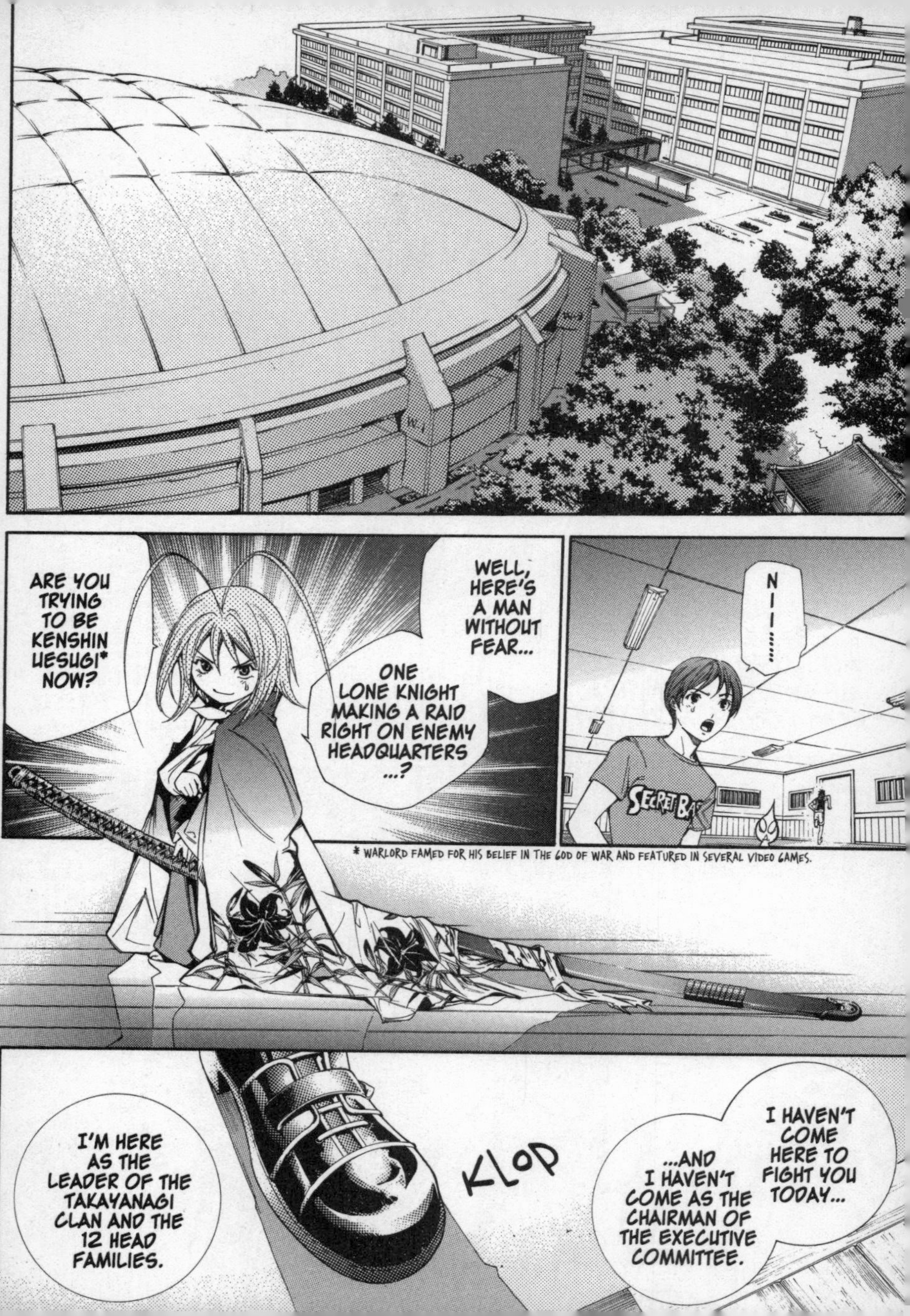
NIII......
WELL, HERE'S A MAN WITHOUT FEAR...
ONE LONE KNIGHT MAKING A RAID RIGHT ON ENEMY HEADQUARTERS ...?
ARE YOU TRYING TO BE KENSHIN UESUGI* NOW?
* WARLORD FAMED FOR HIS BELIEF IN THE GOD OF WAR AND FEATURED IN SEVERAL VIDEO GAMES.
I HAVEN'T COME HERE TO FIGHT YOU TODAY...
...AND I HAVEN'T COME AS THE CHAIRMAN OF THE EXECUTIVE COMMITTEE.
KLOP
I'M HERE AS THE LEADER OF THE TAKAYANAGI CLAN AND THE 12 HEAD FAMILIES.

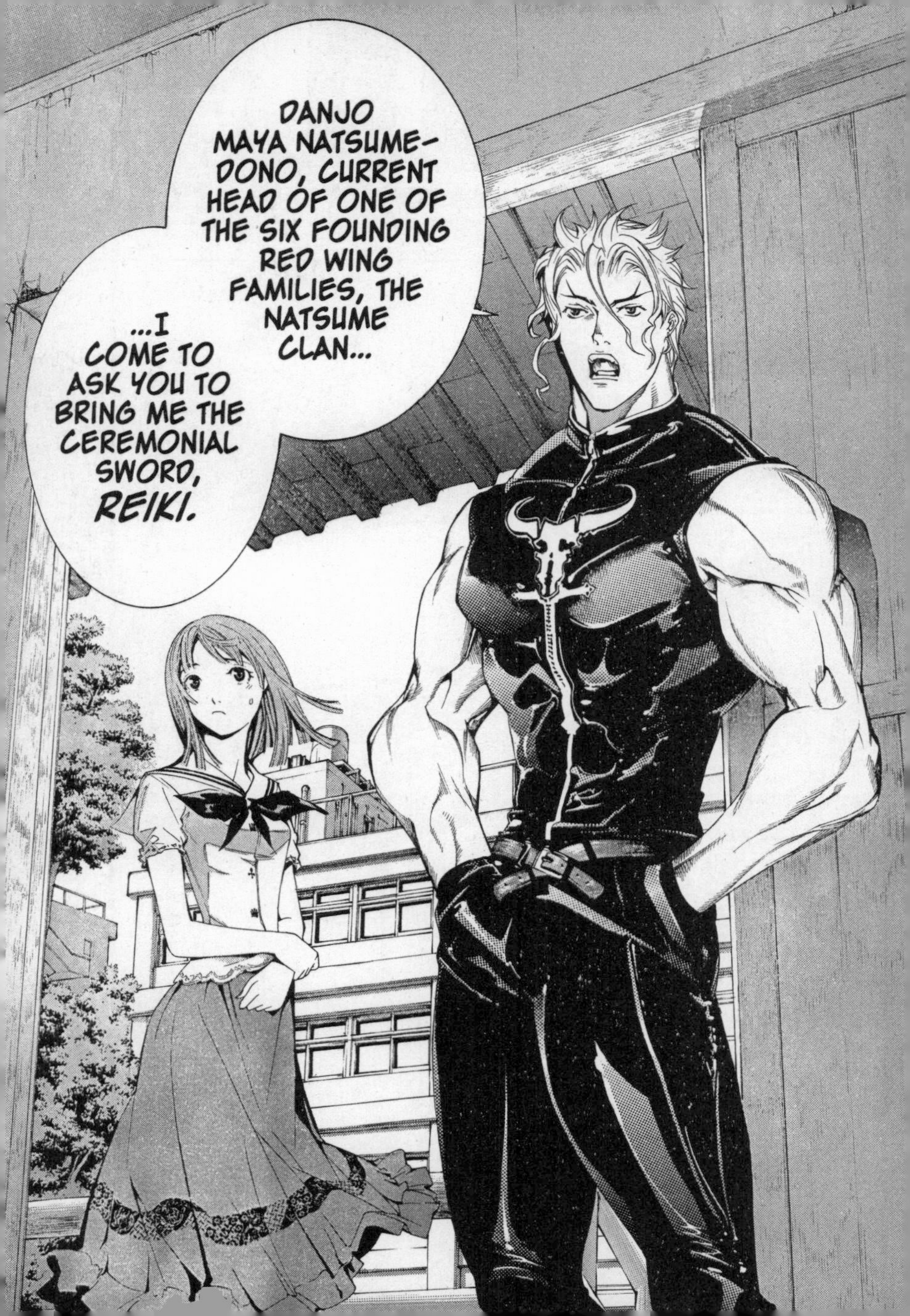
DANJO MAYA NATSUME-DONO, CURRENT HEAD OF ONE OF THE SIX FOUNDING RED WING FAMILIES, THE NATSUME CLAN...
...I COME TO ASK YOU TO BRING ME THE CEREMONIAL SWORD, *REIKI.*

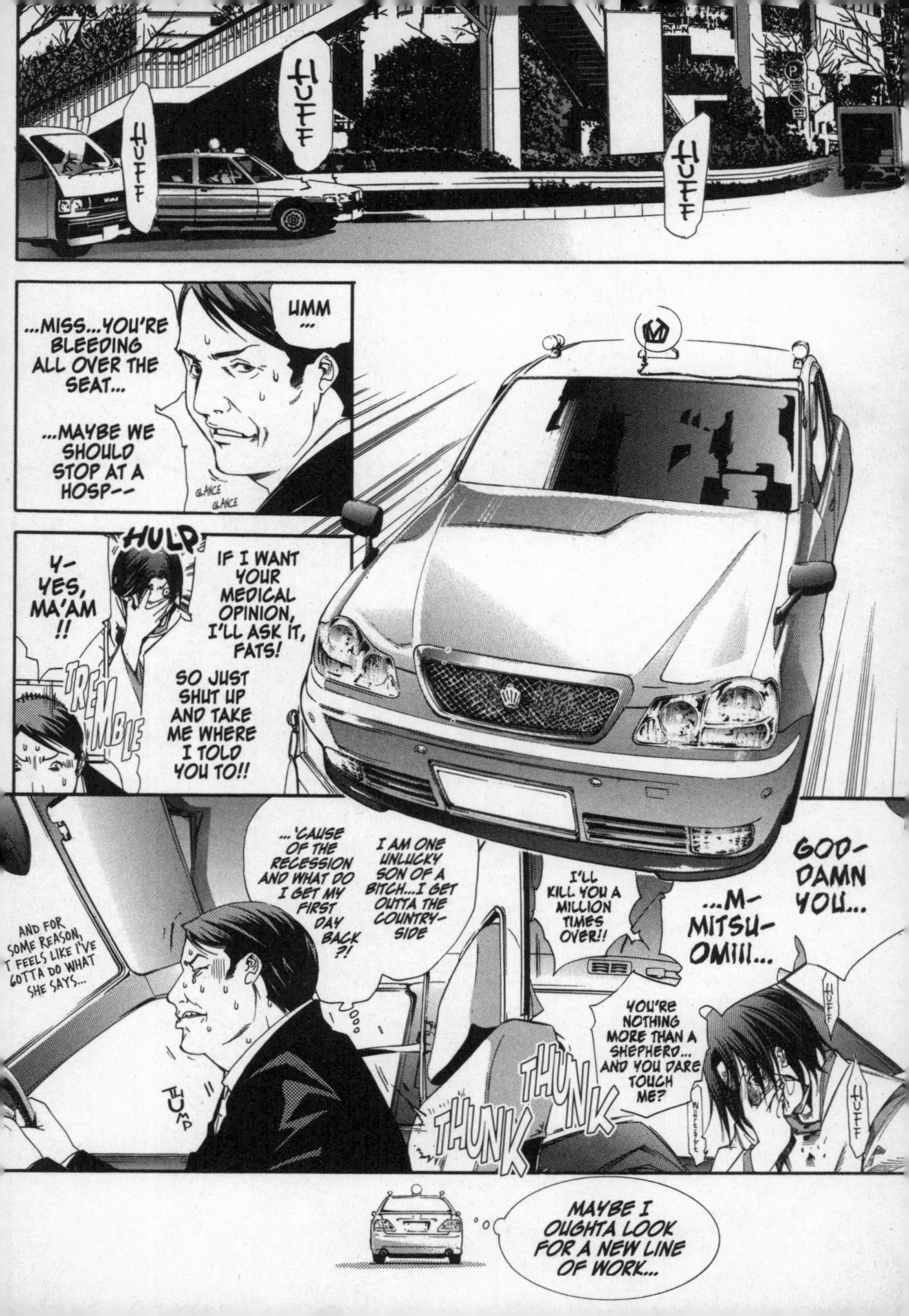
HUFF
HUFF
HUFF
UMM...
...MISS...YOU'RE BLEEDING ALL OVER THE SEAT...
...MAYBE WE SHOULD STOP AT A HOSP--
GLANCE GLANCE
HULP
IF I WANT YOUR MEDICAL OPINION, I'LL ASK IT, FATS!
SO JUST SHUT UP AND TAKE ME WHERE I TOLD YOU TO!!
Y-YES, MA'AM!!
TREMBLE
GOD-DAMN YOU...
HUFF
...M-MITSU-OMIII...
I'LL KILL YOU A MILLION TIMES OVER!!
YOU'RE NOTHING MORE THAN A SHEPHERD... AND YOU DARE TOUCH ME?
HUFF
THUNK
THUNK
I AM ONE UNLUCKY SON OF A BITCH...I GET OUTTA THE COUNTRYSIDE
...'CAUSE OF THE RECESSION AND WHAT DO I GET MY FIRST DAY BACK?!
AND FOR SOME REASON,
T FEELS LIKE I'VE GOTTA DO WHAT SHE SAYS...
THUMP
MAYBE I OUGHTA LOOK FOR A NEW LINE OF WORK...

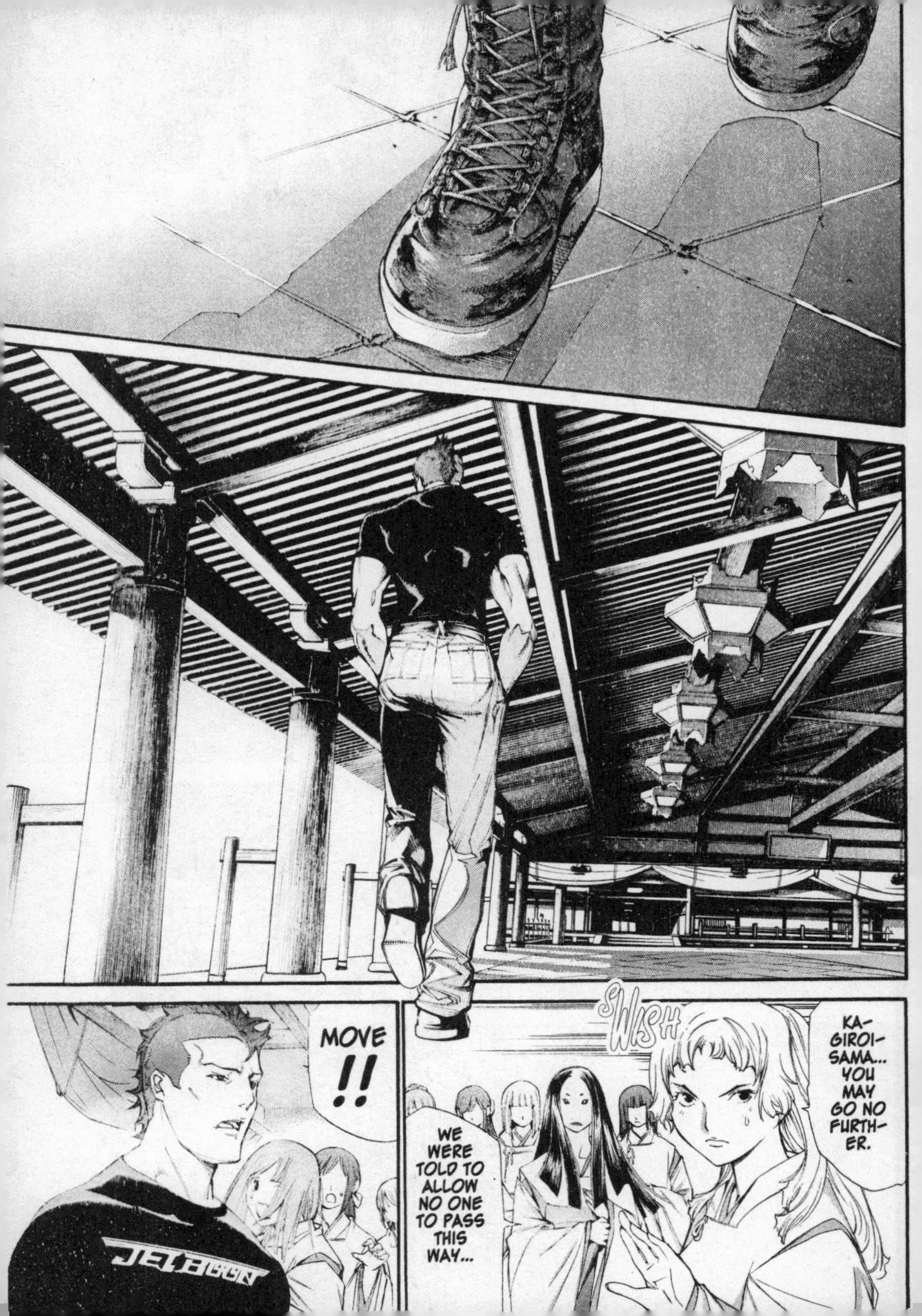
SWISH
KA-GIROI-SAMA... YOU MAY GO NO FURTH-ER.
WE WERE TOLD TO ALLOW NO ONE TO PASS THIS WAY...
MOVE !!
JETBOON

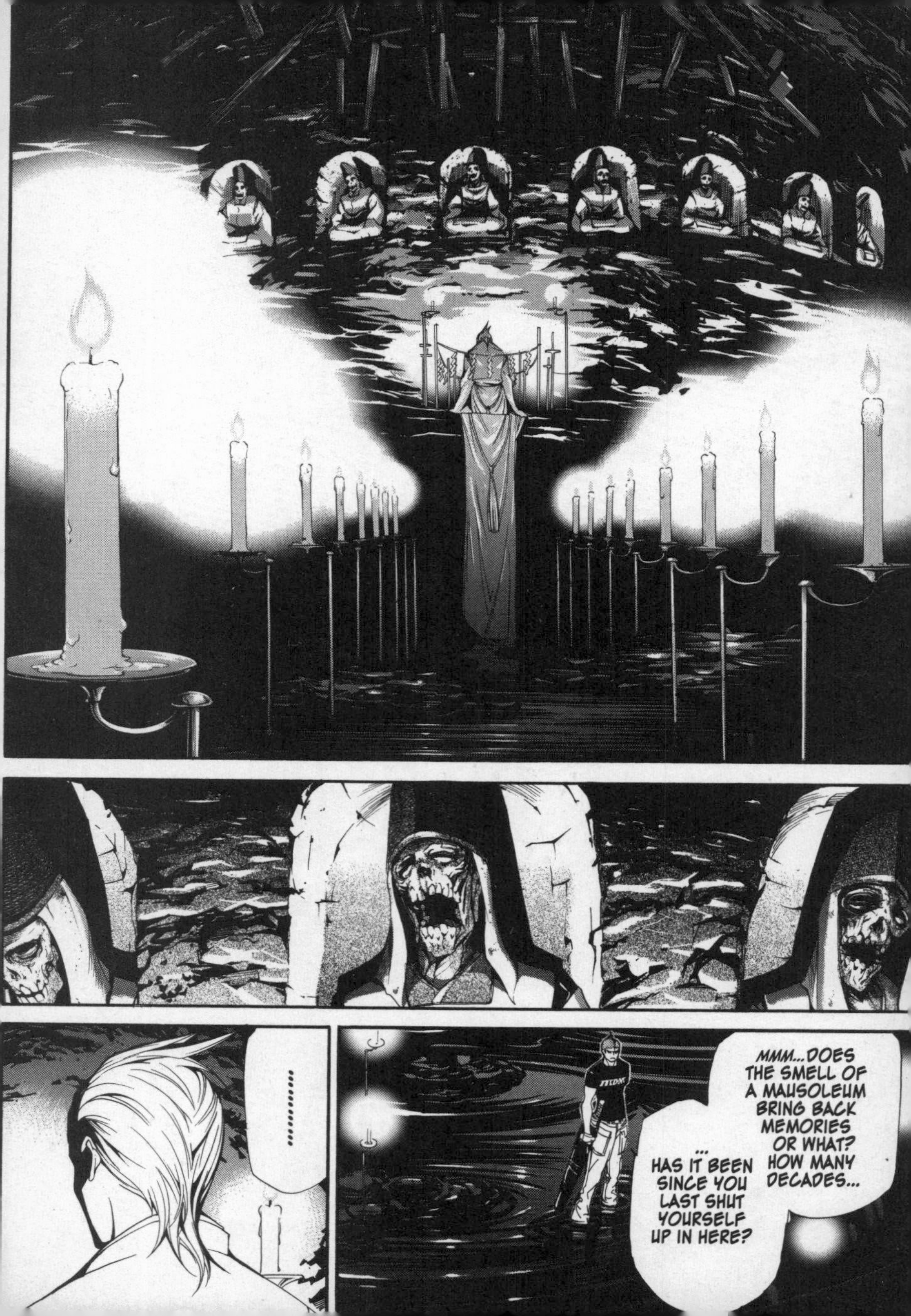
MMM...DOES THE SMELL OF A MAUSOLEUM BRING BACK MEMORIES OR WHAT? HOW MANY DECADES...
...HAS IT BEEN SINCE YOU LAST SHUT YOURSELF UP IN HERE?
....

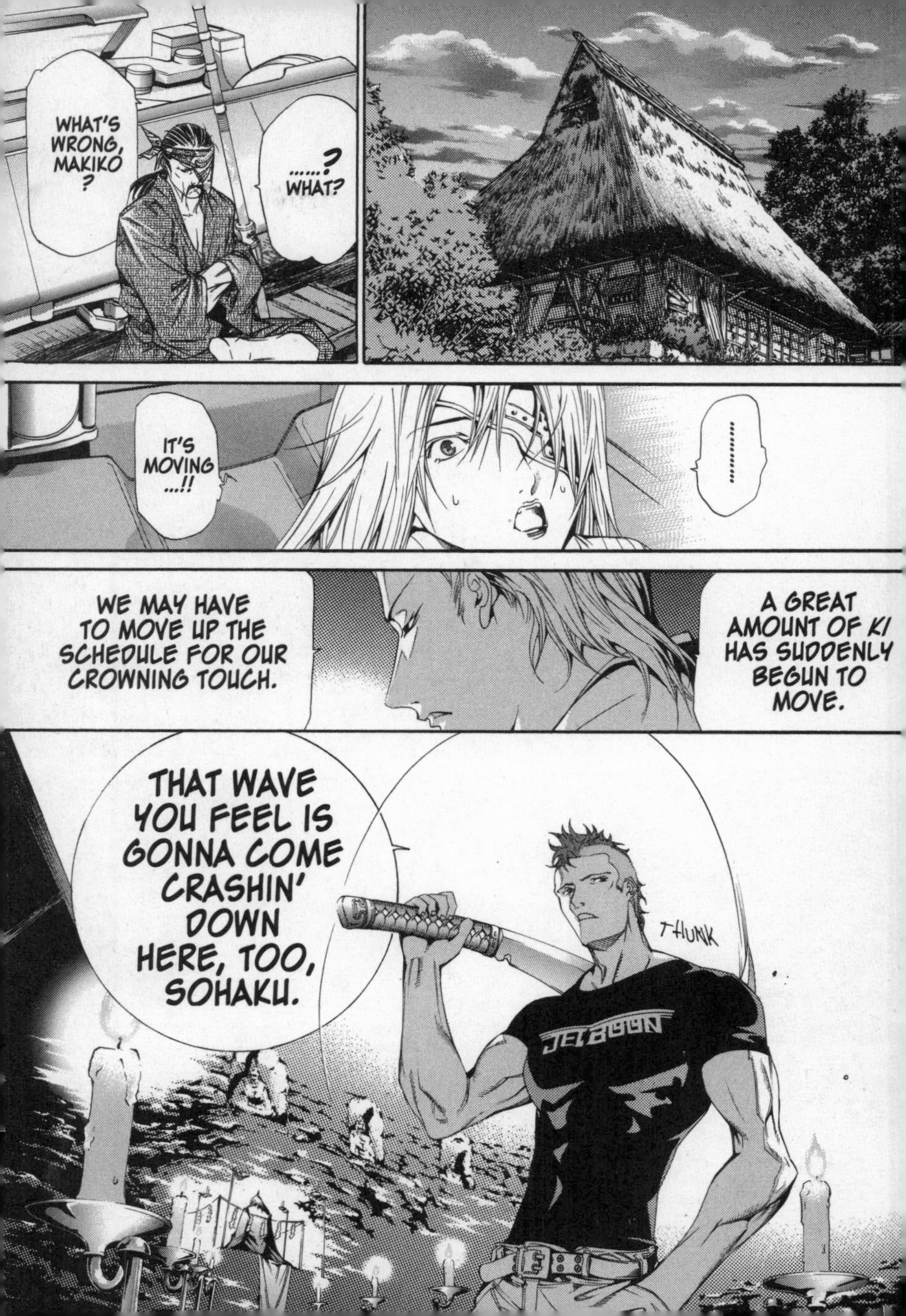
WHAT'S WRONG, MAKIKO?
......? WHAT?
....
IT'S MOVING ...!!
A GREAT AMOUNT OF KI HAS SUDDENLY BEGUN TO MOVE.
WE MAY HAVE TO MOVE UP THE SCHEDULE FOR OUR CROWNING TOUCH.
THAT WAVE YOU FEEL IS GONNA COME CRASHIN' DOWN HERE, TOO, SOHAKU.
THUNK

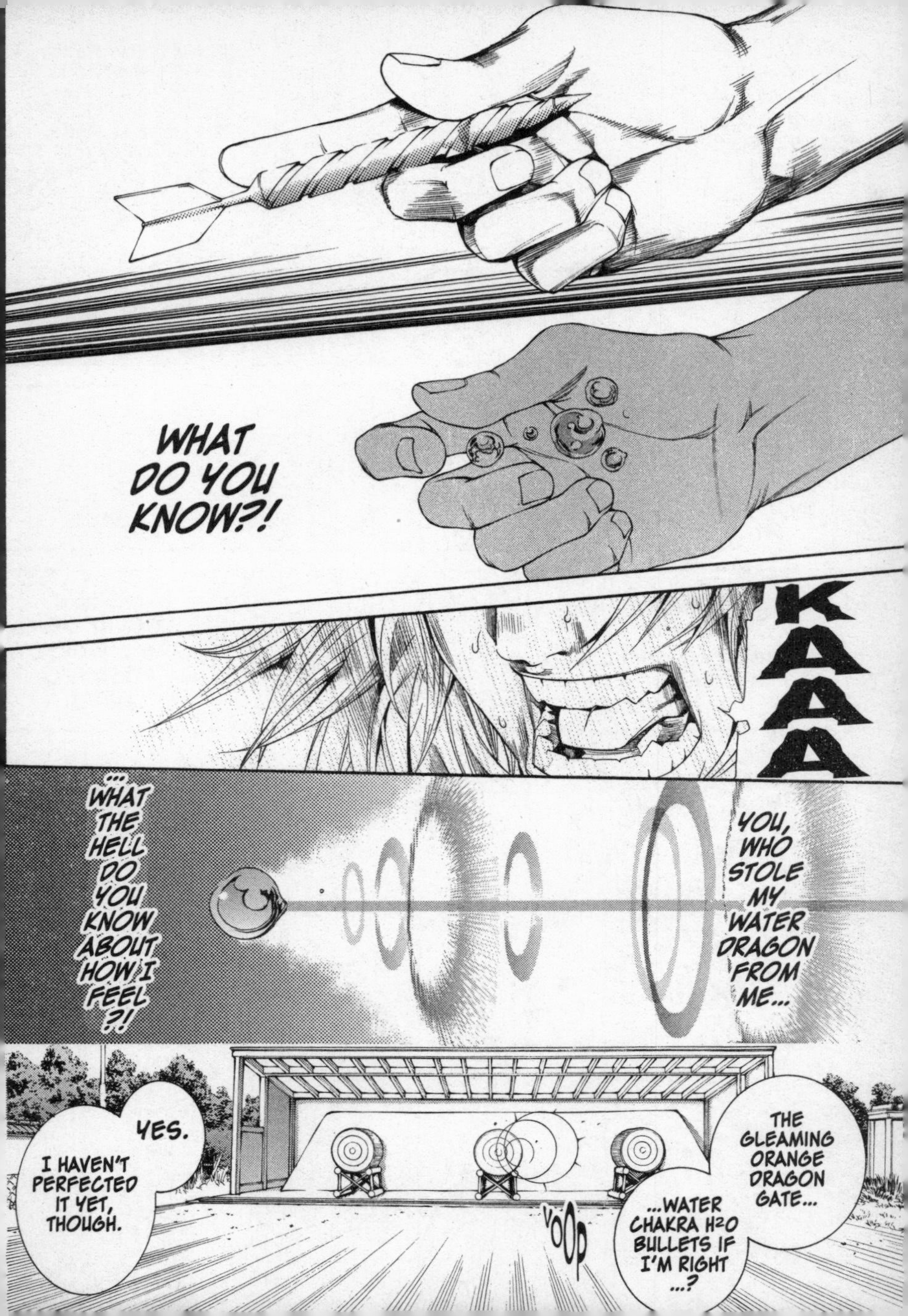
WHAT DO YOU KNOW?!
KAAA
YOU, WHO STOLE MY WATER DRAGON FROM ME...
...WHAT THE HELL DO YOU KNOW ABOUT HOW I FEEL?!
THE GLEAMING ORANGE DRAGON GATE...
...WATER CHAKRA H_2O BULLETS IF I'M RIGHT...?
VOOP
YES.
I HAVEN'T PERFECTED IT YET, THOUGH.

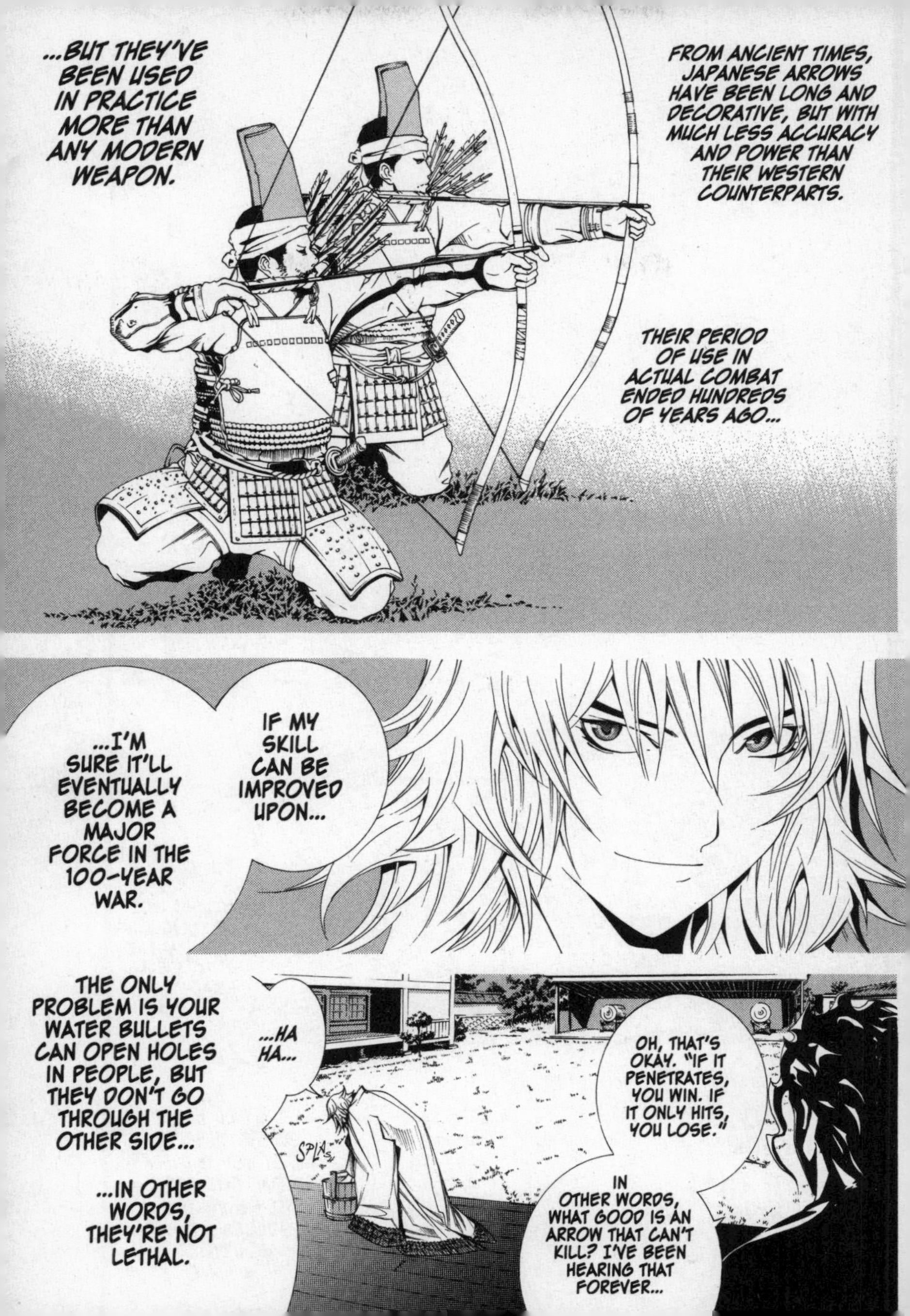
FROM ANCIENT TIMES, JAPANESE ARROWS HAVE BEEN LONG AND DECORATIVE, BUT WITH MUCH LESS ACCURACY AND POWER THAN THEIR WESTERN COUNTERPARTS.
THEIR PERIOD OF USE IN ACTUAL COMBAT ENDED HUNDREDS OF YEARS AGO...
...BUT THEY'VE BEEN USED IN PRACTICE MORE THAN ANY MODERN WEAPON.
IF MY SKILL CAN BE IMPROVED UPON...
...I'M SURE IT'LL EVENTUALLY BECOME A MAJOR FORCE IN THE 100-YEAR WAR.
OH, THAT'S OKAY. "IF IT PENETRATES, YOU WIN. IF IT ONLY HITS, YOU LOSE."
IN OTHER WORDS, WHAT GOOD IS AN ARROW THAT CAN'T KILL? I'VE BEEN HEARING THAT FOREVER...
...HA HA...
SPLASH
THE ONLY PROBLEM IS YOUR WATER BULLETS CAN OPEN HOLES IN PEOPLE, BUT THEY DON'T GO THROUGH THE OTHER SIDE...
...IN OTHER WORDS, THEY'RE NOT LETHAL.

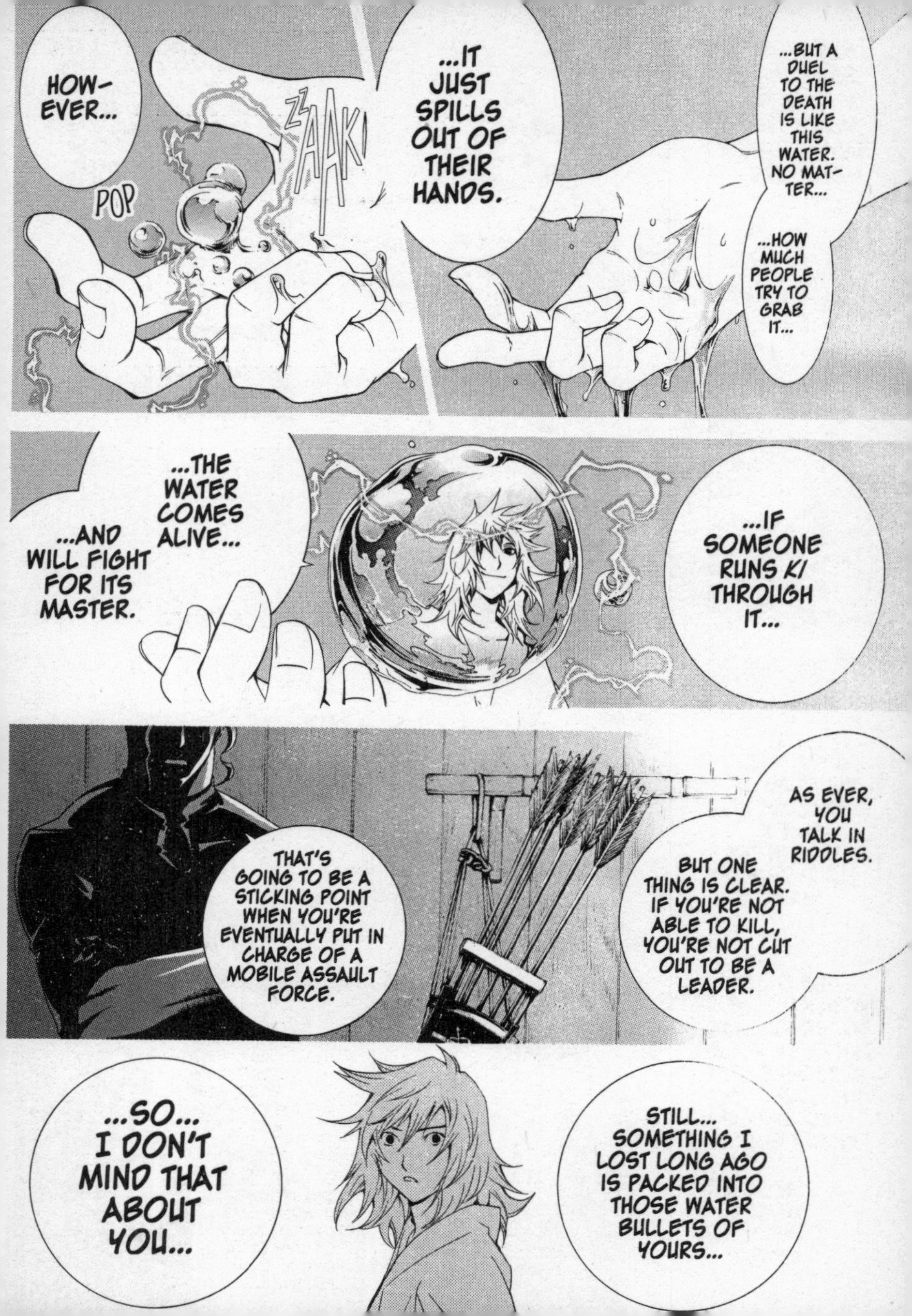
...BUT A DUEL TO THE DEATH IS LIKE THIS WATER. NO MATTER...
...HOW MUCH PEOPLE TRY TO GRAB IT...
...IT JUST SPILLS OUT OF THEIR HANDS.
HOW-EVER...
ZZAAK!
POP
...IF SOMEONE RUNS KI THROUGH IT...
...THE WATER COMES ALIVE...
...AND WILL FIGHT FOR ITS MASTER.
AS EVER, YOU TALK IN RIDDLES.
BUT ONE THING IS CLEAR. IF YOU'RE NOT ABLE TO KILL, YOU'RE NOT CUT OUT TO BE A LEADER.
THAT'S GOING TO BE A STICKING POINT WHEN YOU'RE EVENTUALLY PUT IN CHARGE OF A MOBILE ASSAULT FORCE.
STILL... SOMETHING I LOST LONG AGO IS PACKED INTO THOSE WATER BULLETS OF YOURS...
...SO... I DON'T MIND THAT ABOUT YOU...

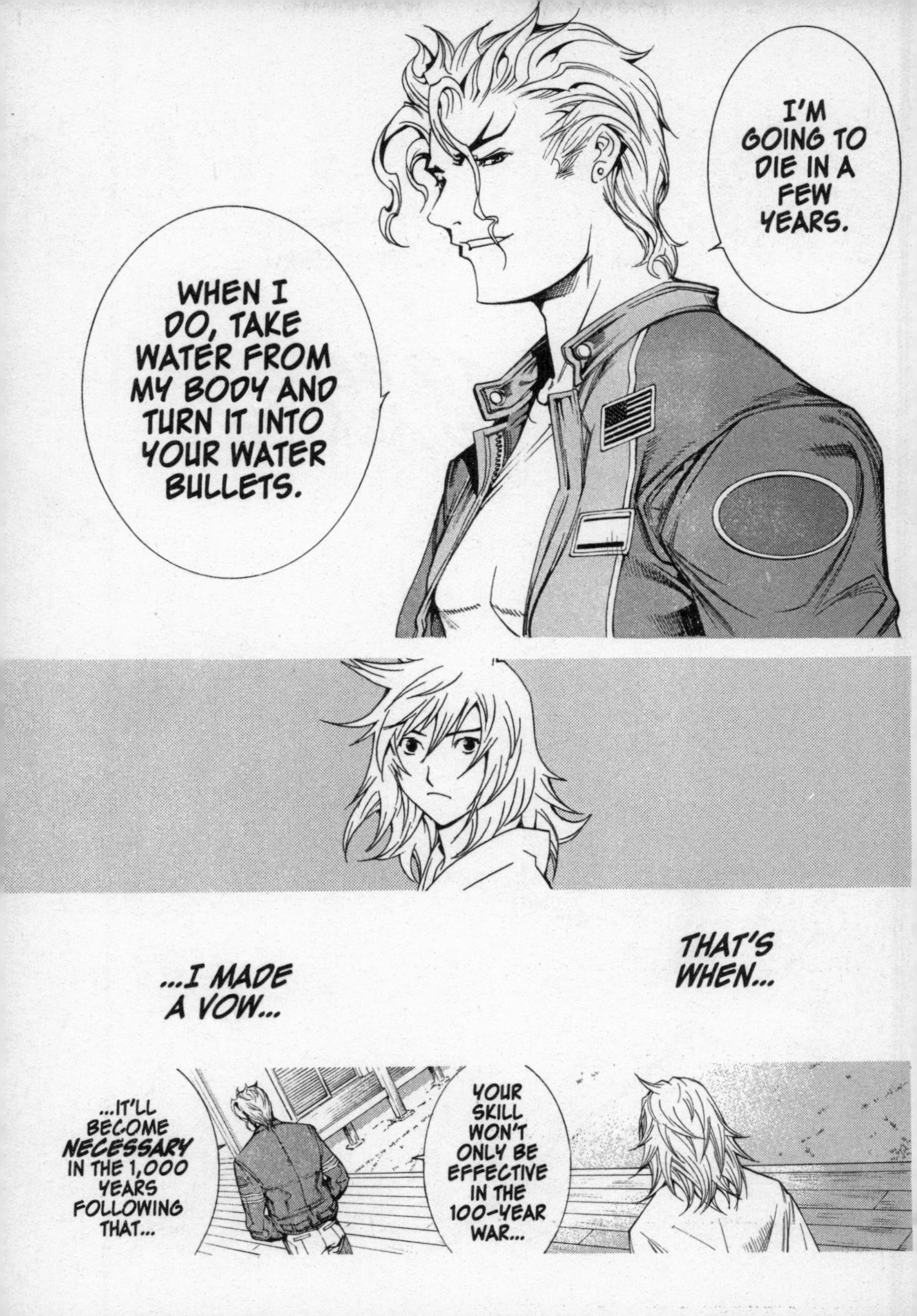
I'M GOING TO DIE IN A FEW YEARS.
WHEN I DO, TAKE WATER FROM MY BODY AND TURN IT INTO YOUR WATER BULLETS.
THAT'S WHEN...
...I MADE A VOW...
YOUR SKILL WON'T ONLY BE EFFECTIVE IN THE 100-YEAR WAR...
...IT'LL BECOME NECESSARY IN THE 1,000 YEARS FOLLOWING THAT...

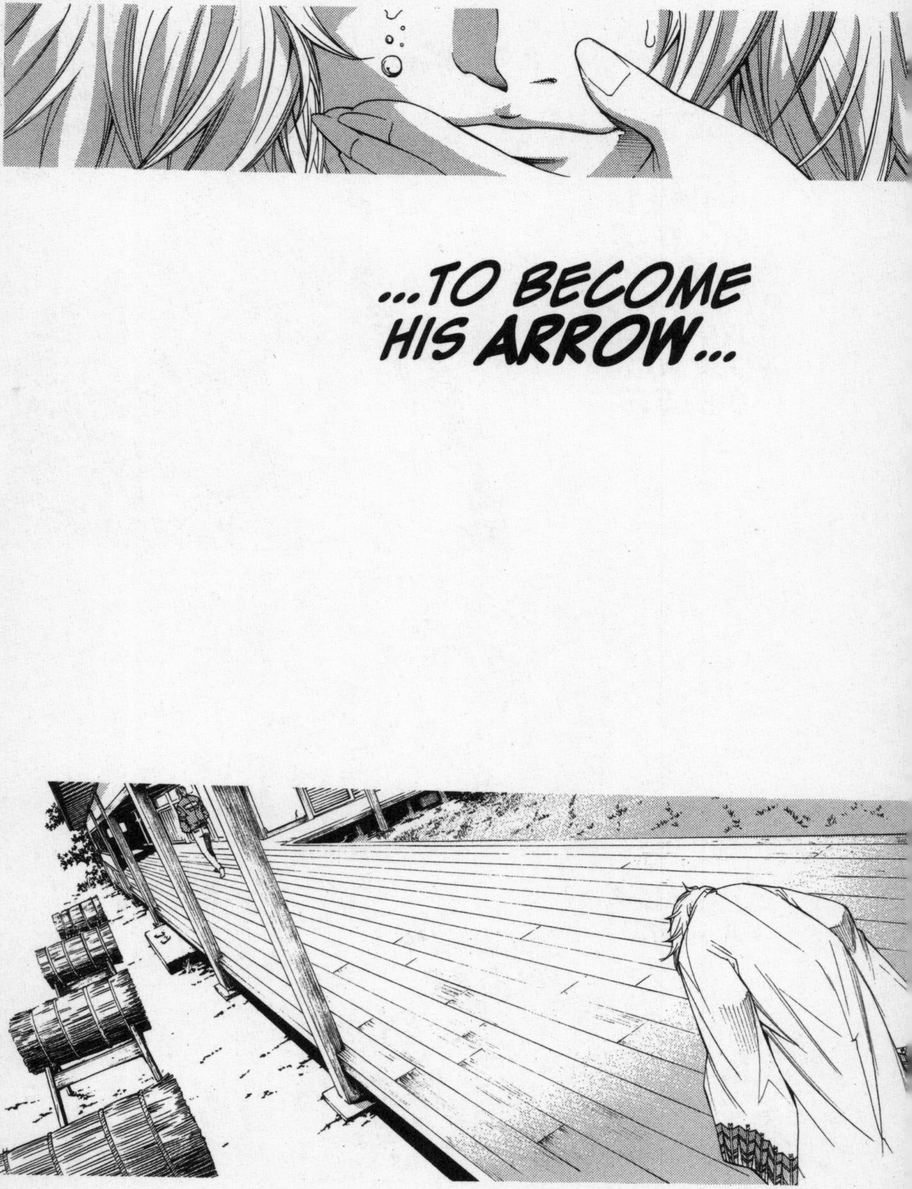
...TO BECOME HIS ARROW...

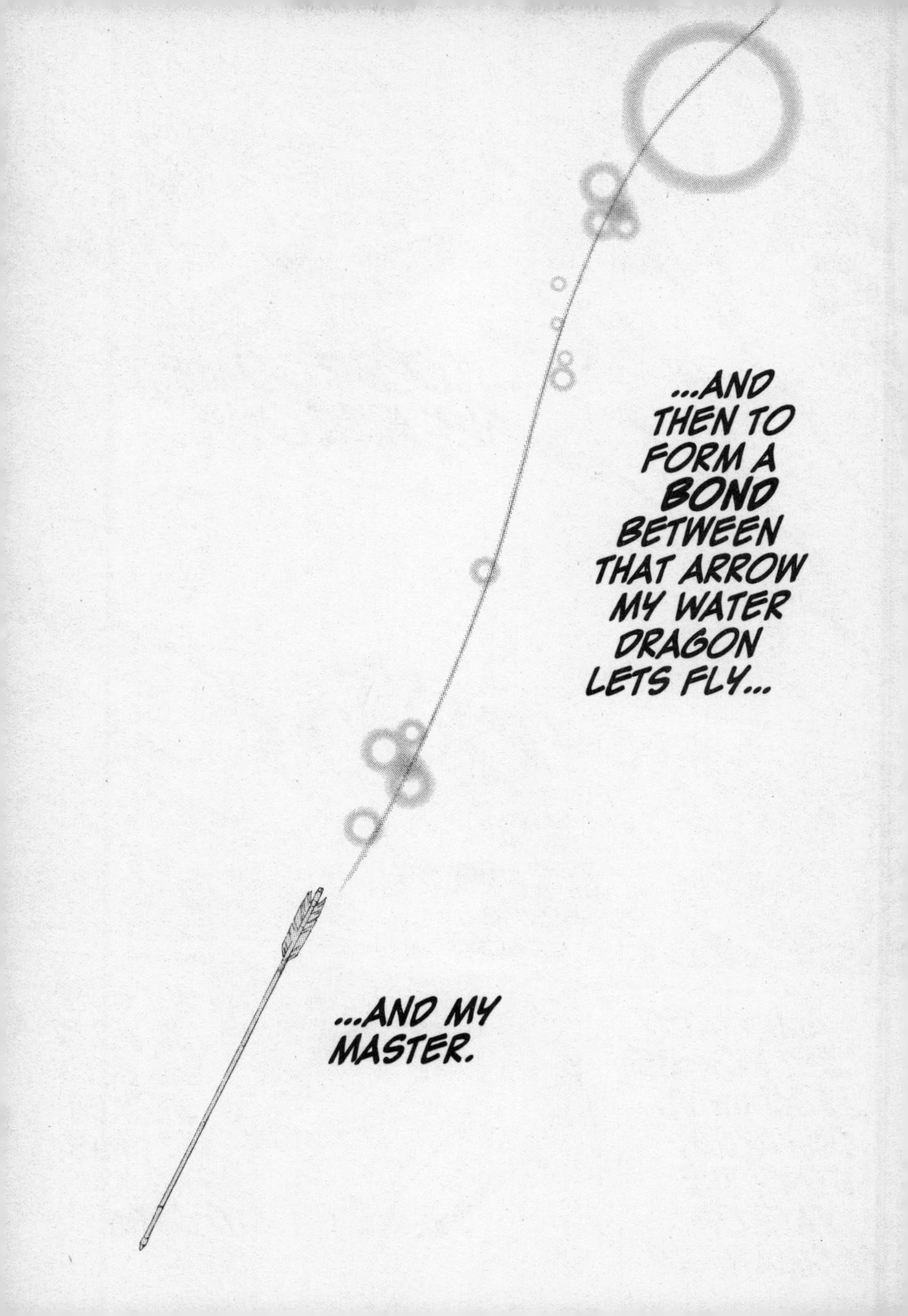
...AND THEN TO FORM A BOND BETWEEN THAT ARROW MY WATER DRAGON LETS FLY...
...AND MY MASTER.

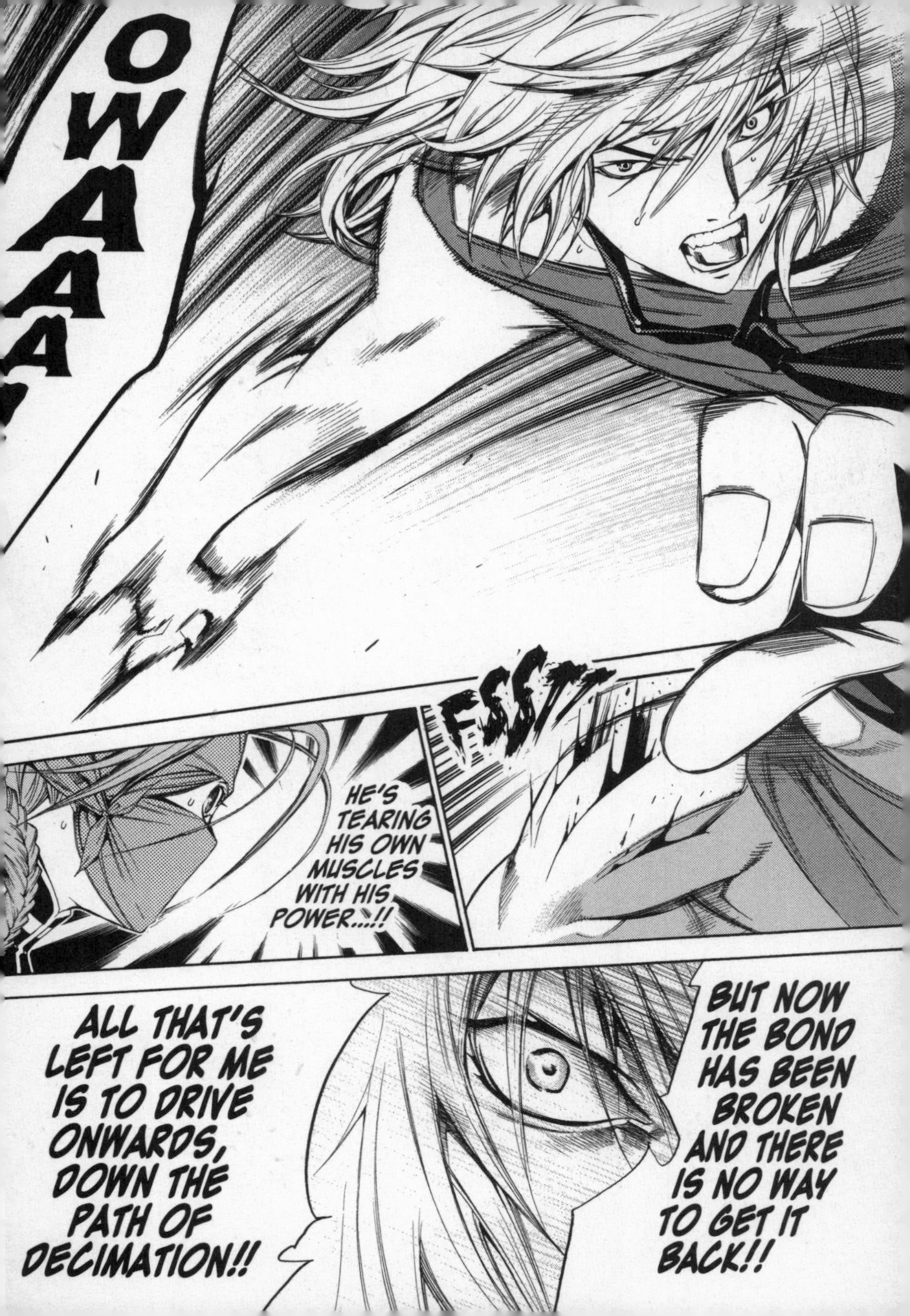
OWAAA
FSST
HE'S TEARING HIS OWN MUSCLES WITH HIS POWER...!!
BUT NOW THE BOND HAS BEEN BROKEN AND THERE IS NO WAY TO GET IT BACK!!
ALL THAT'S LEFT FOR ME IS TO DRIVE ONWARDS, DOWN THE PATH OF DECIMATION!!

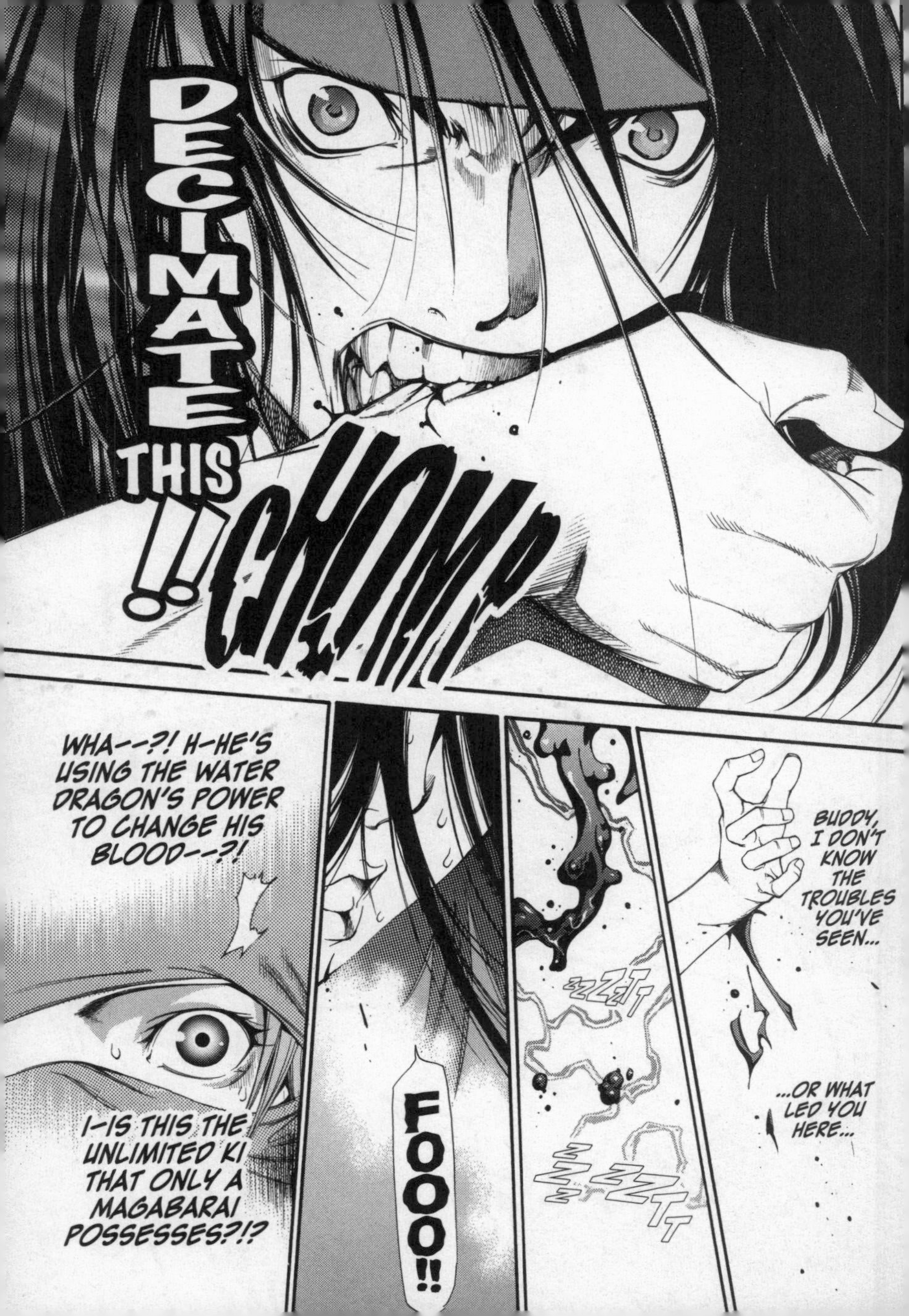

DECIMATE THIS!!
CHOMP
BUDDY, I DON'T KNOW THE TROUBLES YOU'VE SEEN...
...OR WHAT LED YOU HERE...
ZZZZTT
ZZZZZTT
FOOOO!!
WHA--?! H-HE'S USING THE WATER DRAGON'S POWER TO CHANGE HIS BLOOD--?!
I-IS THIS THE UNLIMITED KI THAT ONLY A MAGABARAI POSSESSES?!?

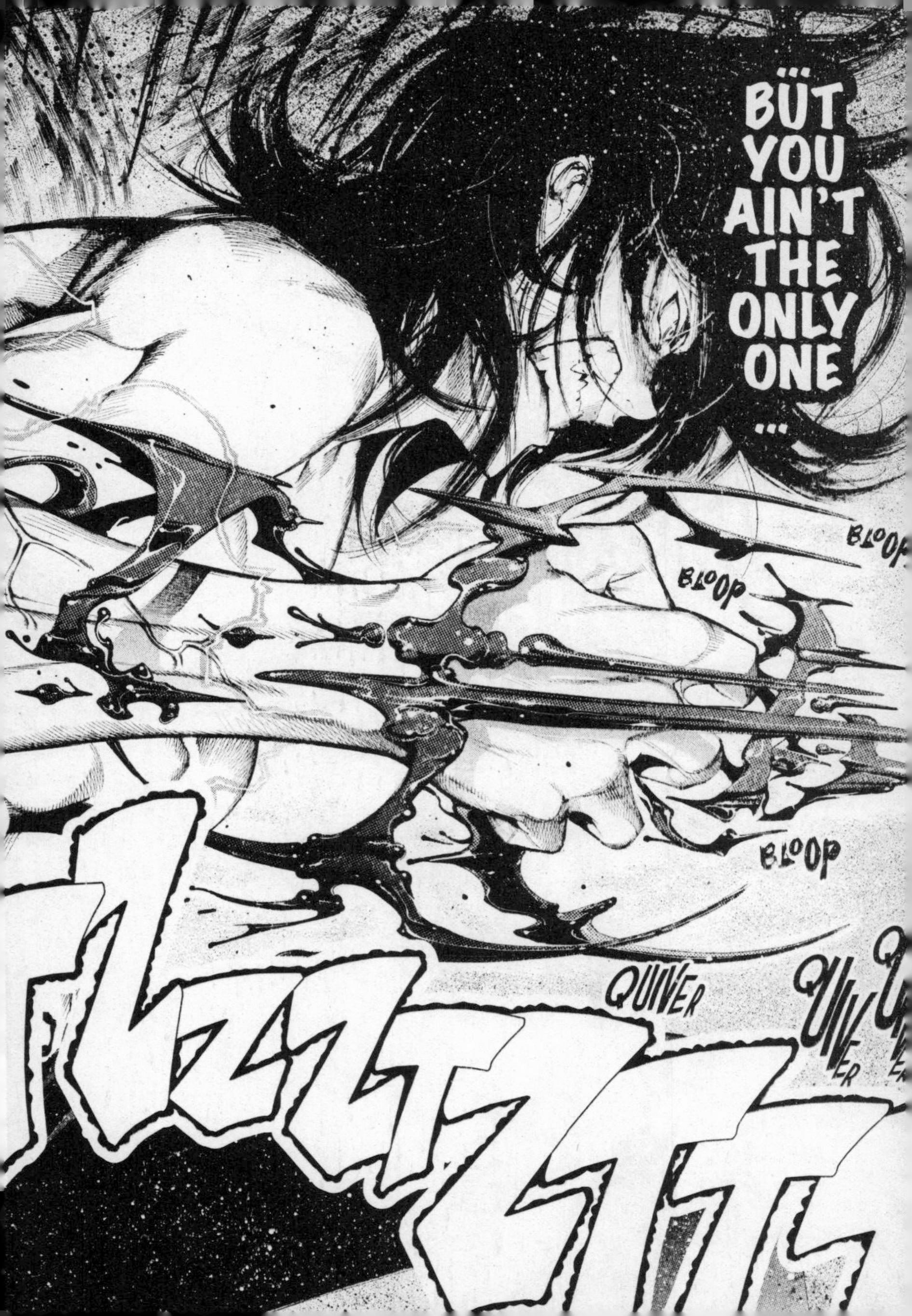
BÜT YOU AIN'T THE ONLY ONE ...
BLOOP
BLOOP
BLOOP
QUIVER
QUIVER

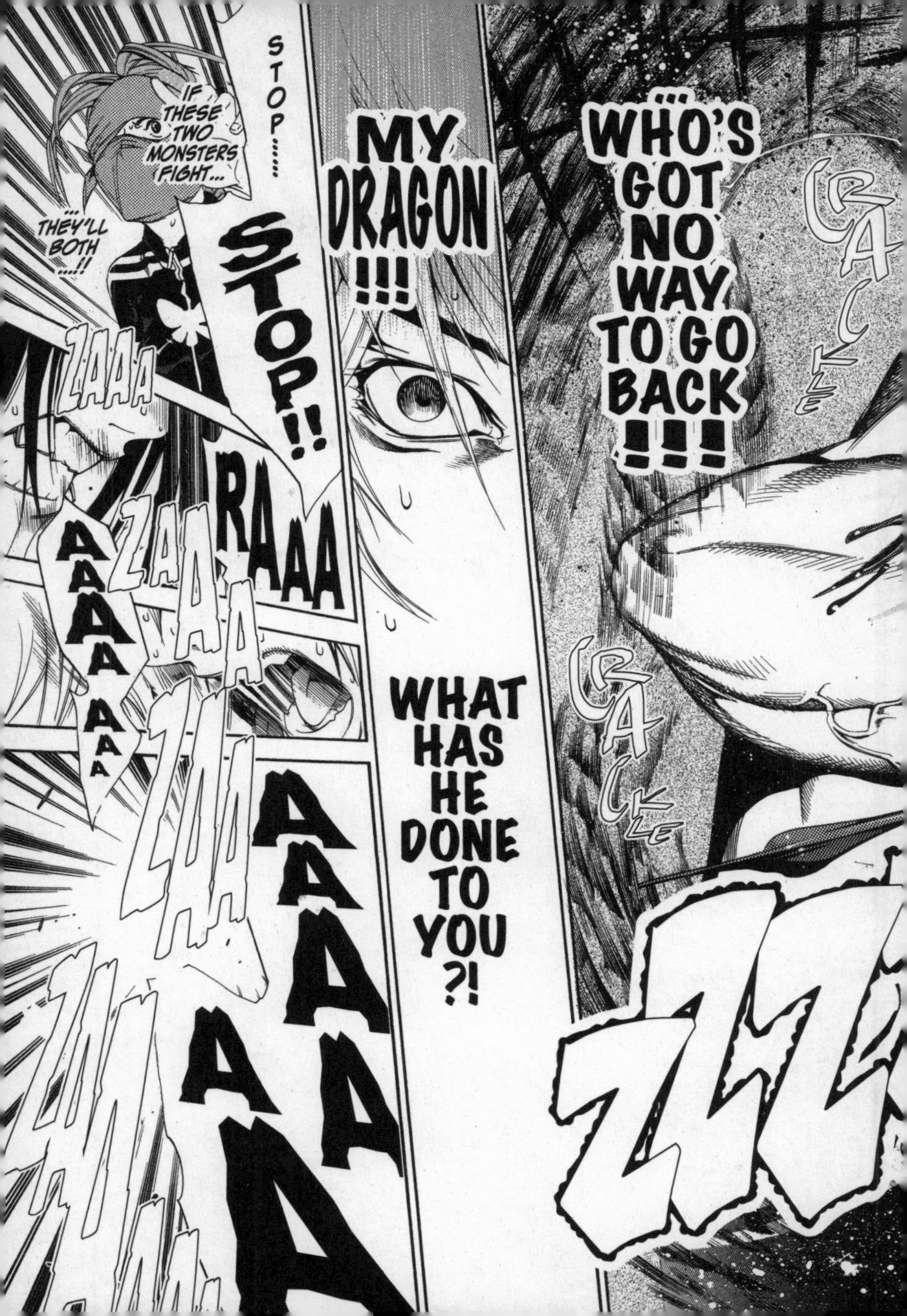
...WHO'S GOT NO WAY TO GO BACK!!!
CRACKLE
CRACKLE
MY DRAGON!!!
WHAT HAS HE DONE TO YOU?!
STOP.....
IF THESE TWO MONSTERS FIGHT...
...THEY'LL BOTH ...!!
STOP!!
RAAAA

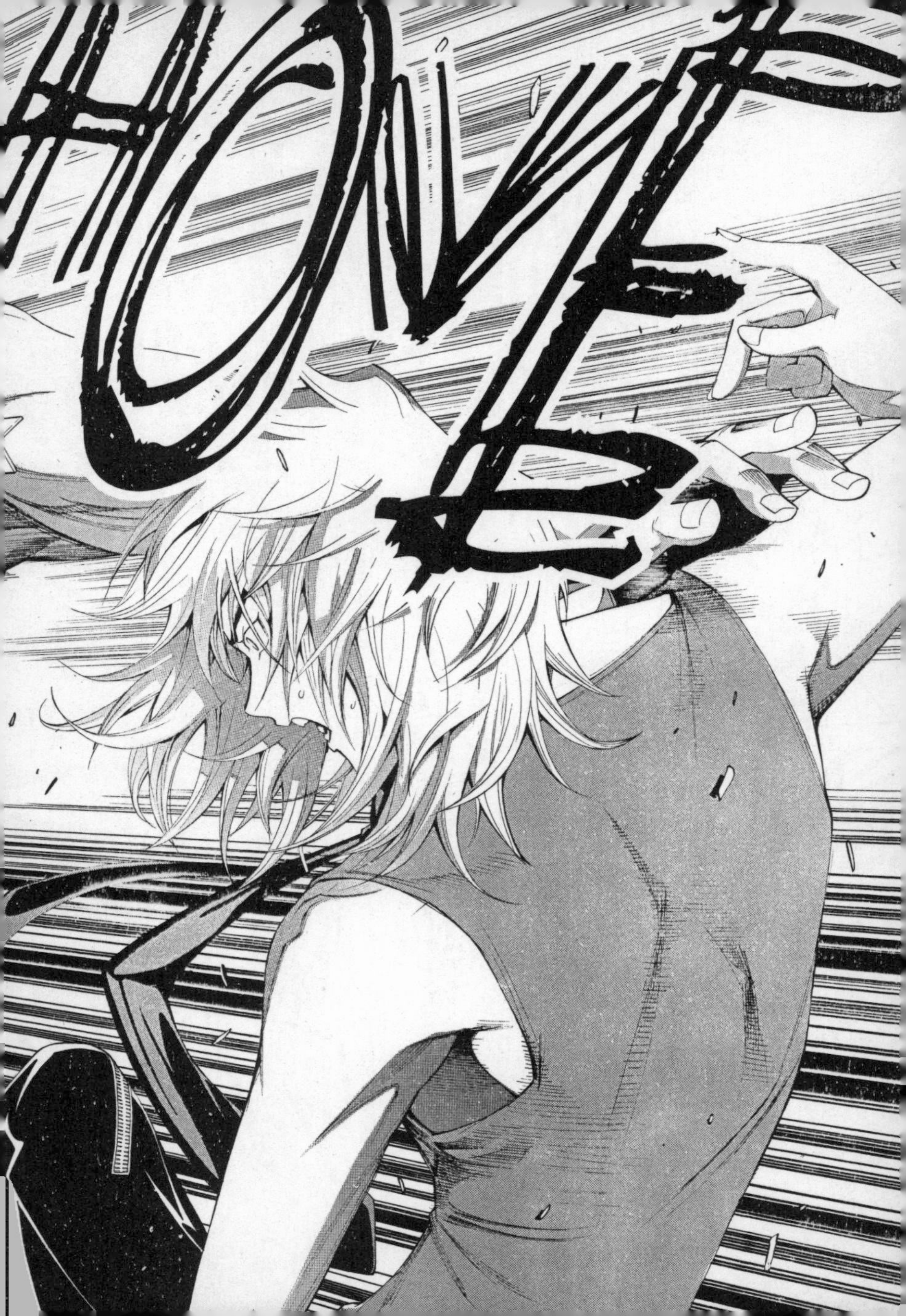

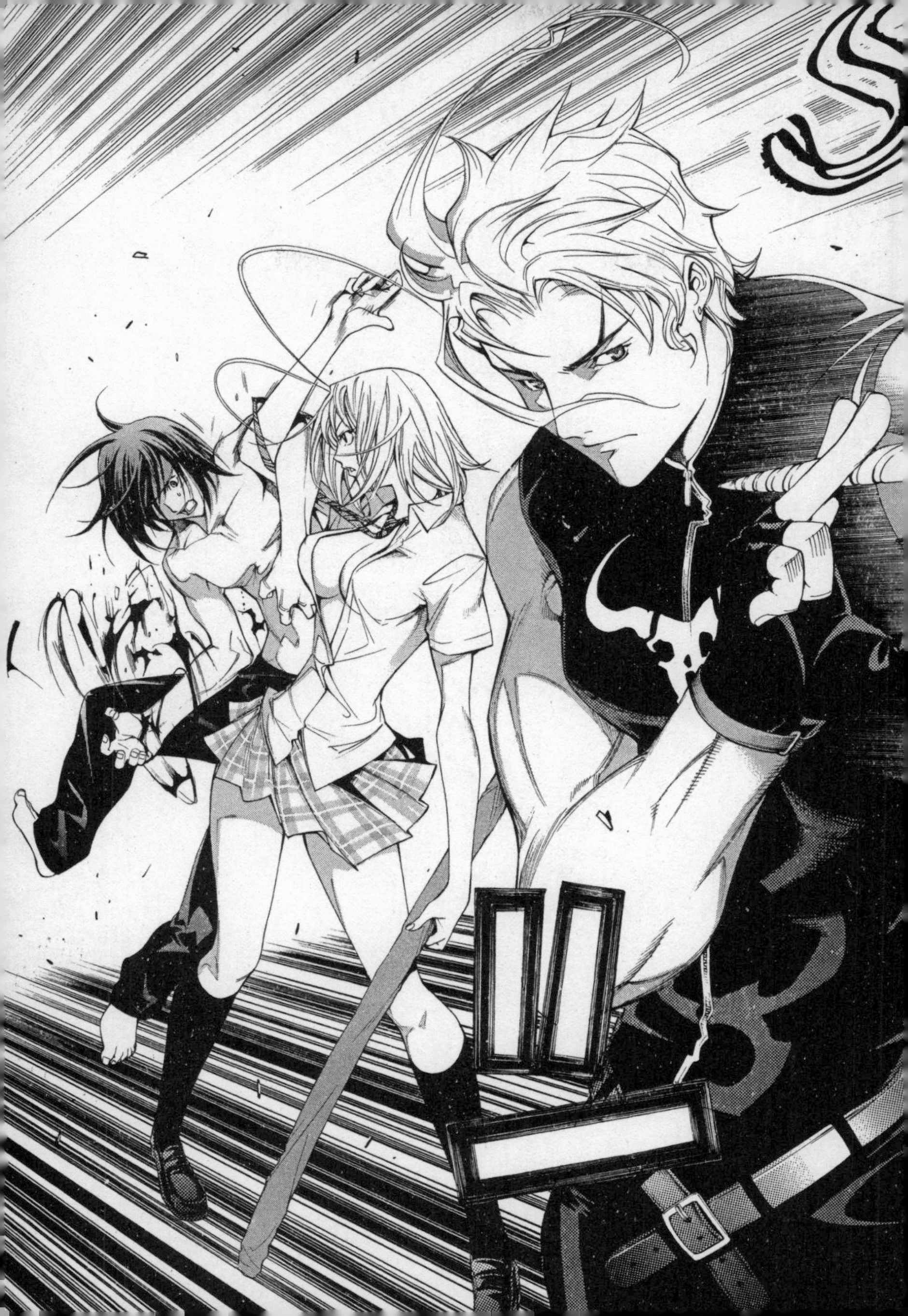

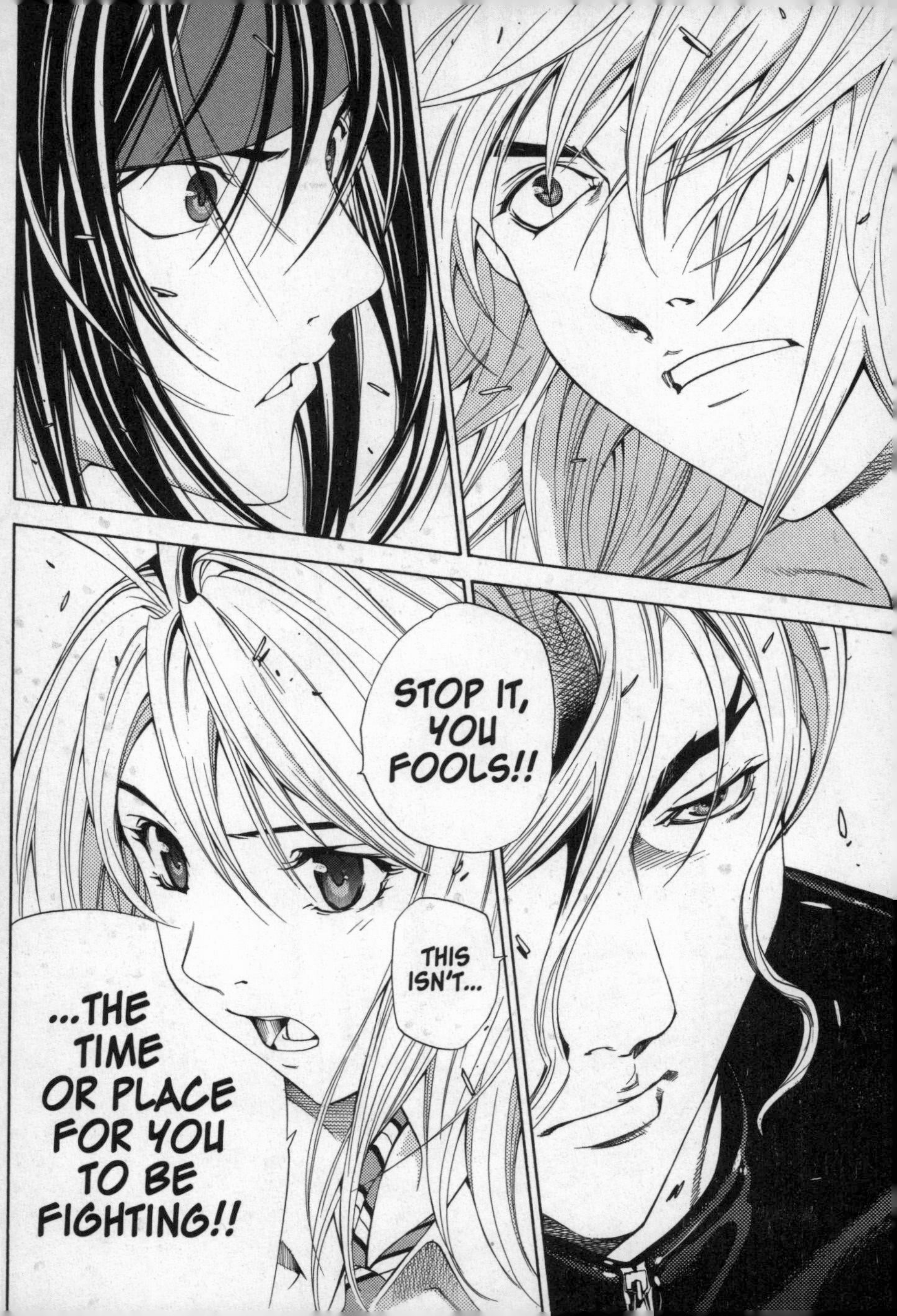
STOP IT, YOU FOOLS!!
THIS ISN'T...
...THE TIME OR PLACE FOR YOU TO BE FIGHTING!!

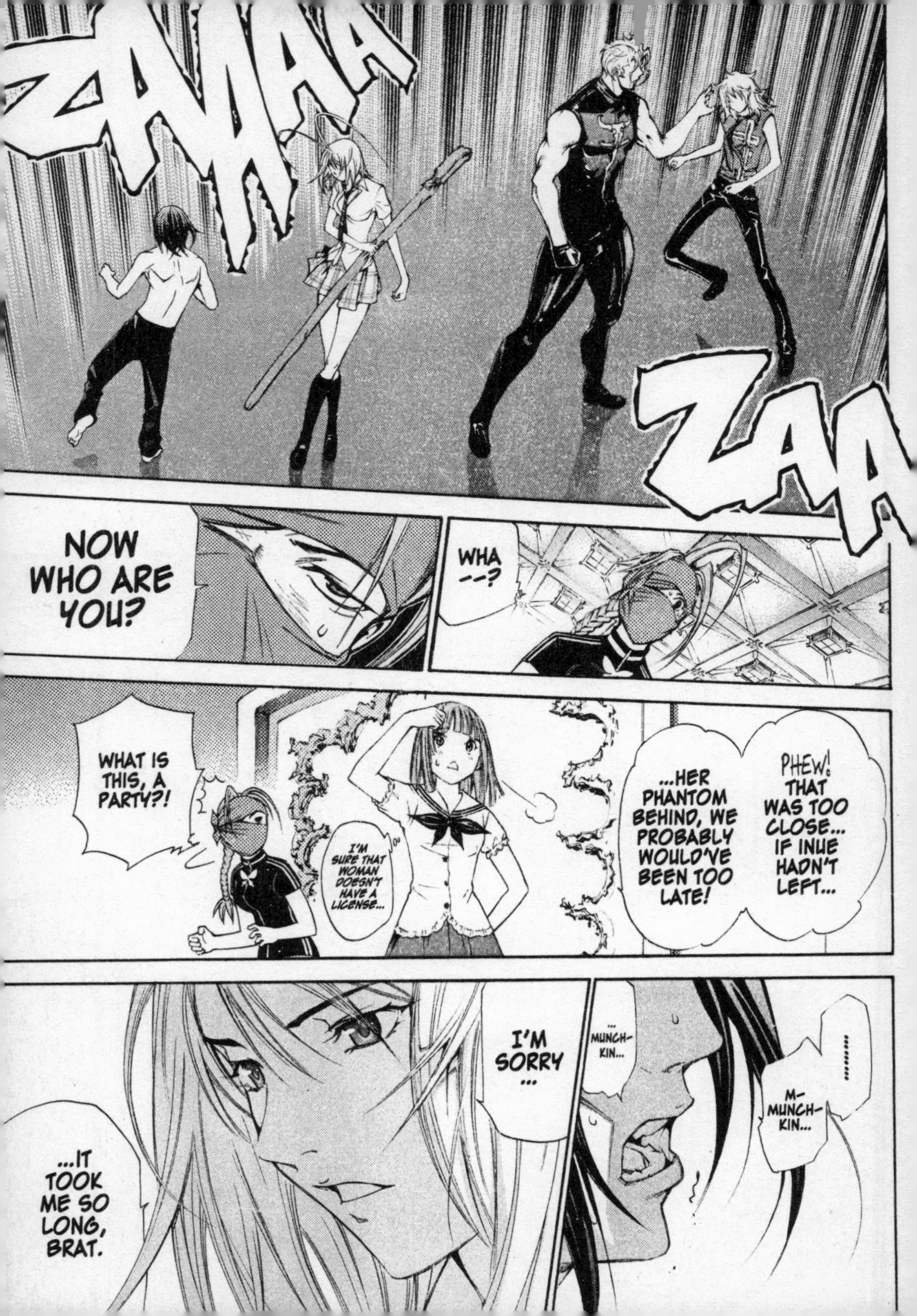
ZAAA
ZAA
WHA--?
NOW WHO ARE YOU?
PHEW! THAT WAS TOO CLOSE... IF INUE HADN'T LEFT...
...HER PHANTOM BEHIND, WE PROBABLY WOULD'VE BEEN TOO LATE!
I'M SURE THAT WOMAN DOESN'T HAVE A LICENSE...
WHAT IS THIS, A PARTY?!
......
M-MUNCH-KIN...
...MUNCH-KIN...
I'M SORRY...
...IT TOOK ME SO LONG, BRAT.

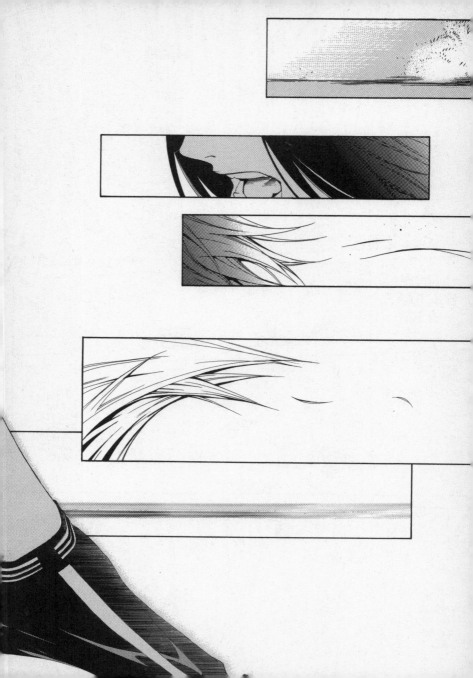

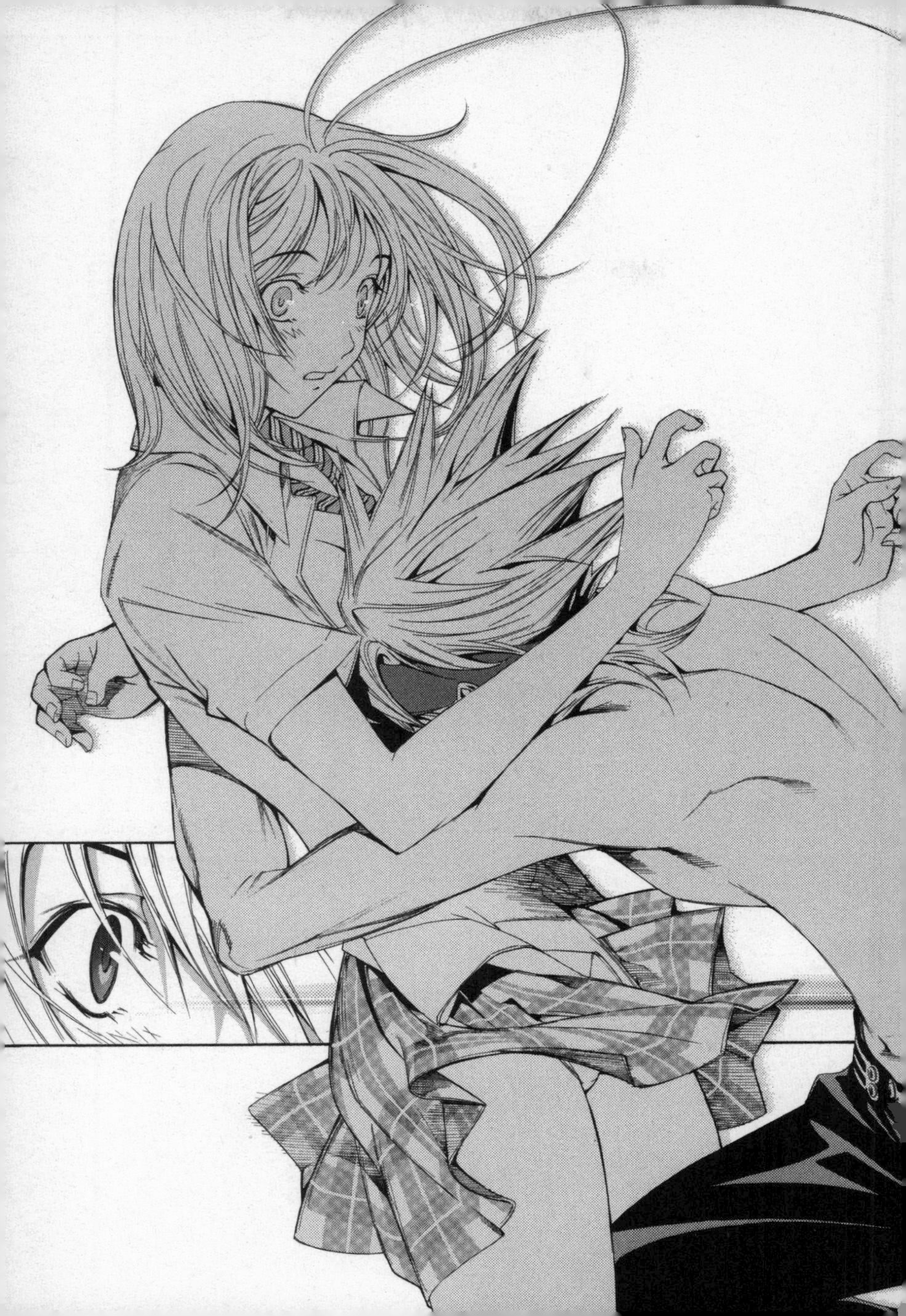

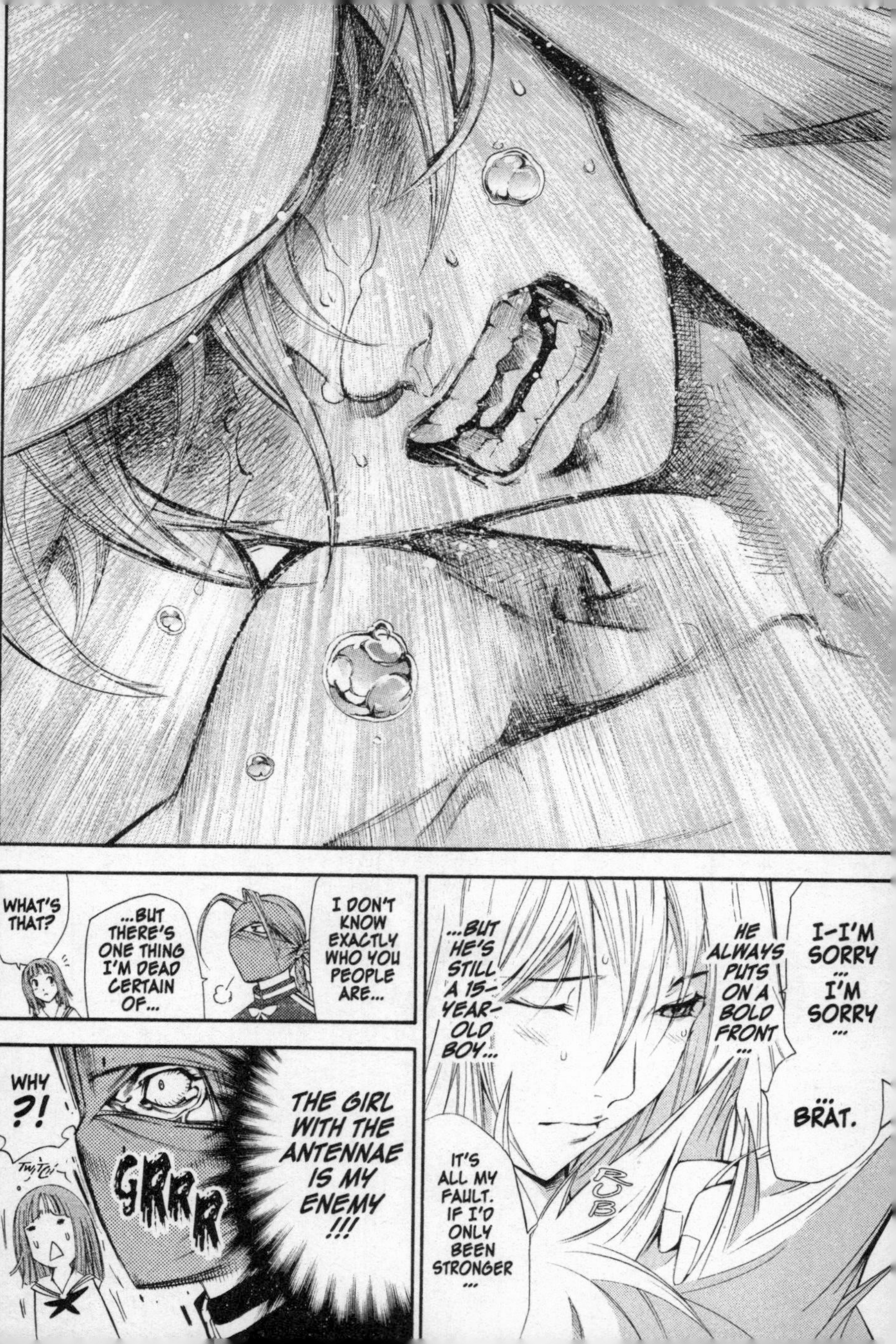
I-I'M SORRY... I'M SORRY...
HE ALWAYS PUTS ON A BOLD FRONT...
...BUT HE'S STILL A 15-YEAR-OLD BOY...
BRÄT.
RUB
IT'S ALL MY FAULT. IF I'D ONLY BEEN STRONGER...
I DON'T KNOW EXACTLY WHO YOU PEOPLE ARE...
...BUT THERE'S ONE THING I'M DEAD CERTAIN OF...
WHAT'S THAT?
THE GIRL WITH THE ANTENNAE IS MY ENEMY!!!
GRRR
WHY?!

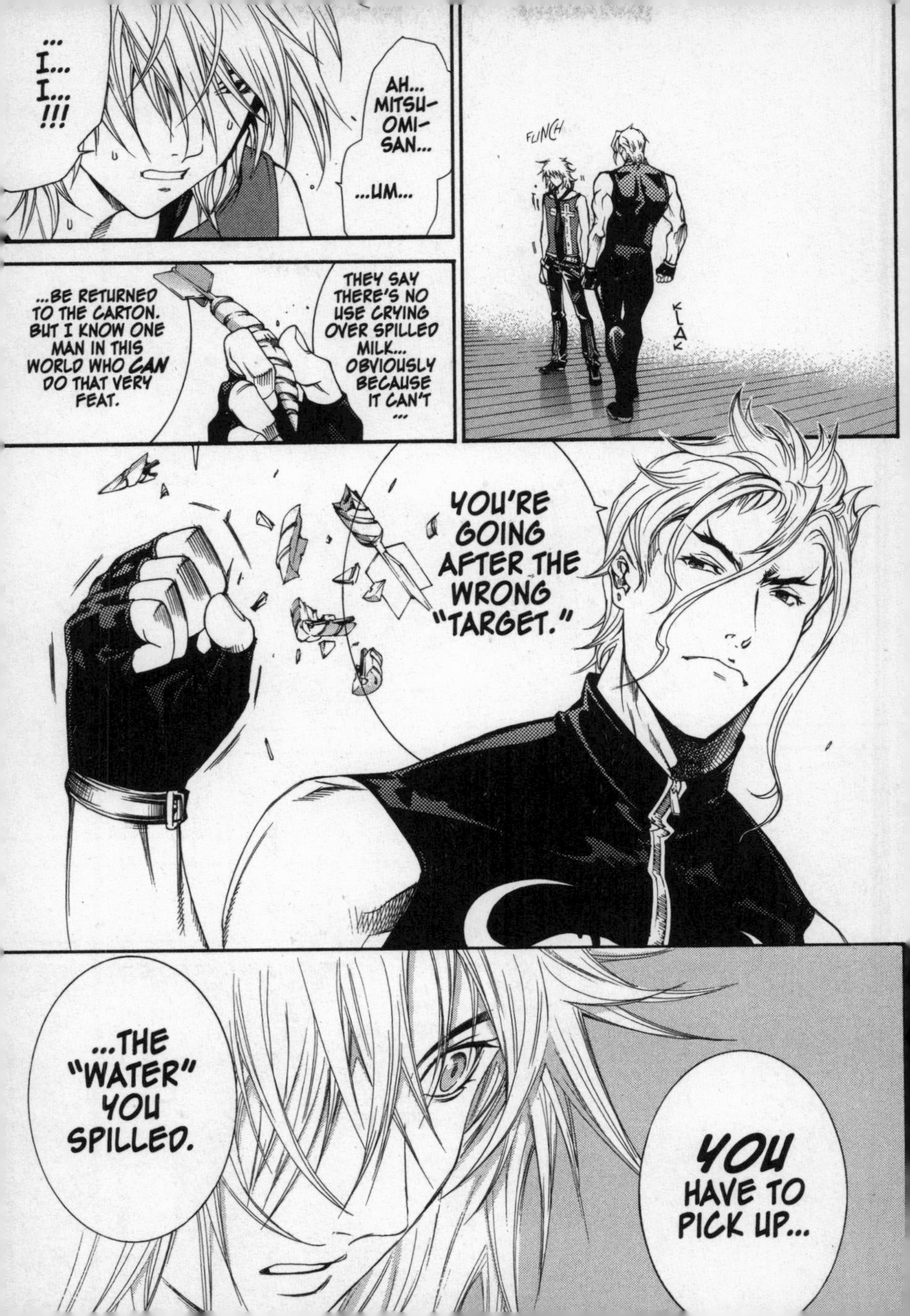
FLINCH
KLAK
AH... MITSUOMI-SAN...
...UM...
... I... I... !!!
THEY SAY THERE'S NO USE CRYING OVER SPILLED MILK... OBVIOUSLY BECAUSE IT CAN'T ...
...BE RETURNED TO THE CARTON. BUT I KNOW ONE MAN IN THIS WORLD WHO CAN DO THAT VERY FEAT.
YOU'RE GOING AFTER THE WRONG "TARGET."
YOU HAVE TO PICK UP...
...THE "WATER" YOU SPILLED.

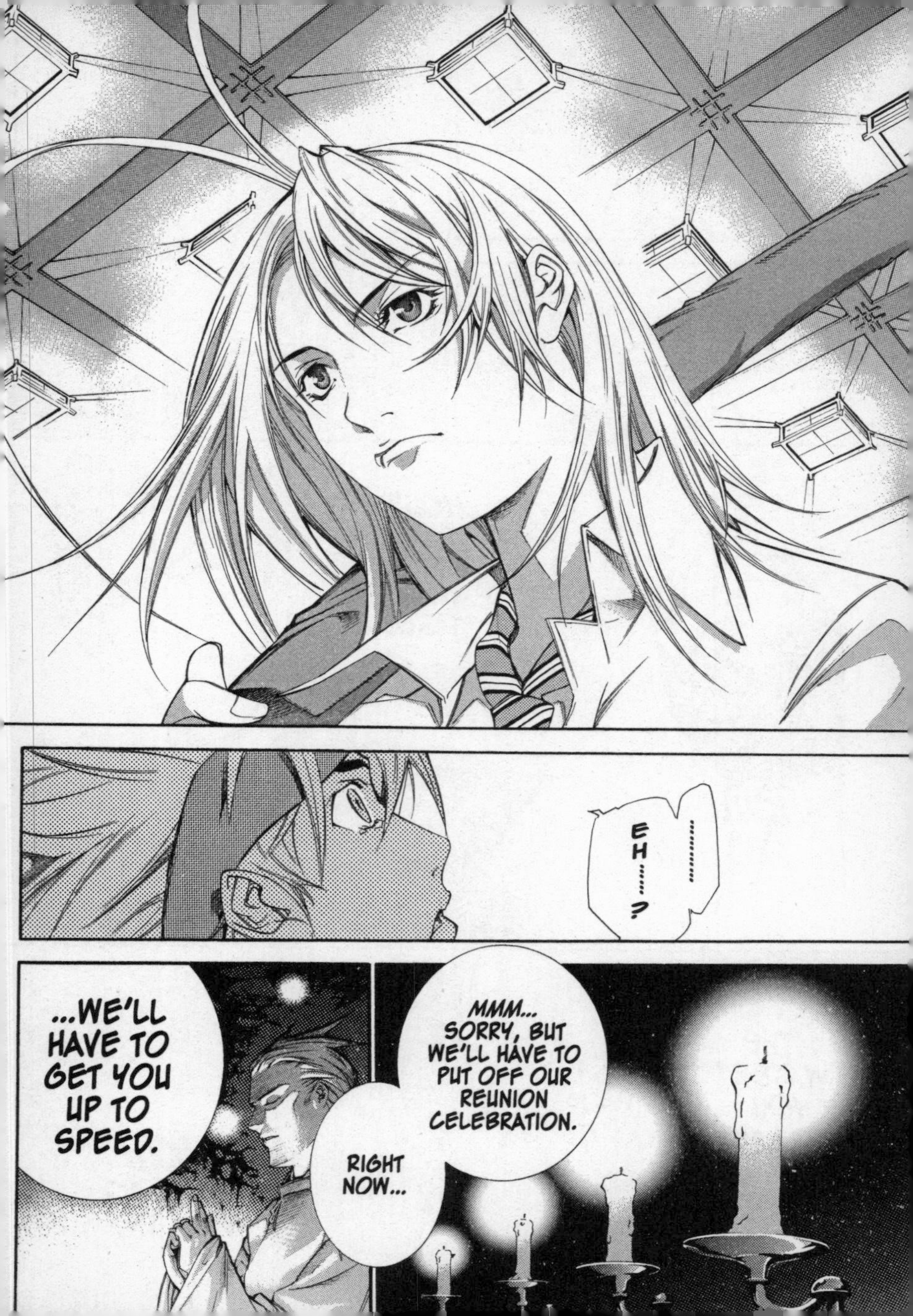
......
EH......?
MMM... SORRY, BUT WE'LL HAVE TO PUT OFF OUR REUNION CELEBRATION.
RIGHT NOW...
...WE'LL HAVE TO GET YOU UP TO SPEED.

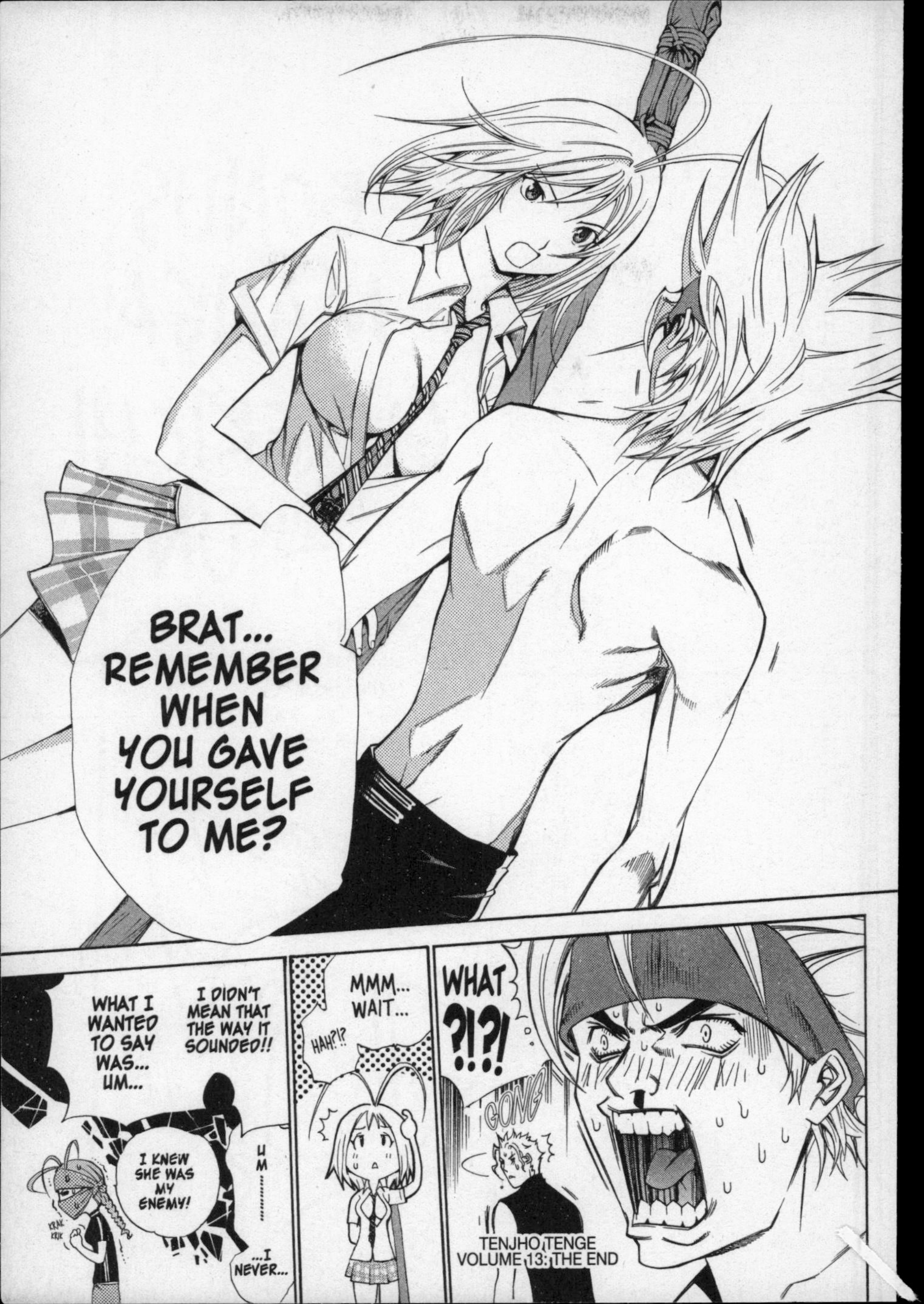
BRAT... REMEMBER WHEN YOU GAVE YOURSELF TO ME?
WHAT ?!?!
GONG
TENJHO TENGE VOLUME 13: THE END
MMM... WAIT...
HAH?!?
UM.........
...I NEVER...
I DIDN'T MEAN THAT THE WAY IT SOUNDED!!
WHAT I WANTED TO SAY WAS... UM...
I KNEW SHE WAS MY ENEMY!
KRAK KRIK

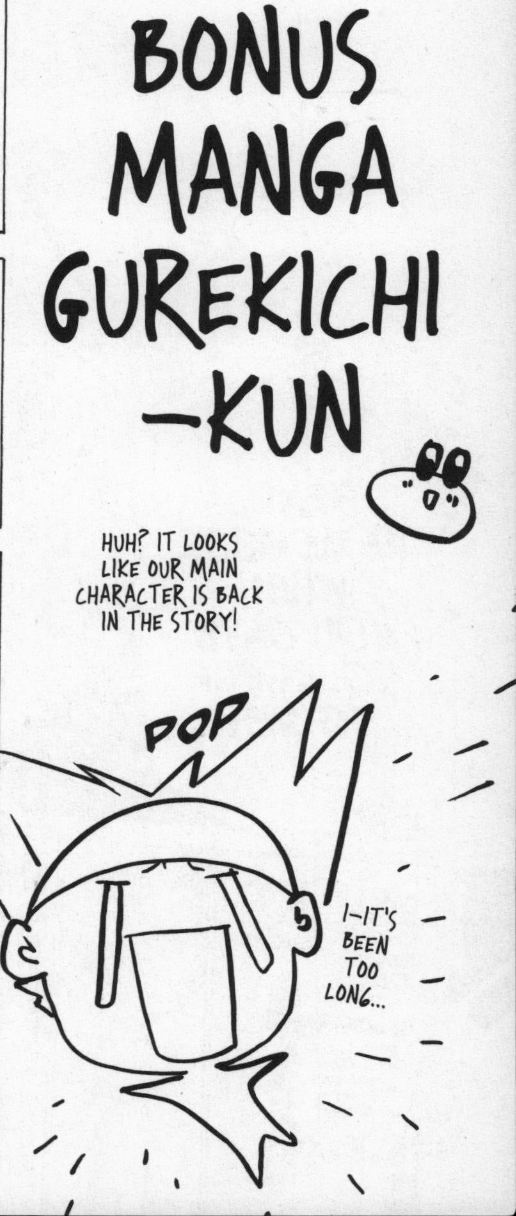
BONUS MANGA GUREKICHI-KUN
HUH? IT LOOKS LIKE OUR MAIN CHARACTER IS BACK IN THE STORY!
POP
I-IT'S BEEN TOO LONG...

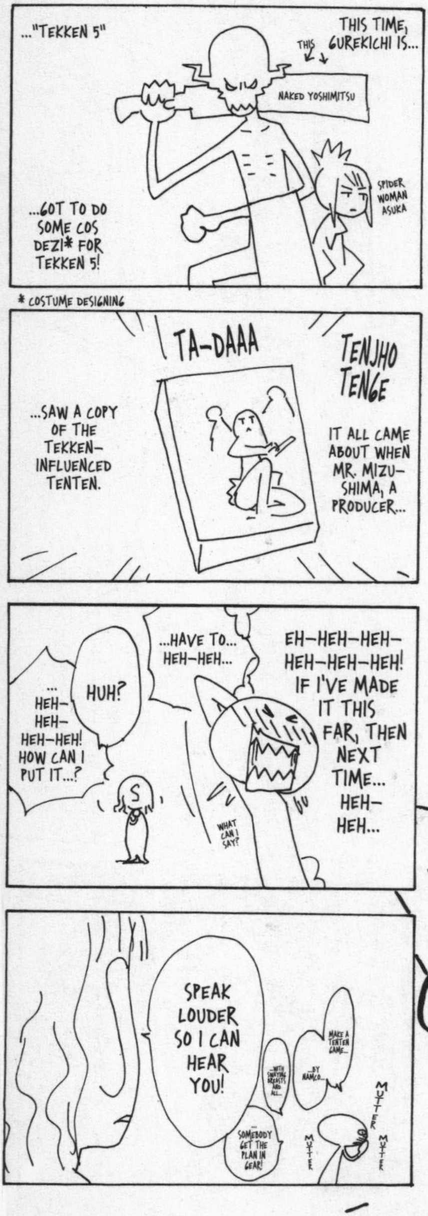
THIS TIME, GUREKICHI IS...
THIS
NAKED YOSHIMITSU
..."TEKKEN 5"
SPIDER WOMAN ASUKA
...GOT TO DO SOME COS DEZI* FOR TEKKEN 5!
* COSTUME DESIGNING
TENJHO TENGE
IT ALL CAME ABOUT WHEN MR. MIZUSHIMA, A PRODUCER...
TA-DAAA
...SAW A COPY OF THE TEKKEN-INFLUENCED TENTEN.
EH-HEH-HEH-HEH-HEH-HEH! IF I'VE MADE IT THIS FAR, THEN NEXT TIME... HEH-HEH...
...HAVE TO... HEH-HEH...
WHAT CAN I SAY?
HUH?
...HEH-HEH-HEH-HEH! HOW CAN I PUT IT...?
MUTTER
MAKE A TENTEN GAME...
...BY NAMCO...
...WITH SWAYING BREASTS AND ALL...
MUTTER
SOMEBODY GET THE PLAN IN GEAR!
MUTTER
SPEAK LOUDER SO I CAN HEAR YOU!

BY POPULAR DEMAND!! (WELL, OKAY, BY MY OWN DEMAND, MAINLY...) GUREKICHI-KUN'S MENTALLY SOOTHING PETS!!

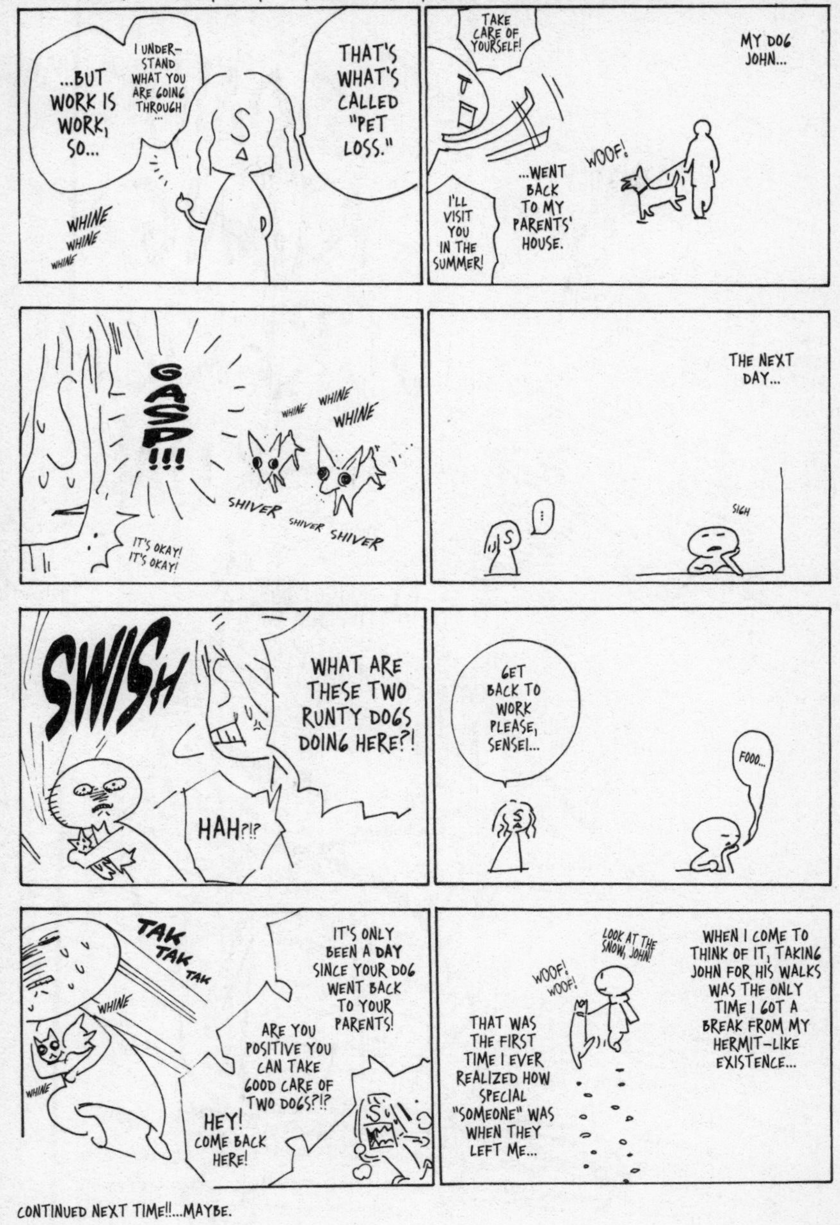
MY DOG JOHN...
WOOF!
...WENT BACK TO MY PARENTS' HOUSE.
TAKE CARE OF YOURSELF!
I'LL VISIT YOU IN THE SUMMER!
THAT'S WHAT'S CALLED "PET LOSS."
I UNDERSTAND WHAT YOU ARE GOING THROUGH...
...BUT WORK IS WORK, SO...
WHINE
WHINE
WHINE
THE NEXT DAY...
SIGH
...
GASP!!!
WHINE
WHINE
WHINE
SHIVER
SHIVER
SHIVER
IT'S OKAY! IT'S OKAY!
FOOO...
GET BACK TO WORK PLEASE, SENSEI...
WHAT ARE THESE TWO RUNTY DOGS DOING HERE?!
SWISH
HAH?!?
WHEN I COME TO THINK OF IT, TAKING JOHN FOR HIS WALKS WAS THE ONLY TIME I GOT A BREAK FROM MY HERMIT-LIKE EXISTENCE...
LOOK AT THE SNOW, JOHN!
WOOF! WOOF!
THAT WAS THE FIRST TIME I EVER REALIZED HOW SPECIAL "SOMEONE" WAS WHEN THEY LEFT ME...
IT'S ONLY BEEN A DAY SINCE YOUR DOG WENT BACK TO YOUR PARENTS!
TAK
TAK
TAK
ARE YOU POSITIVE YOU CAN TAKE GOOD CARE OF TWO DOGS?!?
WHINE
HEY! COME BACK HERE!
WHINE

CONTINUED NEXT TIME!!...MAYBE.

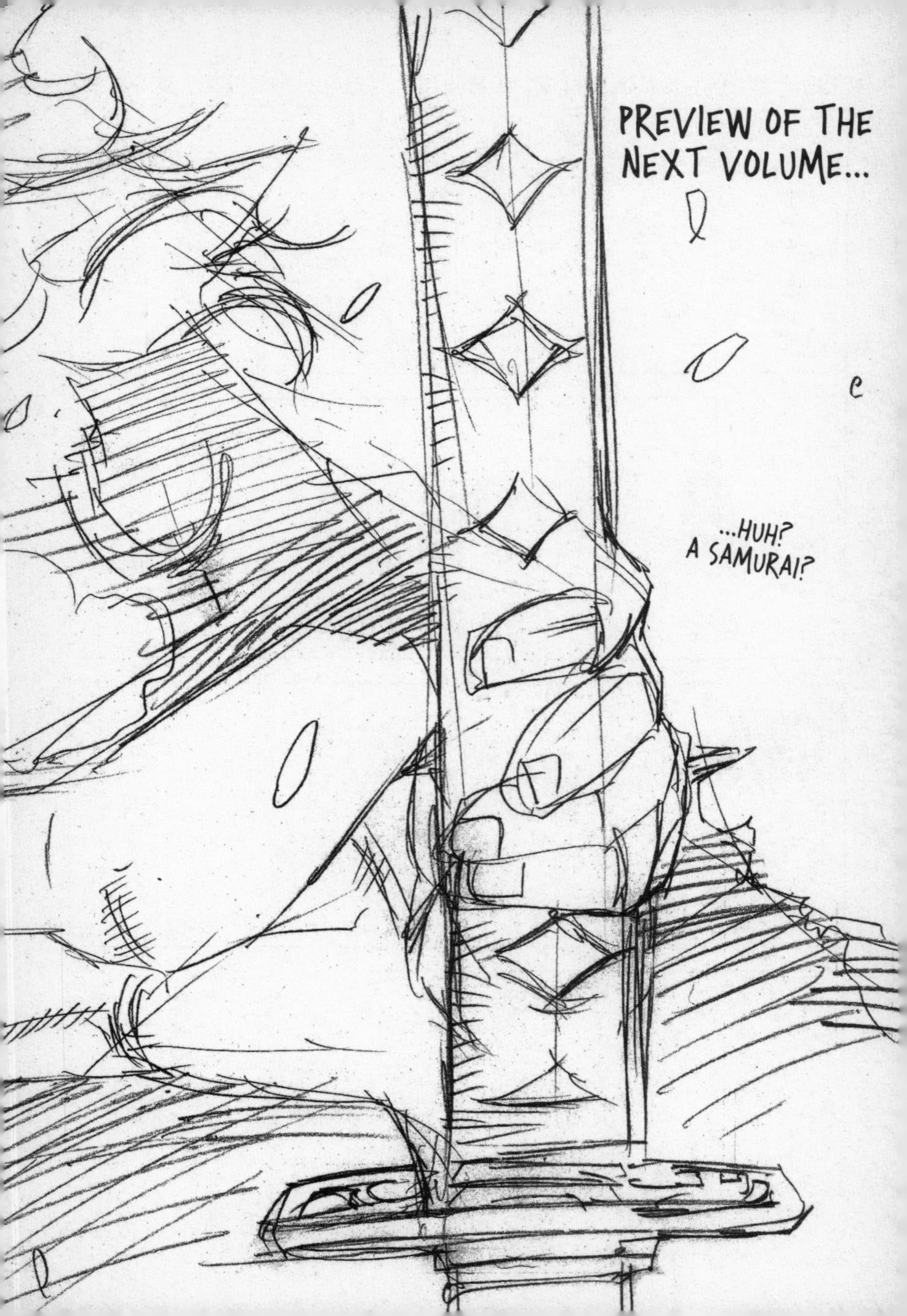
PREVIEW OF THE NEXT VOLUME...
...HUH? A SAMURAI?

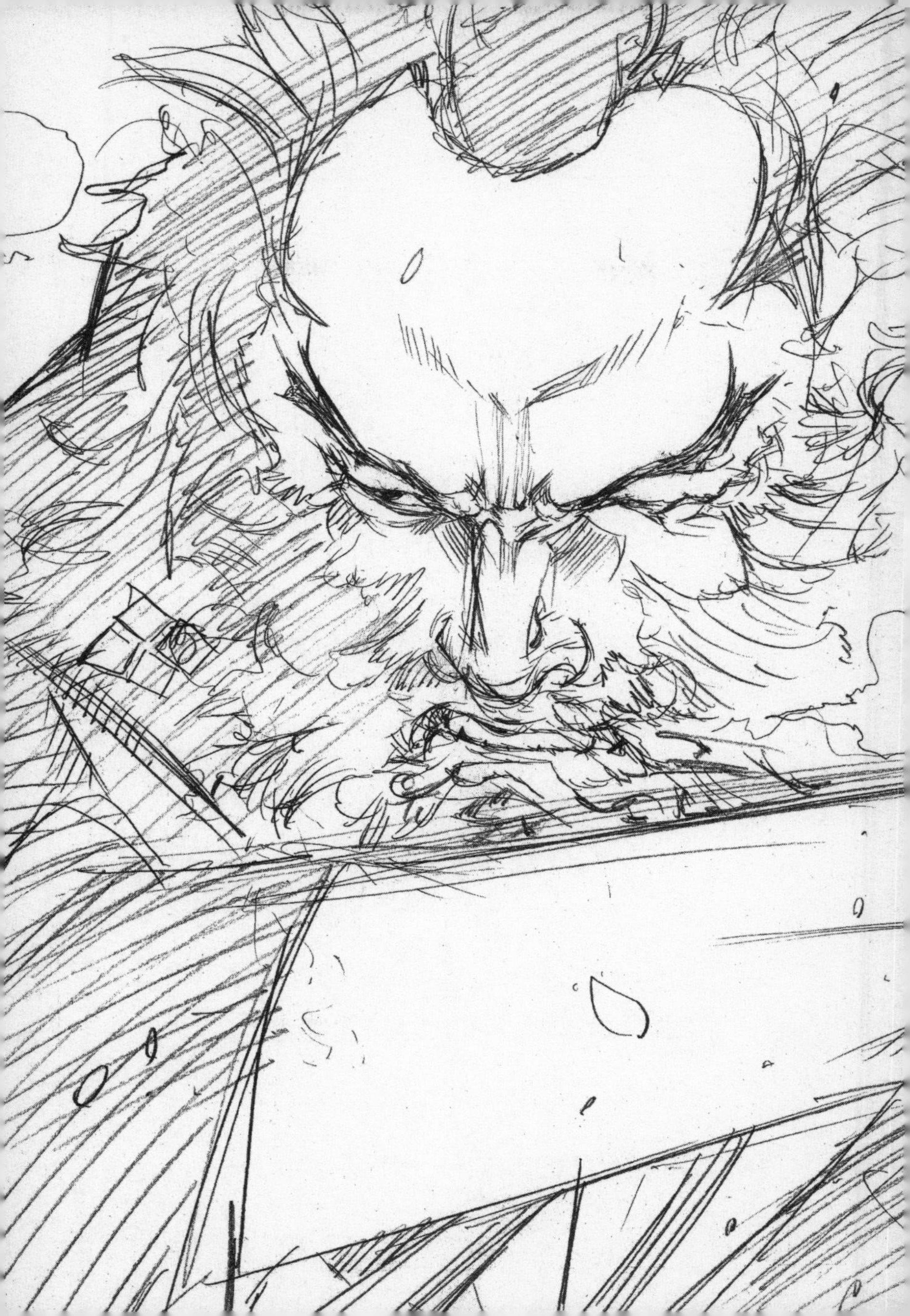

Editor   Yoichi Hasegawa
Chief Editor   Ayami Sakurada
Binding   Michiru Kobayashi

With thanks to: Kokoro Takei, Masayoshi Tazuchi, Yo Mamura, Keisuke
Yamamoto, Masaru Aoki, Yukiko Ishigami, Pacific, Takao Otakuro, Motoko
Shinohara.

The stories in this volume were originally published in "UltraJump" August-
October 2005, January-March 2006.

All the pages in this book were created—and are printed here—in Japanese RIGHT-to-LEFT format. No artwork has been reversed or altered, so you can read the stories the way the creators meant for them to be read.

FLIP IT!

RIGHT TO LEFT?!

Traditional Japanese manga starts at the upper right-hand corner, and moves right-to-left as it goes down the page. Follow this guide for an easy understanding.

For more information and sneak previews, visit cmxmanga.com. Call 1-800-COMIC BOOK for the nearest comics shop or head to your local book store.

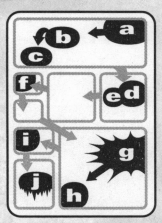

TENJHO TENGE © 1997 by Oh! great. All rights reserved. First published in Japan in 1997 by
SHUEISHA Inc.

TENJHO TENGE Volume 13, published by WildStorm Productions, an imprint of DC Comics. 888
Prospect St. #240, La Jolla, CA 92037. English Translation © 2007. All Rights Reserved. English
translation rights in U.S.A. and Canada arranged by SHUEISHA Inc. through Tuttle-Mori Agency, Inc.,
Tokyo. The stories, characters, and incidents mentioned in this magazine are entirely fictional. Printed
on recyclable paper. WildStorm does not read or accept unsolicited submissions of ideas, stories or
artwork. Printed in Canada.

DC Comics, a Warner Bros. Entertainment Company.

Sheldon Drzka – Translation and Adaptation
Saida Temofonte – Lettering
Larry Berry – Design
Jim Chadwick – Editor

ISBN:1-4012-1285-9
ISBN-13: 978-1-4012-1285-8

WITHOUT AYA'S HELP, WHAT IS MAYA
GOING TO DO?! FIND OUT IN JUNE!

By Oh! great. To get to Juken's archenemy Sohaku, Maya must first defeat
Kagiroi, his mysterious, right-hand man. Kagiroi's iron skin makes it almost
impossible for any blow to hurt him. She needs to activate the latent, mystical
powers of her sword, Reiki. Unfortunately, only her sister Aya can do that, and
she's been spirited away into the past. For Maya, time is running out!